PROPHETS
OUTCAST

PROPHETS
OUTCAST

A CENTURY OF DISSIDENT JEWISH WRITING
ABOUT ZIONISM AND ISRAEL

Edited by
ADAM SHATZ

NATION
BOOKS

Nation Books / New York

This book is for Albert Fried, my mentor

PROPHETS OUTCAST:
A Century of Dissident Jewish Writing about Zionism and Israel

Published by
Nation Books
An Imprint of Avalon Publishing Group
245 West 17th St., 11th Floor
New York, NY 10011

Nation Books is a co-publishing venture of the Nation Institute and Avalon
Publishing Group Incorporated.

Library of Congress Cataloging-in-Publication Data is available.

ISBN 1-56025-509-9

9 8 7 6 5 4 3 2 1

Book design by Paul Paddock
Printed in the United States of America
Distributed by Publishers Group West

CONTENTS

IN PRAISE OF DIASPORISM, OR, THREE CHEERS FOR IRVING BERLIN

by Adam Shatz

I.

At the beginning of Philip Roth's raucous 1993 novel, *Operation Shylock*, the narrator—a novelist named Philip Roth—receives a call from a friend in Israel, the novelist and Holocaust survivor Aharon Appelfeld. A man who calls himself "Philip Roth" and describes himself as "an ardent Diasporist," Appelfeld tells him, has just met with Lech Walesa in Gdansk, urging Ashkenazi Jews in Israel to return to their European countries of origin, including (a Jewish joke if ever there was one) Poland. Translating from an article in an Israeli newspaper, Appelfeld quotes "Roth" as saying:

> The so-called normalization of the Jew was a tragic illusion from the start. But when this normalization is expected to flourish in the very heart of Islam, it is worse than tragic-it is suicidal. Horrendous as Hitler was for us, he lasted a mere twelve years, and what is twelve years to the Jew? The time has come to return to Europe that was for centuries, and remains to this day, the most authentic Jewish homeland there has ever been, the birthplace of rabbinic Judaism, Hasidic Judaism, Jewish secularism, socialism—and on and on. The birthplace, of course, of Zionism too. But Zionism has outlived its historical function. The time has come to renew in the European diaspora our preeminent spiritual and cultural role.

"What swell ideas I have," Roth the novelist says to Appelfeld. "Going to make lots of new pals for me in the Zionist homeland."

"'Anyone who reads this in the Zionist homeland,' said Aharon, 'will only think, "Another crazy Jew."'"

The Roth impersonator's radical proposal is, of course, played for laughs. Israel is a fact of life, and though many of its Jewish citizens have immigrated to Europe and America, fleeing Palestinian suicide bombers and Israel's orthodox religious establishment, most Israeli Jews of European origin are in no hurry to return to their former homes, least of all Poland, where a half-century ago they were nearly exterminated by the Nazis. (Just imagine the slogan: *Next year in Warsaw!*) Roth's imposter is obviously a freak, a demagogue, peddling another crazy solution to the Jewish question to anyone who cares to listen. But, as Roth knows, "crazy" solutions to that insoluble question have been implemented before, most notably Theodor Herzl's project to resettle millions of Jews in their Biblical homeland, which most of them had never seen in two thousand years; a country that, moreover, was now home to another people. "The construction of a counterlife was at its very core," Roth's alter ego, Nathan Zuckerman, once observed of Herzl's Zionism. "It was a species of fabulous utopianism, a manifesto for human transformation as extreme—and, at the outset, as implausible—as any ever conceived."

Although Roth's impersonator in *Operation Shylock* is depicted as a crackpot, Roth—who mischievously subtitles the novel "a confession"— cannot quite shake the shadow of his *doppelganger*. Soon after landing in Israel, in pursuit of the man who has stolen his identity, he begins impersonating his impersonator, with manic brilliance: "Better to be marginal neurotics, anxious assimilationists, and everything else the Zionists despise, better to lose the state than to lose your moral being by unleashing a nuclear war. Better Irving Berlin than Ariel Sharon. Better Irving Berlin than the Wailing Wall. Better Irving Berlin than Holy Jerusalem! What does owning *Jerusalem*, of all places, have to do with being Jews in 1988?"

II.

This is, in fact, a question on the minds of many secular, progressive Jews in 2004, when the security of Jews in Israel and the diaspora— not to mention the human rights and national aspirations of the Palestinian people under Israeli occupation—have fallen hostage to Prime Minister Ariel Sharon's vision of a Greater Israel, a super-armed bunker state, governed by right-wing ideologues and ruling an archipelago of Palestinian ghettos surrounded by a barbed wire "security" fence.

Contrary to what the Jewish establishment would have us believe, to raise this question is not to call for throwing the Jews of Israel into the sea, or, for that matter, back to Europe. The question today is not whether Jews will remain in Israel-Palestine, but where (within the 1967 borders or in a Greater Israel?) and on what terms (in an increasingly theocratic state in which Palestinians remain second-class citizens, or in a democracy based on Arab-Jewish equality?) they will do so. But the impersonator's critique of Zionism—of its romantic attachment to the soil, its glorification of military might and undisguised contempt for the gentle values of the diaspora, its oppressive treatment of Palestine's indigenous inhabitants—contains flashes of undeniable insight. The Zionist solution to the Jewish question has created a whole new set of problems, which it has so far proved incapable of solving. As with the fool in *King Lear*, there is wisdom in his lunacy.

Like Roth's impersonator, Jewish critics of Zionism and Israel have been treated by the Jewish establishment as, at best, innocent oddballs, naïve about the ever-present danger of another Holocaust, and too soft to inflict the brutalities necessary for the preservation of "Jewish democracy" in the Arab world—a "tough neighborhood," as Thomas Friedman constantly reminds us. At worst, such critics have stood accused of being irresponsible, crazy and "self-hating," if not downright disloyal.

I prefer to see them, however, as heirs to a prophetic Jewish tradition of moral criticism, and to the secular, cosmopolitan ideals of the Enlightenment, grounded in a commitment to human equality and solidarity. By opposing the injustices committed in their name, they have shown that there is another way of honoring the memory of Jews who perished in the pogroms and concentration camps of Europe, and that a concern for the fate of the Jews need not come at the expense of the Palestinian people. This book, a collection of writings by Jewish dissidents, pays tribute to a tradition of which few Jews—and even fewer non-Jews—are aware. This is no accident. The Jewish establishment and Israel lobby have done their best to suppress the dissident tradition, and, where they have failed, to vilify it. In these efforts they have enjoyed lamentable success. Today most non-Jews take it for granted that to be Jewish is to support Israel unconditionally. In the Arab world, which has experienced an alarming increase in anti-semitism since the outbreak of the second intifada—perhaps Sharon's most impressive achievement—Jewish critics of Israel are a curiosity. "Are there other Jews like you?" a wide-eyed Palestinian woman once asked me in Lebanon, as if I were an exotic bird. The confusion of Judaism and Israel—a confusion that has placed Jews abroad at increasing risk amid Sharon's ruthless campaign of repression in the Occupied Territories— has been consciously sown by the Israeli government, which seeks to equate all criticism of Israel with anti-semitism.

As I have indicated, Jews themselves have not been immune to such criticisms—a cause of understandable anguish on their part. The title of this book, *Prophets Outcast*, borrowed from the historian Isaac Deutscher, himself a great Jewish dissident, is meant to underscore the terrible price these remarkably prescient men and women have paid for speaking out. Far greater, however, is the price the world has paid for ignoring their warnings. Over the last century, these writers have predicted with uncanny precision the steady deterioration of Arab-Jewish relations under Zionism, the seemingly inexorable drift toward territorial expansionism and theocratic fanaticism in Israel, and the consequent erosion of Jewish ethics. Their dream of Arab-Jewish fraternity, either in the form of two sovereign states or in a single binational state, lost out, tragically, to Ze'ev Jabotinsky's vision of an "Iron Wall" between Israel and the Arab world. Jabotinsky's vision has recently found physical expression in Sharon's "security" fence, an apartheid wall that, by cruelly disrupting the lives of hundreds of thousands of Palestinians, will only breed more insecurity for the Jews it purportedly protects.

But prophetic words, valuable though they are, are not the only legacy of these Jewish dissidents. The rise of a radical protest movement in Israel, where young men and women are refusing to serve in the Occupied Territories, is a homage to their influence. The revival of binationalism among progressive Jews and Palestinians is another, although, for now, a binational state in Israel-Palestine remains a distant dream. It is my hope that *Prophets Outcast* will contribute, in some small way, to rescuing this noble Jewish tradition from what Edward Thompson, the great historian of the English working-class, called "the condescension of posterity."

III.

I began editing this book a year ago, in a state of despair over the situation in Israel-Palestine. There was open talk of "transfer," Israeli code for expelling Palestinians from their land, in Sharon's cabinet, one of whose members, Housing Minister Effi Eitam—a racist, right-wing zealot who heads the National Religious Party—was describing Palestinians as a "cancer." The Bush administration, backed by the Israel lobby and Christian evangelicals, was giving its full support to Sharon, with a few minor quibbles. The Jewish establishment, meanwhile, was practicing a form of McCarthyism against critics of Israeli policy. Roger Cukierman, the leader of the Representative Council of Jewish Institutions in France and a prominent Likudnik, remarked that when Sharon visited France shortly after September 11, "I told him it was essential to get a Minister of Propaganda, like Goebbels." To express sympathy for "the other side" in this climate was to court accusations of "being with the terrorists," even if you were Deputy of Defense Paul Wolfowitz, who was booed at a pro-Israel rally for uttering a few kind words about the suffering of ordinary Palestinians.

You might wonder why I have chosen to speak out on the subject of Israel. I am an American Jew, not an Israeli. Some readers are probably grumbling, *Who are you to judge Israel? You don't live there.* Point taken. But I find it more than a bit curious that Israel's supporters welcome the solidarity of American Jews who don't live there either. And so the question can be thrown back at them: *Who are you to praise Israel?* The fact is, as a Jew and as an American, you are involved in the debate over Israel-Palestine whether you like it or not. The American Jewish establishment and the Israel lobby both claim to speak in your name. Israel, for its part, defines itself not just as a Jewish state, but as *the* Jewish state, whose Jewish majority must be maintained by whatever means necessary, including transfer, which nearly half of Israeli Jews have said they would support. And each year, over $3 billion in American tax dollars flow to Israel, which provides such useful services to our government as training in counter-insurgency and "interrogation" methods to the troops in Iraq. If you don't want to be a party to all this—if you believe that it is rotten for everyone involved, Israelis, Palestinians and Americans—you have no choice but to speak out.

Like most American Jews, I had a Zionist education. In the Sunday school I attended at a Reform Synagogue in Massachusetts, we read about the "birth" of Israel, but not about the expulsion of Palestinians; Zion, after all, had been a barren country, waiting to be rediscovered by hardy Jewish pioneers, "a land without people for a people without land." We were told of the glories of Israeli democracy—but not of its peculiar limitations: for instance, the ways in which it denies equal rights to Palestinian citizens of Israel (the "Israeli Arabs"), in effect turning them into internal exiles. We were told of Arab terrorism, which was real enough, but never of what provoked it. We were told that not only the Arabs but the *goyim* could never be trusted, and that the only conceivable reason someone would have for faulting Israel was animosity toward the Jews. We were taught to think of ourselves as eternal victims, despite the obvious affluence of our suburban surroundings.

I never quite came to think of myself in these terms, being the son of liberal, assimilated Jews who'd marched in civil rights protests, opposed the Vietnam War, and detested ethnic tribalism, no matter who practiced it. My own brand of Zionism, insofar as I had one, was based on the worship not of Herzl and Ben-Gurion, but of Woody Allen, Franz Kafka, and Bob Dylan. As a teenage leftist and reader of *The Nation*, I didn't think "their country, right or wrong" was much of an improvement over "my country, right or wrong." In any event, my causes were putting a stop to American intervention in Central America and ending Reagan's "constructive engagement" with South Africa. The mystical romance of "the land of Israel" and singing *Ha Tikva* never did much for me.

Still, the indoctrination had its effects. When the first intifada erupted in December 1987, my first impulse, as a nice Jewish boy, was to defend Israel. The Arabs, after all, were "terrorists," I mindlessly told my high school history teacher, a left-wing Vietnam veteran who'd become my mentor. Yet I felt ill at ease in my views—or rather, in my half-digested prejudices. The televised images of Israeli soldiers shooting Palestinian children for throwing stones and harassing old women at checkpoints reminded me of pictures I'd seen of the Soweto uprising. And what did I know of "the Arabs"? The only real Arab I knew was my Lebanese friend Jackie, whom our classmates taunted as a "Puerto Rican Jew"—a Semite, like me. My history teacher gently admonished me to read up on the subject.

I followed his advice—and discovered, with a mounting sense of outrage, followed soon thereafter by sorrow, that I had been fed a series of nationalist myths. To my delight, however, I discovered that some of the most eloquent critics of Israel were Jews like Isaac Deutscher, Simha Flapan, Avi Shlaim, Noam Chomsky, I. F. Stone, Pierre Vidal-Naquet, Amira Hass, and Gidon Levy. Their work corroborated the findings of Palestinian writers and historians like Edward Said, Rashid and Walid Khalidi, and Ibrahim Abu-Lughod, whom I also came to admire. Yet these Jewish critics were not romantic fellow-travelers, cheerleaders of another people's movement. They wrote as Jewish humanists, with an anguished understanding of how the question of Palestine fits into the narrative of Jewish history. While insisting on the essentially colonial nature of the Israeli-Palestinian conflict, a struggle between a settler-nationalism and an indigenous one, they also recognized that this was no run-of-the-mill colonial war. They had, in other words, a sense of the tragic. Deutscher, a Polish-Jewish Marxist, captured it best, in a brilliant parable:

> A man once jumped from the top floor of a burning house in which many members of his family had already perished. He managed to save his life; but as he was falling he hit a person standing down below and broke that person's legs and arms. The jumping man had no choice; yet to the man with the broken limbs he was the cause of his misfortune . . . A rational relationship between Israelis and Arabs might have been possible if Israel had at least attempted to establish it, if the man who threw himself down from the burning house had tried to make friends with the innocent victim of his jump and to compensate him. This did not happen. Israel never even recognized the Arab grievance. From the outset Zionism worked toward the creation of a purely Jewish state and was glad to rid the country of its Arab inhabitants.

Unlike Israel's champions, Jews like Deutscher seemed to share my view of the world. They were secular, cosmopolitan, tolerant of diversity and appalled by social injustice. Most were on the left, and many were socialists.

Around the time that I discovered Deutscher's book *The Non-Jewish Jew* in my father's library, my liberal parents were finding their sympathies for Israel sorely tested by the growth of settlements, the repression of the intifada, and by the rise of the radical religious parties in Israel, with their power to define who (and what) is and is not Jewish. A year into the first intifada, they stopped giving money to the local Jewish Federation, concerned that their donations were going to support the creation of more settlements. The federation wouldn't let them off without a fight. First there were the calls to the home, then there were visits from "representatives." Finally a man from the federation showed up at my father's office, accompanied by an Israeli general on an American tour. They proceeded to tell my father he had no right to criticize Israel, no right to ask how his money was being used—and no right to stop giving. My father showed them to the door.

"Who have you been talking to?" they asked him on their way out.

He had been talking to his son.

IV

I can anticipate the protests of some readers.

Isn't Israel a democracy—in fact the region's only democracy?

Indeed it is—for Jews. As the sociologist Baruch Kimmerling notes, Israel's democracy, for all its vitality, remains a *Herrenvolk* democracy, based on blood rather than citizenship. Today, democracies are judged not only by the freedoms they extend to their citizens but, more crucially, by the exceptions they make. It is revealing that those who praise Israel as the "only democracy in the Middle East"—a line most American politicians have committed to memory—have no wish to extend full citizenship rights to the Arabs within its 1967 borders (a fifth of Israel's population and rapidly growing), much less to Palestinians under occupation. In fact, the call for Israel to become a "state of all its citizens," raised by the Arab Knesset member Azmi Bishara, is considered tantamount to a call for "the destruction of Israel."

But isn't Israel a sanctuary for the Jewish people, a guarantee that Jews will always have a place to go if there is another outbreak of virulent Jew hatred?

There is no denying that Israel once provided a refuge for Hitler's victims, a "Jewish hospital in which Jews could begin to recover from the devastation of that horror," as Roth's impersonator puts it. Leaving aside the question as to why this sanctuary should come at the expense of the Palestinians, who played no role in the Holocaust, it is by no means clear today that the existence of a Jewish ethno-state in the Middle East makes Jews safer today, or whether it actually exposes them to greater dangers. What is clear is that, as the Israeli peace activist Uri Avnery recently observed, Israel under Sharon has become a "laboratory for the growing of the anti-Semitic virus."

But haven't the Palestinians committed vile acts of terror? Do they not share some of the blame for the current impasse? Have they not been terribly misled?

The answer to all these questions is yes. Since their expulsion and dispersion in 1948, the Palestinians have suffered a terrible ordeal and, much like the Jews, they have been in many ways hardened, not ennobled, by the experience. As Frantz Fanon once pointed out, "the native is an oppressed person whose permanent dream is to become the persecutor." Some Palestinians have found an awful and quite literally self-destructive way of achieving this "dream" in the suicide bomb. It's also true that Palestinians have not enjoyed the visionary leadership of a Mandela—but then who has, besides the South Africans? Neither the suicide bomb nor Arafat's leadership is the principal obstacle to peace, contrary to the claims of the Jewish establishment and of a distressing number of self-described liberals. The main roadblock is the Israeli government's effort to pursue what Kimmerling calls "politicide," an organized campaign of land confiscation, harassment and violence whose ultimate goal is to destroy the Palestinian will to achieve self-determination. The infernal logic at work today should be obvious by now: Sharon's campaign of politicide fosters terror, and terror reinforces Sharon. The primary responsibility for breaking the current cycle lies with Israel, the vastly more powerful party.

What, then, is to be done?

The writers in *Prophets Outcast* do not speak with one voice. They form a polyphonic ensemble of Zionists, anti-Zionists, and non-Zionists, as well as anarchists, liberals and Marxists. Some espouse a two-state solution, others a binational Arab-Jewish state. What they do share is a commitment to genuine, peaceful coexistence between the Arabs and

Jews of Israel-Palestine. As the Syrian poet Adonis, an Arab dissident who is a spiritual cousin of these prophets outcast, once said to me, "Israelis and Palestinians must find a way to live together. Whether it is in two states, one state or a federation, is up to them. But they must find a way to live together." *Prophets Outcast* does not propose a political framework for resolving the conflict. This is, in form as well as spirit, a Jewish book—a book of questions rather than answers. Readers in search of a unified critique will have to look elsewhere. The emphasis here is on exemplary, individual acts of moral protest, not on ideological rectitude. As Hannah Arendt observed, "in the darkest of times . . . illumination may well come less from theories and concepts than from the uncertain, flickering, and often weak light that some men and women, in their lives and works, will kindle under almost all such circumstances and shed over the time span that was given them on earth." For too long, the Jewish left has been splintered into sectarian camps which have wasted precious energy on quarrels with little echo in the real world. This is no time for petty feuds over doctrinal purity, but for organized resistance to the Occupation, both in solidarity with the Palestinian people and out of concern for Jewish security. The narcissism of small differences is a luxury we can scarcely afford.

PROPHETS
OUTCAST

1 THE NON-JEWISH JEW

Isaac Deutscher, *the son of a strictly observant Jewish printer, was born in 1907 in the Polish town of Chrzanów, at a time of inflamed Polish patriotism that was sometimes indistinguishable from antisemitism. In 1918, a pogrom erupted in Chrzanów, and though the mob passed his house, the experience left a searing imprint. "I lived through three pogroms during the very first week of reborn Poland," he recalled. "This is how the dawn of Polish independence greeted us." Yet, unlike some of his peers, Deutscher gravitated not to Zionism, but to atheism and, before long, revolutionary socialism. As an adolescent he removed his sidelocks, a direct challenge to his father, and stopped attending synagogue. In 1927, while studying in Warsaw, he joined the outlawed Polish Communist Party. Five years later, after organizing an anti-Stalinist faction, he was expelled for exaggerating "the danger of Nazism" and "spreading panic" in communist ranks. In fact, his alarm was clairvoyant; in the fall of 1939 the Nazis invaded Poland, just a few months after Deutscher left Warsaw for London.*

In England, his home until his untimely death in 1967 and where, like Conrad and Nabokov, he learned to write in an English of unerring elegance, Deutscher established himself as a journalist and commentator on European politics. His crowning achievement was his "Trotsky trilogy," a magisterial, three-volume biography of the exiled Soviet leader, with whom he felt a profound affinity as a fellow dissident, anti-Stalinist revolutionary and "non-Jewish" Jew.

Deutscher wrestled throughout his life with the Jewish question, particularly in the wake of the Holocaust, which nearly shattered his faith in human solidarity. In The Non-Jewish Jew, *a posthumously published collection, Deutscher wrote that he had long since abandoned his youthful anti-Zionism, founded as it was on "a confidence in . . . European society and civilization, which that society and civilization have not justified." But the Holocaust did not make him a Zionist. Israel, he said, was a raft for people jumping from "a burning ship," not the "basis of a political orientation." He was repelled by the shrill "nationalist mysticism" he encountered in Israel—"a mysticism which is not free of the old Chosen-People-racialism"—and he deplored the treatment of the Palestinians, who "were made to pay the price for the crimes the West committed toward the Jews." If there was a Jewish tradition worth cultivating, it was that of the great Jewish heretics, "non-Jewish Jews," such as Spinoza, Marx and Freud. In* The Non-Jewish Jew, *Deutscher praised this dissident tradition—secular and tolerant, questioning and innovative, open to the world and averse to tribalism, (Jewish chauvinism included), committed to the ideals of enlightenment and the cause of human emancipation. He is the soul and inspiration of* Prophets Outcast.

THE NON-JEWISH JEW [1]

Isaac Deutscher

from *The Non-Jewish Jew and Other Essays* (1968)

There is an old Talmudic saying: 'A Jew who has sinned still remains a Jew.' My own thinking is, of course, beyond the idea of 'sin' or 'no sin'; but this saying has brought to my mind a memory from childhood which may not be irrelevant to my theme.

I remember that when as a child I read the *Midrash*, I came across a story and a description of a scene which gripped my imagination. It was the story of Rabbi Meir, the great saint and sage, the pillar of Mosaic orthodoxy, and co-author of the *Mishnah*, who took lessons in theology from a heretic, Elisha ben Abiyuh, called Akher (The Stranger). Once on a Sabbath Rabbi Meir was with his teacher, and as usual they became engaged in a deep argument. The heretic was riding a donkey, and Rabbi Meir, as he could not ride on a Sabbath, walked by his side and listened so intently to the words of wisdom falling from his heretical lips that he failed to notice that he and his teacher had reached the ritual boundary which Jews were not allowed to cross on a Sabbath. The great heretic turned to his orthodox pupil and said: 'Look, we have reached the boundary—we must part now; you must not accompany me any farther—go back!' Rabbi Meir went back to the Jewish community, while the heretic rode on—beyond the boundaries of Jewry.

There was enough in this scene to puzzle an orthodox Jewish child. Why, I wondered, did Rabbi Meir, that leading light of orthodoxy, take his lessons from the heretic? Why did he show him so much affection? Why did he defend him against other rabbis? My heart, it seems, was with the heretic. Who was he? He appeared to be in Jewry and yet out of it. He showed a curious respect for his pupil's orthodoxy, when he sent him back to the Jews on the Holy Sabbath; but he himself, disregarding canon and ritual, rode beyond the boundaries. When I was thirteen, or perhaps fourteen, I began to write a play about Akher and Rabbi Meir and I tried to find out more about Akher's character. What made him transcend Judaism? Was he a Gnostic? Was he an adherent of some other school of Greek or Roman philosophy? I could not find the answers, and did not manage to get beyond the first act.

The Jewish heretic who transcends Jewry belongs to a Jewish tradition. You may, if you like, see Akher as a prototype of those great revolutionaries of modern thought: Spinoza, Heine, Marx, Rosa Luxemburg, Trotsky, and Freud. You may, if you wish to, place them within a Jewish tradition. They all went beyond the boundaries of Jewry. They all found Jewry too narrow, too archaic, and too constricting. They all looked for ideals and fulfilment beyond it, and they represent the sum and substance of much that is greatest in modern thought, the sum and substance of the most profound upheavals that have taken place in philosophy, sociology, economics, and politics in the last three centuries.

Did they have anything in common with one another? Have they perhaps impressed mankind's thought so greatly because of their special 'Jewish genius'? I do not believe in the exclusive genius of any race. Yet I think that in some ways they were very Jewish indeed. They had in themselves something of the quintessence of Jewish life and of the Jewish intellect. They were *a priori* exceptional in that as Jews they dwelt on the borderlines of various civilizations, religions, and national cultures. They were born and brought up on the borderlines of various epochs. Their mind matured where the most diverse cultural influences crossed and fertilized each other. They lived on the margins or in the nooks and crannies of their respective nations. Each of them was in society and yet not in it, of it and yet not of it. It was this that enabled them to rise in thought above their societies, above their nations, above their times and generations, and to strike out mentally into wide new horizons and far into the future.

It was, I think, an English Protestant biographer of Spinoza who said that only a Jew could have carried out that upheaval in the philosophy of his age that Spinoza carried out—a Jew who was not bound by the dogmas of the Christian Churches, Catholic and Protestant, nor by those of the faith in which he had been born.[2] Neither Descartes nor Leibnitz could free themselves to the same extent from the shackles of the medieval scholastical tradition in philosophy.

Spinoza was brought up under the influences of Spain, Holland, Germany, England, and the Italy of the Renaissance—all the trends of human thought that were at work at that time shaped his mind. His native Holland was in the throes of bourgeois revolution. His ancestors, before they came to the Netherlands, had been Spanish-Portuguese *Maranim*, crypto-Jews, at heart Jews, outwardly Christian, as were many Spanish Jews on whom the Inquisition had forced the baptism. After the Spinozas had come to the Netherlands, they disclosed themselves as Jews; but, of course, neither they nor their close descendants were strangers to the intellectual climate of Christianity.

Spinoza himself, when he started out as independent thinker and as initiator of modern criticism of the Bible, seized at once the cardinal contradiction in Judaism, the contradiction between the monotheistic and universal God and the setting in which that God appears in the Jewish religion—as a God attached to one people only; the contradiction between the universal God and his 'chosen people'. We know what the realization of this contradiction brought upon Spinoza: banishment from the Jewish community and excommunication. He had to fight against the Jewish clergy which, itself recently a victim of the Inquisition, became infected with the spirit of the Inquisition. Then he had to face the hostility of the Catholic clergy and Calvinistic priests. His whole life was a struggle to overcome the limitations of the religions and cultures of his time.

Among Jews of great intellect exposed to the contradiction of various religions and cultures some were so pulled in various directions by contradictory influences and pressures that they could not find spiritual balance, and broke down. One of these was Uriel Acosta, Spinoza's elder and forerunner. Many times he rebelled against Judaism; and many times he recanted. The rabbis excommunicated him repeatedly; he repeatedly prostrated himself before them on the floor of the Amsterdam Synagogue. Unlike Acosta, Spinoza had the great intellectual happiness of being able to harmonize the conflicting influences and to create out of them a higher outlook on the world and an integrated philosophy.

In almost every generation, whenever the Jewish intellectual, placed at the concatenation of various cultures, struggles with himself and with the problems of his time, we find someone who, like Uriel Acosta, breaks down under the burden, and someone who, like Spinoza, makes of that burden the wings of his greatness. Heine was in a sense the Uriel Acosta of a later age. His relation to Marx, Spinoza's intellectual grandson, is comparable to Uriel Acosta's relation to Spinoza.

Heine was torn between Christianity and Jewry, and between France and Germany. In his native Rhineland there clashed the influences of the French Revolution and of the Napoleonic Empire with those of the old Holy Roman Empire of the German Kaisers. He grew up within the orbit of classical German philosophy and within the orbit of French Republicanism; and he saw Kant as a Robespierre and Fichte as a Napoleon in the realm of the spirit; and so he describes them in one of the most profound and moving passages of *Zur Geschichte der Religion and Philosophie in Deutschland.* In his later years he came in contact with French and German socialism and communism; and he met Marx with that apprehensive admiration and sympathy with which Acosta had met Spinoza.

Marx likewise grew up in the Rhineland. His parents having ceased to be Jews, he did not struggle with the Jewish heritage as Heine did. All the more intense was his opposition to the social and spiritual backwardness of contemporary Germany. An exile most of his life, his thought was shaped by German philosophy, French socialism, and English political economy. In no other contemporary mind did such diverse influences meet so fruitfully. Marx rose above German philosophy, French socialism, and English political economy; he absorbed what was best in each of these trends and transcended the limitations of each.

To come nearer to our time, there were Rosa Luxemburg, Trotsky, and Freud, each of whom was formed amid historic cross-currents. Rosa Luxemburg is a unique blend of the German, Polish, and Russian characters and of the Jewish temperament; Trotsky was the pupil of a Lutheran Russo-German gymnasium in cosmopolitan Odessa on the fringe of the Greek-Orthodox Empire of the Tsars; and Freud's mind matured in Vienna in estrangement from Jewry and in opposition to the Catholic clericalism of the Habsburg capital. All of them had this in common, that the very conditions in which they lived and worked did not allow them to reconcile themselves to ideas which were nationally or religiously limited and induced them to strive for a universal *Weltanschauung*.

Spinoza's ethics were no longer the Jewish ethics, but the ethics of man at large—just as his God was no longer the Jewish God: his God, merged with nature, shed his separate and distinctive divine identity. Yet, in a way, Spinoza's God and ethics were still Jewish, except that his was Jewish monotheism carried to its logical conclusion and the Jewish universal God thought out to the end; and once thought out to the end, that God ceased to be Jewish.

Heine wrestled with Jewry all his life; his attitude towards it was characteristically ambivalent, full of love-hate or hate-love. He was in this respect inferior to Spinoza, who, excommunicated by the Jews, did not become a Christian. Heine did not have Spinoza's strength of mind and character; and he lived in a society which even in the first decades of the nineteenth century was still more backward than Dutch society had been in the seventeenth. At first he pinned his hopes on that pseudo-emancipation of Jews, the ideal which Moses Mendelsohn had expressed in the words: 'be a Jew inside your home and a man outside.' The timidity of that German-Jewish ideal was of a piece with the paltry liberalism of the gentile German bourgeoisie: the German Liberal was a 'free man' inside his home and an *allertreuester Untertane* ('the most faithful subject') outside. This could not satisfy Heine for long. He abandoned Jewry and surrendered to Christianity. At heart he was never reconciled to the abandonment and the conversion. His rejection of Jewish orthodoxy runs through the whole of his work. His Don Isaac says to the Rabbi von Bachrach: 'I could not be one of you. I like your cooking much better than I like your religion. No, I could not be one of you; and I suspect that even at the best of times, under the rule of your King David, in the best of your times, I would have run away from you and gone to the temples of Assyria and Babylon which were full of love and the joy of life.' Yet, it was a fiery and resentful Jew who had, in *An Edom*, *'gewaltig beschworen den tausendjährigen Schmerz.'*

Marx, about twenty years younger, surmounted the problem which tormented Heine. Only once did he come to grips with it, in his youthful and famous *Zur Judenfrage*. This was his unreserved rejection of Jewry. Apologists of Jewish orthodoxy and Jewish nationalism have because of it violently attacked Marx as an 'anti-Semite'. Yet, I think that Marx went to the very heart of the matter when he said that Jewry had survived 'not in spite of history but in history and through history', that it owed its survival to the distinctive role that the Jews had played as agents of a money economy in environments which lived in a natural economy; that Judaism was essentially a theoretical epitome of market, relationships and the faith of the merchant; and that Christian Europe, as it developed from feudalism to capitalism, became Jewish in a sense. Marx saw Christ as the 'theorizing Jew', the Jew as a 'practical Christian' and, therefore, the 'practical' bourgeois Christian as a 'Jew'. Since he treated Judaism as the religious reflection of the bourgeois way of thought, he saw bourgeois Europe as becoming assimilated to Jewry. His ideal was not the equality of Jew and Gentile in a 'Judaized' capitalist society, but the emancipation of Jew and non-Jew alike from the bourgeois way of life, or, as he put it provocatively in his somewhat over-paradoxical Young Hegelian idiom, in the 'emancipation of society from Jewry'. His idea was as universal as Spinoza's, yet advanced in time by two hundred years—it was the idea of socialism and of the classless and stateless society.

Among Marx's many disciples and followers hardly any were, in spirit and temperament, as close to him as Rosa Luxemburg and Leon Trotsky. Their affinity with him shows itself in their dialectically dramatic vision of the world and of its class struggles, and in that exceptional concord of thought, passion, and imagination which gives to their language and style a peculiar clarity, density, and richness. (Bernard Shaw had probably these qualities in mind when he spoke of Marx's 'peculiarly Jewish literary gifts'.) Like Marx, Rosa Luxemburg and Trotsky strove, together with their non-Jewish comrades, for the universal, as against the particularist, and for the internationalist, as against the nationalist, solutions to the problems of their time. Rosa Luxemburg sought to transcend the contradiction between German reformist socialism and Russian revolutionary Marxism. She sought to inject into German socialism something of the Russian and Polish revolutionary *élan* and idealism, something of that 'revolutionary romanticism' which so great a realist as Lenin unabashingly extolled; and occasionally she tried to transplant the Western European democratic spirit and tradition into the socialist underground movements of Eastern Europe. She failed in her main purpose and paid with her life. But it was not only she who paid. In her assassination Hohenzollern Germany celebrated its last triumph and Nazi Germany—its first.

Trotsky, the author of permanent revolution, had before him the vision of a global upheaval transforming mankind. The leader, together with Lenin, of the Russian revolution and the founder of the Red Army, he came in conflict with the State he had helped to create when that State and its leaders put up the banner of Socialism in One Country. Not for him was the limitation of the vision of socialism to the boundaries of one country.

All these great revolutionaries were extremely vulnerable. They were, as Jews, rootless, in a sense; but they were so only in some respects, for they had the deepest roots in intellectual tradition and in the noblest aspirations of their times. Yet whenever religious intolerance or nationalist emotion was on the ascendant, whenever dogmatic narrow-mindedness and fanaticism triumphed, they were the first victims. They were excommunicated by Jewish rabbis; they were persecuted by Christian priests; they were hunted down by the gendarmes of absolute rulers and by the *soldateska;* they were hated by pseudo-democratic philistines; and they were expelled by their own parties. Nearly all of them were exiled from their countries; and the writings of all were burned at the stake at one time or another. Spinoza's name could not be mentioned for over a century after his death—even Leibnitz, who was indebted to Spinoza for so much of his thought, did not dare to mention it. Trotsky is still under anathema in Russia today. The names of Marx, Heine, Freud, and Rosa Luxemburg were forbidden in Germany quite recently. But theirs is the ultimate victory. After a century during which Spinoza's name was covered with oblivion, they put up monuments to him and acknowledged him as the greatest fructifier of the human mind. Herder once said about Goethe: 'I wish Goethe read some Latin books apart from Spinoza's *Ethics.'* Goethe was indeed steeped in Spinoza's thought; and Heine rightly describes him as 'Spinoza who has thrown off the cloak of his geometrical-mathematical formulae and stands before us as a lyrical poet.' Heine himself has triumphed over Hitler and Goebbels. The other revolutionaries of this line will also survive and sooner or later triumph over those who have worked hard to efface their memory.

It is very obvious why Freud belongs to the same intellectual line. In his teachings, whatever their merits and demerits, he transcends the limitations of earlier psychological schools. The man whom he analyses is not a German, or an Englishman, a Russian, or a Jew—he is the universal man in whom the subconscious and the conscious struggle, the man who is part of nature and part of society, the man whose desires and cravings, scruples and inhibitions, anxieties and predicaments are essentially the same no matter to what race, religion, or nation he belongs. From their viewpoint the Nazis were right when they coupled Freud's name with that of Marx and burned the books of both.

All these thinkers and revolutionaries have had certain philosophical principles in common. Although their philosophies vary, of course, from century to century and from generation to generation, they are all, from Spinoza to Freud, determinists, they all hold that the universe is ruled by laws inherent in it and governed by *Gesetzmässigkeiten*. They do not see reality as a jumble of accidents or history as an assemblage of caprices and whims of rulers. There is nothing fortuitous, so Freud tells us, in our dreams, follies, or even in our slips of the tongue. The laws of development, Trotsky says, 'refract' themselves through accidents; and in saying this he is very close to Spinoza.

They are all determinists because having watched many societies and studied many 'ways of life' at close quarters, they grasp the basic regularities of life. Their manner of thinking is dialectical, because, living on borderlines of nations and religions, they see society in a state of flux. They conceive reality as being dynamic, not static. Those who are shut in within one society, one nation, or one religion, tend to imagine that their way of life and their way of thought have absolute and unchangeable validity and that all that contradicts their standards is somehow 'unnatural', inferior, or evil. Those, on the other hand, who live on the borderlines of various civilizations comprehend more clearly the great movement and the great contradictoriness of nature and society.

All these thinkers agree on the relativity of moral standards. None of them believes in absolute good or absolute evil. They all observed communities adhering to different moral standards and different ethical values. What was good to the Roman Catholic Inquisition under which Spinoza's grandparents had lived, was evil to the Jews; and what was good to the rabbis and Jewish elders of Amsterdam was evil to Spinoza himself. Heine and Marx experienced in their youth the tremendous clash between the morality of the French revolution and that of feudal Germany.

Nearly all these thinkers have yet another great philosophical idea in common—the idea that knowledge to be real must be active. This incidentally has a bearing on their views on ethics, for if knowledge is inseparable from action or *Praxis*, which is by its nature relative and self-contradictory, then morality, the knowledge of what is good and what is evil, is also inseparable from *Praxis* and is also relative and self-contradictory. It was Spinoza who said that 'to be is to do and to know is to do'. It was only one step from this to Marx's saying that 'hitherto the philosophers have interpreted the world; henceforth the task is to change it'.

Finally, all these men, from Spinoza to Freud, believed in the ultimate solidarity of man; and this was implicit in their attitudes towards Jewry. We are now looking back on these believers in humanity through the bloody fog of our times. We are looking back at them through the smoke of the gas chambers, the smoke which no wind can disperse from our sight. These 'non-Jewish Jews' were essentially optimists; and their optimism reached heights which it is not easy to ascend in our times. They did not imagine that it would be possible for 'civilized' Europe in the twentieth century to sink to a depth of barbarity at which the mere words 'solidarity of man' would sound as a perverse mockery to Jewish ears. Alone among them Heine had the poet's intuitive premonition of this when he warned Europe to beware of the coming onslaught of the old Germanic gods emerging *'aus dem teutschem Urwalde'*, and when he complained that the destiny of the modern Jew is tragic beyond expression and comprehension—so tragic that 'they laugh at you when you speak of it, and this is the greatest tragedy of all.'

We do not find this premonition in Spinoza or Marx. Freud in his old age reeled mentally under the blow of Nazism. To Trotsky it came as a shock that Stalin used against him the anti-semitic innuendo. As a young man Trotsky had, in most categorical terms, repudiated the demand for Jewish 'cultural autonomy', which the *Bund*, the Jewish

Socialist Party, raised in 1903. He did it in the name of the solidarity of Jew and non-Jew in the socialist camp. Nearly a quarter of a century later, while he was engaged in an unequal struggle with Stalin and went to the party cells in Moscow to expound his views, he was met with vicious allusions to his Jewishness and even with plain anti-semitic insults. The allusions and insults came from members of the party which he had, together with Lenin, led in the revolution and civil war. After another quarter of a century, and after Auschwitz and Majdanek and Belsen, once again, this time much more openly and menacingly, Stalin resorted to anti-semitic innuendo and insult.

It is an indubitable fact that the Nazi massacre of six million European Jews has not made any deep impression on the nations of Europe. It has not truly shocked their conscience. It has left them almost cold. Was then the optimistic belief in humanity voiced by the great Jewish revolutionaries justified? Can we still share their faith in the future of civilization?

I admit that if one were to try and answer these questions from an exclusively Jewish standpoint, it would be hard, perhaps impossible, to give a positive answer. As for myself, I cannot approach the issue from an exclusively Jewish standpoint; and my answer is: Yes, their faith was justified. It was justified at any rate, in so far as the belief in the ultimate solidarity of mankind is itself one of the conditions necessary for the preservation of humanity and for the cleansing of our civilization of the dregs of barbarity that are still present in it and still poison it.

Why then has the fate of the European Jews left the nations of Europe, or the gentile world at large, almost cold? Unfortunately, Marx was far more right about the place of the Jews in European society than we could have realized some time ago. The major part of the Jewish tragedy has consisted in this, that as the result of a long historic development, the masses of Europe have become accustomed to identify the Jew primarily with trade and jobbing, money-lending and money-making. Of these the Jew had become the synonym and symbol to the popular mind. Look up the Oxford English Dictionary and see how it gives the accepted meaning of the term 'Jew': firstly, it is a 'person of the Hebrew race'; secondly—this is the colloquial use—an 'extortionate usurer, driver of hard bargains.' 'Rich as a Jew' says the proverb. Colloquially the word is also used as a transitive verb: to jew, the

Oxford Dictionary tells us, means to 'cheat, overreach'. This is the vulgar image of the Jew and the vulgar prejudice against him, fixed in many languages, not only in English, and in many works of art, not only in *The Merchant of Venice*.

However, this is not only the vulgar image. Remember what was the occasion on which Macaulay pleaded, and the manner in which he pleaded, for political equality of Jew and gentile and for the Jew's right to sit in the House of Commons. The occasion was the admission to the House of a Rothschild, the first Jew to sit in the House, the Jew elected as Member for the City of London. And Macaulay's argument was this: if we allow the Jew to manage our financial affairs for us, why should we not allow him to sit among us here, in Parliament, and have a say in the management of all our public affairs? This was the voice of the bourgeois Christian who took a fresh look at Shylock and hailed him as brother.

I suggest that what had enabled the Jews to survive as a separate community, the fact that they had represented the market economy amidst people living in a natural economy—that this fact and its popular memories have also been responsible, at least in part, for the *Schadenfreude* or the indifference with which the populace of Europe has witnessed the holocaust of the Jews. It has been the misfortune of the Jews that, when the nations of Europe turned against capitalism, they did so only very superficially, at any rate in the first half of this century. They attacked not the core of capitalism, not its productive relationship, not its organization of property and labour, but its externals and its largely archaic trappings which so often were indeed Jewish. This is the crux of the Jewish tragedy. Decaying capitalism has overstayed its day and has morally dragged down mankind; and we, the Jews, have paid for it and may yet have to pay for it.

All this has driven the Jews to see their own State as *the* way out. Most of the great revolutionaries, whose heritage I am discussing, have seen the ultimate solution to the problems of their and our times not in nation-states but in international society. As Jews they were the natural pioneers of this idea, for who was as well qualified to preach the international society of equals as were the Jews free from all Jewish and non-Jewish orthodoxy and nationalism?

However, the decay of bourgeois Europe has compelled the Jew to

embrace the nation state. This is the paradoxical consummation of the
Jewish tragedy. It is paradoxical, because we live in an age when the
nation-state is fast becoming an anachronism, and an archaism—not
only the nation-state of Israel but the nation-states of Russia, the
United States, Great Britain, France, Germany, and others. They are all
anachronisms. Do you not see this yet? Is it not clear that at a time
when atomic energy daily reduces the globe in size, when man has
started out on his interplanetary journey, when a sputnik flies over the
territory of a great nation-state in a minute or in seconds, that at such
a time technology renders the nation-state as ridiculous and outlived
as little medieval princedoms were in the age of the steam-engine?

Even those young nation-states that have come into being as the
result of a necessary and progressive struggle waged by colonial and
semi-colonial peoples for emancipation—India, Burma, Ghana,
Algeria, and others—cannot preserve their progressive character for
long. They form a necessary stage in the history of some peoples; but it
is a stage that those peoples too will have to overcome in order to find
wider frameworks for their existence. In our epoch any new nation-
state, soon after its constitution, begins to be affected by the general
decline of this form of political organization; and this is already showing
itself in the short experience of India, Ghana, and Israel.

The world has compelled the Jew to embrace the nation-state and to
make of it his pride and hope just at a time when there is little or no hope
left in it. You cannot blame the Jews for this; you must blame the world.
But Jews should at least be aware of the paradox and realize that their
intense enthusiasm for 'national sovereignty' is historically, belated. They
did not benefit from the advantages of the nation-state in those centuries
when it was a medium of mankind's advance and a great revolutionary
and unifying factor in history. They have taken possession of it only after
it had become a factor of disunity and social disintegration.

I hope, therefore, that, together with other nations, the Jews will
ultimately become aware—or regain the awareness—of the inade-
quacy of the nation-state and that they will find their way back to the
moral and political heritage that the genius of the Jews who have
gone beyond Jewry has left us—the message of universal human
emancipation.

• • •

Notes

[1] This essay is based on a lecture given during Jewish Book Week to the World Jewish Congress, in February 1958.

[2] 'It is a serious disadvantage resulting from the great outward triumph of Christianity that the thinkers of Christendom rarely come into vital contact with other religions and other modes of world orientation. The consequence of this inexperience is that Christian ways of looking at the world are assumed to be true as a matter of course. . . . The boldest and most original thinker . . . was Spinoza, who stood above the theological prejudices from which the others could not entirely extricate themselves.' *(The Correspondence of Spinoza;* Introduction by A. Wolf.)

Daniel Lazare *has written for numerous publications including* Harper's, The Nation, *and* The New Left Review. *He has also written several books dealing with U.S. politics, constitutional theory, and urban policy, notably* The Frozen Republic *(Harcourt 1996) and* The Velvet Coup *(Verso 2001). In religious terms, he describes himself as an atheist since his bar mitzvah in 1963, an anti-Zionist since his "conversion" to Marxism in college, and a "non-Jewish Jew" since encountering Isaac Deutcher's famous essay on that subject in the 1980s. When asked if he is proud to be Jewish, his standard reply is that he is "too proud to be proud" and that loyalty to the Jewish tradition requires an attitude to that tradition that is stringently critical and combative. He is currently at work on a comparative political study of Judaism, Christianity, and Islam for Pantheon.*

ESTRANGED BROTHERS: RECONSIDERING JEWISH HISTORY

By Daniel Lazare

From *Harper's Magazine* (April 2003)

Discussed in this essay:
The Pity of It All: A History of Jews in Germany, 1743–1933 by Amos Elon. Henry Holt, 2002.

The Tragedy of Zionism: How Its Revolutionary Past Haunts Israeli Democracy by Bernard Avishai. Helios Press, 2002.

G iven the enormity of the event, it is perhaps unsurprising that the tendency since Auschwitz has been to view the history of the Jews through the lens of the Holocaust—to depict two thousand years of the Diaspora as little more than a prelude to catastrophe, and to see events since 1945 as a tale of renewal and democratic progress via the state of Israel. Two Israeli writers, however, are challenging the official mythology. In *The Pity of It All*, Amos Elon shows that the Diaspora was not the vale of tears of modern folklore but, in modern Germany at least, a period of dramatic breakthrough and progress. And in a new edition of *The Tragedy of Zionism*, Bernard Avishai argues that the Israeli state has betrayed Jewish aspirations rather than fulfilled them, promoting democracy for one ethnic group at the expense of another.

Most readers know that the "1933" in Elon's subtitle refers to Hitler's accession to power, but few will recognize the significance of 1743. It's the year that a fourteen-year-old Talmudic student named Moses Mendelssohn entered Berlin through the city gate reserved for Jews, cattle, and pigs. The boy must have been a sad sight—hunchbacked, ragged, nearly penniless, and, Elon surmises, probably barefoot as well, despite having just walked across a hundred miles of hilly countryside. Only a small number of rich Jews, plus the occasional scholar, were allowed to live in the Prussian capital, and the gatekeeper's job was to keep out all others without visible means of support. Accordingly, he questioned the boy as to what he wanted in Berlin. Mendelssohn's reply was succinct: "To learn."

The story is probably apocryphal, but it is nonetheless telling. Products of an Orthodox culture that was at once cerebral and anti-intellectual, devoted to one book (the Talmud) but hostile to all others, young Jews like Mendelssohn were starving men at a banquet. Trained in the life of the mind, they could see the Enlightenment, they fairly quivered in anticipation of all it had to offer, yet they could not get close enough to taste. Mendelssohn, who would go on to become one of Europe's most celebrated philosophers and *littérateurs* (as well as the grandfather of the even more celebrated Felix Mendelssohn-Bartholdy, the composer), was determined to satisfy his intellectual cravings. Berlin's chief rabbi had accepted him as a pupil, and, although it was strictly forbidden, Mendelssohn managed during the next few years to sneak secular books up to his room and teach himself Latin, Greek, French, English, and even proper German. (Most German Jews spoke *Judendeutsch*, a combination of medieval German and Hebrew.) Later, as news of his intellectual abilities began to spread, a few of the more liberal members of the community offered assistance. One helped him with his Latin, another introduced him to mathematics, and a third lent him books by Leibniz and Locke. Eventually, a position as tutor to the son of a wealthy silk merchant provided Mendelssohn with money to buy books of his own; as a consequence, his reading extended to Spinoza, Cicero, Euclid, Aristotle, Plato, Newton, Montesquieu, Rousseau, and Voltaire. Instead of spending his life with his nose pressed to the windowpane, Mendelssohn was now dining happily at the banquet table.

His friend Salomon Maimon was not as lucky. Yet another young Jew who wanted nothing more than to "learn, learn, learn, learn," as he would later write, he grew up poor and homeless in Poland and Lithuania, where he and his parents wandered the countryside "like the

Israelites in the Arabian desert." Maimon was so outstanding a Tal-
mudist that he was ordained a rabbi while still in his teens, yet the "Talmudic darkness"—his term for the medieval obscurantism still
enveloping East European Jewry—was more than he could bear. Forced
to marry at age eleven and a father by age fourteen, he grew tired of
spending his hours in and contemplation over "how many white hairs
a red cow may have and still be a red cow," or whether the high priest
must first "don his shirt and then his pants or vice versa." When he was
twenty-two, Maimon deserted his family and took up the life of a men-
dicant scholar. He studied the cabala, Jewish mysticism, and magic,
and briefly considered conversion to Christianity. He gained entry to
Berlin (on only his second try) but was nearly chased out when the
Jewish police discovered him with a forbidden text by Maimonides.
Although Maimon survived the encounter and went on to write several
well-received philosophical works as well as an autobiography (hailed
by Goethe, Schiller, and Kant as a masterpiece), Elon notes that
Maimon "spent his last years alone on the estate of a philosophically
minded Prussian count, comforted only by his dog, Beline. He died at
age forty-six of apparent alcoholism."

For Maimon, the "Talmudic darkness" proved inescapable. Yet,
although filled with such stories, "The Pity of It All" is not just another
lachrymose tale of Jewish suffering; it is, in fact, best read as an
extended polemic against Daniel Goldhagen's feverish 1996 study,
Hitler's Willing Executioners. The culmination of the "Diaspora as
prelude to catastrophe" school of thought, Goldhagen's book argued
that whereas other countries simply disliked the Jews, Germans by the
early nineteenth century were intent on eliminating them altogether.
Rather than conceiving and executing the Final Solution, the Nazis
merely opened the door to passions that had been building for centuries. If so, Jews like Mendelssohn and Maimon were not heroic pioneers but victims of a monstrous fraud. They fooled themselves into
believing that the Enlightenment offered an escape from prejudice,
that the larger society was beginning to welcome them, and that Germany promised something other than their total destruction.

Fortunately, Elon rejects this tautological approach (in which Germans exterminate the Jews solely because Germans suffer from an
"exterminationist" mind-set) for something a bit more nuanced.

Instead of viewing German-Jewish history backward through the prism of 1933–45, Elon presents it from the perspective of the participants themselves. From their point of view, there was indeed reason for optimism.

Mendelssohn's astonishing success reflected a growing acceptance of Jews in literary and scholarly circles and also seemed to be a harbinger of things to come. Early in his career, Mendelssohn had formed a strategic friendship with two Christian intellectuals: the playwright and journalist Gotthold Lessing and Friedrich Nicolai, a liberal publisher and bookseller. Nicolai published Mendelssohn's first book, Philosophical Dialogues, and Lessing adopted Mendelssohn as the model for his play Nathan the Wise, about a noble Jew during the Crusades who upholds the principle that Judaism, Christianity, and Islam are all of equal moral validity. With the 1767 publication of his third book, *Phaidon* (an adaptation of Plato's dialogue on immortality), Mendelssohn found that he was not only famous throughout Europe but esteemed: Catholic monks asked him for theological instruction, the Prussian Academy of Sciences elected him a member, and the duke of Brunswick offered him a ministerial post. Inspired by Mendelssohn, a Prussian civil servant named Christian von Dohm created a sensation in 1781 with a book calling for full emancipation of the Jews. When the Berlin National Theater performed Shakespeare's *Merchant of Venice* a few years later, the lead actor went on stage before the curtain rose to remind the audience "that intelligent Berliners are now beginning to show a higher regard for the coreligionists of the wise Mendelssohn." Indeed, because of Mendelssohn, German Judeophilia reached a slightly ridiculous point when Goethe, coming across a book by a Polish-Jewish poet named Isachar Falkensohn Behr, was astonished to find that the verses inside were no more than ordinary. A mediocre Jewish poet—who could imagine!

This is not to say that anti-Semitism was absent from the German landscape—it was there, even for someone of Mendelssohn's stature. Prussia's King Frederick II vetoed Mendelssohn's appointment to the Prussian Academy—the French mathematician Pierre-Louis Maupertuis said that the only qualification he lacked was "a foreskin"—and then balked at granting permanent residency status to his wife and children. Despite his fame, Mendelssohn was charged the traditional

Jewish customs duty during a trip to Dresden; although embarrassed local authorities quickly restored the money with an apology, the incident still rankled.

Indeed, German liberalism was more tenuous than most Jews realized. The French Revolution had granted civic equality to the Jews, a reform that Napoleon's troops had helped extend throughout Europe. But with Napoleon's fall in 1815, medieval barriers sprang up anew amid a spirit of romantic nationalism that was fundamentally hostile to a people it saw as foreign interlopers. In 1819, "Hep! Hep!" riots (from the Latin *Hierosolyma est perdita*—"Jerusalem is lost," the rallying cry of the Crusaders) erupted from Bavaria in the south to Hamburg in the north. Formerly so hopeful, German Jews now had to watch as mobs looted and demolished their homes and shops. The revolution of 1848 ushered in an era of liberalism, but the financial crisis of 1873 sent the pendulum back in the other direction, toward another era of prejudice and repression.

But then, as the recession subsided toward the end of the 1870s, German Jews found themselves in a "golden age" that, with the exception of a few years during World War I, would endure until the Nazi seizure of power in January 1933. It would be a serious exaggeration to say that Jews came to dominate German arts and sciences during this period, but, with Einstein, Paul Ehrlich, Walter Benjamin, Kurt Weill, and numerous others, Jews were remarkably well represented in German artistic and scientific ranks—disproportionately so, considering that they constituted less than one percent of the population. And, with Rosa Luxemburg, Eduard Bernstein, and Ferdinand Lassalle, they were similarly represented in political life, mainly on the liberal or radical side. (Elon recounts how, in 1891, the socialist leader August Bebel advised Engels that "'for decent company one must cultivate Jews.'" Although he was not enthusiastic about the idea, Engels nonetheless admitted "that Jews had more brains than 'others of the bourgeoisie.'")

German nationalism was still lurking in the background, ready to lash out at the first sign of political trouble. Yet German Jews lived in a country where the universities were open to them (compare this to the United States, where Harvard maintained a de facto Jewish quota until World War II) and where anti-Semitic mobs did not threaten to topple the government (unlike France during the Dreyfus Affair). As Elon points out, Germany's Jews were not merely grateful for an absence of restrictions but were positively drawn to a society whose values they deeply admired. If Jews were the People of the Book, Germans were *das Volk der Dichter and Denker*—the people of poets and thinkers. Heinrich Heine hailed Jews and Germans as Europe's two "ethical peoples" and even described the ancient Hebrews as "the Germans of the Orient." The poet Stefan George, noting that the German-Jewish relationship was often a troubled one, considered them "estranged brothers," and Kafka observed that they both "have a lot in common. They are ambitious, able, diligent, and thoroughly hated by others. Both are pariahs." Incredible as it may seem, Elon suggests that "before Hitler rose to power, other Europeans often feared, admired, envied, and ridiculed the Germans; only Jews seemed actually to have loved them."

What the Jews loved was not Germans per se but German high culture, a secular religion that for most Jews replaced the old religion of dietary restrictions, tribal ancestor worship, and the endless parsing of sacred texts. "With few exceptions," writes Elon, "the main thrust of [the Jews'] intellectual and political efforts—and of their reckless magnanimity—was a desperate but vain attempt to civilize German patriotism: to base citizenship not on blood but on law, to separate church and state, and to establish what would today be called an open, multicultural society."

Elon tells this story of "reckless magnanimity" extremely well; he has a cinematographer's sense of when to pull back for the long shot and when to tighten the lens for a close-up of some particularly outstanding personality—Mendelssohn, Maimon, Heine, the flamboyant financier and politician Walter Rathenau (assassinated by rightists in 1922), and, of course, Karl Marx, whose close-up is less forgiving. The most controversial of German Jews, Marx is acknowledged as "a serious thinker and social theorist" but also disparaged for founding "a world religion—with disastrous consequences."

Although the word "religion" is clearly meant here in a pejorative sense, the scope of Marx's ideas challenged the parochial confines of tradition and nation. From Mendelssohn to Einstein, many of Germany's Jews went beyond patriotism to embrace a form of universalism that

Marx ultimately came to represent. Notwithstanding their regard for German high culture, the range of their thought was far wider. Judaism could not hold them, and neither could Germany, which is why Marx, despite his often intemperate language and the many failures of the socialist movement, continued to exert such an irresistible pull.

In the late nineteenth century, however, internationalist ideas failed to arrest the momentum of the Jewish nationalist movement. Although one might assume that the Zionists would have been the most realistic in their assessment of German nationalism and the dangers that it represented, Jewish nationalists and German nationalists shared a peculiar fascination for one another. Growing up as a German in Budapest, Theodor Herzl, the founder of modern Zionism, was, Elon writes, "deeply marked by the Jewish love affair with Germany." His hero as a young man was Bismarck, he belonged to a dueling society in college, and he aspired to become a Prussian nobleman. Rather than a democracy, he envisioned the Jewish state as an "aristocratic republic"—that is, one much like Germany or Austria in the 1890s (albeit financed by a board of capitalists in London). Indeed, Herzl conceived of the new Jewish homeland as a kind of German colony:

> Life under the protectorate of this powerful, great, moral, splendidly administered, firmly governed Germany can only have the most salutary effects on the Jewish national character. . . . Strange ways of destiny! Through Zionism it will again be possible for Jews to love this Germany to which our hearts remained attached despite everything.

Despite Wilhelm's well-known anti-Semitism, Herzl struggled to enlist the kaiser in the Zionist cause. As the German monarch put it in a letter to a relative in 1898, there was no reason that Jewish nationalists and German anti-Semites could not work together:

> It would be a tremendous achievement for Germany if the world of the Hebrews looked up to me in gratitude. . . . Moreover, Zionism could harness the creative energies of the tribe of Sem to better purpose than bloodsucking; all the Semites

currently pursuing socialism in the East could engage in useful occupations.

The Tragedy of Zionism, originally published in 1985 and which Avishai has just reissued with a new prologue and epilogue, carries forward the story of this strange offspring of German nationalism to the present. According to Avishai, not only is Israel a good deal less democratic than most Americans realize but Zionism and democracy are mutually antagonistic concepts: rather than a government of, by, and for the people, Zionism entails a government of, by, and for a certain portion thereof. Although the 1948 Israeli declaration of independence promised to extend "complete equality of social and political rights to all . . . inhabitants, irrespective of religion, race or sex," it was all too predictable that, in an expressly Jewish state, some inhabitants would be deemed more equal than others.

Still, the deterioration of the democratic ideal was so gradual, at least initially, as to be all but imperceptible. Herzl may have been an aspiring aristocrat, but the movement he founded in 1896 soon fell under the influence of Russian Jews who had absorbed the rhetoric and much of the thinking of the czarist empire's burgeoning socialist movement. But ideas from one context acquired a very different meaning when transplanted to another. Whereas socialists fought against racial and religious discrimination at home (which is why Jews flocked to the movement in the first place), self-styled socialists agitated against the hiring of non-Jewish workers in Palestine. Labor Zionists had their reasons. If all Jews did was hire Arab *fellahin* to grow their oranges, they would never be more than another group of European sahibs ordering native workers this way and that. Their ties to the land would be nil. The only way to make the soil their own was to work it themselves so that both land and people would be transformed. The combination of nationalist self-sacrifice and Tolstoyan redemption through labor would prove to be a potent one.

It was also an invitation to disaster. The influx of Jewish settlers and Jewish financial contributions generated an economic boom in the future Jewish homeland. This led to an inflow of Arabs eager to improve their own economic lot, which, in turn, caused them to run headlong into restrictive hiring practices that Jewish labor organizers were busily enforcing. As both populations grew, so did the competition between them. (Despite Zionist claims about making the desert bloom, Avishai shows how Arab agricultural production between 1922 and 1938 rose just as smartly.) Clashes between Jews and Arabs soon followed, and once they began, it was impossible to tell who was retaliating for what and who was to blame at any given moment. As nationalist sentiment hardened on both sides, the Yishuv (as the settlement community was known) moved further and further to the right. Although Israel managed to retain a certain socialist gloss for a number of years after independence, the Six-Day War, of 1967, would destroy whatever pretensions to egalitarianism were left.

Indeed, the erosion of Israeli democracy that followed that war echoes the aftermath of the Franco-Prussian War a century before. Politically fragmented and economically backward, Germany was, in many ways, an unlikely victor in 1871. Yet any hope that the underdog's victory would lead to a stable balance of power between the two nations was profoundly mistaken; all it did was tip Germany in a more nationalist and militarist direction. And any hope that Israel would retreat to safe borders after 1967 and seek a modus vivendi with its Arab neighbors was mistaken as well. Instead of withdrawing from the Occupied Territories, the government moved to consolidate its hold on them, even though its new positions left Israel more vulnerable to guerrilla attack. Political command over the military gave way to the increasing militarization of Israeli politics. Before long, Moshe Dayan was delivering weirdly Teutonic speeches about the warrior ethic ("Death in combat is not the end of the fight but its peak; and since combat is a part, and at times the sum total of life, death, which is the peak of combat, is not the destruction of life, but its fullest, most powerful expression"[1]) and religious zealots were beginning to stream into the West Bank. Their numbers were small initially, but these "young men with gleaming eyes," as Avishai calls them, benefited from Zionism's inherent bias in favor of those striving to recapture every last inch of Eretz Yisrael for those proclaimed its rightful inhabitants. For Israel to say no to such expansionism, it would have had to challenge the fundamental tenets of Zionism, which no Israeli government, obviously, was prepared to do.

But this is precisely what Avishai says must now be done. Rather

than a real democracy in which full political rights accrue to the population as a whole, Israel is what Meron Benvenisti, former deputy mayor of Jerusalem, calls a *Herrenvolk* democracy, in which full political rights accrue only to a certain group. The situation is comparable to the United States before the Civil War, when white males carried their citizenship on their backs, so to speak, wherever they went: in the states, in the territories, or in disputed border regions like southern Texas. The arrangement not only permitted them to lord their political privilege over blacks, Indians, and Mexicans; it fairly encouraged them to do so in order to demonstrate that freedom was solely a white man's prerogative. Avishai observes how Israel's Jewish settlers similarly carry their citizenship on their backs into the Occupied Territories, where they, and they alone, vote in elections and benefit from extensive government subsidies. In what is supposedly the only real democracy in the Middle East, 97.5 percent of publicly held land in pre-1967 Israel is reserved exclusively for Jewish use; and a bizarre Law of Return allows any Jew immigrating to Israel from anywhere in the world to apply for a government-subsidized apartment in East Jerusalem, thereby displacing a Palestinian whose roots in the area go back generations. For Zionists, this is perfectly compatible with Yahweh's supposed promise to Abraham some four thousand years ago; but for anybody committed to democratic principles, it is perfectly perverse.

As befits a former technology editor of the *Harvard Business Review,* Avishai's blueprint for change is heavily technocratic. Impressed by Israel's role in the high-tech revolution of the 1990s, he believes that the future lies not with a Zionist state centered around Jerusalem but with a cosmopolitan, knowledge—driven "Hebrew democracy" centered around Tel Aviv. Instead of looking east toward Samaria and Judea, a post–Zionist society will look west to the Mediterranean. According to Avishai, it "will naturally expand along the coastal road and rail link that joins Herzliah, Netanya, and southern Haifa; it will become an international Hebrew-English megalopolis, anchoring the technological development of the whole region up to Turkey." This "megalopolis" would attract, no doubt, hundreds of thousands of Palestinian job-seekers from Israel proper, Gaza, the West Bank, and other points as well. But in a post-ethnic state, an influx of this sort would be no more problematic than Israeli, Russian, or Latin American immigration in multiethnic New York. The so-called demographic dilemma posed by high Palestinian birthrates would disappear, because it would no longer matter, at least not officially, whether Jews are a majority in such a state or merely a substantial minority. The only thing that would matter in this Singapore–on-the-Levant is that the economic machinery keep whirring.

Avishai's remedy is not without its problems. Now that the techno-boom has turned to bust and the country is suffering its worst economic downturn in fifty years, Israel's role in the hightech revolution no longer seems so impressive. A Tel Aviv techno-elite could also have its ugly side as Ashkenazic Jews would turn against poorer, less educated Sephardim from North Africa and the Middle East. And, although a rising economic tide lifts some boats, it often—as Marx would have pointed out—swamps others.

Nevertheless, at least Avishai is searching for some sort of solution. If Israel does not jettison the *Herrenvolk* policies of the last half-century, the outlook is clear: sectarian warfare will continue to escalate and Israeli society will continue its drift to the right. Power will continue to flow to religious fanatics, not only those in Jewish settlements and besieged Palestinian communities in Gaza and the West Bank but their equivalents in Riyadh, Cairo, Karachi, and, for that matter, the United States (where the alliance among Jewish neoconservatives, orthodox rabbis, and Christian fundamentalists is already in bloom). Instead of a post-ethnic future, Israel will retreat further into a tribalist past, and the Talmudic darkness—this time enforced by one of the world's most advanced military regimes—will become all the more enveloping. The legacy of Mendelssohn, Maimon, and, yes, even Marx, will be expunged.

● ● ●

Note

[1] Emphasis in the original

2 THE OTHER ZIONISM

Ahad Ha'am (1856–1927), who was born Asher Ginsberg to a Hasidic family in the Ukraine, was the founding father of "cultural Zionism." With its emphasis on fostering Jewish culture and learning rather than statehood in Palestine, cultural Zionism represented, in the years that led to the creation of Israel, an influential alternative to the ultimately victorious "territorial Zionism" of Theodor Herzl. For Ahad Ha'am and his heirs, notably Judah Magnes and Martin Buber, Palestine was seen as a Jewish cultural center that would spark a spiritual and intellectual renaissance for Jews around the world. Unlike their Herzlian rivals, the cultural Zionists did not aspire to make "Palestine as Jewish as England is English," as the Zionist leader Chaim Weizmann famously put it, but to foster the development of institutions like the Hebrew University in Jerusalem, perhaps the major achievement of the cultural Zionist tradition.

Cultural Zionism's critique of Herzl also entailed a strikingly different view of the Palestinian question. For Ahad Ha'am, who first visited Palestine in 1891 and wrote about his experiences in Hamelitz, a Hebrew daily newspaper published in St. Petersburg, the land of his dreams was not "an abandoned land," a phrase that figures prominently in the writings of early Zionists (later turned into the slogan "a land without a people for a people without a land"). Nor was it an uncultivated desert, waiting for Jewish farmers to make it bloom. On the contrary, "it is hard to find tillable land that is not already tilled." To be sure, Ha'am held many of the same assumptions about the Arabs as his Herzlian rivals, viewing them as a backward, indolent people who stood to benefit from Zionism's successes, and who, with sufficient kindness and charity, could be won over by their conquerors. Yet Ha'am was ahead of his times in appreciating the political dimensions of the problem, and in seeing how power deformed the moral sensibilities of Palestine's Jewish settlers, who, no longer "slaves in their land of exile," displayed "an impulse to despotism, as always happens when 'a slave becomes a king.'"

TRUTH FROM ERETZ ISRAEL (1891)

By Ahad Ha'am (Asher Ginzburg)

From *Israel Studies* (translated by Alan Dowty)

From abroad, we are accustomed to believe that Eretz Israel is presently almost totally desolate, an uncultivated desert, and that anyone wishing to buy land there can come and buy all he wants. But in truth it is not so. In the entire land, it is hard to find tillable land that is not already tilled; only sandy fields or stony hills, suitable at best for planting trees or vines and, even that, after considerable work and expense in clearing and preparing them—only these remain unworked, because the Arabs do not like to exert themselves today for a distant future. And thus it is not possible to find good land for sale every day. Not the peasants alone, but the owners of large properties as well, do not easily part with good land that has no drawbacks. Many of our people who came to buy land have been in Eretz Israel for months, and have toured its length and width, without finding what they seek.

From abroad we are accustomed to believing that the Arabs are all desert savages, like donkeys, who neither see nor understand what goes on around them. But this is a big mistake. The Arab, like all children of Shem, has a sharp intellect and is very cunning. The cities of Syria and Eretz Israel are full of Arab merchants who also know how to exploit the public and to proceed furtively with all those with whom they deal, exactly as in Europe. The Arabs, and especially those in the cities, understand our deeds and our desires in Eretz Israel, but they keep quiet and pretend not to understand, since they do not see our present activities as a threat to their future. Therefore they try to exploit us as well, to extract some benefit from the new visitors as long as they can. Yet they mock us in their hearts. The farmers are happy to have a new

Hebrew colony founded in their midst since they receive a good wage for their labor and get wealthier from year to year, as experience shows; and the owners of large properties are also happy with us, since we pay them a huge price—more than they dreamed possible—for stony and sandy land. However, if the time comes when the life of our people in Eretz Israel develops to the point of encroaching upon the native population, they will not easily yield their place. . .

• • •

There is certainly one thing we could have learned from our *past and present* history: how careful we must be not to arouse the anger of other people against ourselves by reprehensible conduct. How much more, then, should we be careful, in our conduct toward a foreign people among whom we live once again, to walk together in love and respect, and needless to say in justice and righteousness. And what do our brethren in Eretz Israel do? Quite the opposite! They were slaves in their land of exile, and they suddenly find themselves with unlimited freedom, the kind of wild freedom to be found only in a country like Turkey. This sudden change has engendered in them an impulse to despotism, as always happens when "a slave becomes a king,"[1] and behold they walk with the Arabs in hostility and cruelty, unjustly encroaching on them, shamefully beating them for no good reason, and even bragging about what they do, and there is no one to stand in the breach and call a halt to this dangerous and despicable impulse. To be sure our people are correct in saying that the Arab respects only those who demonstrate strength and courage, but this is relevant only when he feels that his rival is acting justly; it is not the case if there is reason to think his rival's actions are oppressive and unjust. Then, even if he restrains himself and remains silent forever, the rage will remain in his heart and he is unrivaled in "taking vengeance and bearing a grudge." [2]

—*21 Iyyar, 5651 (May 29, 1891) on board ship from Jaffa to Odessa*

• • •

Notes

[1] Proverbs 30:22.

[2] Leviticus 19:18.

Yitzhak Epstein, a Russian-born teacher and writer, settled in the Upper Galilee in 1886. A member of the first Aliyah, the opening wave of Jewish immigration to Palestine, Epstein devoted most of his energies to educational reform rather than politics. He might well have been forgotten, had it not been for his taboo-breaking 1905 speech in Basel, Switzerland, before a meeting of the cultural association Ivriya—a conference that happened to coincide with the Seventh Congress of the World Zionist Organization. In that speech, entitled "A Hidden Question," Epstein vividly described the Arab-Jewish struggle as, in essence, a conflict over land, and punctured one of the central myths of Zionism: that the Arabs of Palestine had no national rights which the Zionist movement was bound to respect. He warned: "We are complete illiterates in anything concerning the Arabs, *and all our knowledge about them is folk wisdom. It is time to get smart!"* Epstein's solution—a "benevolent" colonialism that, he suggested, would lead the Palestinians to regard "the day when the Jews came to settle on their land . . . as a day of salvation and redemption"—can hardly be taken seriously today. His analysis of the problem, of Zionism's willful blindness toward "the hidden question" of Palestine's indigenous inhabitants, and of the need for a historic compromise, now has the air of prophecy.

A HIDDEN QUESTION (1907)

Yitzhak Epstein

From *Israel Studies* (translated by Alan Dowty)

Among the difficult questions linked to the idea of the rebirth of our people on its land, there is one question that outweighs all the others: *the question of our attitude toward the Arabs.* This question, upon whose correct solution hangs the revival of our national hope, has not been forgotten, but has been completely *hidden* from the Zionists and in its true form is scarcely mentioned in the literature of our movement. To be sure, in recent years some fragmentary statements on the topic slipped from the mouths of a few writers; but these were the claims of the Territorialists[1] intent on proving the impossibility of practical activity in Eretz Israel, or they were accounts of the Arab Movement.[2] Faithful Zionists have not dealt with the question of what our attitude to the Arabs should be when we come to buy property in Eretz Israel, to found villages, and in general to settle the land. The Zionists certainly did not intentionally ignore one of the main conditions of settlement; they did not recognize its reality because they did not know the country and its inhabitants—and even more, they lacked human and political sensitivity.

That it was possible to avoid such a fundamental question, and that, after thirty years of settlement activity, it must be addressed as a new inquiry—this depressing fact is sufficient demonstration of the superficiality that dominates our movement and shows that we skim over the surface of things without entering into their content or core.

From the day the national movement began, and to this moment, Zionist activists have lost interest in the procedures and laws of Eretz Yisrael, while the question of the people who dwell there—its true workers and rulers—still does not arise either in the arena of actions or in theory. We all saw the prominent splinter and did not sense the hidden beam. Governmental procedures, restrictions imposed on buying land or building houses, the prohibition of Jewish entry and other such matters strikes at all who come to Eretz Israel, while from the Arab side there are not, at first glance, many obstacles. And if our brothers in Eretz Israel did not realize the seriousness of the question, it certainly never arose among Zionists far from the scene. We pay close attention to all the affairs of our land, we discuss and debate everything, we praise and curse everything, but we forget one small detail: that there is in our beloved land an entire people that has been attached to it for hundreds of years and has never considered leaving it.

For many years we have heard that the number of inhabitants in Eretz Israel is six hundred thousand. If we assume this number is correct, and subtract the eighty thousand Jews, we find that in our land there are now more than half a million Arabs, of whom eighty percent live off the land and occupy all the areas suitable for farming without further improvement. The time has come to dismiss the discredited idea, spread among Zionists, that there is in Eretz Israel uncultivated land as a result of lack of working hands and the indifference of the inhabitants. There are no empty fields; to the contrary, every *fellah*[3] tries to enlarge his plot from the land of the adjoining cistern, if it does not require excessive labor. Near cities they also till the sloping hillsides and around the settlement of Metullah the poor *fellahin*, like those in Lebanon, plant between the rocks and do not let a cubit go fallow. And thus, when we come to occupy the land, the question at once arises: what will the *fellahin* do after we buy their fields?

We buy the lands, for the most part, from the owners of large estates; these owners, or their predecessors, acquired their land by deceit and exploitation and lease it to the *fellahin*. Sometimes we buy it from villages that sell part of their property. The *fellah* who leases land is no stranger to it, but a permanent resident who stays in place, and there are *fellahin* whose grandfathers tilled the fields that they, the grandsons, are leasing. It is customary in Eretz Israel for the estate to pass from one owner to another while the tenants remain in their place. But when we buy such a property, we evict the former tillers from it. To be sure, we do not send them away empty-handed, but we pay them well for their hovels and gardens, and in general we are not stingy with money during "the dismissal." From the viewpoint of customary justice and official honesty we are completely righteous, even beyond the strict letter of the law. But, if we do not want to deceive ourselves with a conventional lie, we must admit that we have driven impoverished people from their humble abode and taken bread out of their mouths. Where will the dispossessed, with only a little money, turn? To be sure, the Hebrew settlement sometimes offers him work, at a wage higher than the pitiful income from leased land; but, first, we cannot promise that we will supply him with work permanently, and second, doing so would be a bad idea, because when we employ a *fellah* in a settlement founded on his land, we maintain his connection with the land that raised and nourished him from his birth, and he continues to regard it as his property, expropriated for the moment by foreigners. The work that we give to an Arab will never be seen, in his eyes, as indemnity for the field that was taken from him; he will take the good but not forget the bad.

In general we are making a flagrant error in human understanding toward a great, resolute, and zealous people. While we feel the love of homeland, in all its intensity, toward the land of our fathers, we forget that the people living there now also has a feeling heart and a loving soul. The Arab, like any person, is strongly attached to his homeland. Moreover, the lower his level of development and the more limited his circle of vision, the stronger will be his link to his homeland and to his neighborhood, and the harder it will be for him to leave his village and his field. He will not leave his country, he will not wander far; he is tied to his homeland with moral bonds, one of which is particularly cherished—the graves of his ancestors. In order to appreciate the depth of this feeling one must know how traditional peoples worship their dead and how often they visit their graves and include them in their lives, in their joy and in their grief. The lament of Arab women on the day that their families left Ja'uni—Rosh Pina—to go and settle on the Horan[4] east of the Jordan still rings in my ears today. The men rode on donkeys and the women followed them weeping bitterly, and the valley was filled with their lamentation. As they went they stopped to kiss the stones and the earth.

The question of land purchase can be a problem even when the *fellahin* themselves sell part of the village land. Indeed, in the farmer's distress, crushed by the burden of debts that have accumulated when he was forced to pay heavy taxes, he decides in a moment of desperation (and often in response to urgings of village elders who receive a decent cut) to sell his field; but this sale leaves in his heart a wound that will never heal, and he will always remember the cursed day in which his property fell into alien hands. I knew *fellahin* who, after selling their land, worked together with their wives for the Jews, and given their good wage and low expenses saved money. So long as they earned a good income they kept their silence, but the moment the work stopped they began to grumble about the Jews and to challenge the land sale.

Can we really rely on this way of acquiring land? Will it succeed, and does it suit our purpose? One hundred times no. The children of a people that first decreed the principle that "the land will never be sold," and limited the rights of the buyer in favor of the cultivator, need not and cannot themselves expropriate their land from cultivators who were innocently settled on it. They cannot uproot from it people who, with their ancestors, devoted to it their utmost vigor and their best labor. If there are farmers who water their fields with their own sweat and their own mother's milk, it is the Arabs. Who can appreciate the toil of a *fellah* plowing in torrential rains, harvesting on a summer day in our country, loading and transporting the produce? And what does he get for his labor? A ramshackle house, lowly and dingy, which serves as a general shelter for his family, his ox, and his donkey, the bread of poverty, a worn-out shirt and cloak—these are his clothes, day and night. And his wife and children—how meager is their portion! From her youth until her final days the Arab woman never stops silently bearing her yoke of heavy labor; she draws the water and sometimes also hews the wood, a beast of burden. With a nursing baby on her shoulders, a bundle in her robe, and a jug of water on her head she goes to the shearing and to the gleaning and from morning to evening she works bent under the heat of the blazing sun, and upon her return home, with the sun soon to return, immersed in smoke she bakes the humble bread and boils the thin broth. Yet these we will dispossess, these we will harm, their poverty we will increase?

But let us leave aside for a moment justice and sentimentality and look at the question from the viewpoint of practicality alone. Let us assume for now that in the land of our fathers we need not be concerned with others and that we are permitted—or even also obligated—

to buy any land that comes into our hands. Can such a way of buying land last for long? Will those evicted really hold their peace and calmly accept what was done to them? Will they not in the end rise up to take back with their fists what was taken from them by the power of gold? Will they not press their case against the foreigners who drove them from their land? And who knows, if they will not then be both the prosecutors and the judges . . . And they are brave, all armed, wonderful marksmen, excellent horsemen, devoted to their nation and in particular to their religion. And this people, as yet untouched by the Enlightenment that enervates men's strength, is only a small part of the great nation that occupies all the surrounding areas: Syria, Mesopotamia, Arabia, and Egypt . . .

It is easy to dismiss these words and see them as a betrayal of our ancient and eternal national ideal; but if we weigh the matter soberly, we will have to admit that it would be folly not to ascertain in advance with whom we are dealing, and not bring into account from the outset our own power and the power against us. God forbid that we should close our eyes to what is happening, which is perhaps more imminent than we imagine. It can be said with certainty, *that at the very least there is for now no Arab movement in the national and political sense of that term.* But in truth this people needs no movement; it is mighty and numerous and needs no rebirth, because it never died and never ceased existing for a moment. Physically it is superior to all the European peoples. Being partly vegetarian and drinking water, it is stronger in body than those who eat meat and drink alcohol. We must not ignore its rights, and above all we must not exploit to its disadvantage the evil of the oppressors within its own ranks. We must not provoke the sleeping lion! We must not count on the ash that covers the glowing ember; let one spark escape, and the conflagration will be uncontrollable.

I am averse to the idea that in our land we need to grovel and submit to the inhabitants, but with courage and strength we can gain their respect and dwell securely in our settlements; and in the land of the sun we can gather strength, renew our blood, and awaken. But we will sin against ourselves and our future if we thoughtlessly cast away our best weapon: the justice of our action and the innocence of our ways. So long as we cling to these we are heroes and will fear no one, but if we discard them—our power and heroism are worth nothing.

We must not buy land every time the official owners want to sell it—this the short history of the new *yishuv*[5] has clearly shown. Let me offer some relevant facts from the chronicles of the upper Galilee.

In 1897–1898 the purchase of the Druze village Metullah, in the Iyun valley on our northern border, was completed, and the large, well-known settlement of that name—the crown jewel of the *yishuv*—was founded. Metullah excels in its climate, its land, its water, and its vistas, and it has a great future. The Druze tribe, the mightiest of Arab tribes, is known for its courage, its heroism, it physical strength and beauty, and also for many spiritual qualities. As a mystical Moslem sect it is hated by the [other] Arabs and by the government, but its courage has prevailed and it is free in the land of slavery, because to this day it has never ceased fighting for its freedom. Every Druze rebellion costs the government considerable money and casualties, and so it tries to come to terms with these strong-willed people. On the Druze mountain, in Horan, government officials are sometimes afraid to enter the villages to collect taxes, as it is worth their lives.

And in the village of Metullah were more than a hundred Druze families on leased land that had changed ownership several times. The last owner was a certain pasha who loathed his tenants because he could neither evict them nor collect payment; several times the government was forced to lay siege to the village and wage war upon it in order to extract the tithe. The pasha tried to sell the estate, but found no buyer, because no one wanted to take on or to expel by force such tenants who had grown old on the land (they dwelled there some ninety years). And behold the purchase was proposed to the *pekidut*.[6] I recall that when I went with a settlement official to see the village land for the first time, the young Druze men gathered in the courtyard of their prayer-house and called to us: "If you dare to buy Metullah we will slaughter you!" The *pekidut* was then at the peak of its power, while the local government and the Arabs looked upon it as a mighty force that could sweep all obstacles aside. But in Metullah it was very difficult to overcome the obstacles; it was impossible to remove the Druze. The negotiations continued for four years, and perhaps even then would not have concluded except for an extraordinary event. In the year 1895–1896 the last Druze rebellion broke out; it lasted for a year, the tribal chiefs were exiled to Constantinople—and the *pekidut* made use of the emergency to complete the purchase. The village elders received substantial rewards, and in the circumstances violent resistance was not possible. Nevertheless many of the villagers refused to leave their homes and rejected even the most generous offers for their houses and gardens. And the day came to pass when the settlement official came to Metullah with a bag of gold coins in his carriage, and as though by chance there also appeared an army officer with troops, who came to arrest those evading military service—there are many of these among the Druze and the government does not pursue them diligently—and they were ready to command the hold-outs to sign the bills of sale. All of them of course signed, and within a few days more than six hundred souls left the village of their birth. . . . and within a week some sixty Jewish farmers, the pick of settlement workers, gathered there and occupied the Druze houses. So long as the government was pursuing the Druze and their leaders were forced into hiding—the settlement was at peace. But at the end of a year the government released the tribal chiefs from exile and issued a general amnesty for the tribe. Within a few months the Druze of Metullah submitted a protest against the *pekidut* for occupying their homes and their vineyards, which they had not sold to it. Among the claimants were also the village elders who had received a lavish price for all they had. In discussions with the settlers, they demanded that they be allowed to build houses on a plot of land next to the village, and they complained that they were not offered work or appointed as guards. Privately they warned the Jews that the settlement would come to a bitter end if its inhabitants did not take pity on their wives and children and leave.

Admittedly the Druze of Metullah are totally destitute and when they were expelled from the village, even though each received a few hundred francs, they were suddenly put in a terrible situation. In addition: after they left their village with its pleasant and healthy climate, they found temporary shelter in a Druze village in the Hula Valley, north of Mei-Merom, where marsh fever is prevalent. Thus many of them were stricken and suffered from malaria. In no way could these people come to terms with the idea that they must forget Metullah, and therefore they continued to besiege the settlement and to threaten it and also fired into one of the houses. Once at night they fell upon a Jew who was sleeping on his threshing floor and killed him. And once in broad daylight they robbed a farmer plowing his field of his yoke of oxen. Many times rumors spread that on a certain day the Druze would assault the settlement and destroy it, and the fear of death would seize all the settlers. The men would arm themselves and not get undressed, and when shots would be heard at night around the settlement they would run in panic to the spot where they expected to find the evildoers—and they would find no one. Hundreds of nights like this passed on Metullah, and it could be said that for five straight years the settlement was permeated with terror and hysteria.

The *pekidut* did what it could: it employed excellent lawyers, proved the fairness of the purchase, tried to compromise with the Druze though their tribal chiefs, scattered considerable money in every direction, and all to no effect. Sometimes they thought the disputes were finally at an end: the central government sent a vigorous order to defend the settlement, the local authority threatened the malcontents and arrested the main instigators, the tribal chief advised the protesters to accept conciliatory payments and to leave the Jews alone, and the Druze took his advice—and received a goodly sum. But a few months later some of them announced that they would not be appeased, since they were not after money but rather their land.

In any case, the Druze challenge brought another sorrow upon the settlement. The purchase of Metullah was concluded with the help of the chief of the Mutawalis, a Shi'ite Moslem sect that sucks the blood of its *fellahin* brothers. These robbers received a mediator's fee befitting their station, and in doing so found a good opportunity to get rid of assertive and free-spirited neighbors in exchange for a Jewish settlement that could conveniently be subjugated and milked. And, indeed, they spread their wings over the Jewish community and undertook to guard the settlement, and at the same time never stopped looking for pretexts to pursue pay-offs. The *pekidut* grew weary of bearing such "protection" and tried to remove it from their necks, and then these despots informed on the settlement, instigated villagers subject to their control against it, and allowed them to steal and plunder the Jews' crops. During one summer, Metullah's neighbors turned their animals free in the standing grain and at harvest time came to the fields with their donkeys and loaded on them, before the eyes of the owners, the wheat and the barley, the beans and the peas, and returned peacefully home. And when Druze threats increased, the *pekidut* was forced to ask for help from these informers and instigators, and for a high price they were again the defenders of the settlement. . . .

At last, after legal tangles, threats, and intensive effort from all sides, the *pekidut* managed to compromise with the Druze and to conciliate them with an enormous sum, and Metullah became calm, if it is possible to be calm under the necessary protection of the gang of murderers that dominates this district.

It was ordained and ordered to buy Metullah, this charmed spot, but not in this way (we shall return to this issue), that brought upon us two calamities: it aroused against us the enmity of a mighty tribe, of whose hostility we not only have to be cautious but whose trust and friendship we need, and it saddled us in this region with overlords—from the scum of the earth (this is not rhetoric, but a plain fact). Generally the Metullah affair revealed our impotence and made us an object of scorn and ridicule throughout the Galilee.

In the Iyun Valley we contended with strong opponents who do not concede one hairsbreadth of their rights, while in other settlements we are at odds with the powerless, who submit to their village elders, while the fear of authority and jail forces them to conquer their anger. But their hatred is stored deep in their hearts; they see us as sworn enemies and take their revenge on us whenever they can. Around Tiberias, the *fellahin* challenged several purchases and claimed that the sellers had falsely registered land in their own name by deceit and forgery. For some time the appellants did not allow the Jews to plow the land, and they even began to work it themselves, until the *pekidut* evicted them with the help of armed soldiers.

Indeed, the Jewish *yishuv* has already bestowed considerable bounty on the country's inhabitants: the condition of the cities and villages near the settlements has improved, hundreds of craftsmen—masons, builders, painters, [and] donkey and camel drivers—and thousands of workers find employment in the settlements, commerce has grown, and the demand for dairy products and garden produce has increased. But all of this will not compensate for what we have subverted. Our name is not inscribed on the good, but it is engraved on the bad, the memory of which will not perish. It is hard to attract lovers, but how easy it is to gain enemies among the simple *fellahin*. How strong is the envy of people who have been swept off their land. . . .

It is time to open our eyes regarding our course. If we do not want to undermine our actions, we need to consider each step that we take in our land, and to solve the question of our attitude toward the Arabs soon before it creates a Jewish question there. We have gone too far to be content with the current situation! We dare not divert our attention for a moment from reality, from the future! Every time that the imagined national advantage impinges on human justice, then this advantage also becomes a national sin that has no atonement. Our vision is so elevated, that it is not in vain that our youth aspire to realize the social ideals that move humankind in our days. But if so, then we need "to refrain from ugly deeds and their like"; that is to say, from every ugly enterprise, from every suspect step and from every action that has a tinge of injustice.

But—they will tell us—while you philosophize about every purchase and whether it is acceptable by standards of fairness, the Germans[7] will acquire it without philosophy.

I will respond to this question in a moment. But generally we do not want to resemble the Germans. They do not see the future of their people in our land, and they do not need (and who does, if they do not?) to think about the distant future and to rise above conventional honesty. Moreover, there is much we need to learn from the Germans: science, hard work, perseverance, but not the standards of fairness. The study of justice they learned from us and for some time to come they will need our instruction.

When we enter our land we must rid ourselves of all thoughts of conquest and uprooting. Our watchword must be: live and let live! God forbid that we should harm any people, much less a great people whose hatred is most dangerous to us.

What follows from all this is that, when we come to buy lands in Eretz Israel, we must thoroughly check whose land it is, who works it, and what the rights of the latter are, and we must not complete the purchase until we are certain that no one will be worse off. In this way we will have to forswear most cultivated land. What is left for us, therefore, in our land? Here we reach the critical question to which all the other important questions are secondary: how can we establish ourselves in Eretz Israel without sinning against justice and without harming anyone?

An answer to this question of questions can be found in a basic principle that we must place before ourselves in everything as a guideline for our undertakings in Eretz Israel: *we come to our land to take possession of what is not already possessed by others, to find what others have not found, to reveal for our benefit and for the happiness of all the inhabitants the hidden wealth under its soil and the concealed blessing in its skies and sun.* Regarding settlement, we will try first of all to acquire all the land that is not being cultivated because it requires improvement that is more or less difficult and expensive. This part of our land is perhaps more extensive than the part that is cultivated, since it includes most of the hills and mountains and also many valleys and ravines. A small percentage of this land will never be of use, but the greater part is suitable for trees or vines and especially figs, olives, and grapes, and a considerable part will be suitable, after clearing and deep plowing, for crops as well, and where irrigation is possible—even for intensive cultivation. . . . [8]

The hills, which are for the most part uncultivated, we need to acquire for ourselves. But, while we will take hold of the uncultivated land, we will not wash our hands of the cultivated lands. We will also buy them, not in order to evict the tenants, but instead with the explicit precondition of leaving them on the estate and bettering their condition by instituting improved agricultural methods. In the new, intensive agriculture, when the property is improved and worked scientifically, its land will support Jewish settlers as well as the *fellahin.* As enlightened owners we will devote a certain sum to the betterment of the tenants, because what is good for them is good for us. Wherever we turn we will bring some profit to the residents, but not by giving covert bribes and payoffs to be rid of them. We will bring them a true and lasting profit, material and spiritual. Our agronomists will advise them and instruct them in agricultural science, raising livestock, and selective breeding, and will also show scientific methods of fighting diseases among livestock and poultry, as well as in the field, vineyard, and garden. At a low cost, they will obtain from us medicines for the diseases prevalent in Eretz Israel, and, in time of need, the Jewish doctor will be available to them. Their children will be accepted in our schools, and when we manage to reduce the tithe to the government, it will also be reduced for them. To be sure, at first they will regard us suspiciously and will not believe in the new developments and even less in the developers, but, over time, our good intentions will become clear and they will realize the sincerity of our aspirations and the usefulness of the improvements: it is useful to know that the *fellah* is ahead of farmers of many lands in his cleverness and his practical wisdom. And then our Arab tenants will recognize us as their benefactors and comforters and will not curse the day when the Jews came to settle on their land, but will remember it as a day of salvation and redemption.

We would also use this approach when we buy part of the *fellahin* land. Every new corner of which we take hold in our land should be a ray of light and abundance to its environs and a source of benefit to its primary workers.[9] And above all doubt, after we have made efforts like these in various districts of our land, hundreds of villagers will come to request the Jews to take over their land, and other land buyers in Eretz Israel will not be able to compete with us. Then the government as well will see the great benefit that we have brought to the country's inhabitants, and even our opponents—and they are many—will have to admit that our settling in Eretz Israel brings only benefit.

This approach is not an imaginary dream. It is difficult, but it is easy, reliable, and productive compared to the approaches tried up to now. If instead of dispossessing the Druze of Metullah, we had divided the land with them, then we would not have spent on them even half of what we spent on bribes to scoundrels, on the expulsion of poor families, on legal proceedings and lawyers and on unworkable deals, we would not be in thrall to murderers, and we would surely be living with our neighbors and working our land in peace. The Druze love and respect education and would send their sons and daughters to our schools, and in coming generations we would find them not only honest neighbors, but also loyal friends. And this applies to the rest of the settlements. We wasted much capital in order to create energetic enemies when we could have spent less—but let it be even more—and gained allies, enlarging our reputation, and sanctifying the name of Israel, and bringing us nearer to our goal—opening to us the gates of hearts, which are much more important than the gates of the shore.

Our approach to land purchase must be a direct expression of our general attitude to the Arab people. The principles that must guide our actions when we settle amidst or near this people are:

A. The Hebrew people, first and foremost among all peoples
   in the teaching of justice and law, absolute equality, and

human brotherhood, respects not only the individual rights of every person, but also the national rights of every people and tribe.

B. The people Israel, as it aspires to rebirth, is a partner in thought and in deed to all the peoples who are stirring to life; it honors and respects their aspirations, and when it comes in contact with them, it cultivates their national recognition.

These two principles must be the basis of our attitude toward the Arabs—this mighty people that excels in its physical traits and in its intelligence. From the moment we come into contact, we must respect its rights. It has been attached to our land for more than 20 jubilees,[10] settling there throughout in concentration until there was no room for others, and now our historical claims may not avail us. But, fortunately, this nation occupies such a broad swath of territory that it can allow us, an ancient people so close to it in blood, language, and many spiritual traits, to occupy that part of the land of our fathers that it does not yet occupy. And it not only can, but also must for its own good, let the Jews into their country, because it is powerless to lift itself up alone and to end its poverty and ignorance, but with us alone it can overcome its deficiencies. These two peoples, the Hebrew and the Arab, can supply each other's deficiency, because what we can give to the Arabs they can get from no other people. Every nation that comes to Syria in the guise of an economic savior will seek to conquer, to subjugate, and to assimilate, which is not the case with us, the people without an army and without warships: we are guileless, we have no alien thought of subjugation and of diluting the national character of our neighbors; with a pure heart we come to settle among them in order to better them in all respects. The principle of "Do not do unto others that which is hateful to yourself"[11] we will observe positively: "Do unto others that which is pleasing to yourself"; and while we try to establish our nation, we will also support the revival of the inhabitants and will reinforce their national feeling in the best sense of the term.

We must, therefore, enter into a covenant with the Arabs and conclude an agreement that will be of great value to both sides and to all humankind. We will certainly agree to such a covenant, but the agreement of the other side is also necessary; this we will obtain gradually by means of practical action that benefits the land, us, and the Arabs. In this practical way our neighbors will little by little understand the great blessing that they can derive from the partnership between the Jewish people and the Arab people. Every new factory and every settlement that we found, every public institution that we establish, if we but share the benefit with the residents of Eretz Israel, bring us closer to our goal. Achievement of this living charter, which needs to be inscribed, not on paper or on parchment, but on the heart and mind of an entire people, is an immense undertaking that has no like in the chronicles of humankind's progress and liberation, because its outcome is the rebirth of two ancient Semitic peoples, talented and full of potential, who complement each other. It must be admitted that up to now we had the "wrong address"; in order to acquire our land, we turned to all the powers that had some link to it, we negotiated with all the in-laws but forgot about the groom himself: we ignored the true masters of the land. Without belittling all those who have an interest in our land and particularly in its government, we must deal mostly with the Arab people, and among them mostly with the *fellahin* faction, which is more straightforward and more numerous than the other factions. The most important thing we can do in this regard is to improve the condition of the tenants and the *fellahin* who live on the lands that we buy. The more we continue to buy land and to benefit those who work it, the more numerous will be those wanting to sell their land to us, the more influential we will be in Eretz Israel, and the more recognition there will be of our beneficence and indispensability.

But also in the cities there we have broad scope for action. Let us open our public institutions wide to residents of Eretz Israel: hospitals, pharmacies, libraries, reading rooms, inexpensive restaurants, savings and loan funds; let us arrange popular lectures, plays, and musical performances to their taste and in their language; let us give an important place to the Arabic language in our schools and willingly enroll Arab children in them; let us open our kindergartens to their younger children and in so doing bring great benefit to poor families: an economic, hygienic, but more importantly, spiritual and moral benefit. And through the children we will exercise an enormous influence on the adults. The time has come for us to understand that education is a great political force to which we must devote our best public effort. Indeed, others have already beat us to it, and in the large cities the Jesuits, the English, and the Americans have set up the middle and upper level educational institutions; but if we completely understood the importance of conquest of education[12] in our land and the great value that a higher scientific institute has as a general influence, we could compete with the French and the Anglo-Americans. For to all of them, science and education are only means to a religious and hegemonic end; we are teaching "torah for its own sake" and prescribe complete freedom of opinion and belief in our schools. If we were wise enough to conquer the scientific and educational institutions and to raise them to a high level so that they would be renowned throughout the lands of antiquity, thousands of students from Egypt, Syria, Mesopotamia and Turkey would stream to our schools, and they could also serve as a source of great material resources for Eretz Israel. Every decent educational institution that we found there is one small, but important, word in the charter and is worth thousands of cash payoffs.

And in our schools, as in all our institutions, let us stay away from short-sighted and small-minded nationalism that regards only itself. Let us endow it generously with sciences, crafts, labor, and physical education. Our intention is not to Judaize the Arabs, but to prepare them for a fuller life, to refine them, to develop them, to free them from their narrow vision, so that, in the course of time, they will become loyal allies, friends, and brothers. Let us prepare the inhabitants of the land and make them ready for our *yishuv*, let us be the light of science in our land and let us clear the path for law and justice. Let us do battle with the prejudices of the various nationalists who detest each other. *And all this we can do in the purity of our aspirations and our ideas, we alone and no others.*

And when we come to educate our ally and to deal with him, let us not forget another principle. As a teacher must know his student's inner soul and inclinations, so it is not enough for us to pose the final goal, but we have a duty to become properly acquainted with the Arab people, their attributes, their inclinations, their aspirations, their language, their literature, and especially to gain a deep understanding of their life, their customs, their sufferings and their torments. Let us not make the mistake that has inflicted endless damage on children's education. For thousands of years educators have seen their pupils as short adults; that is to say, they saw childhood in the body but not in the spirit, which, when it confronted the material, was—in the opinion of educators of old—already sufficiently formed, ready and prepared and armed with all the skills to understand, to be educated, and to feel. We are entering an environment that is now living in the sixteenth century, and we must take into account in all our actions the spiritual condition of this people at the moment. If we want to lead a person to a known place, we must take him from where he is now; otherwise he cannot follow us. We need, therefore, to study the psyche of our neighbors and to understand its differences. It is a disgrace that, to date, *nothing whatsoever has been done in this regard*, that so far not even one Jew has devoted himself to this topic, so that we are *complete illiterates in anything concerning the Arabs*, and all of our knowledge about them is folk wisdom. It is time to get smart!

Every item in our program needs to be clarified and systematized, while this lecture touches lightly on the broad outline of our work and shows the necessity of understanding how things really stand, while there is time.

It is possible to reject the arguments in this lecture on various grounds, but the lecturer ventures to rule on one of them: these words were said in the spirit of our nation, in the spirit of universal justice, which left its imprint on our people from the day that it became a nation. The prophet of exile, when he came to speak on the division of the land, said: "You shall allot it as a heritage for yourselves and for the strangers who reside among you, who have begotten children among you. You shall treat them as Israelite citizens; they will receive allotments along with you among the tribes of Israel. You shall give the stranger an allotment within the tribe where he resides" (Ezekiel 47:22–23). And the great prophet from Anatot [Jeremiah], who came before Ezekiel, when he came to prophesy bad tidings for the evil neighbors who were encroaching on Israel's heritage, said at the end: "I will restore them each to his own inheritance and his own land. And if they learn the ways of my people . . . then they shall be built up in the midst of my people" (Jeremiah 12:15–16).

Let us teach them the good ways, let us build them—and we will also be built.

• • •

Notes

[1] Zionists who supported establishment of a Jewish state in a location other than Palestine.

[2] Arab nationalism, which was emerging as a visible movement in the early 1900s.

[3] Arab farmer (pl: *fellahin*).

[4] The Golan Heights.

[5] "Settlement," meaning the Jewish community in Palestine. The "new" *yishuv*, Zionists who began settling in 1882, was distinguished from the "old" *yishuv*, the pre-existing Jewish population.

[6] Loosely, "administration" or "officialdom"; from *pakid*, official or clerk. In this context, *pekidut* is a specific reference to the administrative structure of officials and clerks imposed by Baron Edmond de Rothschild of Paris on the Jewish settlements that he supported. Since this accounted for most of the early settlements, the role of the *pekidut* in settlement and in new land purchases was central.

[7] The German Templars, founders of several colonies in Palestine, who were sometimes competitors for available land.

[8] At this point, a lengthy discussion on improving water use has been deleted.

[9] A play on words in Hebrew; "corner" and "ray" are the same word [keren].

[10] In other words, for over 1000 years (a jubilee is 50 years).

[11] Rabbi Hillel, in the Babylonian Talmud, Shabbat 31a.

[12] A play on "conquest of labor," in which new settlers in Eretz Yisrael (primarily from the Second *Aliyah*, beginning in 1905) rallied for the employment of Jewish workers in Jewish settlements.

In 1929, sixty-seven Jews in Hebron, including women and children, were killed in cold blood by Palestinian rioters armed with clubs, knives and sticks. The massacre followed a series of volatile Muslim-Jewish confrontations at Jerusalem's Western Wall, where Jewish worshippers had tried to put up a partition screen separating men and women, rousing fears among Muslims of Zionist ambitions to wrest control of this shared holy site. (They did so in defiance of the British Mandatory authorities rulers, who feared, correctly, that Muslims would perceive the partition as a provocation.) After the slaughter in Hebron, the violence rapidly spread, engulfing other towns in an orgy of killing by both Arabs and Jews. When the slaughter subsided, 120 Jews and eighty-seven Arabs lay dead, with hundreds of wounded on both sides. Fifty-five Arabs were convicted of murder, twenty-five of whom were sentenced to death. Two of the seventy Jews tried for murder were convicted and sentenced to death, but their sentences were commuted.

The Hebron massacre and the riots that ensued raised an outcry among Jews, many of whom denounced the attacks as a pogrom. In February 1930, **Sigmund Freud,** the founder of psychoanalysis, was asked to add his name to a petition denouncing the Arab riots. He declined to do so, in an eloquent letter underscoring the dangers that religious fanaticism and aggressive nationalism present to Jewish security.

LETTER TO THE KEREN HAJESSOD (DR. CHAIM KOFFLER) OF THE PALESTINE FOUNDATION FUND

Sigmund Freud

Vienna: 26 February 1930

Dear Sir,

I cannot do what you wish. I am unable to overcome my aversion to burdening the public with my name, and even the present critical time does not seem to me to warrant it. Whoever wants to influence the masses must give them something rousing and inflammatory and my sober judgment of Zionism does not permit this. I certainly sympathize with its goals, am proud of our University in Jerusalem and am delighted with our settlements' prosperity. But, on the other hand, I do not think that Palestine could ever become a Jewish state, nor that the Christian and Islamic worlds would ever be prepared to have their holy places under Jewish control. It would have seemed more sensible to me to establish a Jewish homeland on a less historically burdened land. But I know that such a rational viewpoint would never have gained the enthusiasm of the masses and the financial support of the wealthy. I concede with sorrow that the unrealistic fanaticism of our people is in part to be blamed for the awakening of Arab distrust. I can raise no sympathy at all for the misdirected piety which transforms a piece of Herod's wall into a national relic, thereby challenging the feelings of the natives.

Now judge for yourself whether I, with such a critical point of view, am the right person to come forward as the solace of a people deluded by unjustified hope.

Your obedient servant,

Freud

The grandson of a prominent Jewish scholar, **Martin Buber** *(1878–1965) was an influential philosopher and theologian, and a major theorist and exponent of cultural Zionism. Born in Vienna, he began to edit the Zionist weekly,* Die Welt (The World) *in 1901, but later resigned because his views on Zionism clashed with those of Theodor Herzl. In the 1920s, he devoted himself to philosophy, lecturing at the University of Frankfurt and publishing an important treatise,* I and Thou, *a study of Man's dialogue with himself, with the world, and with God. In 1938, he emigrated to Palestine, where he taught at the Hebrew University, and campaigned on behalf of a binational state founded on Arab-Jewish equality. Like Ahad Ha'am and Judah Magnes, an American-born rabbi who became the founder and first president of Hebrew University, he believed that the partition of Palestine and the creation of a Jewish state could only be achieved by violence, and that maintaining such a state in a hostile region was a recipe for permanent warfare—hardly an auspicious climate, in his view, for the spiritual revival of the Jewish people.*

ZIONISM AND "ZIONISM"

Martin Buber

From *A Land of Two Peoples* (May 1948)

Zionism and "Zionism"

From the beginning, modern Zionism contained two basic tendencies which were opposed to each other in the most thoroughgoing way, an internal contradiction that reaches to the depths of human existence. For a long time this contradiction was not felt except in the realm of ideas. However, since the political situation has grown increasingly concrete, and the need for decisive action has arisen alongside it, the internal contradiction has become more and more real, until, during recent years, it has attained shocking actuality.

One can comprehend the two tendencies at the origin as two different interpretations of the concept of [national] rebirth.

One tendency was to comprehend that concept as the intention of returning and restoring the true Israel, whose spirit and life would once again no longer exist beside each other like separate fields, each one of which was subject to its own law, as they existed during the nation's wandering in the wilderness of exile, but rather the spirit would build the life, like a dwelling, or like flesh. Rebirth—its meaning is not simply the secure existence of the nation instead of its present vulnerability, but rather the experience of fulfillment instead of our present state of being, in which ideas float naked in a reality devoid of ideas.

On the other hand, the second tendency grasps the concept of rebirth in its simplest meaning: normalization. A "normal" nation needs a land, a language, and independence. Thus one must only go and acquire those commodities, and the rest will take care of itself. How will people live with each other in this land? What will people say to each other in that language? What will be the connection of their independence with the rest of humanity?—all these questions are of no interest to this interpretation of rebirth. Be normal, and you've already been reborn!

In fact these two tendencies are only a new form of the pair that have been running about next to each other from ancient times: the powerful consciousness of the task of maintaining truth and justice in the total life of the nation, internally and externally, and thus becoming an example and a light to humanity; and the natural desire, all too natural, to be "like the nations." The ancient Hebrews did not succeed in becoming a normal nation.

Today the Jews are succeeding at it to a terrifying degree.

Never in the past have spirit and life been so distant from each other as now, in this period of "rebirth." Or maybe you are willing to call "spirit" a collective selfishness which acknowledges no higher standards and yields to no uplifting decree? Where do truth and justice determine our deeds, either outwardly or inwardly? (I said "inwardly" because unruliness directed outwards inevitably brings on unruliness directed inwards.) This sort of "Zionism" blasphemes the name of Zion; it is nothing more than one of the crude forms of nationalism, which acknowledge no master above the *apparent* (!) interest of the nation. Let us say that it is revealed as a form of *national assimilation*, more dangerous than individual assimilation; for the latter only harms the individuals and families who assimilate, whereas national assimilation erodes the nucleus of Israel's independence.

From the clear recognition of these tendencies, which stand in opposition to each other, derives the principal political question confronting us as we dig out the roots of the political problems of our day. The self-realizing tendency says: we wish to return to the earth in order to acquire the natural foundations of human life which make the spirit real. We do not wish to return to any land whatsoever, but to that land in which we first grew up, since it alone may arouse historical and meta-historical forces into action, coupling spirit with life, life with spirit. This land is not, today, devoid of inhabitants, as it was not in those times in which our nation trod upon it as they burst forth out of the desert. But today we will not tread upon it as conquerers. In the past we were forced to conquer it, because its inhabitants were essentially opposed to the spirit of "Israel." Moreover, the danger of paganization, that is to say, the danger of subjugating the spirit to the rule of the instincts, was not entirely averted even by conquest. Today we are not obliged to conquer the land, for no danger is in store for our spiritual essence or our way of life from the population of the land. Not as in ancient days, today we are permitted to enter into an alliance with the inhabitants in order to develop the land together and make it a pathfinder in the Near East—a covenant of two independent nations with equal rights, each of whom is its own master in its own society and culture, but both united in the enterprise of developing their common homeland and in the federal management of shared matters. On the strength of that convenant we wish to return once more to the union of Near Eastern nations, to build an economy integrated in that of the Near East, to carry out policies in the framework of the life of the Near East, and, God willing, to send the Living Idea forth to the world from the Near East once again. And the path to that? Work and peace—peace founded upon work in common.

In contrast to this view of Zionism, the "protective" tendency makes only one demand: sovereignty. That demand was expressed and presented in two different forms, one beside the other. The first form crystalized around the "democratic" concept of the majority: we must endeavor to create a Jewish majority in a state that will include the whole land of Israel. It was evident that the meaning of that program was war—real war—with our neighbors, and also with the whole Arab nation: for what nation will allow itself to be demoted from the position of majority to that of a minority without a fight?

When that program was revealed to be illusory, a program of tearing off took its place. That is to say, tearing one part of the land away from the rest, and in the torn off portion—once again, a majority, and the thing's name would be a Jewish State. They frivolously sacrificed the completeness of the land which the Zionist movement once set out to "redeem." If only we can attain sovereignty! The life-concept of "independence" was replaced by the administrative concept of "sovereignty." The watchword of peace was exchanged for that of struggle.

This thing was done during a period when the value of the sovereignty of small states is diminishing with frightening rapidity. Instead of the aspiration of becoming a leading and active group within the framework of a Near Eastern Union, there has come the goal of establishing a small state which is endangered in that it stands in perpetual opposition to its geo-political environment and must apply its best forces to military activity instead of applying them to social and cultural enterprises.

This is the demand for which we are waging war today.

Fifty years ago, when I joined the Zionist movement for the rebirth of Israel, my heart was whole. Today it is torn. The war being waged for a political structure risks becoming a war of national survival at any moment. Thus against my will I participate in it with my own being, and my heart trembles like that of any other Israeli. I cannot, however, even be joyful in anticipating victory, for I fear lest the significance of Jewish victory be the downfall of Zionism.

*Best known for his revolutionary contributions to modern physics, **Albert Einstein** (1879–1955) was also a democratic socialist and humanist. As a Jew who had suffered from anti-Semitism in his native Germany—he left Berlin a month before Hitler came to power and settled in Princeton, New Jersey— Einstein gravitated toward Zionism. In the 1920s he made the first of many trips to Jerusalem, where he befriended many Israelis at Hebrew University, to which he left his scientific papers. But, as these three statements reveal, Einstein's Zionism was a tolerant, open one, close in spirit to that of Ha'am and Buber. In the first statement, made just after the Hebron riots of 1929, Einstein laments "the tragic events of late August," and, rather than calling for revenge, expresses his hope that "the two great Semitic peoples . . . may have a great future in common." In the second statement, a 1938 speech, he honors the "productive work in Palestine," but opposes the "creation of a Jewish state," because he is "afraid of the inner damage Judaism will sustain- especially in the development of a narrow nationalism in our own ranks." In the final statement, a group letter published on December 4, 1948 in* The New York Times, *Einstein deplores the forthcoming visit to the United States of Menachem Begin, the leader of the terrorist Irgun party that slaughtered over a hundred unarmed Palestinians in the village of Deir Yassin on April 9 of that year. Einstein's remarks on Begin, whom he did not hesitate to call a fascist, are particularly interesting in light of the Irgun leader's future as a statesman. Begin went on to become Israel's Prime Minister, and, with Ariel Sharon, his Minister of Defense, to carry out the disastrous invasion of Lebanon in 1982. The "revisionist" Zionism that Begin embodied, and which Einstein viewed, with with what now looks like touching innocence, as a fringe phenomenon, is the Israeli mainstream today.*

THREE STATEMENTS

Albert Einstein

Falastin (Palestinian newspaper), 28th January 1930

Letter to the Editor of Falastin

One who, like myself, has cherished for many years the conviction that the humanity of the future must be built up on an intimate community of the nations, and that aggressive nationalism must be conquered, can see a future for Palestine only on the basis of peaceful cooperation between the two peoples who are at home in the country. For this reason I should have expected that the great Arab people will show a truer appreciation of the need which the Jews feel to rebuild their national home in the ancient seat of Judaism; I should have expected that by common effort ways and means would be found to render possible an extensive Jewish settlement in the country.

I am convinced that the devotion of the Jewish people to Palestine will benefit all the inhabitants of the country, not only materially, but also culturally and nationally. I believe that the Arab renaissance in the vast expanse of territory now occupied by the Arabs stands only to gain from Jewish sympathy. I should welcome the creation of an opportunity for absolutely free and frank discussion of these possibilities, for I believe that the two great Semitic peoples, each of which has in its way contributed something of lasting value to the civilisation of the West, may have a great future in common, and that instead of facing each other with barren enmity and mutual distrust, they should support each other's national and cultural endeavours, and should seek the possibility of sympathetic co-operation. I think that those who are not actively engaged in politics should above all contribute to the creation of this atmosphere of confidence.

I deplore the tragic events of last August not only because they revealed human nature in its lowest aspects, but also because they have estranged the two peoples and have made it temporarily more difficult for them to approach one another. But come together they must, in spite of all.

Speech to the National Labor Committee for Palestine, New York, 17th April 1938

Our Debt to Zionism

Rarely since the conquest of Jerusalem by Titus has the Jewish community experienced a period of greater oppression than prevails at the present time. In some respects, indeed, our own time is even more troubled, for man's possibilities of emigration are more limited today than they were then.

Yet we shall survive this period too, no matter how much sorrow, no matter how heavy a loss in life it may bring. A community like ours, which is a community purely by reason of tradition, can only be strengthened by pressure from without. For today every Jew feels that to be a Jew means to bear a serious responsibility not only to his own community, but also toward humanity. To be a Jew, after all, means first of all, to acknowledge and follow in practice those fundamentals in humaneness laid down in the Bible-fundamentals without which no sound and happy community of men can exist.

We meet today because of our concern for the development of Palestine. In this hour one thing, above all, must be emphasized: Judaism owes a great debt of gratitude to Zionism. The Zionist movement has revived among Jews the sense of community. It has performed productive work surpassing all the expectations any one could entertain. This productive work in Palestine, to which self-sacrificing Jews throughout the world have contributed, has saved a large number of our brethren from direst need. In the particular, it has been possible to lead a not inconsiderable part of our youth toward a life of joyous and creative work.

Now the fateful disease of our time—exaggerated nationalism, borne up by blind hatred—has brought our work in Palestine to a most difficult stage. Fields cultivated by day must have armed protection at night against fanatical Arab outlaws. All economic life suffers from insecurity. The spirit of enterprise languishes and a certain measure of unemployment (modest when measured by American standards) has made its appearance.

The solidarity and confidence with which our brethren in Palestine face these difficulties deserve our admiration. Voluntary contributions by those still employed keep the unemployed above water. Spirits remain high, in the conviction that reason and calm will ultimately reassert themselves. Everyone knows that the riots are artificially fomented by those directly interested in embarrassing not only ourselves but especially England. Everyone knows that banditry would cease if foreign subsidies were withdrawn.

Our brethren in other countries, however, are in no way behind those in Palestine. They, too, will not lose heart but will resolutely and firmly stand behind the common work. This goes without saying.

Just one more personal word on the question of partition. I should much rather see reasonable agreement with the Arabs on the basis of living together in peace than the creation of a Jewish state. Apart from practical consideration, my awareness of the essential nature of Judaism resist the idea of a Jewish state with borders, an army , and a measure of temporal power no matter how modest. I am afraid of the inner damage Judaism will sustain-—especially from the development of a narrow nationalism with in our own ranks, against which we have already had to fight strongly, even without a Jewish state. A return to a nation in the political sense of the word would be equivalent to turning away from the spiritualization of our community which we owe to the genius of our prophets. If external necessity should after all compel us to assume this burden, let us bear it with tact and patience.

One more word on the present psychological attitude of the world at large, upon which our Jewish destiny also depends. Anti-Semitism has always been the cheapest means employed by selfish minorities for deceiving the people. A tyranny based on such deception and maintained by terror must inevitably perish from the poison it generates within itself. For the pressure of accumulated injustice strengthens those moral forces in man which lead to a liberation and purification of public life. May our community through its suffering and its work contribute toward the release of those liberating forces.

• • •

Letter to the *New York Times*, December 4, 1948:

New Palestine Party Visit of Menachem Begin and Aims of Political Movement Discussed

To the Editors of the *New York Times*:

Among the most disturbing political phenomena of our times is the emergence in the newly created state of Israel of the "Freedom Party" (Tnuat Haherut), a political party closely akin in its organization, methods, political philosophy and social appeal to the Nazi and Fascist parties. It was formed out of the membership and following of the former Irgun Zvai Leumi, a terrorist, right-wing, chauvinist organization in Palestine.

The current visit of Menachem Begin, leader of this party, to the United States is obviously calculated to give the impression of American support for his party in the coming Israeli elections, and to cement political ties with conservative Zionist elements in the United States. Several Americans of national repute have lent their names to welcome his visit. It is inconceivable that those who oppose fascism throughout the world, if correctly informed as to Mr. Begin's political record and perspectives, could add their names and support to the movement he represents.

Before irreparable damage is done by way of financial contributions, public manifestations in Begin's behalf, and the creation in Palestine of the impression that a large segment of America supports Fascist elements in Israel, the American public must be informed as to the record and objectives of Mr. Begin and his movement.

The public avowals of Begin's party are no guide whatever to its actual character. Today they speak of freedom, democracy and anti-imperialism, whereas until recently they openly preached the doctrine of the Fascist state. It is in its actions that the terrorist party betrays its real character; from its past actions we can judge what it may be expected to do in the future.

Attack on Arab Village

A shocking example was their behavior in the Arab village of Deir

Yassin. This village, off the main roads and surrounded by Jewish lands, had taken no part in the war, and had even fought off Arab bands who wanted to use the village as their base. On April 9 (*The New York Times*), terrorist bands attacked this peaceful village, which was not a military objective in the fighting, killed most of its inhabitants 240 men, women, and children and kept a few of them alive to parade as captives through the streets of Jerusalem. Most of the Jewish community was horrified at the deed, and the Jewish Agency sent a telegram of apology to King Abdullah of Trans-Jordan. But the terrorists, far from being ashamed of their act, were proud of this massacre, publicized it widely, and invited all the foreign correspondents present in the country to view the heaped corpses and the general havoc at Deir Yassin.

The Deir Yassin incident exemplifies the character and actions of the Freedom Party.

Within the Jewish community they have preached an admixture of ultranationalism, religious mysticism, and racial superiority. Like other Fascist parties they have been used to break strikes, and have themselves pressed for the destruction of free trade unions. In their stead they have proposed corporate unions on the Italian Fascist model.

During the last years of sporadic anti-British violence, the IZL and Stern groups inaugurated a reign of terror in the Palestine Jewish community. Teachers were beaten up for speaking against them, adults were shot for not letting their children join them. By gangster methods, beatings, window-smashing, and wide-spread robberies, the terrorists intimidated the population and exacted a heavy tribute.

The people of the Freedom Party have had no part in the constructive achievements in Palestine. They have reclaimed no land, built no settlements, and only detracted from the Jewish defense activity. Their much-publicized immigration endeavors were minute, and devoted mainly to bringing in Fascist compatriots.

Discrepancies Seen

The discrepancies between the bold claims now being made by Begin and his party, and their record of past performance in Palestine bear the imprint of no ordinary political party. This is the unmistakable stamp of a Fascist party for whom terrorism (against Jews, Arabs, and

British alike), and misrepresentation are means, and a "Leader State" is the goal.

In the light of the foregoing considerations, it is imperative that the truth about Mr. Begin and his movement be made known in this country. It is all the more tragic that the top leadership of American Zionism has refused to campaign against Begin's efforts, or even expose to its own constituents the dangers to Israel from support to Begin.

The undersigned therefore take this means of publicly presenting a few salient facts concerning Begin and his party; and of urging all concerned not to support this latest manifestation of fascism.

ISIDORE ABRAMOWITZ, HANNAH ARENDT, ABRAHAM BRICK, RABBI JESSURUN CARDOZO, ALBERT EINSTEIN, HERMAN EISEN, M.D., HAYIM FINEMAN, M. GALLEN, M.D., H.H. HARRIS, ZELIG S. HARRIS, SIDNEY HOOK, FRED KARUSH, BRURIA KAUFMAN, IRMA L. LINDHEIM, NACHMAN MAISEL, SEYMOUR MELMAN, MYER D. MENDELSON, M.D., HARRY M. OSLINSKY, SAMUEL PITLICK, FRITZ ROHRLICH, LOUIS P. ROCKER, RUTH SAGIS, ITZHAK SANKOWSKY, I.J. SHOENBERG, SAMUEL SHUMAN, M. SINGER, IRMA WOLFE, STEFAN WOLFE.

A German-Jew, a refugee from Nazism, and one of the most gifted moral and political thinkers of the last century, **Hannah Arendt** *(1906–1975) is best remembered for her writings on totalitarianism. But woven into all her work is a profound concern with the history of Jews in modern Europe, as they struggled to find a place for themselves under hostile, and sometimes life-threatening conditions. Some members of the Jewish elite, she wrote, became* parvenus, *seeking in vain to escape their Jewish identity by assimilating into Gentile society (often to the point of conversion), while others found a sanctuary from anti-Semitism within the framework of Jewish religion and tradition. Neither self-abnegating assimilation nor tribal insularity appealed to Arendt, who praised instead the tradition of "conscious pariahs," Jews like Heinrich Heine, Franz Kafka and Walter Benjamin, who "were great enough to transcend the bounds of nationality and to weave the strands of their Jewish genius into the texture of European life." Arendt epitomized the "conscious pariah," as surely as Isaac Deutscher epitomized the "non-Jewish Jew." She thereby incurred the wrath of the Jewish establishment, of which she was a scalding critic. For as much as she despised antisemitism, she also believed that Jews had suffered since their emancipation from their own tribalism and from the excessive trust that their leaders placed in the state. And because she did not mince words, she found herself attacked—and finally ostracized—as a "self-hating Jew." In a famous exchange of letters that followed the publication of* Eichmann in Jerusalem, *her controversial book on the trial of Nazi leader Adolf Eichmann and the "banality of evil," Gershom Scholem said he found "little trace" in Arendt's writing of* Ahabath Israel, *or "love of the Jewish people." Arendt sharply replied: "You are quite right—I am not moved by any 'love' of this sort, and for two reasons: I have never in my life 'loved' any people or collective—neither the German people, nor the French, nor the American, nor the working class or anything of that sort. I indeed love 'only' my friends and the only kind of love I know of and believe in is the love of persons."*

Nevertheless, Arendt did not hesitate to support Jewish causes she considered just. The creation of a "Jewish homeland" in Palestine was one such cause. But, she pointedly added, "This goal must never be sacrificed to the pseudo-sovereignty of a Jewish State." As Israel constructs a "separation fence" confining the Palestinian people to the sort of ghetto Jews have known all too well in their history, we would do well to heed Arendt's warning at the close of this remarkable essay: "Chauvinism of the Balkan type could use the religious concept of the chosen people and allow its meaning to degenerate into hopeless vulgarity."

"THE JEW AS PARIAH": PEACE OR ARMISTICE IN THE NEAR EAST?

Hannah Arendt

From *The Jew as Pariah: Jewish Identity and Politics in the Modern Age* (1950)

Peace in the Near East is essential to the State of Israel, to the Arab people and to the Western world. Peace, as distinguished from an armistice, cannot be imposed from the outside, it can only be the result of negotiations of mutual compromise and eventual agreement between Jews and Arabs.

The Jewish settlement in Palestine may become a very important factor in the development of the Near East, but it will always remain a comparatively small island in an Arab sea. Even in the event of maximum immigration over a long period of years the reservoir of prospective citizens of Israel is limited to roughly two million, a figure that could be substantially increased only by catastrophic events in the United States or the Soviet Union. Since, however, (apart from the improbability of such a turn of events) the State of Israel owes its very existence to these two world powers, and since failure to achieve a genuine Jewish-Arab understanding will necessarily make its survival even more dependent upon continued sympathy and support of one or the other, a Jewish catastrophe in the two great surviving centers of world Jewry would lead almost immediately to a catastrophe in Israel.

The Arabs have been hostile to the building of a Jewish homeland almost from the beginning. The uprising of 1921, the pogrom of 1929,

Note: This paper was written in 1948 upon the suggestion of Judah L. Magnes, the late President of the Hebrew University in Jerusalem, who from the close of World War I to the day of his death in October, 1948, had been the outstanding Jewish spokesman for Arab-Jewish understanding in Palestine. It is dedicated to his memory.

the disturbances from 1936 to 1939 have been the outstanding land-marks in the history of Arab-Jewish relations under British rule. It was only logical that the evacuation of British troops coincided with the outbreak of a Jewish-Arab war; and it is remarkable how little the accomplished fact of a State of Israel and Jewish victories over Arab armies have influenced Arab politics. All hopes to the contrary notwithstanding, it seems as though the *one* argument the Arabs are incapable of understanding is force.

As far as Arab-Jewish relations are concerned, the war and the Israeli victories have not changed or solved anything. Any settlement short of genuine peace will give the Arabs time to grow stronger, to mend the rivalries between the Arab states, possibly to promote revolutionary changes, social, economic and political. Probably such changes in the Arab world will come about in any event, but the question is whether they will be inspired by the thought of *revanche* and crystallize around a common hostility against Israel, or whether they will be prompted by an understanding of common interests and crystallize around close economic and political cooperation with the Jews, the most advanced and Westernized people of the region. Arab reluctance, on the one hand, to begin direct peace talks and the (implied) admission that they may prefer a peace imposed by an outside power, and Israeli handling of the Arab refugee problem on the other, argue in favor of the first possibility. But all considerations of the self-interest of both peoples speak for the second. To be sure, these reasons are weak in a century when political issues are no longer determined by common sense and when the representatives of great powers frequently behave more like gamblers than statesmen.

To such general considerations must be added the education in irre-sponsibility which was the concomitant of the mandate system. For twenty-five years, the peoples of Palestine could rely upon the British government to uphold adequate stability for general constructive pur-poses and feel free to indulge in all kinds of emotional, nationalistic, illusionary behavior. Occasional outbreaks, even if they enlisted almost unanimous popular support (as, for instance, the disturbances of 1936 to 1939 which were preceded by a successful Arab general strike, or the Jewish fight against Arab labor 1934–1935–1936 which was supported by practically the whole Jewish population), led to nothing more serious than another Inquiry Commission or another turn in the complicated game of British imperialist policy.

It is only natural that in an atmosphere where nothing was quite serious both parties grew more and more reckless, were more and more inclined to consider only their own interests and to overlook the vital realities of the country as a whole. Thus the Arabs neglected to take into account the rapid growth of Jewish strength and the far-reaching consequences of economic development, while the Jews ignored the awakening of colonial peoples and the new nationalist solidarity in the Arab world from Iraq to French Morocco. In hope or in hate both peoples have focused their attention so exclusively upon the British that they practically ignored each other: the Jews forgot that the Arabs, not the English, were the permanent reality in Near Eastern policies and the Arabs that Jewish settlers, and not British troops, intended to stay permanently in Palestine.

The British, on the other hand, were quite content with this state of affairs, because it prevented both a working agreement between Jews and Arabs, which might have resulted in a rebellion against British rule, and an open conflict between them, which might have endangered the peace of the country. No doubt, "if the British Government had really applied itself with energy and good will to the establishment of good relations between the Jews and the Arabs, such could have been accomplished" (Chaim Weizmann). Yet, British interest in Arab-Jewish understanding awoke only when the British had decided to evacuate the country—a decision by the way which was caused neither by Jewish terrorism nor by the Arab League, but came as a consequence of the Labor Government's liquidation of the British rule in India. Since then the British have been genuinely interested in an Arab-Jewish settlement and in the prevention of the Balkanization of the region which may again attract a third power. But although the interests of the peoples of the Near East certainly coincide with British interests at this moment, the past record of British imperialism has made it impossible for her to negotiate a reasonable settlement.

But the choice between genuine peace and armistice is by no means only, or even primarily, an issue of foreign policy. The internal structure of the Arab as well the Jewish states will depend upon it. A mere armistice would force the new Israeli state to organize the whole people for permanent potential mobilization; the permanent threat of armed intervention would necessarily influence the direction of all economic and social developments and possibly end in a military dictatorship. The cultural and political sterility of small thoroughly militarized nations has been sufficiently demonstrated in history. The examples of Sparta and similar experiments are not likely to frighten a generation of European Jews who are trying to wipe out the humiliation of Hitler's slaughterhouses with the newly-won dignity of battle and the triumph of victory. Nevertheless, even this generation should be able to realize that an independent Spartan existence will be possible only after the country has been built up and after the Jewish homeland has been definitely established, by no means the case now. Excessive expenditures on armaments and mobilization would mean not only the stifling of the young Jewish economy and the end of the country's social experiments, but lead to an increasing dependence of the whole population upon financial and other support from American Jewry.

A condition of no-peace and no-war will be far easier for the Arabs to bear precisely because of the stagnation of their economic life and the backwardness of their social life. In the long run, however, the poverty-stricken, undeveloped and unorganized Near East needs peace as badly as the Jews; it needs Jewish cooperation in order quickly to achieve the strength to prevent its remaining a power vacuum and to assure its independence. If the Arab states are not just pretending but really are afraid of Russian aggression, their only salvation lies in sincere collaboration with the State of Israel. The Arabs' argument that they can do without Jewish help and prefer to grow slowly and organically rather than be influenced by "foreign" Western methods and ideas may sound very attractive to a few romantics inside and outside the Arab world. The simple truth of the matter is that the world's political pace will not allow them enough time for "organic" development; the Arabs, though potentially stronger than the Jews, are not a great power either and hardly on the way to becoming one. The victories of the Israeli army are dangerous to them not so much because of possible Jewish domination as because of the demonstrated power vacuum. If they continue to be anti-Western, to spend their energies fighting the tiny Jewish state and indulging their sterile pride in keeping the national character intact, they are threatened with something far worse, and much more real, than the bogey of Jewish domination.

In terms of international politics, the danger of this little war between two small peoples is that it inevitably tempts and attracts the great powers to interfere, with the result that existing conflicts explode because they can be fought out by proxy. Until now, neither the Jewish charge of an *Anglo*-Arab invasion nor the Arab countercharge of a *Russian*-Jewish aggression has contained any truth at all. The reason, however, why both legends sound so plausible and are so frequently accepted is that such a situation can indeed develop.

Moreover, the last war showed all too clearly that no better pretext or greater help exists for would-be aggressors than petty national conflicts fought out in chauvinist violence. The peoples of the Near East who show such a disturbing resemblance in psychology and political mentality to the small nations of Central and Eastern Europe, would do well to consider how easily these latter were conquered by Stalin as well as by Hitler, and to compare them with the more fortunate small nations, like the Scandinavian countries and Switzerland, who were not devoured by hate and not torn by chauvinistic passion.

The great good fortune of Jews as well as Arabs at this moment is that America and great Britain not only have no interest in further hostilities, but, on the contrary, are genuinely eager to bring about an authentic pacification of the whole region. Mutual denunciations by Jews and Arabs to the effect that they are either British or Russian agents serve only to cloud the real issues: Jewish determination to keep and possibly extend national sovereignty without consideration for Arab interests, and Arab determination to expel the Jewish "invaders" from Palestine without consideration for Jewish achievements there. If this "independent and sovereign" behavior (Arab unwillingness during the war to take British advice, and the Jewish inclination to interpret as pressure any device which America may offer, for instance, in the question of Arab refugees) goes on unabated, then all independence and sovereignty will be lost. Since a trusteeship under the United Nations has become impossible, continuance of this stubbornness leaves only three kinds of peace which the world may finally be willing to offer the Near East: a Pax Britannica which is very unlikely at the moment, a Pax

Americana which is even more unlikely, or a Pax Moscovita which, alas, is the only actual danger.

The Incompatibility of Claims

A good peace is usually the result of negotiation and compromise, not necessarily of a program. Good relationships between Jews and Arabs will depend upon a changed attitude toward each other, upon a change in the atmosphere in Palestine and the Near East, not necessarily upon a formula. Hardly any conflict in the history of the world has given rise to so many programs and formulae from the outside; yet none of them has ever been acceptable to either side. Each has been denounced as soon as it was published as pro-Jewish by the Arabs and pro-Arab by the Jews.

The reception of the two Bernadotte Peace Proposals is typical. The first report to the United Nations concluded with a series of recommendations, made in the spirit of the United Nations' decision of partition; they provided for political implementation of economic cooperation through a "coordinated foreign policy" and "measures of common defense," for negotiated boundaries and for a limited guarantee of Jewish immigration. The second report, on the contrary, recommended two completely sovereign and independent political entities, separated by neutralized zones, and temporarily supervised by a UN commission. Both reports were denounced equally by both sides. The differences between the two Peace Proposals were hardly recognized because they had one thing in common: the recognition of the existence of a State of Israel on one side, and the Existence of an Arab population in Palestine and the Near East on the other.

Since no formula, however good and sensible, seems to be acceptable to either side while the present mood of the two peoples persists, it may well be that any plan, however rudimentary, will be a sufficient basis of negotiations as soon as this mood is changed.

The past two years will stand out in Jewish history for many decades, and perhaps for many centuries to come. Even if the establishment of a Jewish State and the outbreak of an Arab-Jewish war may turn out ultimately to be one of many ephemeral episodes in an unhappy history of a country that has known many changes of rulers and fortune, their place as a turning point in Jewish history has already been decided. The majority of the Jewish people feel that the happenings of the last years have a closer relation to the destruction of the Temple in 70 A.D. and the Messianic yearnings of two thousand years of dispersion, than to the United Nations' decision of 1947, the Balfour Declaration of 1917, or even to fifty years of pioneering in Palestine. Jewish victories are not fudged in the light of present realities in the Near East but in the light of a very distant past; the present war fills every Jew with "such satisfaction as we have not had for centuries, perhaps not since the days of the Maccabees" (Ben-Gurion).

This feeling of historical momentum, this determination to regard these recent events as a final verdict of history, is doubtless strengthened by success, but success is not its source. The Jews went into battle against the British occupation troops and the Arab armies with the "spirit of Masadah," inspired by the slogan "or else we shall go down," determined to refuse all compromise even at the price of national suicide. Today the Israeli government speaks of accomplished facts, of Might is Right, of military necessities, of the law of conquest, whereas two years ago, the same people in the Jewish Agency spoke of justice and the desperate needs of the Jewish people. Palestinian Jewry bet on one card—and won.

Against Jewish determination to regard the outcome as final stands the determination of the Arabs to view it as an interlude. Here, too, we are confronted with a decision which is neither deducible from events nor changed in the least by them. Defeats seem to confirm the Arabs' attitude as much as victories do that of the Jews. Arab policy in this respect is very simple and consists mainly in a diplomacy which discounts defeats and states and restates with undisturbed stubbornness the old claim to ownership of the country and refusal to recognize the State of Israel.

This mutual refusal to take each other seriously is perhaps the clearest sign of the seriousness of the situation. During the war, it expressed itself in the dangerous inclination to interpret the whole conflict as the result of a sinister behind-the-scenes conspiracy in which the Arabs were not confronted with 700,000 or 800,000 Palestinian Jews but with the overwhelming strength of American or Russian imperialism or both, while the Jews insisted that they fought not so much the members of the Arab League as the entire might of the British Empire. That the Arabs should attempt to find a plausible explanation for the fact that six Arab states could not win a single victory against the tiny forces of Palestinian Jewry, and that the Jews should shrink from the idea of being permanently surrounded by hostile neighbors who so hopelessly outnumbered them, is understandable enough. The net result, however, of a propaganda (by itself hardly worthy of consideration) which treats the real opponent as a kind of ghost or tool is an atmosphere where negotiations are impossible: for what is the point of taking statements and claims seriously if you believe that they serve a conspiracy?

This utterly unreal situation is not new. For more than twenty-five years, Jews and Arabs have made perfectly incompatible claims on each other. The Arabs never gave up the idea of a unitary Arab state in Palestine, though they sometimes reluctantly conceded limited minority rights to Jewish inhabitants. The Jews, with the exception of the Revisionists, for many years refused to talk about their ultimate goals, partly because they knew only too well the uncompromising attitude of the Arabs and partly because they had unlimited confidence in British protection. The Biltmore program of 1942 for the first time formulated Jewish political aims officially—a unitary Jewish state in Palestine with the provision of certain minority rights for Palestinian Arabs who then still formed the majority of the Palestinian population. At the same time, the transfer of Palestinian Arabs to neighboring countries was contemplated and openly discussed in the Zionist movement.

Nor is this incompatibility only a matter of politics. The Jews are convinced, and have announced many times, that the world—or history or higher morality—owes them a righting of the wrongs of two thousand years and, more specifically, a compensation for the catastrophe of European Jewry which, in their opinion, was not simply a crime of Nazi Germany but of the whole civilized world. The Arabs, on the other hand, reply that two wrongs do not make a right and that "no code of morals can justify the persecution of one people in an attempt to relieve the persecution of the other." The point of this kind of argumentation is that it is unanswerable. Both claims are nationalistic because they make sense only in the closed framework of one's own people and history, and legalistic because they discount the concrete factors of the situation.

Social and Economic Separation

The complete incompatibility of claims which until now has frustrated every attempt to compromise and every effort to find a common denominator between two peoples whose common interests are patent to all except themselves is only the outward sign of a deeper, more real incompatibility. It is incredible and sad, but it is true, that more than three decades of intimate proximity have changed very little the initial feeling of complete strangeness between Arabs and Jews. The way the Arabs conducted this war has proved better than anything else how little they knew of Jewish strength and the will to fight. To the Jews, similarly, the Arabs they met for so many years in every city, village and rural district, with whom they had constant dealing and conflicts, have remained phantoms, beings whom they have considered only on the irrelevant levels of folklore, nationalist generalizations, or idle idealistic dreams.

The Jewish and Arab failure to visualize a close neighbor as a concrete human being has many explanations. Outstanding among them is the economic structure of the country in which the Arab and Jewish sectors were separated by, so to speak, watertight walls. The few exceptions, such as common export organizations of Jewish and Arab orange growers or a few factories that employed both Jewish and Arab labor, only confirmed the rule. The building of the Jewish homeland, the most important economic factor in the recent history of the entire Near East, never depended on Jewish-Arab cooperation, but exclusively on the enterprise and pioneering spirit of Jewish labor and the financial support of world Jewry. Jewish economy may eventually have to depend heavily if not exclusively on the Arab markets of the Near East. But this stage of mutual dependence is still far off and will be reached only after Palestine has been fully industrialized and the Arab countries have reached a level of civilization that could offer a market for high-quality merchandise, which only Jewish economy will probably be able to produce profitably.

The struggle for political sovereignty, necessarily accompanied by heavy expenditure for armaments and even more decisive losses in work hours, has retarded considerably the development toward economic independence. As long as outside financial support on a large scale is assured, Jewish-Arab cooperation can hardly become an economic necessity for the new Israeli state. The same has been true in the past. The financial support of world Jewry, without which the whole experiment would have failed, signified economically that the Jewish settlement could assert itself without much thought of what was going on in the surrounding world, that it had no vital interest, except on humanitarian grounds, in raising the Arab standard of living and that economic issues could be fought out as though the Jewish National Home were completely isolated from its neighbors.

Naturally economic and social isolation had its good and its bad aspects. Its advantage was that it made possible such experiments as the collective and cooperative settlements, that an advanced and in many respects very promising economic structure could impose itself upon an environment of hopeless misery and sterility. Its economic disadvantage was that the experiment dangerously resembled a hothouse plant and that the social and political problems which arose from the presence of a native population could be handled without consideration of objective factors.

Organized Jewish labor fought and won a relentless battle against cheap Arab labor; the old-time Arab *fellahin*, even though they were not deprived of their soil by Jewish settlement, quickly became a kind of relic, unfit for and superfluous to the new modernized structure of the country. Under the leadership of Jewish labor, Palestine underwent the same industrial revolution, the same change from a more or less feudal to a more or less capitalist order, as European countries did 150 years ago. The decisive difference was only that the industrial revolution had created and employed its own fourth estate, a native proletariat, whereas in Palestine the same development involved the importation of workers and left the native population a potential proletariat with no prospect of employment as free laborers.

This unhappy potential Arab proletariat cannot be argued away by statistics about land sales nor can it be counted in terms of the destitute. Figures do not show the psychological changes of the native population, their deep resentment against a state of affairs which seemingly left them untouched, and in reality demonstrated to them the possibility of a higher standard of living without ever fulfilling the implied promises. The Jews introduced something new into the country which, through sheer productivity, soon became the decisive factor.

Compared to this new life, the primitive Arab economy assumed a ghostlike appearance, and its backwardness and inefficiency seemed to await a catastrophe to sweep it away.

It was, however, no accident that Zionist officials allowed this economic trend to take its course and that none of them ever made, in Judah L. Magnes' words, Jewish-Arab cooperation "the chief objective of major policy." Zionist ideology, which after all is at least thirty years older than the Balfour Declaration, started not from a consideration of the realities in Palestine but from the problem of Jewish homelessness. The thought that "the people without a country needed a country without a people" so occupied the minds of the Zionist leaders that they simply overlooked the native population. The Arab problem was always "the veiled issue of Zionist politics" (as Isaac Epstein called it as long ago as 1907), long before economic problems in Palestine forced Zionist leadership into an even more effective neglect.

The temptation to neglect the Arab problem was great indeed. It was no small matter, after all, to settle an urban population in a poor, desertlike country, to educate thousands of young potential tradesmen and intellectuals to the arduous life and ideas of pioneerdom. Arab labor was dangerous because it was cheap; there was the constant temptation for Jewish capital to employ Arabs instead of the more expensive and more rights-conscious Jewish workers. How easily could the whole Zionist venture have degenerated in those crucial years into a white man's colonial enterprise at the expense of, and based upon, the work of natives. Jewish class struggle in Palestine, was for the most part a fight against Arab workers. To be anti-capitalist in Palestine almost always meant to be practically anti-Arab.

The social aspect of Jewish-Arab relationships is decisive because it convinced the only section of the population that had not come to Palestine for nationalistic reasons that it was impossible to come to terms with the Arabs without committing national and social suicide. The crude nationalist demand of "a country without a people," seemed so indisputably right in the light of practical experience that even the most idealistic elements in the Jewish labor movements let themselves be tempted first into forgetfulness and neglect, and then into narrow and inconsiderate nationalistic attitudes.

British administration which, according to the terms of the mandate, was supposed to prepare "the development of self-governing institutions," did nothing to bring the two peoples together and very little to raise the Arab standard of living. In the twenties, this may have been a half-conscious policy of *divide et impera;* in the late thirties, it was open sabotage of the Jewish National Home which the colonial services had always held to be dangerous to imperialist interests and whose ultimate survival, as the British knew perhaps better than Zionist leadership, depended upon cooperation with the Arabs. Much worse, however, though much less tangible, was the romantic attitude of the colonial services; they adored all the charming qualities of Arab life which definitely impeded social and economic progress. The urban Jewish middle class and especially the free professions in Jerusalem, were for a certain time inclined to imitate the British society they met among the administrative personnel. Here they learned, at best, that it was fashionable to be interested in Arab folk life, to admire the noble gestures and customs of the Bedouins, to be charmed by the hospitality of an ancient civilization. What they overlooked was that Arabs were human beings like themselves and that it might be dangerous not to expect them to act and react in much the same way as Jews; in other words, that because of the presence of the Jews in the country, the Bedouins were likely to want even more urgently land to settle down (a revival of the "inherent tendency in nomad society to desert the weariness and hopelessness of pastoral occupations for the superior comforts of agriculture"—H. St. J. B. Philby), the *fellahin* to feel for the first time the need for machines with which one obtained better products with less toil, and the urban population to strive for a standard of living which they had hardly known before the arrival of the Jews.

The Arab masses awoke only gradually to a spirit of envy and frustrated competition. In their old disease-stricken poverty, they looked upon Jewish achievements and customs as though they were images from a fairy-tale which would soon vanish as miraculously as they had appeared to interrupt their old way of life. This had nothing to do with neighborliness between Jewish and Arab villages which was the rule rather than the exception for a long time, which survived the disturbances of 1936–1939 and came to an end only under the impact of Jewish terrorism in 1947 and 1948. These relations, however, could be so easily destroyed without harming Jewish municipal and economic interests because they had always been without consequence, a simple, frequently touching expression of human neighborliness. With the exception of the Haifa municipality, not a single common institution, not a single common political body had been built up on this basis in all those years. It was as though, by tacit agreement, the neighbors had decided that their ways of life were different to the point of mutual indifference, that no common interests were possible except their human curiosity. No neighborliness could alter the fact that the Jews regarded the Arabs as an interesting example of folk life at best, and as a backward people who did not matter at worst, and that the Arabs considered the whole Jewish venture a strange interlude out of a fairy tale at best, and, at worst, an illegal enterprise which one day would be fair game for looting and robbery.

The Uniqueness of The Country

While the mood of the country was only too typical, quite like other small nations' fierce chauvinism and fanatic provincialism, the realities of Jewish achievement in Palestine were unique in many respects. What happened in Palestine was not easy to judge and evaluate: it was extraordinarily different from anything that had happened in the past.

The building of a Jewish National Home was not a colonial enterprise in which Europeans came to exploit foreign riches with the help and at the expense of native labor. Palestine was and is a poor country and whatever riches it possesses are exclusively the product of Jewish labor which are not likely to survive if ever the Jews are expelled from the country. Exploitation or robbery, so characteristic of the "original accumulation" in all imperialist enterprises, were either completely absent or played an insignificant role. American and European capital that flooded the country, came not as dividend-paying capital held by absentee shareholders but as "charity" money which the recipients were free to expend at will. It was used for the acquisition and nationalization of the soil, the establishment of collective settlements, long-term loans to farmers' and to workers' cooperatives, social and health services, free and equal education, and generally for the building of an economy with a pronounced socialist physiognomy. Through these efforts, in thirty years the land was changed as completely as if it had been transplanted to another continent, and this without conquest and with no attempt at extermination of natives.

The Palestinian experiment has frequently been called artificial, and it is true that everything connected with the building of a Jewish national home—the Zionist movement as well as the realities in Palestine—has not been, as it were, in the nature of things not according to the ways of the world. No economic necessities prompted the Jews to go to Palestine in the decisive years when immigration to America was the natural escape from misery and persecution; the land was no temptation for capital export, did not in itself offer opportunities for the solution of population problems. The collective rural settlements, the backbone of Palestinian society and the expression of pioneerdom, can certainly not be explained by utilitarian reasons. The development of the soil, the erection of a Hebrew University, the establishment of great health centers, were all "artificial" developments, supported from abroad and initiated by a spirit of enterprise which paid no heed to calculations of profit and loss.

A generation brought up in the blind faith in necessity—of history or economy or society or nature—found it difficult to understand that precisely this artificiality gave the Jewish achievements in Palestine their human significance. The trouble was that Zionists as well as anti-Zionists thought that the artificial character of the enterprise was to be reproached rather than praised. Zionists, therefore, tried to explain the building of a Jewish National Home as the only possible answer to a supposedly eternal antisemitism, the establishment of collective settlements as the only solution to the difficulties of Jewish agricultural labor, the foundation of health centers and the Hebrew University in terms of national interests. Each of these explanations contains part of the truth and each is somehow beside the point. The challenges were all there, but none of the responses was "natural." The point was that the responses were of much more permanent human and political value than the challenges, and that only ideological distortions made it appear that the challenges by themselves—antisemitism, poverty, national homelessness—had produced something.

Politically, Palestine was under a British mandate, that is a form of government supposedly devised only for backward areas where primitive peoples have not yet learned the elementary rules of self-government. But under the not too sympathetic eye of the British trustee the

Jews erected a kind of state within a non-existent state, which in some respects was more modern than the most advanced governments of the Western world. This non-official Jewish government was represented only on the surface by the Jewish Agency, the recognized political body of world Zionism, or by the Vaad Leumi, the official representative of Palestinian Jewry. What actually ruled the Jewish sector of the country much more efficiently than either and became more decisive in everyday life than British administration was the Histadruth, the Palestinian trade unions in which the overwhelming majority of Jewish labor, that is, the majority of the population, were organized. The trade unions stepped into all those areas which are usually regulated by municipal or national government as well as into a great number of activities which in other countries are the domain of free enterprise. All sorts of functions, such as administration, immigration, defense, education, health, social services, public works, communications, etc., were developed upon the initiative and under the leadership of the Histadruth which, at the same time, grew into the largest single employer in the country. This explains the miraculous fact that a mere proclamation of Jewish self-government eventually sufficed to bring a state machine into being. The present government of Israel, though a coalition government in appearance, is actually the government of the Histadruth.

Although the Jewish workers and farmers had an emotional awareness of the uniqueness of their achievements, expressed in a new kind of dignity and pride, neither they nor their leaders realized articulately the chief features of the new experiment. Thus Zionist leadership could go on for decades talking about the natural coincidence between Jewish interests and British imperialism, showing how little they understood themselves. For while they were talking this way, they built up a country that was economically so independent of Great Britain that it fitted into neither the Empire nor the Commonwealth; and they educated the people in such a way that it could not possibly fit into the political scheme of imperialism because it was neither a master nor a subject nation.

This would have been greatly to the credit of the Israeli State and even to its advantage today, if it had only been realized in time. But even now this is not the case. To defend their nationalist aggressiveness Israeli leadership today still insists on old truisms like "no people ever gets anything, least of all freedom, as a gift but has to fight for it," thus proving that they do not understand that the whole Jewish venture in Palestine is an excellent indication that some changes have occurred in the world and one may conquer a country by transforming its deserts into flourishing land.

Ideological explanations are those which do not fit realities but serve some other ulterior interests or motives. This does not mean that ideologies are ineffective in politics; on the contrary, their very momentum and the fanaticism they inspire frequently overwhelm more realistic considerations. In this sense, almost from the beginning, the misfortune of the building of a Jewish National Home has been that it was accompanied by a Central European ideology of nationalism and tribal thinking among the Jews, and by an Oxford-inspired colonial romanticism among the Arabs. For ideological reasons, the Jews overlooked the Arabs, who lived in what would have been an empty country, to fit their preconceived ideas of national emancipation. Because of romanticism or a complete inability to understand what was actually going on, the Arabs considered the Jews to be either old-fashioned invaders or newfangled tools of imperialism.

The British-inspired romanticization of poverty, of "the gospel of bareness" (T. E. Lawrence) blended only too well with the new Arab national consciousness and their old pride, according to which it is better to accept bribes than help. The new nationalist insistence on sovereignty, supported by an older desire to be left alone, served only to bolster exploitation by a few ruling families and prevent the development of the region. In their blind ideological hostility against Western civilization, a hostility which, ironically enough, was largely inspired by Westerners, they could not see that this region would be modernized in any case and that it would be far wiser to form an alliance with the Jews, who naturally shared the general interests of the Near East, than with some big faraway power whose interests were alien and who would necessarily consider them a subject people.

The Non-Nationalist Tradition

Against this background of ideological thinking the few protagonists of Jewish-Arab cooperation find their true stature. So few in number that they can hardly be called a real opposition force, so isolated from the masses and mass propaganda media that they were frequently ignored

or suffocated by that peculiar praise which discredits a man as impractical by calling him an "idealist" or a "prophet," they nevertheless created, on the Jewish as well as the Arab side, an articulate tradition. At
least their approach to the Palestinian problem begins in the objective
realities of the situation.

Since it is usually asserted that good will toward the Jewish National
Home in Palestine was always completely lacking on the Arab side and
that Jewish spokesmen for Arab-Jewish understanding never could produce a single Arab of any standing who was willing to cooperate with
them, a few instances of Arab initiative in trying to bring about some
kind of Jewish-Arab agreement may be mentioned. There was the
meeting of Zionist and Arab leaders in Damascus in 1913 charged with
preparing an Arab-Jewish conference in Lebanon. At that time the
whole Near East was still under Turkish rule and the Arabs felt that as
an oppressed people they had much in common with the Eastern
European sections of the Jewish people. There was the famous friendship treaty of 1919 between King Feisal of Syria and Chaim Weizmann
which both sides allowed to slip into oblivion. There was the Jewish-
Arab conference of 1922 in Cairo when the Arabs showed themselves
willing to agree to Jewish immigration within the limitations of the
economic capacity of Palestine.

There were negotiations carried on between Judah L. Magnes (with
the subsequent knowledge of the Jewish Agency) and the Palestinian
Arab Higher Committee at the end of 1936, immediately after the
outbreak of the Arab disturbance. A few years later, tentative consula-
tions were carried out between leading Egyptians and the Jews. "The
Egyptians," reports Weizmann in his autobiography, "were
acquainted and impressed by our progress and suggested that perhaps
in the future they might serve to bridge the gulf between us and the
Arabs of Palestine. They assumed that the White Paper . . . would be
adopted by England, but its effects might be mitigated, perhaps even
nullified, if the Jews of Palestine showed themselves ready to cooperate with Egypt."

And last but not least, as late as 1945, Azzam Bey, then Secretary of
the Arab League, stated that "the Arabs (were) prepared to make far-
reaching concessions toward the gratification of the Jewish desire to see
Palestine established as a spiritual and even a material home." To be

sure, such Arabs had as little Arab mass support as their Jewish counterparts. But who knows what might have happened if their hesitating
and tentative efforts had gotten a more sympathetic reception on the
other side of the table? As it was, these Arabs were discredited among
their own people when they discovered that the Jews either ignored them
(as happened to Azzam Bey's statement), or broke off negotiations as
soon as they hoped to find support from an outside ruling power (the
Turkish government in 1913 and the British in 1922), and generally
made the solution of the problem dependent upon the British who
naturally "found its difficulties insuperable" (Ch. Weizmann). In the
same way Jewish spokesmen for Arab-Jewish understanding were discredited when their very fair and moderate demands were distorted
and taken advantage of, as happened with the efforts of the Magnes
group in 1936.

The necessity of Jewish-Arab understanding can be proved by
objective factors; its possibility is almost entirely a matter of subjec-
tive political wisdom and personalities. Necessity, based on economic, military and geographic considerations, will make itself felt in
the long run only, or possibly, at a time when it is too late. Possibility
is a matter of the immediate present, a question of whether there is
enough statesmanship on both sides to anticipate the direction of
long-range necessary trends and channel them into constructive political institutions.

It is one of the most hopeful signs for the actual possibility of a
common Arab-Jewish policy that its essentials have only recently been
formulated in very cogent terms by at least one outstanding Arab,
Charles Malik, the representative of Lebanon to the United Nations,
and one outstanding Palestinian Jew, Judah L. Magnes, the late President of the Hebrew University and Chairman of the Palestinian group
of Ihud (Unity).

The speech Dr. Malik made on May 28, 1948, before the Security
Council of the United Nations on the priority of Jewish-Arab agree-
ment over all other solutions of the Palestinian problem is noteworthy
for its calm and open insistence on peace and the realities of the Near
East, and also because it found a "responsive echo" in the Jewish
Agency's delegate, Major Aubrey Eban.

Dr. Malik, addressing the Security Council, warned the great powers against a policy of *fait accompli*. "The real task of world statesmanship," he said, was "to help the Jews and the Arabs not to be permanently alienated from one another." It would be a grave disservice to Jews to give a Jewish state a false sense of security as the result of successful manipulation of international machinery, for this would distract them from the fundamental task of establishing a "reasonable, workable, just, abiding understanding with the Arabs."

Dr. Malik's words sound like a late echo to Martin Buber's (the philosopher of the Hebrew University) earlier denunciation of the Zionist Biltmore program as "admitting the aim of the minority to 'conquer' the country by means of international maneuvers." But Dr. Magnes' statement of the case and the conditions for Jewish-Arab cooperation before the Anglo-American Committee of Inquiry in 1946, when the White Paper's ban on Jewish immigration was still in force, read like an anticipated response from the Jewish side to the Arab challenge: "Our view is based on two assumptions, first that Jewish-Arab cooperation is not only essential, it is also possible. The alternative is war. . . ."

Dr. Magnes recognized that Palestine is a Holy Land for three monotheistic religions. To it the Arabs have a natural right and the Jews historical rights, both of equal validity. Thus, Palestine was already a bi-national state. This means political equality for the Arabs and justifies numerical equality for the Jews, that is, the right of immigration to Palestine. Dr. Magnes did not believe that all Jews would be satisfied with his proposal but he thought that many would accept it since they wanted the Jewish State mainly because they wanted a place to which to migrate. He urged the necessity of revising the whole concept of the state. To the Arabs he argued that sovereign independence in tiny Palestine was impossible. Indeed, he called for Palestinian participation in a middle east regional federation as both a practical necessity and as a further assurance to the Arabs. "What a boon to mankind it would be if the Jews and Arabs of Palestine were to strive together in friendship and partnership to make this Holy Land into a thriving peaceful Switzerland in the heart of this ancient highway between East and West. This would have incalculable political and spiritual influence in all the Middle East and far beyond. A bi-national Palestine could become a beacon of peace in the world."

The Hebrew University and The Collective Settlements

If nationalism were nothing worse than a people's pride in outstanding or unique achievement, Jewish nationalism would have been nourished by two institutions in the Jewish National Home: the Hebrew University and the collective settlements. Both are rooted in permanent non-nationalist trends in Jewish tradition—the universality and predominance of learning and the passion for justice. Here was a beginning of something true liberals of all countries and nationalities had hoped for when the Jewish people, with its peculiar tradition and historical experience, were given freedom and cultural autonomy, a hope no one expressed better than Woodrow Wilson who called for "not merely the rebirth of the Jewish people, but the birth also of new ideals, of new ethical values, of new conceptions of social justice which shall spring as a blessing for all mankind from that land and that people whose lawgivers and prophets . . . spoke those truths which have come thundering down the ages." (Quoted from Selig Adler, "The Palestine Question in the Wilson Era" in *Jewish Social Studies,* October 1948).

These two institutions, the *Kibbutzim* (collective settlements) on one hand, the Hebrew University on the other, supported and inspired the non-nationalist, anti-chauvinist trend and opposition in Zionism. The University was supposed to represent the universalism of Judaism in the particular Jewish land. It was not conceived just as the University of Palestine, but as the University of the Jewish people.

It is highly significant that the most consistent and articulate spokesmen for Jewish-Arab understanding came from the Hebrew University. The two groups that made cooperation with the Arabs the cornerstone of their political philosophy, the Brith Shalom (Covenant of Peace) in the twenties and the Ihud (Unity) Association in the forties—both founded and inspired by Judah L. Magnes, the co-founder and President of the Hebrew University since 1925—are not simply the expression of Western-educated intellectuals who find it difficult to swallow the crude slogans of a Balkanized nationalism. From the beginning Zionism contained two separate tendencies that met only in their agreement about the necessity of a Jewish homeland.

The victorious trend, the Herzlian tradition, took its chief impulse from the view of antisemitism as an "eternal" phenomenon in all countries of Jewish dispersion. It was strongly influenced by other nineteenth

century small national liberation movements and denied the possibility of Jewish survival in any country except Palestine, under any conditions except those of a full-fledged sovereign Jewish state. The other
trend, dating back to Ahad Haam, saw in Palestine the Jewish cultural
center which would inspire the spiritual development of all Jews in
other countries, but would not need ethnic homogeneity and national
sovereignty. As far back as the nineties of the last century, Ahad Haam
insisted on the presence in Palestine of an Arab native population and
the necessity for peace. Those who followed him never aimed to make
"Palestine as Jewish as England is English" (in the words of Weizmann),
but thought that the establishment of a center of higher learning was
more important for the new revival movement than the foundation of
a State. The main achievement of the Herzlian tradition is the Jewish
State; it came about (as Ahad Haam feared at the turn of the century
and as Judah L. Magnes warned for more than twenty-five years) at the
price of an Arab-Jewish war. The main achievement of the Ahad Haam
tradition is the Hebrew University.

Another part of the movement, influenced by though not connected
with Ahad-Haam Zionism, grew out of Eastern-European socialism,
and ultimately led to the foundation of collective settlements. As a new
form of agricultural economy, social living and workers' cooperatives,
it became the mainstay of the economic life of the Jewish homeland.
The desire to build a new type of society in which there would be no
exploitation of man by man did more to attract the best; elements of
Eastern European Jewry—that is, the powerful revolutionary ferment in
Zionism without which not a single piece of land would have been
tilled or a single road built—than the Herzlian analyses of Jewish
assimilation, or Jabotinsky's propaganda for a Jewish State, or the cultural Zionists' appeal for a revival of the religious values of Judaism. In
the rural collective settlements, an age-old Jewish dream of a society
based on justice, formed in complete equality, indifferent to all profit
motives, was realized, even if on a small scale. Their greatest achievement was the creation of a new type of man and a new social elite, the
birth of a new aristocracy which differed greatly from the Jewish
masses in and outside of Palestine in habits, manners, values and way
of life, and whose claim to leadership in moral and social questions
was clearly recognized by the population. Completely free and

unhampered by any government, a new form of ownership, a new type of farmer, a new way of family life and child education, and new approaches to the troublesome conflicts between city and country, between rural and industrial labor were created. Just as the very universalism of teaching and learning at the Hebrew University could be trusted to secure firm links between the Jewish National Home, world Jewry and the international, world of scholarship, so could the collective settlements be trusted to keep Zionism within the highest tradition of Judaism whose "principles call for the creation of a visible tangible society founded upon justice and mercy" (M. Buber). At the same time these experiments hold out hope for solutions that may one day become acceptable and applicable for the large mass of men everywhere whose dignity and humanity are today so seriously threatened by the standard of a competitive and acquisitive society.

The only larger groups who ever actively promoted and preached Jewish-Arab friendship came from this collective settlement movement. It was one of the greatest tragedies for the new State of Israel that these labor elements, notably the Hashomer Hatzair, sacrificed their bi-national program to the *fait accompli* of the United Nations' partition decision.

The Results of the War

Uninfluenced by the voices raised in a spirit of understanding, compromise and reason, events have been allowed to take their course. For more than twenty-five years, Dr. Magnes and the small group of his followers in Palestine and in Zionism had predicted that there would be either Jewish-Arab cooperation or war, and there has been war; that there could be either a bi-national Palestine or domination of one people by the other, and there has been the flight of more than 500,000 Arabs from Israeli-dominated territory; that the British White-Paper policy and its ban on immigration in the years of the Jewish European catastrophe had to be immediately annulled or the Jews would risk everything to obtain a State if only for the sake of immigration, and, with no one on the British side willing to make any concessions, there is the fact that the Jews obtained a sovereign state.

Similarly, and despite the great impression which Dr. Malik's speech made on his colleagues in the Security Council of the United Nations, the whole policy not only of Israel but of the United Nations and the

United States itself is a policy of *fait accompli*. True, on the surface it looks as though the armed forces of Israel had created the *fait accompli* of which Dr. Malik warned so eloquently. Yet, who would doubt that no number of victories in themselves would have been sufficient to secure Israel's existence without the support of the United States and American Jewry?

The most realistic way to measure the cost of the peoples of the Near East of the events of the past year is not by casualties, economic losses, war destruction or military victories, but by the political changes, the most outstanding of which has been the creation of a new category of homeless people, the Arab refugees. These not only form a dangerous potential irredenta dispersed in all Arab countries where they could easily become the visible uniting link; much worse, no matter how their exodus came about (as a consequence of Arab atrocity propaganda or real atrocities or a mixture of both), their flight from Palestine, prepared by Zionist plans of large-scale population transfers during the war and followed by the Israeli refusal to readmit the refugees to their old home, made the old Arab claim against Zionism finally come true: the Jews simply aimed at expelling the Arabs from their homes. What had been the pride of the Jewish homeland, that it had not been based upon exploitation, turned into a curse when the final test came: the flight of the Arabs would not have been possible and not have been welcomed by the Jews if they had lived in a common economy. The reactionary Arabs of the Near East and their British protectors were finally proved right: they had always considered "the Jews dangerous not because they exploit the *fellaheen*, but because they do not exploit them" (Ch. Weizmann).

Liberals in all countries were horrified at the callousness, the haughty dismissal of humanitarian considerations by a government whose representatives, only one year ago, had pleaded their own cause on purely humanitarian grounds, and were educated by a movement that, for more than fifty years, had based its claims exclusively on justice. Only one voice eventually was raised in protest to Israel's handling of the Arab refugee question, the voice of Judah L. Magnes, who wrote a letter to the editor of *Commentary* (October 1948):

> It seems to me that any attempt to meet so vast a human situation except from the humane, the moral point of view will lead

us into a morass. . . . If the Palestine Arabs left their homesteads "voluntarily" under the impact of Arab propaganda and in a veritable panic, one may not forget that the most potent argument in this propaganda was the fear of a repetition of the Irgun-Stern atrocities at Deir Yassin, where the Jewish authorities were unable or unwilling to prevent the act or punish the guilty. It is unfortunate that the very men who could point to the tragedy of Jewish Displaced Persons as the chief argument for mass immigration into Palestine should now be ready, as far as the world knows, to help create an additional category of DP's in the Holy Land.

Dr. Magnes, feeling the full significance of actions which forfeited the old proud claim of Zionist pioneerdom that theirs was the only colonizing venture in history not carried out with bloody hands, based his protest on purely humanitarian grounds—and laid himself wide open to the old accusations of quixotic morality in politics where supposedly only advantage and success count. The old Jewish legend about the thirty-six unknown righteous men who always exist and without whom the world would go to pieces says the last word about the necessity of such "quixotic" behavior in the ordinary course of events. In a world like ours, however, in which politics in some countries has long since outgrown sporadic sinfulness and entered a new stage of criminality, uncompromising morality has suddenly changed its old function of merely keeping the world together and has become the only medium through which true reality, as opposed to the distorted and essentially ephemeral factual situations created by crimes, can be perceived and planned. Only those who are still able to disregard the mountains of dust which emerge out of and disappear into the nothingness of sterile violence can be trusted with anything so serious as the permanent interests and political survival of a nation.

Federation or Balkanization?

The true objectives of a non-nationalist policy in the Near East and particularly in Palestine are few in number and simple in nature. Nationalist insistence on absolute sovereignty in such small countries as Palestine, Syria, Lebanon, Iraq, Transjordan, Saudi Arabia and Egypt can lead only to the Balkanization of the whole region and its transformation into a battlefield for the conflicting interests of the great powers to the detriment of all authentic national interests.

In the long run, the only alternative to Balkanization is a regional federation, which Magnes (in an article in *Foreign Affairs*) proposed as long ago as 1943, and which more recently was proclaimed as a distant but desired goal by Major Aubrey Eban, Israeli representative at the United Nations. While Dr. Magnes' original proposal comprised only those countries which the Peace Treaties of 1919 had dismembered but which had formed an integrated whole under Turkish government, that is, Palestine, Transjordan, Lebanon and Syria, the concept of Aubrey Eban (as published in an article in *Commentary* in 1948) aimed at a "Near Eastern League, comprising all the diverse nationalities of the area, each free within its own area of independence and cooperating with others for the welfare of the region as a whole." A federation which according to Eban might possibly include "Turkey, Christian Lebanon, Israel and Iran as partners of the Arab world in a league of non-aggression, mutual defense and economic cooperation" has the great advantage that it would comprise more than the two peoples, Jews and Arabs, and thus eliminate Jewish fears of being outnumbered by the Arabs.

The best hope for bringing this federation nearer would still be a Confederation of Palestine, as Dr. Magnes and Ihud proposed after partition and a sovereign Jewish State had become an accomplished fact. The very term Confederation indicates the existence of two independent political entities as contrasted with a federal system which is usually regarded "as a multiple government in a single state," *(Encyclopedia of Social Sciences)* and could well serve also as a model for the difficult relationships between Moslem Syria and Christian Lebanon. Once such small federated structures are established, Major Eban's League of Near Eastern countries will have a much better chance of realization. Just as the Benelux agreement was the first hopeful sign for an eventual federation of Europe, so the establishment of lasting agreement between two of the Near Eastern peoples on questions of defense, foreign policy and economic development could serve as a model for the whole region.

One of the chief advantages of federal (or confederate) solutions of the Palestinian problem has been that the more moderate Arab, statesmen (particularly from Lebanon) agreed to them. While the plan for a federal state was proposed only by a minority of the United Nations' Special Committee on Palestine in 1947, namely by the delegates of India, Iran and Yugoslavia, there is no doubt that it could very well have served as a basis for a compromise between Jewish and Arab claims. The Ihud group at that time practically endorsed the minority report; it was in basic accordance with the principles set down and best expressed in the following sentence: "The federal state is the most constructive and dynamic solution in that it eschews an attitude of resignation towards the question of the ability of Arabs and Jews to cooperate in their common interest, in favor of a realistic and dynamic attitude, namely, that under changed conditions the will to cooperate can be cultivated." Mr. Camille Chamoun, representative of Lebanon, speaking before the United Nations' General Assembly on November 29, 1947, in a desperate effort to reach a compromise formula on the very day partition was decided, called once more for an independent state of Palestine to be "constituted on a federal basis and . . . [comprise] a federal government and Cantonal governments of Jewish and Arab cantons." Like Dr. Magnes in his explanation of the plan for a Confederation of Palestine, he invoked the Constitution of the United States of America to serve as a model for the future constitution of the new state.

The plan for a Confederate Palestine with Jerusalem as a common capital, was nothing more or less than the only possible implementation of the UN partition decision, which made economic union a prerequisite. The purely economic approach of the United Nations would have met with difficulty under any circumstances because, as Major Eban rightly stressed, "the economic interdependence of all Palestine was much overrated by the General Assembly." It would, moreover, have run into the same difficulties as the European Recovery Program, which also pre-supposed the possibility of economic cooperation without political implementation. These inherent difficulties in an economic approach became plain impossibility with the outbreak of the war, which first of all can be concluded only by political measures. Moreover the war has destroyed all sectors of a combined Jewish-Arab economy and eliminated, with the explusion of almost all Arabs from Israeli-held territories, the very small common economic basis upon which hopes for a future development of common economic interests had rested.

Indeed, an obvious shortcoming of our arguments for peace as against a precarious armistice and for confederation as against further Balkanization, is that they can hardly be based upon anything like economic necessity. In order to arrive at a correct estimate of the impact of war on the Israeli economy, one cannot simply add up the staggering losses in working hours and destruction of property which Israel has suffered. Against them stands a very substantial increase in income from "charity" which never would have been given without the establishment of a state and the present tremendous immigration, both of which were the direct causes of the Jewish-Arab war. Since Jewish economy in Palestine in any case depended largely upon investment through donation, it may even be possible that the gains obtained through emergency outweigh the losses suffered through war.

Pacification of the region might well attract more dividend paying investment capital from American Jewry and even international loans. Yet it would also automatically diminish the Israeli income in nondividend paying money. At first glance, such a development may seem to lead to a sounder economy and greater political independence. Actually it may well mean greatly reduced resources and even increased interference from the outside for the simple reason that the investing public is likely to be more businesslike and less idealistic than mere donors.

But even if we assume that American Jewry, after the European catastrophe, would not have needed the emergency of war and the stimulation of victories to mobilize support to the extent of a hundred and fifty million dollars a year, the economic advantages of the war probably outweigh its losses. There are first the clear gains resulting from the flight of the Arabs from Israeli-occupied territory. This evacuation of almost fifty per cent of the country's population in no way disrupted Jewish economy because it had been built in almost complete isolation from its surroundings. But more important than these gains, with their heavy moral and political mortgage, is the factor of immigration itself. The new immigrants, who are partly settled in the deserted homesteads of Arab refugees, were urgently needed for reconstruction purposes and to offset the great loss in manpower brought about by mobilization; they are not only an economic burden to the country, they constitute also its surest asset. The influx of American money, chiefly raised and used for the resettlement of DP's, combined with the influx of man-power, may stimulate Israeli economy in much the same way, only on a much larger scale, as, ten years ago, the influx of American money together with the immigration of youngsters (Youth Aliya) helped the enlargement and modernization of the collective settlements.

The same absence of economic necessity marks the argument for confederation. As things stand today, the Israeli State is not only a Jewish island in an Arab sea and not only a Westernized and industri-alized outpost in the desert of a stagnant economy: it is also a producer of commodities for which no demand exists in its immediate neigh-borhood. Doubtless this situation will change some time in the future, but nobody knows how close or how distant this future may be. At the moment, at any rate, federation could hardly base itself on existing economic realities, on a functioning interdependence. It could become a working device only if—in the words of Dr. Magnes in 1947—"Jewish scientific ability, Jewish organizing power, perhaps finance, perhaps the experience of the West, which many of the countries of this part of the world have need of, [would] be placed at their disposal for the good of the whole region."

Such an enterprise would call for great vision and even sacrifices, though the sacrifices might be less difficult to bear if the channeling of Jewish pioneering skill and capital into Arab countries were connected with some agreement about the resettlement of Arab DP's. Without such a modernization of the Near East, Israel will be left in economic isolation, without the prerequisites for a normal exchange of its prod-ucts, even more dependent on outside help than now. It is not and never has been an argument against the great achievements of the Jewish National Home that they were "artificial," that they did not follow economic laws and necessities but sprang from the political will of the Jewish people. But it would be a tragedy if, once this home or this state has been established, its people continued to depend upon "miracles" and were unable to accommodate themselves to objective necessities, even if these are of a long-range nature. Charity money can be mobilized in great quantities only in emergencies, such as in the recent catastrophe in Europe or in the Arab-Jewish war; if the Israeli government cannot win its economic independence from such money it will soon find itself in the unenviable position of being forced to create emergencies, that is, forced into a policy of aggressiveness and expansion. The extremists understand this situation very well when they propagate an artificial prolongation of the war which, according to them, never should have ended before the whole of Palestine and Transjordan are conquered.

In other words, the alternative between federation and Balkanization is a political one. The trouble is not that rampant nationalism has disrupted a common economic structure, but that justified national aspirations could develop into rampant nationalism because they were not checked by economic interests. The task of a Near East Federation would be to create a common economic structure, to bring about economic and political cooperation and to integrate Jewish economic and social achievements. Balkanization would isolate even further the new Jewish pioneer and worker who have found a way to combine manual labor with a high standard of culture and to introduce a new human element into modern life. They, together with the heirs of the Hebrew University, would be the first victims of a long period of military insecurity and nationalistic aggressiveness.

But only the first victims. For without the cultural and social *hinterland* of Jerusalem and the collective settlements, Tel Aviv could become a Levantine city overnight. Chauvinism of the Balkan type could use the religious concept of the chosen people and allow its meaning to degenerate into hopeless vulgarity. The birth of a nation in the midst of our century may be a great event; it certainly is a dangerous event. National sovereignty which so long had been the very symbol of free national development has become the greatest danger to national survival for small nations. In view of the international situation and the geographical location of Palestine, it is not likely that the Jewish and Arab peoples will be exempt from this rule.

3 MARXISTS ON THE JEWISH QUESTION

Leon Trotsky (1879–1940) *was one of the most extraordinary "non-Jewish Jews" of modern history. With Lenin he helped lead the Russian revolution, only to spend the rest of his life battling his erstwhile comrade Joseph Stalin, whom Trotsky accused of being the revolution's gravedigger. Trotsky was no saint. By presiding over the militarization of labor during the Russian civil war, by advocating the absorption of trade unions into the state apparatus, and by assailing those who "have made a fetish of democratic principles," he arguably helped lay the foundations of the Soviet dictatorship ruled by Stalin, who banished him in 1928 and had him assassinated twelve years later. Ruthless, intolerant of opposition, fired by a millennial vision of permanent revolution, Trotsky is the very embodiment of a Leninist tradition that has fallen into discredit. Yet Trotsky's towering achievements as a military strategist, historian, political theorist, journalist, and man of letters cannot be so easily dismissed, while his personal integrity and unbending courage—particularly in his years of exile, when he was a stateless outcast, denied refuge by Europe's "democratic" governments—are beyond reproach.*

Trotsky was an atheist, with little direct involvement in questions of specifically Jewish concern. Yet, as George Steiner once observed of him, "Like Marx, he was Jewish in his instinctive commitment to internationalism, in his strategic and personal disregard of national barriers and antagonis . . . If one forgets Trotsky's Jewishness, moreover, it is not easy to get into right focus his passionate concern with survival through the word, his sense of the written book as weapon and watchman's cry . . . Like Marx, Trotsky was one of the great Jewish seers and exiles of the modern age." Trotsky's internationalism and cosmopolitan ethos made him especially sensitive to the rise of fascism, whose dangers he foresaw more clearly than anyone.

As Trotsky understood, fascism does not carry a passport; nationalism can all too easily degenerate into barbarism, especially when inflamed by war. And though he did not live to see the creation of Israel, he showed a perceptive awareness that Zionism, far from resolving the Jewish question, was likely to exacerbate it: "the conflict between the Jews and Arabs in Palestine acquires a more and more tragic and more and more menacing character," he observed in a 1937 interview. At the same time, Trotsky had no illusions about the "progressive" nature of the Palestinian resistance to Zionism, an inchoate mixture, he indicated in an earlier interview, of both "national liberationists (anti-imperialists) and reactionary Mohammedans and anti-Semitic pogromists." Trotsky's solution to the "Jewish problem," world revolution, is touchingly of its time. But his insistence that neither Zionism nor Arab chauvinism can bring peace to Israel-Palestine rings as true today as it did then.

ON THE "JEWISH PROBLEM"
Leon Trotsky

Excerpts from *On the Jewish Problem*

This interview appeared in Class Struggle, *February 1934. The journal was the organ of a short-lived group, the Communist League of Struggle, led by Albert Weisbord.*

Question: *Does the Left Opposition have to make special demands to win the Jewish working class in America?*

Answer: *The role of the foreign-born Jewish worker in the American prole-tarian revolution will be a very great one, and in some respects decisive. There is no question but that the Left Opposition must do all it can to penetrate into the life of the Jewish workers.*

Question: *What is your attitude towards the Jewish language? Why do you in your autobiography characterize it as "jargon"?*

Answer: *My attitude towards the Jewish language is similar to that of all lan-guages. If I really used in my autobiography the term "jargon," it is because in the years of my youth in Odessa the Jewish language was not called Yid-dish, as today, but "jargon." Such was the expression of Jews themselves, who did not consider it a sign of superciliousness. The word Yiddish is in universal use for the last fifteen or twenty years. I can see this even in France.*

Question: *In the Jewish circles you are considered to be an "assimilator." What is your attitude towards assimilation?*

Answer: *I do not understand why I should be considered as an "assimilator." I do not know, generally, what kind of a meaning this word holds. I am, it is* understood, opposed to Zionism and all such forms of self-isolation on the part of the Jewish workers. I call upon the Jewish workers of France to better acquaint themselves with the problems of French life and of the French working class. Without that it is difficult to participate in the working class movement of that country in which they are being exploited. As the Jewish proletariat is spread in different countries it is necessary for the Jewish worker, outside of his own language, to strive to know the language of other countries as a weapon in the class struggle. What has that to do with "assimilation"?

Question: The official Communist Party characterized, without question, the Jewish-Arab events in 1929 in Palestine as the revolutionary uprising of the oppressed Arabian masses. What is your opinion of this policy?

Answer: Unfortunately, I am not thoroughly familiar with the facts to venture a definite opinion. I am now studying the question. Then it will be easier to see in what proportion and in what degree there were present those elements such as national liberationists (anti-imperialists) and reactionary Mohammedans and anti-Semitic pogromists. On the surface, it seems to me that all these elements were there.

Question: What is your attitude about Palestine as a possible Jewish "homeland" and about a land for the Jews generally? Don't you believe that the anti-Semitism of German fascism compels a different approach to the Jewish question on the part of Communists?

Answer: Both the fascist state in Germany, as well as the Arabian-Jewish struggle, bring forth new and very clear verifications of the principle that the Jewish question cannot be solved within the framework of capitalism. I do not know whether Jewry will be built up again as a nation. However, there can be no doubt that the material conditions for the existence of Jewry as an independent nation could be brought about only by the proletarian revolution. There is no such thing on our planet as the idea that one has more claim to land than another.

The establishment of a territorial base for Jewry in Palestine or any other country is conceivable only with the migrations of large human masses. Only a triumphant socialism can take upon itself such tasks. It can be foreseen that it may take place either on the basis of a mutual understanding, or with the *aid of a kind of international proletarian tribunal which should take up this question and solve it.*

The blind alley in which German Jewry finds itself as well as the blind alley in which Zionism finds itself is inseparably bound up with the blind alley of world capitalism, as a whole. Only when the Jewish workers clearly see this interrelationship will they be forewarned against pessimism and despair.

Interview with Jewish correspondents in Mexico

This interview, done January 18,1937, is printed below as it appeared in the magazine Fourth International, December 1945. The correspondents represented the ITA (Jewish Telegraphic Agency) and Der Weg, a Jewish paper published in Mexico. A Yiddish version of the interview also appeared in the Jewish liberal daily Der Tog, and in the socialist daily Forwaerts, January 24, 1937.

Before trying to answer your questions I ought to warn you that unfortunately I have not had the opportunity to learn the Jewish language, which moreover has been developed only since I became an adult. I have not had and I do not have the possibility of following the Jewish press, which prevents me from giving a precise opinion on the different aspects of so important and tragic a problem. I cannot therefore claim any special authority in replying to your questions. Nevertheless I am going to try and say what I think about it.

During my youth I rather leaned toward the prognosis that the Jews of different countries would be assimilated and that the Jewish question would thus disappear in a quasi-automatic fashion. The historical development of the last quarter of a century has not confirmed this perspective. Decaying capitalism has everywhere swung over to an exacerbated nationalism, one part of which is anti-Semitism. The Jewish question has loomed largest in the most highly developed capitalist country of Europe, in Germany.

On the other hand the Jews of different countries have created their press and developed the Yiddish language as an instrument adapted to modern culture. One must therefore reckon with the fact that the Jewish nation will maintain itself for an entire epoch to come. Now the nation cannot normally exist without a common territory. Zionism springs from this very idea. But the facts of every passing day demonstrate to us that Zionism is incapable of resolving the Jewish question. The conflict between the Jews and Arabs in Palestine acquires a more and more tragic and more and more menacing character. I do not at all believe that the Jewish question can be resolved within the framework of rotting capitalism and under the control of British imperialism.

And how, you ask me, can socialism solve this question? On this point I can but offer hypotheses. Once socialism has become master of our planet or at least of its most important sections, it will have unimaginable resources in all domains. Human history has witnessed the epoch of great migrations on the basis of barbarism. Socialism will open the possibility of great migrations on the basis of the most developed technique and culture. It goes without saying that what is here involved is not compulsory displacements, that is, the creation of new ghettos for certain nationalities, but displacements freely consented to, or rather demanded by certain nationalities or parts of nationalities. The dispersed Jews who would want to be reassembled in the same community will find a sufficiently extensive and rich spot under the sun. The same possibility will be opened for the Arabs, as for all other scattered nations. *National topography will become a part of the planned economy.* This is the grand historical perspective that I envisage. To work for international socialism means also to work for the solution of the Jewish question.

You ask me if the Jewish question still exists in the USSR. Yes, it exists, just as the Ukrainian, the Georgian, even the Russian questions exist there. The omnipotent bureaucracy stifles the development of national culture just as it does the whole of culture. Worse still, the country of the great proletarian revolution is now passing through a period of profound reaction. If the revolutionary wave revived the finest sentiments of human solidarity, the Thermidorian reaction has stirred up all that is low, dark and backward in this agglomeration of 170 million people. To reinforce its domination the bureaucracy does not even hesitate to resort in a scarcely camouflaged manner to chauvinistic tendencies, above all to anti-Semitic ones. The latest Moscow trial, for example, was staged with the hardly concealed design of presenting internationalists as faithless and lawless Jews who are capable of selling themselves to the German Gestapo.

Since 1925 and above all since 1926, anti-Semitic demagogy, well camouflaged, unattackable, goes hand in hand with symbolic trials against avowed pogromists. You ask me if the old Jewish petty bourgeoisie in the USSR has been socially assimilated by the new Soviet environment. I am indeed at a loss to give you a clear reply. The social and national statistics in the USSR are extremely tendentious. They serve not to set forth the truth, but above all to glorify the leaders, the chiefs, the creators of happiness. An important part of the Jewish petty bourgeoisie has been absorbed by the formidable apparatuses of the state, industry, commerce, the cooperatives, etc., above all in their lower and middle layers. This fact engenders an anti-Semitic state of feeling and the leaders manipulate it with a cunning skill in order to canalize and to direct especially against the Jews the existing discontent against the bureaucracy.

On Birobidjan I can give you no more than my personal evaluations. I am not acquainted with this region and still less with the conditions in which the Jews have settled there. In any case it can be no more than a very limited experience. The USSR alone would still be too poor to resolve its own Jewish question, even under a regime much more socialist than the present one. The Jewish question, I repeat, is indissolubly bound up with the complete emancipation of humanity. Everything else that is done in this domain can only be a palliative and often even a two-edged blade, as the example of Palestine shows.

The Belgian-Trotskyist **Abraham Leon** lived an itinerant, cruelly menaced existence at the violent extremities of European history, a Jew and a revolutionary in an era that saw the rise of fascism and murderous antisemitism. Leon was born in Warsaw, Poland, to Zionist parents who took the family to Palestine, with the intention of staying. In 1926, however, the family left Palestine for Brussels, where Leon was drawn into the ranks of Hashomer Hatzair, the Socialist Zionist movement. The young man showed a talent for political organizing, and soon became a leader of the the group's Brussels section. But Leon's relentlessly questioning spirit led him to break with Hashomer Hatzair, and later with Zionism itself. Hashomer Hatzair, a pro-Soviet organization, remained supportive of Stalin throughout the Moscow trials, something Leon could not abide. Electrified by the speeches of Walter Dauge, the young leader of the Revolutionary Socialist Party, he embraced Trotskyism; meanwhile, his readings of Jewish history and of Marx persuaded him that socialist universalism and Jewish nationalism were irreconcilable. The issue of Jewish—indeed of human—survival was no abstract matter to Leon, whose country was occupied by the Nazis in 1940. While writing his study, "The Jewish Question: A Marxist Interpretation," Leon was organizing resistance to the Nazis with an illegal Trotskyist cell among miners, factory workers, and, still more daringly, among German soldiers. In 1944, after two years underground, he resurfaced with his wife in the region of Charleroi, his hopes raised by growing unrest in the mines and by the news of the Allies landing in Europe. That very evening, his house was searched. After being detained and tortured, he was sent to Auschwitz, where he perished in the gas chambers. He was twenty six when he died.

Ungenerous readers of Leon's essay on Zionism will point out that neither world revolution nor his beloved proletariat protected him from the flames of European anti-Semitism, and they are right. Yet his critique of Zionism remains rich in insights, offering a perceptive analysis of the conflict in Palestine, still-pithy observations about the relationship between the Jews in Israel and in the Diaspora, and a prescient warning that Jewish state might have to depend for its survival on the protection of an imperial power. He was tragically wrong about world revolution as the only solution to the Jewish problem; he was tragically right about Zionism, the false messiah of modern Jewish ideology.

"ZIONISM"

Abraham Leon

From *The Jewish Question: A Marxist Interpretation* (1940)

Zionism was born in the light of the incendiary fires of the Russian pogroms of 1882 and in the tumult of the Dreyfus Affair—two events which expressed the sharpness that the Jewish problem began to assume at the end of the Nineteenth Century.

The rapid capitalist development of Russian economy after the reform of 1863 made the situation of the Jewish masses in the small towns untenable. In the West, the middle classes, shattered by capitalist concentration, began to turn against the Jewish element whose competition aggravated their situation. In Russia, the association of the "Lovers of Zion" was founded. Leo Pinsker wrote *Auto-Emancipation*, in which he called for a return to Palestine as the sole possible solution of the Jewish question. In Paris, Baron Rothschild, who like all the Jewish magnates viewed with very little favor the mass arrival of Jewish immigrants in the western countries, became interested in Jewish colonization in Palestine. To help "their unfortunate brothers" to return to the land of their "ancestors," that is to say, to go as far away as possible, contained nothing displeasing to the Jewish bourgeoisie of the West, who with reason feared the rise of anti-Semitism. A short while after the publication of Leo Pinsker's book, a Jewish journalist of Budapest, Theodor Herzl, saw anti-Semitic demonstrations at Paris provoked by the Dreyfus Affair. Soon he wrote *The Jewish State*, which to this day remains the bible of the Zionist movement. From its inception, Zionism appeared as a reaction of the Jewish petty bourgeoisie (which still forms the core of Judaism), hard hit by the mounting anti-Semitic wave, kicked from one country to another, and striving to attain the Promised Land where it might find shelter from the tempests sweeping the modern world.

Zionism is thus a very young movement; it is the youngest of the European national movements. That does not prevent it from pretending, even more than all other nationalism, that it draws its substance from a far distant past. Whereas Zionism is in fact the product of the last phase of capitalism, of capitalism beginning to decay, it pretends to draw its origin from a past more than two thousand years old. Whereas Zionism is essentially a reaction against the situation created for Judaism by the combination of the destruction of feudalism and the decay of capitalism, it affirms that it constitutes a reaction against the state of things existing since the fall of Jerusalem in the year 70 of the Christian era. Its recent birth is naturally the best reply to these pretensions. As a matter of fact, how can one believe that the remedy for an evil existing for two thousand years was discovered only at the end of the Nineteenth Century? But like all nationalisms—and even more intensely—Zionism views the historic past in the light of the present. In this way, too, it distorts the present-day picture. Just as France is represented to French children as existing since the Gaul of Vercingetorix; just as the children of Provence are told that the victories that the kings of Ile de France won over their ancestors were their own successes, in the same way Zionism tries to create the myth of an eternal Judaism, eternally the prey of the same persecutions. Zionism sees in the fall of Jerusalem the cause of the dispersion, and consequently, the fountain-head of all Jewish misfortunes of the past, present and future. "The source of all the misfortunes of the Jewish people is the loss of its historic country and its dispersion in all countries," declares the Marxist delegation of the "Poale-Zion" to the Dutch-Scandinavian committee. After the violent dispersion of the Jews by the Romans, their tragic history continues. Driven out of their country, the Jews did not wish (oh beauty of free will!) to assimilate. Imbued with their "national cohesiveness," "with a superior ethical feeling," and with "an indestructible belief in a single God," they have resisted all attempts at assimilation. Their sole hope during these somber days which lasted two thousand years has been the vision of a return to their ancient country.

Zionism has never seriously posed this question: Why, during these two thousand years, have not the Jews really tried to return to this country? Why was it necessary to wait until the end of the Nineteenth

Century for a Herzl to succeed in convincing them of this necessity? Why were all the predecessors of Herzl, like the famous Sabbatai Zebi, treated as false Messiahs? Why were the adherents of Sabbatai Zebi fiercely persecuted by orthodox Judaism?

Naturally, in replying to these interesting questions, refuge is sought behind religion. "As long as the masses believed that they had to remain in the Diaspora until the advent of the Messiah, they had to suffer in silence," states Zitlovski,[1] whose Zionism is moreover quite conditional. Nevertheless this explanation tells us nothing. What is required is precisely an answer to the question of why the Jewish masses believed that they had to await the Messiah in order to be able to "return to their country." Religion being an ideological reflection of social interests, it must perforce correspond to them. Today religion does not at all constitute an obstacle to Zionism.[2]

In reality just so long as Judaism was incorporated in the feudal system, the "dream of Zion" was nothing but a dream and did not correspond to any real interest of Judaism. The Jewish tavern owner or "farmer" of Sixteenth-Century Poland thought as little of "returning" to Palestine as does the Jewish millionaire in America today. Jewish religious Messianism was no whit different from the Messianism belonging to other religions. Jewish pilgrims who went to Palestine met Catholic, Orthodox and Moslems pilgrims. Besides it was not so much the "return to Palestine" which constituted the foundation of this Messianism as the belief in the rebuilding of the temple of Jerusalem.

All of these idealist conceptions of Zionism are naturally inseparable from the dogma of eternal anti-Semitism. "As long as the Jews will live in the Diaspora, they will be hated by the 'natives.' " This essential point of view for Zionism, its spinal column so to speak, is naturally given different nuances by its various currents. Zionism transposes modern anti-Semitism to all of history; it saves itself the trouble of studying the various forms of anti-Semitism and their evolution. However, we have seen that in different historical periods, Judaism made up part of the possessing classes and was treated as such. To sum up [the idealist conception] the sources of Zionism must be sought in the impossibility of assimilation because of "eternal" anti-Semitism and of the will to safeguard the "treasures of Judaism."[3]

In reality, Zionist ideology, like all ideologies, is only the distorted reflection of the interests of a class. It is the ideology of the Jewish petty bourgeoisie, suffocating between feudalism in ruins and capitalism in decay. The refutation of the ideological fantasies of Zionism does not naturally refute the real needs which brought them into being. It is modern anti-Semitism, and not mythical "eternal" anti-Semitism, which is the best agitator in favor of Zionism. Similarly, the basic question to determine is: To what extent is Zionism capable of resolving not the "eternal" Jewish problem but the Jewish question in the period of capitalist decay?

Zionist theoreticians like to compare Zionism with all other national movements. But in reality, the foundations of the national movements and that of Zionism are altogether different. The national movement of the European bourgeoisie is the consequence of capitalist development; it reflects the will of the bourgeoisie to create the national bases for production, to abolish feudal remnants. The national movement of the European bourgeoisie is closely linked with the ascending phase of capitalism. But in the Nineteenth Century, in the period of the flowering of nationalisms, far from being "Zionist," the Jewish bourgeoisie was profoundly assimilationist. The economic process from which the modern nations issued laid the foundations for integration of the Jewish bourgeoisie into the bourgeois nation.

It is only when the process of the formation of nations approaches its end, when the productive forces have for a long time found themselves constricted within national boundaries, that the process of expulsion of Jews from capitalist society begins to manifest itself, that modern anti-Semitism begins to develop. The elimination of Judaism accompanies the decline of capitalism. Far from being a product of the development of the productive forces, Zionism is precisely the consequence of the complete halt of this development, the result of the petrifaction of capitalism. Whereas the national movement is the product of the ascending period of capitalism, Zionism is the product of the imperialist era. The Jewish tragedy of the Twentieth Century is a direct consequence of the decline of capitalism.

Therein lies the principal obstacle to the realization of Zionism. *Capitalist decay—basis for the growth of Zionism—is also the cause of the impossibility of its realization.* The Jewish bourgeoisie is compelled to create a national state, to assure itself of the objective framework for the development of its productive forces, precisely in the period when the conditions for such a development have long since disappeared. The conditions of the decline of capitalism which have posed so sharply the Jewish question make its solution equally impossible along the Zionist road. And there is nothing astonishing in that. An evil cannot be suppressed without destroying its causes. But Zionism wishes to resolve the Jewish question without destroying capitalism, which is the principal source of the suffering of the Jews.

At the end of the Nineteenth Century, in the period when the Jewish problem was just beginning to be posed in all its sharpness, 150,000 Jews each year left their countries of origin. Between 1881 and 1925, nearly four million Jews emigrated. Despite these enormous figures, the Jewish population of Eastern Europe rose from 6 to 8 million.

Thus, even when capitalism was still developing, even when the countries across the ocean were still receiving immigrants, the Jewish question could not even begin to be resolved (in the Zionist sense); far from diminishing, the Jewish population showed a bad penchant of wanting to grow. In order to begin to resolve the Jewish question, that is to say, in order to begin really to transplant the Jewish masses, it would be necessary for the countries of immigration to absorb at least a little more than the natural growth of Jews in the Diaspora, that is at least 300,000 Jews per year. And if such a figure could not be reached before the first imperialist war, when all the conditions were still favorable for emigration, when all developed countries such as the United States were permitting the mass entry of immigrants, then how can we think that it is possible in the period of the continuous crisis of capitalism, in the period of almost incessant wars?

Naturally there are enough ships in the world to transport hundreds of thousands, even millions of Jews. But if all countries have closed their doors to immigrants, it is because there is an overproduction of labor forces just as there is an overproduction of commodities. Contrary to Malthus, who believed that there would be too many people because there would be too few goods, it is precisely the abundance of goods which is the cause of the "plethora" of human beings. By what miracle, in a period when the world markets are saturated with goods, in a period when unemployment has everywhere become a permanent fixture, by what miracle can a country, however great and rich it may be (we pass over the data relating to poor and small Palestine), develop its productive forces to the point of being able to welcome 300,000 immigrants each year? In reality the possibilities for Jewish emigration diminish at the same time that the need for it increases. The causes which promote the need for emigration are the same as those which prevent its realization; they all spring from the decline of capitalism.

It is from this fundamental contradiction between the *necessity for* and the *possibility of* emigration that the political difficulties of Zionism flow. The period of development of the European nations was also the period of an intensive colonization in the countries across the ocean. It was at the beginning and middle of the Nineteenth Century, in the golden age of European nationalism, that North America was colonized; it was also in this period that South America and Australia began to be developed. Vast areas of the earth were practically without a master and lent themselves marvelously to the establishment of millions of European emigrants. In that period, for reason that we have studied, the Jews gave almost no thought to emigrating.

Today the whole world is colonized, industrialized and divided among the various imperialisms. Everywhere Jewish emigrants come into collision at one and the same time with the nationalism of the "natives" and with the ruling imperialism. In Palestine, Jewish nationalism collides with an increasingly aggressive Arab nationalism. The development of Palestine by Jewish immigration tends to increase the intensity of this Arab nationalism. The economic development of the country results in the growth of the Arab population, its social differentiation, the growth of a national capitalism. To overcome Arab resistance the Jews need English imperialism. But its "support" is as harmful as is Arab resistance. English imperialism views with a favorable eye a weak Jewish immigration to constitute a counterweight to the Arab factor, but it is intensely hostile to the establishment of a big Jewish population in Palestine, to its industrial development, to the growth of its proletariat. It merely uses the Jews as a counterweight to the Arab threat but does everything to raise difficulties for Jewish immigration. Thus, to the increasing difficulties flowing from Arab resistance, there is added the perfidious game of British imperialism.

Finally, we must draw still one more conclusion from the fundamental premises which have been established. Because of its necessarily artificial character, because of the slim perspectives for a rapid and normal development of Palestinian economy in our period, the task of Zionist colonization requires considerable capital. Zionism demands incessantly increasing sacrifices from the Jewish communities of the world. But so long as the situation of the Jews is more or less bearable in the Diaspora, no Jewish class feels the necessity of making these sacrifices. To the extent that the Jewish masses feel the necessity of having a "country," to the extent also that persecutions mount in intensity, so much the less are the Jewish masses able to contribute to Zionist construction. "A strong Jewish people in the Diaspora is necessary for Palestinian reconstruction," states Ruppin. But so long as the Jewish people is strong in the Diaspora, it feels no need for Palestinian reconstruction. When it strongly feels this necessity, the possibility for realizing it no longer exists. It would be difficult today to ask European Jews, who have a pressing need to emigrate, to give aid for the rebuilding of Palestine. The day when they will be able to do it, it is a safe assumption that their enthusiasm for this task will have considerably cooled.

A relative success for Zionism, along the lines of creating a Jewish majority in Palestine and even of the formation of a "Jewish state," that is to say, a state placed under the complete domination of English or American imperialism, cannot, naturally, be excluded. This would in some ways be a return to the state of things which existed in Palestine before the destruction of Jerusalem and, from this point of view, there will be "reparation of a two-thousand-year-old injustice." But this tiny "independent" Jewish state in the midst of a world-wide Diaspora will be only an apparent return to the state of things before the year 70. It will not even be the beginning of the solution of the Jewish question. The Jewish Diaspora of the Roman era was in effect based on solid economic ground; the Jews played an important economic role in the world. The existence or absence of a Palestinian mother country had for the Jews of this period only a secondary importance. Today it is not a question of giving the Jews a political or spiritual center (as Ahad Ha'am would have it). It is a question of saving Judaism from the annihilation which threatens it in the Diaspora. But in what way will the existence of a small Jewish state in Palestine change anything in the situation of the Polish or German Jews? Admitting even that all the Jews in the world were today Palestinian citizens, would the policy of Hitler have been any different?

One must be stricken with an incurable juridical cretinism to believe that the creation of a small Jewish state in Palestine can change anything at all in the situation of the Jews throughout the world, especially in the present period. The situation after the eventual creation of a Jewish state in Palestine will resemble the state of things that existed in the Roman era only in the fact that *in both cases the existence of a small Jewish state in Palestine could in no way influence the situation of the Jews in the Diaspora.* In the Roman era, the economic and social positions of Judaism in the Diaspora was very strong, so that the disappearance of this Jewish state did not in any way compromise it. Today the situation of the Jews in the world is very bad; so the reestablishment of a Jewish state in Palestine cannot in any way restore it. In both cases the situation of the Jews does not at all depend on the existence of a state in Palestine but is a function of the general economic, social and political situation. Even supposing that the Zionist dream is realized and the "secular injustice" is undone—and we are still very far from that—the situation of Judaism throughout the world will in no way be modified by that. The temple will perhaps be rebuilt but the faithful will continue to suffer.

The history of Zionism is the best illustration of the insurmountable difficulties that it encounters, difficulties resulting, in the last analysis, from the fundamental contradiction which tears it apart: The contradiction between the growing necessity of resolving the Jewish question and the growing impossiblity of resolving it under the conditions of decaying capitalism. Immediately following the first imperialist war, Jewish emigration to Palestine encountered no great osbtacles in its path. Despite that, there were relatively few immigrants; the economic conditions of capitalist countries after the war made the need to emigrate less pressing. It was, moreover, because of this light emigration that the British government did not feel obliged to set up bars to the entry of Jews into Palestine. In the years 1924, 1925, 1926, the Polish bourgeoisie opened an economic offensive against the Jewish masses. These years are also the period of a very important immigration into Palestine. But this massive immigration soon collided with insurmountable economic difficulties. The ebb was almost as great as was

the floodtide. Up to 1933, the date of Hitler's arrival to power, immigration was of little importance. After this date, tens of thousands of
Jews began to arrive in Palestine. But this "conjuncture" was soon
arrested by a storm of anti-Jewish demonstrations and massacres. The
Arabs seriously feared becoming a minority in the country. The Arab
feudal elements feared being submerged by the capitalist wave. British
imperialism profited from this tension by piling up obstacles to the entry
of the Jews, by working to deepen the gulf existing between the Jews
and the Arabs, by proposing the partition of Palestine. Up to the second
imperialist war, Zionism thus found itself in the grip of mounting difficulties. The Palestinian population lived in a state of permanent
terror. Precisely when the situation of the Jews became ever more desperate, Zionism showed itself absolutely incapable of providing a
remedy. "Illegal" Jewish immigrants were greeted with rifle fire by their
British "protectors."

The Zionist illusion began to lose its attractiveness even in the eyes
of the most uninformed. In Poland, the last elections revealed that the
Jewish masses were turning completely away from Zionism. The
Jewish masses began to understand that Zionism not only could not
seriously improve their situation, but that it was furnishing weapons
to the anti-Semites by its theories of the "objective necessity of Jewish
emigration." The imperialist war and the triumph of Hitlerism in
Europe are an unprecedented disaster for Judaism. Judaism is confronted with the threat of total extinction. What can Zionism do to
counteract such a disaster? Is it not obvious that the Jewish question
is very little dependent upon the future destiny of Tel Aviv but very
greatly upon the regime which will be set up tomorrow in Europe and
in the world? The Zionists have a great deal of faith in a victory of
Anglo-American imperialism. But is there a single reason for believing
that the attitude of the Anglo-American imperialists will differ after
their eventual victory from their prewar attitude? It is obvious that
there is none. Even admitting that Anglo-American imperialism will
create some kind of abortive Jewish state, we have seen that the situation of world Judaism will hardly be affected. A great Jewish immigration into Palestine after this war will confront the same difficulties as
previously. Under conditions of capitalist decay, it is impossible to
transplant millions of Jews. Only a world-wide socialist planned

economy would be capable of such a miracle. Naturally this presupposes the proletarian revolution.

But Zionism wishes precisely to resolve the Jewish question independently of the world revolution. By misconstruing the real sources of the Jewish question in our period, by lulling itself with puerile dreams and silly hopes, Zionism proves that it is ideological excrescence and not a scientific doctrine."4

• • •

Notes

[1] *Materialism and the National Question.*

[2] There is a religious Zionist bourgeois party, *Misrakhi,* and are religious Zionist workers' party, *poale-Misrakhi.*

[3] Adolf Böhm, *Die Zionistische Bewegung,* Berlin, 1935, vol. I, Chap. 3.

[4] In this chapter, Zionism has been treated only insofar as it is linked with the Jewish question. The role of Zionism in Palestine naturally constitutes another problem.

4

THE BIRTH OF ISRAEL AND THE DESTRUCTION OF PALESTINE

In 1948, Israel achieved its independence, on the ruins of Palestine, another country that still has yet to achieve statehood. Until the 1980s, it was common for Israeli historians to argue that the Palestinians had only themselves to blame for the loss of their homeland. In this account, the Zionist movement, content with an equitable partition of mandate Palestine, had generously extended an olive branch to the indigenous inhabitants, only to be rejected, and finally attacked in a war to drive the Jews into the sea. During that war, the story continued, some 750,000 Palestinians left their homes voluntarily, having been promised by the invading Arab armies that they would soon return in triumph. After the war, Israel reached out to its neighbors, only to be shot down once again.

In the 1980s, this tale, a self-congratulatory fable passing for history, came under withering assault from Israel's "new historians." (Palestinian historians had always recognized the fable for what it was.) American students of the conflict might be familiar with the names Benny Morris, Tom Segev, Avi Shlaim and Ilan Pappé. But the true pioneer among the new historians was an Israeli peace activist named **Simha Flapan,** who, from 1954 to 1981, had served as the National Secretary of the left-Zionist Mapam party. Drawing upon recently declassified Israeli sources, and upon unpublished material from Arab sources, Flapan offered a forceful and systematic challenge to Israel's official history in his final work, The Birth of Israel: Myths and Realities. He showed, among other things, that Zionist support for partition was tactical, not principled, and that its aims were in fact expansionist; that the Palestinians were expelled, sometimes in fear for their lives; and that Arab leaders were far more open to compromise with the Zionist movement than commonly portrayed.

One of Israel's bravest peace activists, Flapan was born in Tomaszow, Poland, in 1911, four years after his compatriot Isaac Deutscher. In 1930 he emigrated to Palestine, where he enjoyed a distinguished career as a writer, publisher and political activist. Flapan always defined himself as a Zionist, yet his belief in human equality, his loathing of racism, and his internationalist vision led him far afield of the Israeli mainstream, which was just beginning to use the word "Palestinian" when he died in 1987. As the founder and editor in chief of New Outlook, a monthly journal on Middle East affairs, Flapan presided over a trailblazing forum of Arab-Jewish dialogue, and his work earned him the admiration of many progressive Arab as well as Jewish intellectuals. The introduction and conclusion of his great book—the opening salvo in the battle over the writing of history that continues to rage today in Israel—remain as compelling, and troubling, as ever.

THE BIRTH OF ISRAEL

Simha Flapan

Introduction and Conclusion from *The Birth of Israel: Myths and Reality* (1987)

Introduction

Nothing is absolute or eternal in relations between peoples. Neither friendship nor hatred is immutable. Who could have imagined, forty years ago, when the smoke of Auschwitz had hardly receded, that the peoples of Israel and Germany would so soon enter into relations of mutual respect? Today, in the heat of an apparently insoluble conflict between Jews and Arabs, amid the devastation of dead and wounded strewn over airports and refugee camps, supermarkets and bombed-out suburbs, it requires a tremendous effort of imagination and analysis to realize that change is possible, that recrimination and intransigence could give way to understanding and peace. One of the major obstacles in the conflict, as in any long-standing national conflict, is the impasse arising from opposing demonologies.

Neither the Arabs, traumatized by their successive defeats at the hands of the Israelis, nor the Israelis, intoxicated by their astounding victories, are able to cut through the web of myth and distortion that envelops their reasoning. This generalization, I am sorry to say, applies even to some Israelis in the forefront of the peace movement.

Friends and colleagues with whom I have worked closely for many years advised me not to present the subject of my research as a challenge to Israel's long-held and highly potent myths. They suggested that I simply make my contribution in a noncommittal, academic manner, describing the evolution of the Arab-Israeli conflict and leaving the conclusions to the reader. Out of respect for their work and our many years of collaboration, I gave considerable thought to their proposal. But I concluded that such an approach would defeat the very purpose of this book. It would have produced a detailed historical study interesting only to historians and researchers, whereas, in my opinion, what is required is a book that will undermine the propaganda structures that have so long obstructed the growth of the peace forces in my country. It is not the task of intellectuals and friends of both peoples to offer ad hoc solutions but to hold the roots of the conflict up to the light of intelligent inquiry, in the hope of sweeping away the distortions and lies that have hardened into sacrosanct myth. I do not for a moment believe that my contribution here will work wonders. I do believe, however, that it is a necessary step in the right direction.

I originally planned to survey and analyze the evolution of the Israeli-Palestinian conflict from the War of Independence in 1948 to the Six-Day War of June 1967, and so continue the work I began in my book *Zionism and the Palestinians, 1917–1947*. The 1967 war was a watershed: Israel occupied the West Bank and Gaza, gaining control over the lives of 1,000,000 more Palestinians, in addition to the 325,000 already within its borders; the majority of Palestinians were now, one way or another, under Israeli control. But during the course of my research, I changed my mind and decided to concentrate entirely on what I see as the crucial formative years in the shaping of Arab-Israeli relations: 1948 to 1952. The events of these four years, beginning shortly after the UN Resolution on the Partition of Palestine, remain central to Israel's self-perception.

The War of Independence, which erupted less than six months after the passage of the UN resolution, was to prove the single most traumatic event in Jewish-Arab relations, a turning point for both Jews and Palestinians. In its wake, the Jewish people achieved a state of their own after two thousand years of exile and more than fifty years of intensive Zionist colonization. Israel became the focal point of Jewish life all over the world and a powerful political factor in the Middle East. The Palestinians, meanwhile, became a nation of refugees, deprived of their homeland and any real hope for sovereignty, subjected to oppression and discrimination by Jews and Arabs alike. The Arab world as a whole, suffering from its humiliating defeat at the hands of Israel, fell prey to convolutions and turbulence that continue to this day.

The war determined the subsequent attitudes and strategies of Israel, the Arab states, and the Palestinians. It transformed the local

Jewish-Palestinian confrontation into a general Arab-Israeli conflict. It generated another four wars, each one more destructive and dangerous. It led to an escalating arms race and an unending cycle of terror and reprisals, constituting a grave threat to the peace and stability of the whole world. And it left a tragic legacy of mutual fears, suspicions, prejudices, passionate recriminations, preposterous self-righteousness, and blindness to the legitimate rights of an adversary.

Nonetheless, in spite of all its disastrous consequences, the 1948 war is generally believed to have been inevitable. Yet this apparently self-evident and unassailable truth was suddenly opened to question during the latest and most crucial political event in the Israeli-Palestinian conflict, the Lebanon War.

The invasion, the saturation bombing and siege of Beirut, and the massacres in the Palestinian refugee camps of Sabra and Shatila produced a sharp schism in Israeli society. Massive antiwar opposition erupted—for the first time, in Israel's history—while the guns were still firing. Significantly, in defending the actions of his government, then-Prime Minister Menahem Begin referred to the policies of David Ben-Gurion, Israel's first prime minister, in 1948. Begin claimed that the only difference between them was that Ben-Gurion had resorted to subterfuge, whereas he was carrying out his policy openly. He cited Ben-Gurion's plan to divide Lebanon by setting up a Christian state north of the Litani River, his relentless efforts to prevent the creation of a Palestinian state, and, during the 1948 war, his wholesale destruction of Arab villages and townships within the borders of Israel and the expulsion of their inhabitants from the country—all in the interest of establishing a homogeneous Jewish state.

At first, Begin's claim to historical continuity and his attempt to vindicate his policies by invoking the late Ben-Gurion sounded preposterous. After all, the fiercest internal struggles in Zionist history had occurred between Ben-Gurion's socialist labor movement and the right-wing Revisionist party (of which Begin's party, Herut, was the Israeli successor). Before independence, the split nearly caused civil war within the Jewish community in Palestine. With the establishment of the state of Israel, Ben-Gurion and Begin remained implacable enemies. Ben-Gurion refused even to allow the bones of Zeev Jabotinsky, the founder of the Revisionist movement, to be buried in Israel.

It seemed, therefore, that there was something bizarre, if not repugnant, in trying to justify the Lebanon War by drawing parallels with the War of Independence. The 1948 war had never been a subject of controversy. It was always considered a war of self-defense, a struggle for survival. It was fought in the wake of the UN resolution that proclaimed the right of the Jewish people to statehood. The war in Lebanon, on the other hand, was an invasion by the Israel Defense Forces (IDF) in contravention of both the UN Charter and international law.

But Pandora's box had been opened. Israeli historians, investigative journalists, and political analysts examined the evidence—some to defend Begin, some to unmask what they were sure was demagoguery, and some to get at the truth of his assertions. Nearly all, myself included, had to admit that, political opinions and prejudices notwithstanding, Begin's quotations and references were, indeed, based on fact.

In the final chapter of my previous book, which appeared long before the Lebanon War, I discussed whether the War of Independence had been inevitable. I raised this question in connection with a claim made in 1975 by Dr. Nahum Goldmann, one of the architects of the UN Partition Resolution. Since the Jewish state existed de facto, Goldmann asserted, the war could have been prevented by postponing the proclamation of independence and accepting a last-minute, US-inspired truce proposal. On the basis of the material available to me at that time, I had to conclude that although the claim was corroborated by the logic of events and the pattern of behavior of the Arab states, no documents had yet been uncovered to substantiate it.

In 1982, the Israeli Ministry of Defense published the *War Diaries* of Ben-Gurion, who is generally credited with the victory in the War of Independence. Moreover, the Israeli State Archives, in conjunction with the Central Zionist Archives in Jerusalem, had already begun publishing thousands of declassified documents dealing with the foreign policy of the Jewish Agency and the Israeli government and their contacts with the Arab world in the period between the passage of the UN Partition Resolution on November 29, 1947, and the signing of the armistice treaties between Israel and Egypt, Jordan, Lebanon, and Syria in 1949. Although much material remains classified, the carefully edited selection of documents and files now accessible casts an entirely new light on this most crucial period in Israeli-Arab relations, and I began to peruse them very closely.

I was also fortunate enough to obtain unpublished material from Arab sources, among them the Arab Studies Society in Jerusalem, founded in 1948 and headed by Faisal Husseini, the son of the leader of the Palestinian fighting forces, Abd al-Qadir Husseini; and a number of Palestinian and Egyptian friends. For reasons that should be apparent, I must withhold their names for the time being. The only persons I can mention freely are, unfortunately, those whose activities were cut off by brutal assassinations: Said Hamami, the PLO representative in London, who was the first to initiate contacts with known Zionists; Dr. Issam Sartawi, Yasser Arafat's special envoy to Europe, who maintained an ongoing dialogue with Israeli peace organizations; and Aziz Shihada, a lawyer from Ramallah who founded the Arab refugee congress in 1949 and worked tirelessly until his death for a just solution to this tragic problem, which is, to be sure, the crux of the Israeli-Arab conflict. I was now able to compare Israeli and Arab versions of events and to verify both against the historical record.

This new material enabled me to reexamine and document Goldmann's claim. In taking up the matter, I was motivated by both personal friendship and our many years of cooperation in promoting a Jewish-Arab dialogue. Goldmann's position had led him, despite his prominent position in Jewish life, to an abiding conflict with the Israeli establishment which lasted until his death in 1982. I hoped, perhaps, to vindicate him on this matter. But even more important, I became convinced that the new evidence was exceptionally relevant to the present state of Israeli-Palestinian relations. In fact, it was a *sine qua non* for understanding the course of the entire conflict leading up to and including the Lebanon War.

Indeed, the historical parallel between, the War of Independence and the Lebanon War raises many crucial questions for Israelis interested in peace and for Americans and American Jews who have Israel's fundamental interests at heart. Was the policy of the Zionist leadership in 1948 and that of Israel's subsequent leaders actually aimed at attaining a homogeneous Jewish state in the whole or most Palestine? If this was the case, then the attempted destruction and further dispersal of the Palestinian refugees in Lebanon appears to be a more advanced application of the same policy. Does this mean that socialist leadership of the Jewish community in 1948 and their successors up

until 1977—when Begin's party came to power—were no different
from their hated Revisionist rivals on this issue? And even more frightening, to what extent does the growing support for the theocratic racist
Rabbi Meir Kahane—who talks openly of deporting the Palestinians
from Israel and the West Bank and Gaza—have its roots in the events
of 1948?

Like most Israelis, I had always been under the influence of certain
myths that had become accepted as historical truth. And since myths
are central to the creation of structures of thinking and propaganda,
these myths had been of paramount importance in shaping Israeli
policy for more than three and a half decades. Israel's myths are located
at the core of the nation's self-perception. Even though Israel has the
most sophisticated army in the region and possesses an advanced
atomic capability, it continues to regard itself in terms of the Holocaust, as the victim of an unconquerable, bloodthirsty enemy. Thus
whatever Israelis do, whatever means we employ to guard our gains or
to increase them, we justify as last-ditch self-defense. We can, therefore,
do no wrong. The myths of Israel forged during the formation of the
state have hardened into this impenetrable, and dangerous, ideological
shield. Yet what emerged from my reading was that while it was precisely during the period between 1948 and 1952 that most of these
myths gained credence, the documents at hand not only failed to substantiate them, they openly contradicted them.

Let us look briefly at these myths—and the realities:

**Myth One: Zionist acceptance of the United Nations Parti-
tion Resolution of November 29, 1947, was a far-reaching
compromise by which the Jewish community abandoned the
concept of a Jewish state in the whole of Palestine and recognized the right of the Palestinians to their own state. Israel
accepted this sacrifice because it anticipated the implementation of the resolution in peace and cooperation with the
Palestinians.** My research suggests that it was actually only a tactical move in an overall strategy. This strategy aimed first at
thwarting the creation of a Palestinian Arab state through a
secret agreement with Abdallah of Transjordan, whose annexation of the territory allocated for a Palestinian state was to be the

first step in his dream of a Greater Syria. Second, it sought to increase the territory assigned by the UN to the Jewish state.

Myth Two: The Palestinian Arabs totally rejected partition and responded to the call of the mufti of Jerusalem to launch an all-out war on the Jewish state, forcing the Jews to depend on a military solution. This was not the whole story. While the mufti was, indeed, fanatical in his opposition to partition, the majority of Palestinian Arabs, although also opposed, did not respond to his call for a holy war against Israel. On the contrary, prior to Israel's Declaration of Independence on May 14, 1948, many Palestinian leaders and groups made efforts to reach a *modus vivendi*. It was only Ben-Gurion's profound opposition to the creation of a Palestinian state that undermined the Palestinian resistance to the mufti's call.

Myth Three: The flight of the Palestinians from the country, both before and after the establishment of the state of Israel, came in response to a call by the Arab leadership to leave temporarily, in order to return with the victorious Arab armies. They fled despite the efforts of the Jewish leadership to persuade them to stay. In fact, the flight was prompted by Israel's political and military leaders, who believed that Zionist colonization and statehood necessitated the "transfer" of Palestinian Arabs to Arab countries.

Myth Four: All of the Arab states, unified in their determination to destroy the newborn Jewish state, joined together on May 15, 1948, to invade Palestine and expel its Jewish inhabitants. My research indicates that the Arab states aimed not at liquidating the new state, but rather at preventing the implementation of the agreement between the Jewish provisional government and Abdallah for his Greater Syria scheme.

Myth Five: The Arab invasion of Palestine on May 15, in contravention of the UN Partition Resolution, made the 1948 war inevitable. The documents show that the war was not inevitable. The Arabs had agreed to a last-minute American proposal for a three-month truce on the condition that Israel temporarily postpone its Declaration of Independence. Israel's provisional government rejected the American proposal by a slim majority of 6 to 4.

Myth Six: The tiny, newborn state of Israel faced the onslaught of the Arab armies as David faced Goliath: a numerically inferior, poorly armed people in danger of being overrun by a military giant. The facts and figures available point to a different situation altogether. Ben-Gurion himself admits that the war on self-defense lasted only four weeks, until the truce of June 11 when huge quantities of arms reached the country. Israel's better trained and more experienced armed forces then attained superiority in weapons on land, sea, and air.

Myth Seven: Israel's hand has always been extended in peace, but since no Arab leaders have ever recognized Israel's right to exist, there has never been anyone to talk to. On the contrary from the end of World War II to 1952, Israel turned down successive proposals made by Arab states and by neutral mediators that might have brought about an accommodation.

It is the purpose of this book to debunk these myths, not as an academic exercise but as a contribution to a better understanding of the Palestinian problem and to a more constructive approach to its solution.

There is also a personal issue—for me as for tens of thousands of Israelis, ardent Zionists and socialists, whose public and private lives have been built on a belief in those myths, along with a belief in Zionism and the state of Israel as embodying not only the national liberation of the Jewish people but the great humanitarian principles of Judaism and enlightened mankind. True, we did not always agree with many official policies and even opposed them publicly. And developments since 1967 have created realities contradictory to these beliefs. But we still believed that Israel was born out of the agony of a just and inevitable war, guided by the principles of human dignity, justice, and equality. Perhaps it was naiveté. Perhaps it was the effect of the Holocaust that made us unable, unwilling to be fundamentally critical of our country and ourselves. Whatever its sources, the truth cannot be shunned. It must be used even now in the service of the same universal principles that inspired us in our younger days.

My commitment to socialist Zionism dates back to my youth in Tomashov, Poland, where I was born just before World War I, and has continued unabated ever since. In 1930, when I was nineteen, I came to Palestine and joined Kibbutz Gan Shmuel. There my children and grandchildren were born, and there I remained for forty-two years, until personal considerations forced me to move to Tel Aviv, where I now live. I became active in political affairs in 1948, I served as the national secretary of MAPAM, the United Worker-party associated with the Kibbutz Artzi-Hashomer Hatzair movement. In 1954, I was appointed director of MAPAM's Arab affairs department, a post I held for eleven years. Since 1957, when I founded the monthly journal *New Outlook*, devoted to Middle Eastern affairs, I have come into steady contact with Palestinians and other Arabs prepared to hold a dialogue on our common problems. I have retained an abiding interest in Israel-Arab relations, and all my work in Israel and abroad has been motivated by one overriding concern—a quest for a just solution to the Israeli-Palestinian conflict through mutual recognition of both peoples' right to self-determination.

I have never believed that Zionism inherently obviates the rights of the Palestinians, and I do not believe so today. I do believe, however, that I have been more ignorant of some of the facts than I should have been. It wasn't until I was studying Arab-Zionist relations from 1917 to 1947, for example, that I made the painful discovery that the "father" of the idea that the Palestinians were not entitled to national independence was none other than Zionism's most outstanding leader, Chaim Weizmann, the architect of the Balfour Declaration and Israel's first president. He was the man I had most admired as the personification of the liberal, humanist, and progressive values of Zionism. Granted, he favored equal rights for the Arab population within the Jewish state, but he did not accord the Palestinians the same national

rights or aspirations that he considered inalienable for the Jews. Unfortunately, his successors—with the notable exception of Nahum Goldmann, but including Ben-Gurion and Golda Meir—were not even
prepared to grant equal rights to the Arabs of Israel, who were viewed
as a potential fifth column. Instead, these leaders chose to deprive
them of many civil rights while perpetuating the myths that justified
their doing so.

A critical review of the past is indispensable for the new generation
or Jews and Palestinians who reached maturity after the Six-Day War
of 1967. This generation is now taking over decision making bodies
and managing the political, social, and economic affairs of their
respective peoples. Their opinions and concepts have been shaped
largely by the fact of Israeli rule over the lives of nearly 1,500,000
Palestinians in the West Bank, Gaza, and East Jerusalem. For the generation of Israelis, control over the whole of Palestine is something
natural, something that has always been and always will be. The Palestinians are considered "outsiders" who aim to destroy the Jewish state
or, failing this, to grab a part of it for themselves.

For the young Palestinians, on the other hand, Israel is a "crusader"
state that stole their land, expelled their people, and now oppresses those
who remain, hoping eventually to evict them, too. Furthermore, Israel is
viewed as an outpost of Western imperialism, blocking the way not only
to Palestinian independence but to Arab unity and progress as well.

In addition to their distorted views and an unwillingness to recognize the legitimate rights of one another, both peoples have yet something else in common: Neither believes in the possibility of
reconciliation. If the stereotypes and false history continue to dominate the minds of the young, disaster must follow.

In order to stimulate new thinking, it is necessary to undermine the
myths that have determined structures of thinking. Some of my findings may cause storms of controversy. But they may also serve as a cat-
alyst in evolving new positions and alternate solutions.

In treating the subject of the Israeli-Palestinian conflict through a discussion of Israel's foundation myths, I am well aware of the constraints
and limitations involved. First of all, I am dealing with only one side of
the problem. I am restricting myself to an analysis of Israeli policies and
Israeli propaganda structures. I choose to do it this way not because I

attribute to Israel sole responsibility for their failure to find a solution to this century-old problem—the Palestinians, too, were active players in the drama that has brought upon them the calamity of defeat and the loss of their homeland. But a review of the contributing Arab myths, misconceptions, and fallacious policies must be done by an Arab—only then will it be credible, only then can it have some influence in shaping new Arab policies. Furthermore, the outsider faces the barriers of language, the problem of access to primary sources (many of which are still classified), and the difficulties of personal verification. I have no doubt, however, that in the future Arab and Palestinian scholars will realize that self-criticism is not a sign of weakness, and that a critical review of Arab history and policies will follow.

Certainly, the ideal way to fulfill this undertaking would have been a joint project by an Israeli-Palestinian Historical Society. I hope this is not wishful thinking, and that someday such a common effort will produce a study free of the deficiencies and limitations of this one.

Conclusion

My efforts to undermine the propaganda structures surrounding the War of Independence and its aftermath have been motivated not only by a penchant for accuracy and a desire to correct the record, but by the relevance of the myths to the present-day situation in Israel. The labor party and Likud, despite the historical rivalry of their political conceptions within the Zionist movement, have joined together in a "national unity" government that controls up to 90 seats in the 120-seat Knesset. Their union is based not on any consensus about the fundamental problems facing Israel—the continuation of the peace process and the future of the occupied territories—but, rather, on the removal of these problems from the national agenda. Yet clear-cut decisions on these issues cannot be postponed for long.

A choice will have to be made between pursuing the goal of a greater Israel—which means the annexation of the territories occupied since 1967, continued rule over an unwilling subject population, and increased military activism—and meeting the basic economic, social, and educational needs of the society and preserving its democratic character.

Maintaining the status quo can only increase the already devastating polarization of Israel society along with the resulting tensions and conflicts, and erode the moral and ethical values from which Israel traditionally drew its strength. It is clear that the liberal, humanist, and socialist elements that aspire to peace and coexistence with the Palestinians and the rest of the Arab world face a difficult struggle with the ever-growing ethnocentric, militaristic, fundamentalist camp, for whom power and territory are primary objectives, to be achieved, if necessary, by the continued oppression and subjugation of the Palestinian people.

In this struggle, ideology plays a primary role. Menahem Begin justified his invasion of Lebanon in 1982 with the argument of "historical continuity," referring to Ben-Gurion's policies in 1948. Labor on the other hand, presents Ben-Gurion's ideas and strategies as the other alternative to Likud's concept of a Greater Israel, pointing out that he totally rejected rule over another people and was unconditionally committed to the preservation of the Jewish and democratic character of the state. As I acknowledged at the outset of this study, an analysis of Ben-Gurion's concepts and strategies during the most crucial and traumatic period in Jewish-Arab relations is not, therefore, a mere academic exercise, and Begin's claim cannot be ignored. Indeed, in spite of the fundamental differences between the two wars and their objectives, the War of Independence (to be exact, its first stage, from November 1947 to May 1948) and the Lebanon War have many features in common that differentiate them from the other Israeli-Arab wars.

The first is the identity of the enemy: the Palestinian people, who claimed the right to independence and statehood in Palestine. In both cases Israel's aim was to thwart such possibilities and eliminate any Palestinian leadership struggling to attain those rights. In 1948 this was achieved by a tactical agreement with King Abdallah, who furthered Israel's aims insofar as he wanted to liquidate the mufti-dominated Arab Higher Committee and annex the West Bank to Transjordan. In 1982 Begin attempted to do the same by liquidating the PLO in Lebanon—seen as the major obstacle to Israeli annexation of the West Bank and to the creation of a collaborationist Arab leadership there that would accept a miserly autonomy, deprived of legislative powers and the right to self-determination.

The second feature the two wars share is that in both instances the

Israeli army confronted not only soldiers but a civilian population. True, in the wars of 1956, 1967, and 1973, the civilian populations, especially the Arabs along the Suez Canal and in the Golan Heights, suffered from bombing and shelling, and hundreds of thousands became refugees, but the Israel Defense Forces confronted only regular Arab armies. In 1948 and 1982, on the other hand, Israeli soldiers had to shell villages, blow up houses, schools, and mosques (killing innocent men, women, and children), and detain "able-bodied" men or drive them from their homes into forced exile.

These parallels reveal yet others. In 1948, the Palestinians did not have an army. Their struggle was carried out by scattered groups of volunteers, mobilized by local leaders or by commanders appointed by the Arab League. In 1982, the PLO did not have an army either, only arsenals of weapons and fighting units trained by different political organizations for infiltration, sabotage, and guerrilla warfare. In 1948, the eradication of the Palestinian fighting groups was planned and executed by the destruction of villages and towns; in 1982, by the destruction of the refugee camps that served as their bases. In 1948 about 360 Arab villages and 14 towns within the borders of Israel were destroyed and their inhabitants forced to flee. In 1982, the order given to the Israeli army to liquidate the "terrorist organizations" in Lebanon meant the destruction of refugee camps and urban suburbs with a Palestinian population, though the members of the organizations were also the leaders of the Palestinian communities, their hospitals, schools, workshops, and social and cultural societies.

In such circumstances, the dehumanization of the Israeli soldiers was inevitable, leading to brutal behavior and violation of elementary human rights. In a society like Israel's, which claims the deep sense of justice and respect for life inherent in Judaism, the erosion of these moral values could not be admitted without a significant rationalization. In both cases, therefore, the enemy had to be dehumanized as well. Thus Ben-Gurion described the Arabs as "the pupils and even the teachers of Hitler, who claim that there is only one way to solve the Jewish question—one way only: total annihilation." For his part, Begin described the PLO fighters as "two-legged animals" and justified the terrible suffering caused by the siege of Beirut by comparing the attacks on Yasser Arafat's last stronghold in the city to the Allied bombing of Berlin, aimed at destroying Hitler's bunker.

There was in 1948, as in Israel today, a basic "philosophy of expulsion." Today it is expressed in the racist ideology of the rabble-rousing rabbi Meir Kahane, with his anti-Arab provocations. In 1947 and 1948 it was couched in the seemingly more benign conception of a homogeneous Jewish state struggling for survival. The man who, with Ben-Gurion's approval, launched a campaign to persuade the Palestinians to lock their homes, sell their land, and immigrate, with compensation, to other countries, was the director of the colonization department of the Jewish National Fund, Joseph Weitz. Weitz did not employ theocratic, racist slogans or propose the abolition of democracy, as does Kahane today. But he and Ben-Gurion did not refrain from harassment by a Military Administration claiming security considerations, and ultimately their aim was the same: a homogeneous Jewish state in all or most of Palestine.

Indeed, it was under Ben-Gurion's leadership in the crucial years 1947 to 1949 that the planks in Zionism's traditional Arab policy became cudgels. Nonrecognition of the Palestinians' right to self-determination turned into an active strategy to prevent, at all costs the creation of the Palestinian state as called for in the UN Partition Resolution. The comprehensive social, political, cultural, and economic separation of Jews and Arabs that had always characterized the Yishuv was accelerated, first, by the proposed political partition; second, by the stimulation of a mass exodus of Palestinians from the areas controlled by the Israeli forces; third, by the wholesale destruction of Arab villages and townships to prevent their return; and finally, by the forceful segregation of the remaining Arab minority through the imposition of a Military Administration in Arab areas. The "civilizing mission" of Zionism in the Arab world, as formulated in the Weizmann-Faisal agreement of 1919, was transformed into support for King Abdallah of Transjordan, and the effective political splintering of the Arab movement for independence and unity.

This transformation in Zionist strategy became the model for Israel's policies toward the Arabs in general and the Palestinians in particular. Ben-Gurion's conceptions were molded into the official doctrines of the Israeli establishment, the armed forces, and the political and economic elite—regardless of class or political affiliation.

In retrospect, Ben-Gurion's contribution to the creation of the state cannot be disputed—in the victorious War of Independence, in the absorption of mass immigration, and in the country's successful industrial, technological, and scientific development. But today, in the centenary year of Ben-Gurion's birth, the Labor party is proposing the philosophy of the "state-builder," the "armed prophet," the "prophet of fire"—Ben-Gurionism—as the only ideological, political, and social alternative to right-wing, reactionary nationalism now so entrenched in Israeli society. Indeed, the concept of a democratic Jewish society might conceivably provide such an alternative were it free from the impulse toward territorial expansionism—for whatever reason: historical, religious, political, or strategic. But the fact is that Ben-Gurion built his political philosophy precisely on these two contradictory elements: a democratic *Jewish* society in the *whole*, or in most, of Palestine.

Israel's success in 1948 and in the armistice talks in 1949 seems to have vindicated Ben-Gurion's policy of not recognizing the Palestinians as a national entity. For a number of years after the war, most Israelis shared the perception that the Palestinian people had ceased to exist; in their view, only the humanitarian problem of the refugees remained (as did, of course, the determination of final borders and the signing of peace treaties with the Arab states). The Palestinian problem was obliterated from Israel's political thinking despite the refugees' struggle for repatriation and the restoration of their rights and property. Between 1948 and 1967, no Israeli studies on the Arab world appear to have predicted the reemergence of the Palestinian national movement in the refugee camps. The fedayeen were seen only as agents of Arab military rulers preparing for wars of revenge. Ben-Gurion viewed them as instruments of the Arab states' deliberate policy of guerrilla warfare, harassment; and violation of the tenuous armistice treaties. In response, he initiated massive retaliations and severe and humiliating punishments intended to force them to stop this policy. As Moshe Sharett wrote in 1955, "In the thirties we restrained the emotions of revenge and we educated the public to consider revenge as an absolutely negative impulse. Now, on the contrary, we justify the system of reprisals out of pragmatic considerations . . . we have eliminated the mental and moral brakes on this instinct and made it possible . . . to uphold revenge as a moral value."

Nearly twenty years had to pass before it became clear that the eviction of the Palestinians from their lands and the creation of the refugee problem only intensified the national aspirations of the Palestinians, whose dispersion and homelessness created a problem greatly resembling that of the Jewish people in past times. Ben-Gurion's policies led to a vicious circle of escalating violence: large-scale battles created dangerous political tensions and rendered the whole area prey to a feverish arms race and great-power rivalry, culminating finally in full-scale wars. The Palestinians themselves became a factor in this sequence of events, seeking to channel political and social unrest into a pan-Arab movement for the restoration of their rights. They became the most committed militants, spearheading the move toward Arab unity and confrontation with Israel.

Thus, Ben-Gurion's nonrecognition of Palestinian nationalism created the very danger he was most afraid of. He knew that the victory of 1948 was achieved not because the Israeli army was more heroic but because the Arab armies were corrupt and the Arab world divided. He became obsessed with the fear that a charismatic leader would modernize Arab education, develop their economies unite all the Arab states:

> The Arab people have been beaten by us. Will they forget it quickly? Seven hundred thousand people beat 30 million. Will they forget this offense? It can be assumed that they have a sense of honor. We will make peace efforts, but two sides are necessary for peace. Is there any security that they will not want to take revenge? Let us recognize the truth: we won not because we performed wonders, but because the Arab army is rotten. Must this rottenness persist forever? Is it not possible that an Arab Mustafa Kemal will arise? The situation in the world beckons toward revenge: there are two blocs; there is a fear of world war. This tempts anyone with a grievance. We will always require a superior defensive capability.

This fear led Ben-Gurion to concentrate on building a military force (including a nuclear option) to match the combined force of all the Arab countries and to prevent any unfavorable changes in the political structure of the region. It also led Israel to subordinate its foreign, economic, and social policies to the end of acquiring or producing better and more sophisticated weapons than the Arabs. This in turn involved Israel in the great-power rivalry in the Middle East and required the country to "take sides" in the struggles between Arab nationalism and its adversaries on the principle that "the enemy of my enemy is my friend." This policy has continued unabated till today. Its efficacy, as shown in the Suez War of 1956 and the Six-Day War of 1967, has made its underlying concepts axiomatic for both the public and the political elite. The 1967 victory was so overwhelming that Israelis increasingly came to believe that they could live forever without peace. It induced a demand for new territorial dimensions and new strategic frontiers, enthusiastically acclaimed by the disciples of Jabotinsky, who never stopped dreaming of a Jewish state on both sides of the Jordan, and by the religious nationalists, who insisted on Israel's God-given right to the historical borders of the biblical covenant.

Until 1967, the labor movement in Israel had maintained its hegemony, although its traditional, pre-state social values were being gradually undermined—both in education and in its egalitarian economic conceptions—as a result of the free rein given to capitalist rather than cooperative enterprise and the growth of a large sector of underprivileged people. With the blitz victory in 1967 and the occupation of the West Bank and Gaza, the sudden expansion of Israel's borders gave rise to a more rapid erosion of the socialist and humanist values that had once been the hallmark of labor Zionism: prominent political leaders, poets, writers, and intellectuals, whose roots had been in the labor movement, joined the new, dynamic Greater Israel movement, which sought to turn Israel's most recent conquests into an integral part of the country.

The 1.25 million Palestinians who came under Israeli rule provided cheap labor for the Israeli economy, supplying nearly 100,000 workers for agriculture, public works, construction, light industries, and private services. The Palestinians became Israel's "water carriers and hewers of wood." Jewish workers moved up the social ladder to positions of management, the professions, trade, and public service. The influx of enormous quantities of capital stimulated the growth of a war economy, huge investments in the occupied territories in an Israeli-controlled infrastructure, and a boom in private enterprise. The formerly labor-oriented economy was turned into an unbridled capitalist one, with a typical consumer mentality, out for quick profits, speculation, and tax evasion. Diaspora Jewry, basking in Israel's military glory, provided unconditional moral and financial support, and massive economic and military aid from the United States hastened the further militarization of Israel's political thinking and self-image as a mini-superpower and an indispensable ally of the United States in its global policy of confrontation with the USSR. Chatting with American friends, the late prime minister Golda Meir once said: "I don't know why you fancy a French word like détente when there is a good English phrase for it—Cold War."

The first settlements in the West Bank were built at the inspiration of Yigal Allon, a kibbutz member, a minister in the Labor government, and the former left-wing MAPAM commander of the Palmach; it was also Allon who gave his approval to attempts of the fundamentalist rabbi Moshe Levinger to establish a Jewish community in the heart of Arab Hebron.

In the new circumstances, any attempts made to preach a return to the old values of the labor movement were bound to fail. Labor leaders did not understand that only by ending the occupation of the Arab territories and reaching a peace settlement with the Arabs could they reverse this erosion of "pioneering socialist values."

The religious-nationalistic Gush Emunim, the Bloc of the Faithfill, was not long in emerging as the spiritual leader of new Israel expansionism, and with the traumatic experience of the Yom Kippur War of 1973, when Israel's military superiority was called into question, the soil was fertile for the appearance of a gun-toting, messianic ethnocentric, expansionist movement, of which Meir Kahane was only the most extreme example.

The Labor government tried to curb the movement for religious and messianic expansion by insisting on "strategic" expansion only that is, permanent Israeli control over those areas delineated in the Allon plan and ostensibly necessary for Israel's security: the Jordan Valley, the Golan Heights, Sharm al-Sheikh. But the Labor party both failed to curb the right and continued to rationalize its own policy of unilateral settlement in the occupied territories by arguing that it would prompt the Arabs to negotiate peace out of a fear that loss of time would mean loss of territory. This argument was the primary article of faith for Meir, who, while insisting that there were no Palestinians, bemoaned the moral decline of Israeli society and the labor movement. Meanwhile, Israeli society as a whole was moving more and more to the right, and its widespread disregard, both official and otherwise, of the human and national rights of others was masked as a return to the religious, traditional, and historical rights and values of Judaism.

There is no intrinsic connection between Judaism and democracy. There always was an orthodox, fundamentalist current in Judaism, characterized by racial prejudice toward non-Jews in general and Arabs in particular. A substantial portion—perhaps even the overwhelming majority—of the religious movements, and a growing part of the population in general, came to conceive of the West Bank not as the homeland of the Palestinian people but as Judea and Samaria, the birthplace of the Jewish faith and homeland of the Jewish people. Many people not only became indifferent to the national rights of the Palestinians living there, *they did not even see the necessity for granting them civil rights.* Israel's experience prior to the war in 1967 proved that it was quite possible to exclude the Arab minority from the democratic system by means of a Military Administration, justified by Arab belligerence and the necessity for a very high level of classified "security" and concomitant measures. Ben-Gurion had maintained such a regime within Israel for eighteen years, and all of his labor successors, before 1967 and after, followed suit: Levi Eshkol, Golda Meir, and Yitzhak Rabin. Little wonder that when Likud came to power in 1977, Menahem Begin had his work cut out for him, especially after Moshe Dayan, the first son of the trail-blazing labor-Zionist Kibbutz Degania, crossed party lines to help him out as foreign minister. Begin hoped to wipe out the "trauma" of the Yom Kippur War and assure the success of Greater Israel by eliminating Egypt from the military confrontation through the return of the Sinai Peninsula and then by giving the *coup de grâce* to the Palestinians with the war in Lebanon. Had he succeeded he would have indeed come full circle: Jabotinsky's star pupil and successor would have completed the job that Ben-Gurion, in his own view, had left unfinished.

The Labor party and the labor movement as a whole are now trying to regain the influence they lost in 1977. While Shimon Peres, Ben-Gurion's stalwart lieutenant, shares the offices of prime minister and foreign minister with Yitzhak Shamir, Begin's lieutenant, and the occupation continues unabated, Labor is trying to present Ben-Gurion's idea of a democratic Jewish state as the alternative to a Greater Israel.

But the glorification of the War of Independence and of Ben-Gurion's strategy cannot serve as an alternative. For the line from Ben-Gurion to Begin is direct. Both leaders based their policies on the negation of the binational reality of Palestine: two peoples claiming the same land as a basis for national independence. And in both cases, this negation has doomed their policies. Lebanon became a watershed. It proved that force and oppression cannot eradicate from the hearts and minds of a homeless people its aspiration for freedom and independence. The moral and political failure of that war improved Labor's chances for a return to power. But this would depend heavily on the movement's readiness and ability to submit its own past policies to a serious critical review. Such a step implies an analysis of Ben-Gurion's whole political philosophy and his strategy in the crucial 1947–48 period. He may have assured us of the creation of a Jewish state, but as long as he left the Israeli-Palestinian conflict unresolved, he left us a heritage of war and destruction as well, for which three generations of Israelis and Palestinians are still paying.

The question that remains is this: Can one reasonably hope for a change? The answer is not easy. If there is to be a way out of the present impasse, both Israelis and Palestinians will have to take giant steps in changing their attitudes, priorities, and practices.

There is a consensus among Israeli peace groups that an end must come to the occupation and to Israeli rule over Palestinians. There is also a growing awareness of the fact that the best way to negotiate a real peace is with the PLO. But this will be possible only if both negotiating partners adopt a clear-cut policy in favor of a peace settlement.

There are those who view the Palestine National Covenant—the founding document of the Palestine Liberation Organization—as insignificant and unimportant. I am not of this opinion. In my view it expresses an ideological credo that became a program for action when al-Fatah assumed leadership of the PLO. The covenant, proclaimed on May 28, 1964, declares that the 1947 partition plan and the establishment of Israel "are illegal and false" and calls for the liberation of Palestine as an Arab homeland. The most controversial points of the covenant are articles 6 and 7, which define Palestinians as "those Arab citizens who were living normally in Palestine up to 1947," and declare that only "Jews of Palestinian origin"—i.e., those living in Palestine before 1948—are eligible to remain. But precisely because the covenant has become a plan of action, one should also take the changes in PLO positions very seriously. They have resulted from failures and setbacks in attempts to implement the covenant.

In the past twenty years most of the PLO's efforts to abide by the covenant—guerrilla tactics in the West Bank and Gaza, the establishment of a territorial sanctuary in Jordan, attempts to maintain their independence from Syria and other host countries, the diplomatic attempt to "de-Zionize" Israel or have it expelled from the UN—failed to produce results. The PLO did succeed in gaining moral and political support all over the world for its claim to be the sole legitimate representative of the Palestinian people in their struggle for self-determination and statehood.

The PLO was deeply affected by the passivity of the Arab regimes during the war in Lebanon, their submission to US pressures, their consent to the dismantling and evacuation of PLO bases in Lebanon, and the stormy and massive demonstrations in Israel against the war, the destruction of the refugee camps, and the massacre of the Palestinians. Against this background one must view as serious and important the signals and indications from the PLO of a readiness to negotiate a political solution to the conflict. The PLO is now compelled to develop a new strategy, and there are already instances or feelers being put out to encourage a dialogue with Israelis—most recently at the conference of PLO leaders and members of the Israeli peace camp held in Rumania in November 1986.

Until the Lebanon War, most of the PLO and other Arab leaders viewed the struggle between Zionists of different outlooks as a "Jekyll and Hyde" phenomenon. They viewed Jabotinsky, and later Begin, as the true spokesmen of Zionism. Chaim Weizmann and the labor Zionists were considered merely hypocritical cover-ups for Zionism's real expansionist aims. Although the policies of Israel's successive governments, both Labor and Likud, have done nothing to alter this view—and the present national unity government only reinforces it—the war in Lebanon did reveal deep divisions within Israeli society, divisions not always discernible according to party affiliation.

Israel is in the midst of a deep moral, social, economic, and political crisis, one that will surely become exacerbated if there is no dramatic change of policy. Many young people, as well as a substantial number of artists, journalists, and other intellectuals, including a growing number of people from the so-called Oriental communities, find themselves unable to accept the undemocratic and reactionary religious, military, and moral codes that are now representative of "official" Israel. The outcome of the struggle between two diametrically opposed visions of Israel—an enlightened, democratic state or a fundamentalist, militarist one—will have a significant effect on the future of the Palestinian people as well as on peace in the region.

The objective asymmetry of the situation places the major responsibility for the solution of the conflict on Israel, but it does not release the PLO from adopting a strategy that will enable the progressive forces of peace in Israel to strengthen their positions.

At the same time, it must be recognized that the support of the Israeli peace camp for Palestinian self-determination, mutual recognition, and coexistence is not enough. Diaspora Jewry and friends of Israel abroad must realize that present Israeli policy is doomed to reproduce over and over again the cycle of violence that shocks our sensibilities every time we read or hear of wanton murder and bloodshed, whether the hand that perpetrates it detonates a bomb or fires a pistol. The collective revenge of an army for the murder of one of its citizens is no more righteous or admirable than the individual revenge of a desperate youth for the murder of one of his people. It is only propaganda and distorted vision that labels one "terrorism" and the other "national defense."

It is, then, in the hope of clarifying the distorted vision on our side of the conflict—that is, on the Jewish, Israeli side—that I have written this book.

In order for Israel to be "born," Palestine had to be destroyed—its villages razed, its people dispersed and stripped of their nationality, its history suppressed. In his essay "Erasures," **Gabriel Piterberg**—*an associate professor of history at the University of California, Los Angeles, raised on a kibbutz by Argentine Jewish parents—offers a disquieting analysis of how "Palestine was 'emptied' to enable the creation of Israel."*

ERASURES

Gabriel Piterberg

From *The New Left Review* 10, July–August 2001

Three foundational myths underlie Israeli culture to this day. These are the 'negation of exile' (*shelilat ha-galut*), the 'return to the land of Israel' (*ha-shiva le-Eretz Yisrael*), and the 'return to history' (*ha-shiva la-historia*). They are inextricably intertwined in the master-narrative of Zionism, the story that explains 'how we got to where we are and where we should go henceforth'. The negation of exile establishes a continuity between an ancient past, in which there existed Jewish sovereignty over the land of Israel, and a present that renews it in the resettlement of Palestine. Between the two lies no more than a kind of interminable interim. Depreciation of the period of exile is shared by all Zionists, if with differing degrees of rigidity, and derives from what is, in their outlook, an uncontestable presupposition: from time immemorial, the Jews constituted a territorial nation. It follows that a non-territorial existence must be abnormal, incomplete and inauthentic. In and of itself, as a historical experience, exile is devoid of significance. Although it may have given rise to cultural achievements of moment, exile could not by definition have been a wholesome realization of the nation's *Geist*. So long as they were condemned to it, Jews—whether as individuals or communities—could lead at best a partial and transitory existence, waiting for the redemption of 'ascent' (*aliyah*) once again to the land of Israel, the only site on which the nation's destiny could be fulfilled. Within this mythical framework, exilic Jews always lived provisionally, as potential or proto-Zionists, longing 'to return' to the land of Israel.[1]

Here the second foundational myth complements the first. In Zionist terminology, the recovery by the people of its home promised to deliver the *normalization* of Jewish existence; and the site designated for the re-enactment of Exodus would be the territory of the Biblical story, as elaborated in the Protestant culture of the eighteenth and nineteenth centuries. Zionist ideology defined this land as *empty*. This did not mean Zionist leaders and settlers were ignorant of the presence of Arabs in Palestine, or mulishly ignored them. Israel was 'empty' in a deeper sense. For the land, too, was condemned to an exile as long as there was no Jewish sovereignty over it: it lacked any meaningful or authentic history, awaiting redemption with the return of the Jews. The best-known Zionist slogan, 'a land without a people to a people without a land', expressed a twofold denial: of the historical experience both of the Jews in exile, and of Palestine without Jewish sovereignty. Of course, since the land was not literally empty, its recovery required the establishment of the equivalent of a colonial hierarchy—sanctioned by Biblical authority—of its historic custodians over such intruders as might remain after the return. Jewish settlers were to be accorded exclusive privileges deriving from the Pentateuch, and Palestinian Arabs treated as part of the natural environment. In the *macho* Hebrew culture of modern times, to know a woman, in the Biblical sense, and to know the land became virtually interchangeable as terms of possession. The Zionist settlers were collective subjects who acted, and the native Palestinians became objects acted upon.

The third foundational myth, the 'return to history', reveals, more than any other, the extent to which Zionist ideology was underpinned by the emergence of Romantic nationalism and German historicism in nineteenth-century Europe. Its premise is that the natural and irreducible form of human collectivity is the nation. From the dawn of history peoples have been grouped into such units, and though they might at one time or another be undermined by internal divisions or oppressed by external forces, they are eventually bound to find political self-expression in the shape of sovereign nation-states. The nation is the autonomous historical subject *par excellence*, and the state is the telos of its march toward self-fulfillment. According to this logic, so long as they were exiles, the Jews remained a community outside history, within which all European nations dwelt. Only nations that occupy the soil of their homeland, and establish political sovereignty over it, are capable of shaping their own destiny and so entering history by this logic. The return of the Jewish nation to the land of Israel, overcoming its docile passivity in exile, could alone allow it to rejoin the history of civilized peoples.

Cleansing Palestine

Metaphorically empty, factually inhabited by Arabs, how was Palestine 'emptied' to enable the creation of Israel? Recently, long overdue controversies have broken out over the origins of the present state, prompted by the work of historians who are not committed to its founding myths. This is a welcome development: much hallowed mystification has been cleared away. But there is a danger that debate could become too narrowly focused on the single issue of whether or not there was an Israeli master plan to effect a comprehensive expulsion of the Palestinian Arabs from their homes in 1948.[2] The moral pressure behind this obsessive question is understandable, and should be respected. But it is also true that it takes for granted that what matters is the framework of the perpetrators, not the perspective of the victims. The existence or otherwise of an explicit Zionist intention to unleash ethnic cleansing, under cover of war, poses problems that Israelis certainly need to confront. But to Palestinians who lost their homes, their goods, their rights and their identities, it matters little whether the disaster that befell them resulted from decisions taken by military commanders and local bureaucrats on the spot, or from an implicit understanding that this was the wish of the Zionist political leadership, or through a diffuse atmosphere and ideology that treated massive expulsions as desirable—or any combination of the above. What counted for the Arabs driven off their lands was the fact of their dispossession and transformation into refugees. Retrospective rituals of bad conscience risk becoming luxuries that only the victor can afford, without consequence for the victims who have had to live with the results.

The reality is that the eventuality of massive expulsions was inherent in the nature of Zionist colonization in Palestine long before war broke out in 1948. Consideration of notions of population 'transfer' ceased to be just an abstract idea after the report of the Peel Commission in the late 1930s. After all, as Zeev Sternhell correctly observes, Zionism was in many ways a typical example of the 'organic'—as distinct from 'civic'—nationalism of Central and Eastern Europe.[3] This kind was feral in its demand for ethnic homogeneity, ruling out from the beginning any possibility of the Zionist movement accepting a bi-national state in Palestine. Given the demography of Palestine in 1947, the establishment of a Jewish state inexorably required the removal of Palestinians from their farms and towns. However, the form that this 'population transfer' was to take did not need a premeditated plan of expulsion by the Israeli government (as distinct from the calculation of individual officials and bureaucratic agencies). Rather, the crucial decision was *to prevent Palestinian Arabs at all costs from returning to their homes*, regardless of the circumstances in which they had 'left' them, and no matter how plainly their 'departure' had been envisaged as a temporary move made under duress, in the midst of war. There were, of course, deliberate and massive expulsions. The infamous Operation Danny of July 10–14, 1948, which resulted in a massacre at Lydda and the forcible transfer of the entire population of the townships of Ramlah and Lydda—ten miles south-east of Tel Aviv—to Jordan, is a well-known case in point.[4] But the really crucial decision, which was fully conscious and explicit, was to make sure that the collapse of the Palestinian community that unfolded under the pressures of all-out war between Israel and the Arab states would be irreversible.

For what followed, we are indebted to outstanding recent research by Haya Bombaji-Sasportas of Ben-Gurion University in the Negev.[5] In April 1948, Haifa fell to an Israeli assault. In June, Foreign Minister Moshe Sharett—a darling of Israeli 'moderates' to this day—said to his colleagues:

> To my mind this is the most surprising thing: the emptying of the country by the Arab community. In the history of the land of Israel this is more surprising than the establishment of the Hebrew State itself . . . This has happened amidst a war that the Arab nation declared against us, because the Arabs fled of their own accord—and their departure is one of those revolutionary changes after which history does not revert to its previous course, as we see from the outcome of the war between Greece and Turkey. We should be willing to pay for land. This does not mean that we should buy holdings from each and every [Arab]. We shall receive assets and land, which can be used to help settle

Arabs in other countries. But they do not return. And this is our policy: they do not return.[6]

A day before, in a letter to an important official in the Jewish Agency, Sharett defined the emptying of the land of its Arab inhabitants as 'a wonderful thing in the history of the country and in a sense even more wonderful than the establishment of the State of Israel.'[7]

'Retroactive transfer'

Bureaucrats everywhere have particular ways of thought and forms of expression, which sometimes produce chillingly apt terms. Yosef Weitz, the director of the Jewish National Fund's Lands Department, and one of the most relentless proponents of transfer, serves as an outstanding example. As early as May 28, 1948, when he headed the semi-official three-member Transfer Committee, he noted in his diary a meeting with Sharett. On this occasion, Weitz asked Sharett whether he thought orderly action should be taken to ensure that the flight of Arabs from the war zone was an irreversible fact, and described the aim of such action as a 'retroactive transfer' (*transfer be-di 'avad*). Sharett said yes.[8]

Weitz's term underlay the confidential discourse of Israeli officials and politicians of the time. Probably from the seizure of Haifa, and with increasing intensity and ferocity during the autumn of 1948, Palestinian territories conquered by Israeli arms were voided of Arabs, without a master plan being needed to remove them. There was a range of ways in which the land became 'Arabless': flight of the wealthy; temporary escape of civilians from areas under threat of heavy fighting; encouragement of panic by Israeli military violence, terror and propaganda; and full-fledged expulsion.[9] What is amply documented and demonstrable is the cold deliberation of the policy of 'retroactive transfer' which issued from these movements. This was the fundamental decision that was systematized, bureaucratized and legalized in the 1950s, with far-reaching consequences for both Palestinians and Jews, within Israel and without. To this day, what structurally defines the nature of the Israeli state is the return of Jews and the non-return of Arabs to Palestine. If this dynamic of return/non-return were to disappear, the Zionist state would lose its identity.

Official narratives

The physical implementation of the policy of non-return meant the brutal wartime demolition of occupied villages, and in some cases of urban neighbourhoods; the confiscation of lands and properties; the settlement of Jews in places rendered Arab-free. The results were completed with systematic legal measures in the 1950s, affecting both refugees outside Israel and those within, whom the state defined as its (second-class) citizens. But the erasure of Arab existence in Palestine was not just physical. It was also discursive. A group of officials in command of what was considered expert knowledge of 'the Arab question' was responsible for this side of the operation. It comprised two distinct types of functionary. One had come through the foreign-policy department of the Jewish Agency or the intelligence unit of Haganah, in the pre-state period. These could speak Arabic, had experience of dealing with Arabs, took pride in being field-experts, and were known as Arabists (*Arabistim*). The other contingent were the better educated products of European-mostly German-universities, and/or the Hebrew University in Jerusalem; they knew written Arabic (*fusha*), believed they had a wider and deeper understanding of the enemy than their field counterparts, and were known as Orientalists (*mizrahanim*). Once the state was established, most of them held posts in its intelligence machinery, or in the research and Middle East departments of the Foreign Office, or were advisers on 'Arab affairs' to the Prime Minister.[10] After the war, an early key move of this apparatus was to define the plight of Palestinian refugees as a 'humanitarian' issue tied inextricably to an overall resolution of the Arab-Israeli conflict, in the full knowledge that such a resolution would not be forthcoming. Bombaji-Sasportas correctly observes that this strategy was instrumental in cancelling the subjectivity of the victims of Israeli expansion: ignoring their identity, memory and aspirations in favour of a deliberately constructed Gordian knot that has been accepted as a fact of life ever since by Israeli scholarship, whether mainstream or critical.[11] In his own way, Asher Goren—an official in the Israeli Foreign Office—also noticed this. In a memorandum of September 27, 1948, summarizing the refugee problem, he concluded, after reiterating that it was pendant on the conflict with the Arab states as a whole: 'The compromise-seekers [among Arab statesmen] want return [of the refugees to their homes]. The warmongers object to it. The will of the refugees is unknown nor does anyone ask them.'[12]

It was the semi-official Transfer Committee headed by Weitz, which submitted its first report in November 1948, that formulated what would later become the official Israeli narrative of the 'refugee problem'.[13] The Committee's main function was to execute and oversee the policy of non-return by systematic demolition and erasure of Palestinian villages and neighbourhoods, and then the systematic seizure of land and property owned by Palestinians. The report was a massive document containing much detailed information on the Palestinians and the activities of the Committee. Its textual purpose was to enforce the conclusion, laid out with every appearance of authority and objectivity, that the only solution for the refugees was their resettlement in Arab countries. In hindsight this report may be seen as the Ur-text of all Israeli discourse—academic, bureaucratic, political—on the fate of 'those who left', at least until the publication of Benny Morris's work in the 1980s and 1990s. It supplied the account that became the standard version of history for propaganda and foreign-policy purposes.

The narrative was fraudulent, and there is reason to believe that it was consciously fraudulent.[14] Its burden was that the Palestinians themselves, their leaders, and accomplices in the Arab states bore sole responsibility for the creation of the 'refugee problem'. The Mufti of Jerusalem, Hajj Amin al-Husayni, had advised the Palestinians to leave their homes in order to return with the victorious Arab armies, and claim not only their property but also that of the defeated Jews. It was therefore the responsibility of the Arab states to see that the refugees were resettled there—not just because they had incited their displacement but also because it was a 'scientific fact' that Arab societies were now the only appropriate home for such people, since the map of Palestine had been transformed and Israel had its hands full with the absorption of Jewish refugees driven out of the Arab world.

The disappearance of Shaykh Mu'nis
A logical concomitant of this schema was a sustained campaign to wipe out any traces of the Palestinian past on conquered soil. A striking example of how this policy worked in practice is offered by the recent memoir of Zvi Yavetz, Professor Emeritus of Roman History, a founder

of Tel Aviv University and a powerful kingmaker in its Faculty of Humanities for three decades. Reminiscing about his role in the early negotiations with academics, politicians and bureaucrats to set up the university, he describes how a decision was taken to move the nascent campus from provisional quarters in the heart of Tel Aviv to Shaykh Mu'nis.[15] It so happens that Golda Meir (then Myerson) also mentioned Shaykh Mu'nis, in early May 1948—just after the fall of Haifa. Speaking to the Central Committee of Mapai, she said she wished to raise the question of what was to be done with locations that had become substantially Arab-less. A distinction, she told her colleagues, should be drawn between 'hostile' and 'friendly' villages. 'What do we do with the villages that were deserted . . . without a battle by [Arab] friends?' she asked. 'Are we willing to preserve these villages so that their inhabitants may return, or do we wish to erase any trace [*limhok kol zekher*] that there was a village in a given place?'[16] Meir's answer was unequivocal. It was unthinkable to treat villages 'like Shaykh Mu'nis', which had fled because they did not want to fight the Yishuv, in the way that hostile villages had been treated—i.e., subjected to 'retroactive transfer'.

But the inhabitants of Shaykh Mu'nis did not gain much from their classification as 'friendly'. Until late March 1948, the leaders of this large village north of Tel Aviv had prevented Arab irregulars from entering it, and even loosely collaborated with the Haganah. Then, however, the Irgun abducted five of the village notables. Thereupon the population fled *en masse*, and Shaykh Mu'nis literally vanished—a disappearance confirmed three months later by IDF intelligence. Golda Meir's seemingly poignant question in early May, in other words, was asked in the full knowledge that it had ceased to exist at the end of March—a typical soul-searching in the manner of Labour Zionism: crocodile tears over a *fait accompli*. What was once Shaykh Mu'nis became part of an affluent neighbourhood in northern Tel Aviv, which took the name of Ramat Aviv. There, in the 1960s, the University of Tel Aviv was built on the site where Shaykh Mu'nis had been less than twenty years before. Yavetz, a well-known 'leftist' veteran of the war of 1948, not to say an eminent historian, utters not a word of this. Shaykh Mu'nis was no longer there, and for thirty years it could not be remembered. But eventually there was one twisted, colonial exception. In the

1990s, as the university grew larger and wealthier, a luxurious VIP club was built on the campus, called the Green House. Its architecture is an Orientalist Israeli version of an 'Arab mansion', and its location is the hill where the house of the mukhtar of Shaykh Mu'nis once stood (it is a VIP club, after all). The information on the site's past, and who owned it, may be found in the menu of the Green House.

From the start, Israeli officials were well aware of the significance of memory and the need to erase it. Repression of what had been done to create the state was essential among the Jews themselves. It was still more important to eradicate remembrance among Palestinians. Shamai Kahane composed one of the most striking documents of the official campaign to this end. A high-ranking functionary in the Foreign Office, Kahane served as personal and diplomatic secretary to Sharett in 1953–54, and was instrumental in the creation of the huge bureaucratic archive known as 'Operation Refugee File'.[17] On March 7, 1951, he made a proposal to the Acting Director of the Middle East Department of the Foreign Office, Divon. Here is the text of his memorandum:

PROPAGANDA AMONG THE REFUGEES IN ORDER TO SOBER THEM FROM ILLUSIONS OF RETURN TO ISRAEL

You should be efficiently assisted by propaganda of photos that would very tangibly illustrate to them [the refugees] that they have nowhere to return. The refugees fancifully imagine that their homes, furniture and belongings are intact, and they only need to return and reclaim them. Their eyes must be opened to see that their homes have been demolished, their property has been lost, and Jews who are not at all willing to give them up have seized their places. All this can be conveyed in an indirect way that would not provoke feelings of vengeance unnecessarily, but would show reality as it is, however bitter and cruel.

Ways of infiltrating such material: a brochure or a series of articles accompanied by photos published in Israel or abroad, in a limited circulation that would not make waves in the non-Arab world, but would find its way to Arab journalists who by prearrangement would bring the pertinent materials within it to the notice of the refugees. Another way: to print the photos with appropriate headings (the headings are what matters!) in a brochure that was supposedly published in one of the Arab countries. The photographic material should draw a contrast between Arab villages in the past and how they look today, after the war and the settlement of Jews in the abandoned sites. These photos ought to prove that the Jewish settlers found everything in ruins and have put a great deal of work into restoring the deserted villages, that they tie their future to these places, look after them and are not at all willing to give them up.

There is a certain risk in this proposal, but I think that its benefits would be greater than any damage it could do, and we should consider very carefully how to carry it out efficiently.[18]

Kahane's memorandum is a faithful illustration of the ruthless state of mind of the Israeli establishment as it set out to transform the consciousness and memory of its victims. It can be seen as a preamble to a thorough report on every imaginable aspect of 'the refugee problem' that Kahane prepared later that year, with an eye to the activities of the UN Appeasement Committee and a conference it was sponsoring in Paris.[19] This is a remarkable document in a number of ways: evidence of how swiftly the Arab heritage of Palestine had become a transient episode in the official mind; and of how completely any return by the refugees was now presented as an objective impossibility, rather than as an eventuality that the state itself was resolved at any cost to block. Reaffirming the familiar thesis that Arabs were the culprits of their own displacement, Kahane revealed the extent to which Palestine had already become Arab-less for him. 'Nationally', he wrote, 'the growth of an Arab minority will hinder the development of the state of Israel as a homogeneous state.' Repatriation, he added altruistically, would be a misfortune for the refugees themselves:

If the refugees had returned to Israel they would have found themselves in a country whose economic, social and political structures differed from those of the country they left behind. The cities and most of the deserted Arab villages have since been settled by Jews who are leaving their ineradicable imprint on them . . . If the refugees had come back to the realities that have developed in Israel, they would have certainly found it difficult to adjust to them. Urban professionals, merchants and officials would have had to wage a desperate battle for survival in a national economy within which all the key positions are held by Jews. Peasants would have been unable, in most cases, to return to their lands.

Here Kahane was rehearsing the argument of an earlier Foreign Office report, of March 16, 1949, also composed with a view to the Appeasement Committee which had just been set up under UN Resolution 194. Its authors seem to have been Michael Comay, director of the Commonwealth Department in the Foreign Office, and Zalman Lifshitz, former member of the Transfer Committee and adviser to Ben-Gurion on land issues. Written in English and entitled 'The Arab Refugee Problem', this document too emphasizes the impossibility of any Palestinian 'repatriation' in a detached, reality-has-changed, rhetorical register.[20] It adds, however, a tragic emplotment. In this narrative the plight of the refugees is depicted as if it were the result of a natural disaster, whose outcome is mournful, but inevitable and irrevocable. The perpetrator of expatriation, the state for which the document speaks, and which the authors serve, has nothing to do with it. Note the use of impersonal constructions and of the passive voice:

During the war and the Arab exodus, the basis of their [the refugees'] economic life crumbled away. Moveable property which was not taken away with them has disappeared. Livestock has been slaughtered or sold. Thousands of town and village dwellings have been destroyed in the course of the fighting, or in order to deny their use to enemy forces, regular or irregular; and of those which remain habitable, most are serving as temporary homes for [Jewish] immigrants . . . But even if repatriation were economically feasible, is it politically desirable? Would it make sense to recreate that dual society, which has bedevilled Palestine for so long, until it led eventually to open war? Under the happiest of circumstances, a complex and uncertain situation is created where a single state must be shared by two or more people who differ in race, religion, language and culture.

'Present absentees'

Weitz's chillingly precise administrative term, 'retroactive transfer', tells the story of the Israeli drive to transform Palestine into an unreturnable and irrecollectible country for the external refugees who lost their homes during or after the war. Another term, of similar administrative and legal effect, and moral bearing, was coined for internal refugees within the borders of the state. These became known as 'present absentees' (*nokhehim nifkadim*).[21] Of course, as Bombaji-Sasportas amply demonstrates, in this context 'external' and 'internal' are further markers of the determination of the Israeli establishment to objectify, control and dispossess the refugees.[22] If we use them here, it is to show the realities behind them. What the term 'present absentees' designates is the history of the dispossession and displacement of those Palestinians—their number is estimated at 160,000—who found themselves within the state of Israel between 1948 and 1952. It tells of the tacit axis of apartheid that defines the state of Israel to this day: the interplay between the formal inclusion of Palestinians as citizens and their structural exclusion from equal rights within the state. This is the particular dialectic of oppression—of a population formally present but in so many crucial ways absent—that makes the legal-administrative definition of these Palestinians so coldly accurate.

The category of 'absentees' was originally a juridical term for those refugees who were 'absent' from their homes but 'present' within the boundaries of the state as defined by the Armistice Agreements of 1949. The vast majority of the Palestinians so classified were not allowed to return to their homes, to reclaim their property, or to seek compensation. Instead the state promulgated the Law of Absentees' Properties in 1950, which legalized the plundering of their possessions. The looting of Arab property was given the guise of a huge land transaction that the state had conducted with itself. A thinly disguised official entity called 'The Custodian' was authorized to sell absentees' land (defined in Clause 1[b] of the Law) to the Development Agency, a government body created specifically to acquire it. This agency then sold it on to the Jewish National Fund. At the end of the chain these lands were privately farmed out to Jews only (this was the procedural significance of the JNF), and gradually became *de facto* private property, while remaining *de jure* in the keeping of the state.[23]

Cultural obliteration

If such was the outcome of the legal status of absentee, the fully dialectical notion of 'present absentees' was devised in more literary fashion by yet another high-ranking bureaucrat in the Foreign Office, Alexander Dotan. In the early summer of 1952 he was working in its Department for International Institutions when UNRWA wound up its activities in the country and passed responsibility for 'internal' refugees to the Israeli government. In July, Dotan was appointed inter-ministerial coordinator and chair of the Advisory Committee on Refugees. After some research, he then wrote a series of memoranda that offered background briefing and solutions for 'the refugee problem'. The first document, dated November 9, 1952, was specifically concerned with those refugees within Israel who had not been allowed to return to their homes, and many of whom dwelt in other Palestinian villages and towns. Dotan identified and defined these people—for the first time, it would seem— as 'present absentees'.[24] The literary features of the memorandum are striking. Tragic emplotment, ostensible empathy and anthropological detachment are all deployed to generate a Realist depiction of the way 'present absentees' are likely to remember the past:

> The fundamental problem of the refugee, who is wholly dependent on government policy, is land. The current position is that a refugee will often live in a village in Galilee, adjacent to his deserted lands and village, as if at an observation post. The distance is usually just a few kilometres and, in most cases, the refugees would have been able to cultivate their land from their present place of residence, if they had been allowed to do so, even without returning to the deserted and destroyed village. From his place of observation and present shelter the refugee follows what is happening on his land. He hopes and yearns to return to it, but he sees the new [Jewish] immigrants who are trying to strike roots in the land, or those who have farmed it out from the Custodian, or the way the orchards are gradually deteriorating because no one looks after them. The refugee desires to

return to his land, if only to some of it when it is mostly already settled by Jews, and he therefore usually seeks to farm it out from the Custodian, something that is denied to him.

Dotan was adamant that prolongation of these conditions was politically and culturally impossible. His conclusion, however, was not to return the properties and grant real citizenship to the 'internal' refugees, at least. The foundational myths of Zionism made—as they still do—any conjunction of the words 'return' and 'Arabs' or 'Palestinians' unthinkable. What Dotan had in mind was something else: a comprehensive assimilation (*hitbolelut*) of these Palestinians into the Jewish state and society of Israel by obliterating their memory, identity and culture. Dotan deliberately used the very term that was pivotal in the self-justification of the Zionist movement: *hitbolelut* was the disaster that recovery of the land of Israel would prevent—the disappearance of the Jewish people through assimiliation in the Diaspora. Such was the future now to be benignly extended to the Arabs within Israel. In a second memorandum, of November 12, 1952, Dotan warned that current state policies could induce the Palestinians within Israel to feel that they were 'a persecuted national minority that identifies with the Arab nation.' [25] To avert this risk, he proposed a new strategy that would aim on the one hand 'to integrate the Arabs into the state' by 'opening the gates of assimilation to them', while on the other it would 'fiercely combat those who are unwilling or unable to adapt to the [Jewish] state'. Dotan was aware of the likely objections to such a policy, and met them head on. 'It may rightly be asked: what are the prospects that the Arabs would assimilate? This can be answered only through experience, but if one wished to draw a lesson from history one could say that assimilation has been a very common feature in the Middle East since time immemorial.'

The colonial logic of this conception was spelt out with arresting clarity, as Dotan went on to explain how an irreversible obliteration of Palestinian identity might be achieved:

The realization of such a new policy requires a comprehensive onslaught upon the Arab minority by both the state and the Jewish public in the country, and it seems that an important instrument of it might be the formation of a secular Jewish cultural mission. The mission would act as the emissary of the Jewish people and Israeli progress in the Arab village. Under no circumstances should party politics be allowed within or through it. This mission would establish special training seminars for Jewish counsellors to operate in Arab villages, on the lines of our counsellors in the *ma'abarot* or in the new settlements, and like *the missions to the Indian villages in Mexico.* [26] These counsellors would infiltrate the villages together with the refugees, who would begin to settle them, and would accompany the refugees from the first day of their installation . . . Missions of two to three male and female counsellors for every twenty to thirty villages should suffice to effect agrarian changes within them. Such a mission would reside in a village; teach Hebrew; offer agricultural instruction, medical assistance and welfare; supply social guidance; act as natural mediator between the village and the authorities and the Hebrew community; and keep a security check on everything that happens in and around the village. Such a mission could acquire influence on all village matters and fundamentally alter them within a few years.

Dotan's proposal incurred the wrath of Ben-Gurion's powerful and ruthless adviser on Arab affairs, Josh Palmon, who favoured the continuation of a notoriously oppressive military government in the hope that this would extend the process of 'retroactive transfer'—i.e., *de facto* expulsion—to the 'internal' refugees as well. But Dotan reiterated his argument undeterred. His next report, of November 23, 1952, warning that outside powers might otherwise try to impose 'cultural autonomy' for the Palestinian minority on Israel, pressed home his scheme for an Arab *hitbolelut.* There could hardly be a more tangible example of the deliberate attempt to erase the very memory of an Arab Palestine than the final brick of Dotan's assimilationist edifice. This is what he wrote to the Foreign Minister:

An important tool for us is accelerated reconstruction of ancient geographical names and Hebraicization [*shi 'abur*] of Arabic toponyms. In this respect the most important task is to disseminate

the practical use of the new names, a process that has run into difficulties among Jews too. In Jaffa the name 'Jibaliyya' is still current, although 'Giv'at Aliya' is gradually disinheriting it. By
contrast, a Hebrew name has not been found yet for 'Ajami', and
some new immigrants still incorrectly call the Arab neighbourhood within it the 'Ghetto' or 'Arab Ghetto'. It is possible, by
being strictly formal and with adequate indoctrination, to make
the Arab inhabitants of 'Rami' [in the Upper Galilee] get used to
calling their village, in speech and writing, 'Ha-Rama' (Ramat
Naftali), or to make the inhabitants of 'Majd al-Krum' [also in
the Upper Galilee] become used to calling their village 'Beit ha-
Kerem'. From the inhabitants of what the Arabs called
'Shafa'amer [near Haifa], I have already heard the [Hebraicized]
name 'Shefar'am'.[27]

Dotan described his second memorandum as a 'Final Solution of
the Refugee Problem in Israel'. The easy use of the term is striking. Here
lie the historical roots of the obsessive refusal to concede to the Palestinians the right of return, which—more than the unity of Jerusalem—
is the widest consensual basis of Israeli politics today. It is this which
explains the genuine—preposterous—belief that withdrawal from the
territories occupied in 1967 and dismantling of the settlements would
be a painful compromise.

• • •

Notes

[1] This article is based on part of a longer essay, entitled 'Can The Subaltern
Remember? A Pessimistic View of the Victims of Zionism', to appear in a
volume edited by Ussama Makdisi and Paul Silberstein on memory and
violence in the Middle East and North Africa. My definition of the foundational myths is obviously critical. It is informed by Boas Evron, *National
Reckoning* [Hebrew], 1986; Yitzhak Laor, *Narratives with no Natives: Essays on
Israeli Literature* [Hebrew], 1995; David Myers, *Re-Inventing the Jewish Past*,
Oxford 1995; Amnon Raz-Krakotzkin, 'Exile within Sovereignty' [Hebrew],
2 parts, *Theory and Criticism*, 4, 1993, pp. 23-56 and 5, 1994, pp. 113-32; see
also my 'Domestic Orientalism', *British Journal of Middle Eastern Studies*, 23,
1996, pp. 125-45.

[2] The literature on this question is substantial. For notable examples, see
Ibrahim Abu-Lughod, ed., *The Transformation of Palestine*, Evanston 1971;
Christopher Hitchens and Edward Said, eds, *Blaming the Victims*, Verso:
London and New York 1988; Benny Morris, *The Birth of the Palestinian
Refugee Problem, 1947-49*, Cambridge 1987 and *1948 and After*, Oxford
1990; Yigal Elam, *The Executors* [Hebrew], 1990, pp. 31-53; Nur Masalha,
*Expulsion of the Palestinians: The Concept of 'Transfer' in Zionist Political
Thought 1882-1948*, Washington, DC 1992, and 'A Critique of Benny
Morris', in Ilan Pappé, ed., *The Israel/Palestine Question*, London 1999, pp.
211-20. For a recent and qualitative addition, see Eugene Rogan and Avi
Shlaim, eds, *The War for Palestine: Rewriting the History of 1948*, Cam-
bridge 2001.

[3] Zeev Sternhell, *The Founding Myths of Israel*, Princeton 1998, pp. 3-47.

[4] Morris, *Birth of the Palestinian Refugee Problem*, pp. 203-12.

[5] Haya Bombaji-Sasportas, 'Whose Voice is Heard/Whose Voice is Silenced:
the Construction of the Palestinian Refugee Problem in the Israeli Establishment, 1948-52', unpublished MA thesis, 2000. I am deeply grateful to
the author for making the documents available to me.

[6] Elam, *The Executors*, p. 31; emphasis added.

[7] Elam, *The Executors*, p. 43.

[8] See Morris, *1948 and After*, pp. 89-144.

[9] See especially Morris's careful attempt to classify each and every case on
which he could gather information, in the maps, appendix and invaluable
index to the maps, in Morris, *Birth*, pp. ix-xx.

[10] See Bombaji-Sasportas, 'Whose Voice is Heard', pp. 17-22; Joel Beinin,
'Know Thy Enemy, Know Thy Ally', in Ilan Pappé, ed., *Arabs and Jews during
the Mandate* [Hebrew], 1995, pp. 179-201; Gil Eyal, 'Between East and West:
The Discourse on "the Arab Village" in Israel' [Hebrew], *Theory and Criti-
cism*, 3, 1993, pp. 39-55; Dan Rabinovich, *Anthropology and the Palestinians*
[Hebrew], 1998.

[11] Bombaji-Sasportas, 'Whose Voice is Heard', pp. 31-3.

[12] Israeli State Archives/Foreign Office/Corpus of the Minister and Director
General 19-2444, vol. II, p. 6: henceforth SA/FO/CMDG.

[13] SA/FO/CMDG, 3/2445. This particular file contains documents of the
period August-November 1948, including the report of the Transfer Committee, so named by Weitz.

[14] Comparison between the official narrative and the confidential papers of the period strongly suggest deliberate deceit; Yaacov Shimoi, a high-ranking functionary of the time, admitted in 1989 that a 'fraudulent version' had been concocted. See Elam, *The Executors,* endnote 17, pp. 48-9.

[15] Zvi Yavetz, 'On the First Days of Tel Aviv University: Memories', *Alpayim,* 11, 1995, pp. 101-29.

[16] See Morris, *Birth of the Palestinian Refugee Problem,* p. 133. The translation of Meir's words is mine, from the 1991 Hebrew edition of Morris's book, p. 185.

[17] For more details on Shamai Kahane, see Bombaji-Sasportas, 'Whose Voice is Heard', pp. 100, 119 and 163-8.

[18] SA/FO/CMDG 18/2402.

[19] SA/FO/CMDG 18/2406.

[20] SA/FO/CMDG 19/4222, vol. II; for the identification of the authors, see Morris, *Birth of the Palestinian Refugee Problem,* p. 255 and Bombaji-Sasportas, 'Whose Voice is Heard', p. 148.

[21] The haunting nature of this term was also noticed by David Grossman, who duly entitled his Hebrew book on the Palestinian Israelis *Present Absentees* (1992). The English translation is *Sleeping on a Wire.*

[22] See especially her discussion of 'the construction of a body of knowledge and the framing of the refugees as a scientific object', and 'the categorization of the refugees', pp. 44–99.

[23] The text of this law is rather long, but is accessible in any official collection of Knesset legislation. For critical comments on the law, see Alina Korn, *The Arab Minority in Israel during the Military Government* (1948-1966), unpublished Ph.D. dissertation, the Hebrew University of Jerusalem, 1991, pp. 91-6, and Tom Segev, 1949: *The First Israelis,* Jerusalem 1984, pp. 93–5 [both in Hebrew].

[24] SA/FO/A/2/2445 (a-948 II).

[25] SA/FO/CMDG 2/2445 A (a-948 II).

[26] *Ma'abarot:* the transition camps built for the massive Jewish immigration of the 1950s—transitory for Ashkenazi arrivals, less so for Sephardi; emphasis added.

[27] Cited in Yitzhak Laor, *Narratives with no Natives,* p. 132. Laor's critical

work is the most sensitive attempt to date to show how the literary establishment has been co-opted by the Israeli state to write the hegemonic
script that deletes the memories of the Palestinians. See especially 'The
Sex Life of the Security Forces: On Amos Oz', and 'We Write Thee Oh
Homeland', pp. 76–105, 115–71.

5 | FROM PREEMPTIVE CONQUEST TO PROTRACTED OCCUPATION

In May of 1967 Egyptian leader Gamal Abdel Nasser massed troops in the Sinai, and closed the Straits of Tiran to Israeli shipping, after the Soviets informed him that Israel was about to attack Syria. Although the rumor turned out to be false, Nasser had reason for believing it. The border war between Israel and Syria had escalated over the previous year, and in April 1967, Israel shot down six Syrian planes, one over Damascus. Western diplomats believed it was only a matter of time before Israel attacked Syria; the question was not whether but when and how.

The answer came on June 5, 1967, when Israel launched its surprise offensive. By June 10, Israel had taken over the remainder of historical Palestine—the West Bank, East Jerusalem, and the Gaza Strip—along with the Syrian Golan Heights. Israeli spokesmen have long insisted that the war was fought wholly in self-defense, under the threat of annihilation.

But the words of Israel's generals suggest a more complicated picture. As General Mattiyahu Peled said, "To pretend that the Egyptian forces concentrated on our borders were capable of threatening Israel's existence does not only insult the intelligence of any person capable of analyzing this kind of situation, but is primarily an insult to the Israeli army."

The 1967 war not only transformed the lines of the conflict over Palestine; it also transformed the political culture of world Jewry. The "Six Day War" was widely seen as an event of Biblical significance, a "miraculous" victory by which Jews had succeeded in "unifying" Jerusalem, and washing away the terrible shame and stigma of victimhood. As feelings of relief turned to euphoria, and as Israel established itself as America's Sparta in the region, there arose among Jews a triumphalist culture that exalted Israel's military might. History's eternal victims were now invincible warriors, in what Peter Novick has described as a "folk theology of 'Holocaust and Redemption.'"

Powerful narcotic though it was, the 1967 victory would prove to be anything but a redemption. Far from enhancing Israel's security, it made Israel even less secure, further inflaming the hatred of the Jewish state among Arabs and Muslims, while engendering the slow yet inexorable erosion of Israeli democracy. "This 'six days wonder,' this latest, all-too-easy triumph of Israeli arms will be seen one day, in a not very remote future, to have been a disaster in the first instance for Israel itself," **Isaac Deutscher** writes in this searing essay—a prophetic analysis of the consequences of Israel's victory.

THE ISRAELI-ARAB WAR, JUNE 1967[1]

Isaac Deutscher

From *The Non-Jewish Jew and Other Essays* (1968)

The war and the 'miracle' of Israel's victory have solved none of the problems that confront Israel and the Arab states. They have, on the contrary, aggravated all the old issues and created new, more dangerous ones. They have not increased Israel's security, but have rendered it more vulnerable than it had been before 5 June 1967. This 'six days wonder', this latest, all-too-easy triumph of Israeli arms will be seen one day, in a not very remote future, to have been a disaster in the first instance for Israel itself.

Let us consider the international background. We have to relate this war to the great power struggle and ideological conflicts in the world which form its context. In these last years American imperialism, and the forces associated with it and supported by it, have been engaged in a tremendous political, ideological, economic, and military offensive over a vast area of Asia and Africa; while the forces opposed to the American penetration, the Soviet Union in the first instance, have barely held their ground or have been in retreat. This trend emerges from a long series of events: the Ghanaian upheaval, in which Nkrumah's government was overthrown; the growth of reaction in various Afro-Asian countries; the bloody triumph of anti-Communism in Indonesia, which was a huge victory for counter-revolution in Asia; the escalation of the American war in Vietnam; and the 'marginal' right-wing military coup in Greece. The Arab-Israeli war was not an isolated affair; it belongs to this category of events. The counter-trend has manifested itself in revolutionary ferment in various parts of India, the radicalization of the political mood in Arab countries, the effective struggle of the National Front of Liberation in Vietnam; and the world-wide growth of opposition to American intervention. The advance of

American imperialism and of Afro-Asian counter-revolution has not gone unopposed, but its success everywhere outside Vietnam has been evident.

In the Middle East the American forward push has been of relatively recent date. During the Suez war, the United States still adopted an 'anti-colonialist' stance. It acted, in seeming accord with the Soviet Union, to bring about the British and French withdrawal. The logic of American policy was still the same as in the late 1940s, when the State of Israel was in the making. As long as the American ruling class was interested primarily in squeezing out the old colonial Powers from Africa and Asia, the White House was a mainstay of 'anti-colonialism'. But having contributed to the debacle of the old Empires, the United States took fright at the 'power vacuum' that might be filled by native revolutionary forces or the Soviet Union or a combination of both. Yankee anti-colonialism faded out, and America 'stepped in'. In the Middle East this happened during the period between the Suez crisis and the last Israeli war. The American military landings in Lebanon in 1958 were designed to stem a high tide of revolution in that area, especially in Iraq. Since then the United States, no doubt relying to some extent on Soviet 'moderation', has avoided open and direct military involvement in the Middle East and maintained a posture of detachment. This posture does not make the American presence there any less real.

The Israelis have, of course, acted on their own motives, and not merely to suit the convenience of American policy. That their leaders and the great mass of Israelis believe themselves to be menaced by Arab hostility need not be doubted. That some 'bloodthirsty' Arab declarations about 'wiping Israel off the map' made Israeli flesh creep is evident. The Israelis are haunted by the memories of the Jewish tragedy in Europe and now feel isolated and encircled by the 'teeming' millions of a hostile Arab world. Nothing was easier for their own propagandists, aided by Arab verbal excesses, than to play up the fear of another 'final solution' threatening the Jews, this time in Asia. Conjuring up Biblical myths and all the ancient religious-national symbols of Jewish history, the propagandists whipped up that frenzy of belligerence, arrogance, and fanaticism of which the Israelis gave such startling displays as they rushed to Sinai and the Wailing Wall and to Jordan and the walls of Jericho. Behind the frenzy and arrogance there lay Israel's suppressed sense of guilt towards the Arabs, the feeling that the Arabs would never forget or forgive the blows Israel had inflicted on them: the seizure of their land, the fate of a million or more refugees, and repeated military defeats and humiliations. Driven half-mad by fear of Arab revenge, the Israelis have, in their overwhelming majority, accepted the 'doctrine' inspiring their government's policy, the 'doctrine' that holds that Israel's security lies in periodic warfare which every few years must reduce the Arab states to impotence.

Yet, whatever their own motives and fears, the Israelis are not and cannot be independent agents. The factors of Israel's dependence were to some extent 'built in' in its history over the last two decades. All Israeli governments have staked Israel's existence on the 'Western orientation'. This alone would have sufficed to turn Israel into a Western outpost in the Middle East, and so to involve it in the great conflict between imperialism (or neo-colonialism) and the Arab peoples struggling for their emancipation. Other factors have been in play as well. Israel's economy has depended for its tenuous balance and growth on foreign Zionist financial aid, especially on American donations. These donations have been a curse in disguise for the new state. They have enabled the government to manage its balance of payments in a way in which no country in the world can do it, without engaging in any trade with its neighbours. The influx of foreign funds has distorted Israel's economic structure by encouraging the growth of a large, unproductive sector and a standard of living which is not related to the country's own productivity and earnings.[2] This has, of course, unfailingly kept Israel well within the 'western sphere of influence'. Israel has in effect lived far above its means. Over many years nearly half of Israel's food was imported from the West. As the American administration exempts from taxation earnings and profits earmarked as donations for Israel, the Treasury in Washington has held its hand on the purses on which Israel's economy depends. Washington could at any time hit Israel by refusing the tax exemption (even though this would lose it the Jewish vote in elections). The threat of such a sanction, never uttered but always present, and occasionally hinted at, has been enough to align Israeli policy firmly with the United States.

Years ago, when I visited Israel, a high Israeli official listed to me the factories that they could not build because of American objections—among them steel mills and plants producing agricultural machinery. On the other hand, there was a list of virtually useless factories turning out fantastic amounts of plastic kitchen utensils, toys, etc. Nor could any Israeli administration ever feel free to consider seriously Israel's vital, long-term need for trade and close economic ties with its Arab neighbours or for improving economic relations with the U.S.S.R. and Eastern Europe.

Economic dependence has affected Israel's domestic policy and 'cultural atmosphere' in other ways as well. The American donor is also the most important foreign investor operating in the Holy Land. A wealthy American Jew, a 'worldly businessman' among his gentile associates and friends in New York, Philadelphia or Detroit, is at heart proud to be a member of the Chosen People, and in Israel he exercises his influence in favour of religious obscurantism and reaction. A fervent believer in free enterprise, he views with a hostile eye even the mild socialism' of the Histradruth and the kibbutzim, and has done his bit in taming it. Above all, he has helped the rabbis to maintain their stranglehold on legislation and much of the education and so to keep alive the spirit of racial-talmudic exclusiveness and superiority. All this has fed and inflamed the antagonism towards the Arabs.

The cold war imparted great momentum to the reactionary trends in Israel and exacerbated the Arab-Jewish conflict. Israel was firmly committed to anti-communism. True, Stalin's policy in his last years, outbreaks of and-semitism in the U.S.S.R., anti-Jewish *motifs* in the trials of Slansky, Rajk, and Kostov, and Soviet encouragement of even the most irrational forms of Arab nationalism, all bear their share of responsibility for Israel's attitude. Yet it should not be forgotten that Stalin had been Israel's godfather; that it was with Czechoslovak munitions, supplied on Stalin's orders, that the Jews had fought the British occupation army—and the Arabs—in 1947–48; and that the Soviet envoy was the first to vote for the recognition of the State of Israel by the United Nations. It may be argued that Stalin's change of attitude towards Israel was itself a reaction to Israel's alignment with the West. And in the post-Stalin era the Israeli governments have persisted in this alignment.

Irreconcilable hostility to Arab aspirations to unity and national emancipation from the West thus became *the* axiom of Israeli policy. Hence Israel's role in 1956, in the Suez war. Israel's Social Democratic ministers, no less than Western colonialists, have embraced a *raison d'état* which sees its highest wisdom in keeping the Arabs divided and backward and in playing their reactionary Hashemite and other feudal elements against the Republican, national-revolutionary forces. Early in 1967, when it seemed that a republican uprising or coup might overthrow King Hussein, Mr. Eshkol's government made no bones, about it that, in case of a 'Nasserite coup' in Amman, Israeli troops would march into Jordan. And the prelude to the events, of last June was provided by Israel's adoption of a menacing attitude towards Syria's new regime which it denounced as 'Nasserite' or even 'ultra-Nasserite' (for Syria's government appeared to be a shade more anti-imperialist and radical than Egypt's).

Did Israel, in fact, plan to attack Syria some time in May, as Soviet Intelligence Services believed and as Moscow warned Nasser? We do not know. It was as a result of this warning, and with Soviet encouragement, that Nasser ordered mobilization and concentration of troops on the Sinai frontier. If Israel had such a plan, Nasser's move may have delayed the attack on Syria by a few weeks. If Israel had no such plan, its behaviour gave to its anti-Syrian threats the kind of plausibility that Arab threats had in Israeli eyes. In any case, Israel's rulers were quite confident that their aggressiveness *vis-à-vis* either Syria or Egypt would meet with Western sympathy and bring them reward. This calculation underlay their decision to strike the preemptive blow on June 5th. They were absolutely sure of American, and to some extent British, moral, political, and economic support. They knew that no matter however far they went in attacking the Arabs, they could count on American diplomatic protection or, at the very least, on American official indulgence. And they were not mistaken. The White House and the Pentagon could not fail to appreciate men who for their own reasons, were determined to put down the Arab enemies of American neo-colonialism. General Dayan acted as a kind of Marshal Ky for the Middle East and appeared to be doing his job with startling speed, efficiency, and ruthlessness. He was, and is, a much cheaper and far less embarrassing ally than Ky.

The Arab behaviour, especially Nasser's divided mind and hesitation on the eve of hostilities, presents a striking contrast to Israel's determination and uninhibited aggressiveness. Having, with Soviet encouragement, moved his troops to the Sinai frontier, and even put his Russian-made missiles in position, Nasser then, without consulting Moscow, proclaimed the blockade of the Straits of Tiran. This was a provocative move, though practically of very limited significance. The western powers did not consider it important enough to try and 'test' the blockade. It provided Nasser with a prestige gain and enabled him to claim that he had wrested from Israel the last fruit of their 1956 victory. (Before the Suez war Israeli ships could not pass these Straits.) The Israelis played up the blockade as a mortal danger to their economy, which it was not; and they replied by mobilizing their forces and moving them to the frontiers.

Soviet propaganda still continued to encourage the Arabs in public. However, a conference of Middle Eastern Communist Parties held in May (its resolutions were summarized in *Pravda*) was strangely reticent about the crisis and allusively critical of Nasser. More important were the curious diplomatic manoeuvres behind the scenes. On 26 May, in the dead of night (at 2:30 A.M.) the Soviet Ambassador woke up Nasser to give him a grave warning that the Egyptian army must not be the first to open fire. Nasser complied. The compliance was so thorough that he not only refrained from starting hostilities, but took no precautions whatsoever against the possibility of an Israeli attack: he left his airfields undefended and his planes grounded and uncamouflaged. He did not even bother to mine the Tiran Straits or to place a few guns on their shores (as the Israelis found to their surprise when they got there).

All this suggests hopeless bungling on Nasser's part and on the part of the Egyptian Command. But the real bunglers sat in the Kremlin. Brezhnev's and Kosygin's behaviour during these events was reminiscent of Khrushchev's during the Cuban crisis, though it was even more muddle-headed. The pattern was the same. In the first phase there was needless provocation of the other side and a reckless move towards the 'brink'; in the next sudden panic and a hasty retreat; and then followed frantic attempts to save face and cover up the traces. Having excited Arab fears, encouraged them to risky moves, promised to stand by

them, and having brought out their own naval units into the Mediterranean to counter the moves of the American Sixth Fleet, the Russians
then tied Nasser hand and foot.

Why did they do it? As the tension was mounting, the 'hot line'
between the Kremlin and the White House went into action. The two
super-powers agreed to avoid direct intervention and to curb the parties to the conflict. If the Americans went through the motions of
curbing the Israelis, they must have done it so perfunctorily, or with so
many winks that the Israelis felt, in fact, encouraged to go ahead with
their plan for the pre-emptive blow. (We have, at any rate, not heard of
the American Ambassador waking up the Israeli Prime Minister to
warn him that the Israelis must not be the first to open fire.) The Soviet
curb on Nasser was heavy, rude, and effective. Even so, Nasser's failure
to take elementary military precautions remains something of a puzzle.
Did the Soviet Ambassador in the course of his nocturnal visit tell
Nasser that Moscow was sure that the Israelis would not strike first?
Had Washington given Moscow such an assurance? And was Moscow
so gullible as to take it at face value and act on it? It seems almost—
incredible that this should have been so. But only some such version
of the events can account for Nasser's inactivity and for Moscow's
stunned surprise at the outbreak of hostilities. Behind all this bungling
there loomed the central contradiction of Soviet policy. On the one
hand the Soviet leaders see in the preservation of the international
status quo, including the social status quo, the essential condition of
their national security and of 'peaceful co-existence'. They are therefore
anxious to keep at a 'safe distance' from storm centres of class conflict
in the world and to avoid dangerous foreign entanglements. On the
other hand, they cannot, for ideological and power-political reasons,
avoid altogether dangerous entanglements. They cannot quite keep at
a safe distance when American neo-colonialism clashed directly or
indirectly with its Afro-Asian and Latin-American enemies, who look
to Moscow as their friend and protector. In normal times this contradiction is only latent, Moscow works for détente and rapprochement
with the U.S.A.; and it cautiously aids and arms its Afro-Asian or
Cuban friends. But sooner or later the moment of crisis comes and
the contradiction explodes in Moscow's face. Soviet policy must then
choose between its allies and protegés working against the status quo,

and its own commitment to the *status quo*. When the choice is pressing and ineluctable, it opts for the *status quo*.

The dilemma is real and in the nuclear age dangerous enough. But it confronts the U.S.A. as well, for the U.S.A. is just as much interested as is the U.S.S.R. in avoiding world war and nuclear conflict. This, however, limits its freedom of action and of political-ideological offensive far less than it restricts Soviet freedom. Washington is far less afraid of the possibility that some move by one of its protégés, or its own military intervention, might lead to a direct confrontation of the super powers. After the Cuban crisis and the war in Vietnam, the Arab-Israeli war has once again sharply illuminated the difference.

To some extent the present situation has been determined by the whole course of Arab-Israeli relations since the second World War and even since the first. Yet I believe that some options were open to the Israelis. There is a parable with the help of which I once tried to present this problem to an Israeli audience.

A man once jumped from the top floor of a burning house in which many members of his family had already perished. He managed to save his life; but as he was falling he hit a person standing down below and broke that person's legs and arms. The jumping man had no choice; yet to the man with the broken limbs he was the cause of his misfortune. If both behaved rationally, they would not become enemies. The man who escaped from the blazing house, having recovered, would have tried to help and console the other sufferer; and the latter might have realized that he was the victim of circumstances over which neither of them had control. But look what happens when these people behave irrationally. The injured man blames the other for his misery and swears to make him pay for it. The other, afraid of the crippled man's revenge, insults him, kicks him, and beats him up whenever they meet. The kicked man again swears revenge and is again punched and punished. The bitter enmity, so fortuitous at first, hardens and comes to overshadow the whole existence of both men and to poison their minds.

You will, I am sure, recognize yourselves (I said to my Israeli audience), the remnants of European Jewry in Israel, in the man who jumped from the blazing house. The other character represents, of course, the Palestine Arabs, more than a million of them, who have lost their lands and their homes. They are resentful; they gaze from across the frontiers on their old native places; they raid you stealthily, and swear revenge. You punch and kick them mercilessly; you have shown that you know how to do it. But what is the sense of it? And what is the prospect?

The responsibility for the tragedy of European Jews, for Auschwitz, Majdanek, and the slaughters in the ghetto, rests entirely on our western bourgeois 'civilization', of which Nazism was the legitimate, even though degenerate, offspring. Yet it was the Arabs who were made to pay the price for the crimes the West committed towards the Jews. They are still made to pay it, for the 'guilty conscience' of the West is, of course, pro-Israeli and anti-Arab. And how easily Israel had allowed itself to be bribed and fooled by the false 'conscience money'.

A rational relationship between Israelis and Arabs might have been possible if Israel had at least attempted to establish it, if the man who threw himself down from the burning house had tried to make friends with the innocent victim of his jump and to compensate him. This did not happen. Israel never even recognized the Arab grievance. From the outset Zionism worked towards the creation of a purely Jewish state and was glad to rid the country of its Arab inhabitants. No Israeli government has ever seriously looked for any opportunity to remove or assuage the grievance. They refused even to consider the fate of the huge mass of refugees unless the Arab states first recognized Israel, unless, that is, the Arabs surrendered politically before starting negotiations. Perhaps this might still be excused as bargaining tactics. The disastrous aggravation of Arab-Israeli relations was brought about by the Suez war, when Israel unashamedly acted as the spearhead of the old bankrupt European imperialisms in their last common stand in the Middle East, in their last attempt to maintain their grip, on Egypt. The Israelis did not have to align themselves with the shareholders of the Suez Canal Company. The pros and cons were clear; there was no question of any mixture of rights and wrongs on either side. The Israelis put themselves totally in the wrong, morally and politically.

On the face of it, the Arab-Israeli conflict is only a clash of two rival nationalisms, each moving within the vicious circle of its self-righteous

and inflated ambitions. From the viewpoint of an abstract internationalism nothing would be easier than to dismiss both as equally worth-
less and reactionary. However, such a view would ignore the social and
political realities of the situation. The nationalism of the people in
semi-colonial or colonial countries, fighting for their independence,
must not be put on the same moral-political level as the nationalism
of conquerors and oppressors. The former has its historic justification
and progressive aspect which the latter has not. Clearly, Arab nationalism, unlike the Israeli, still belongs to the former category.

Yet even the nationalism of the exploited and oppressed should not
be viewed uncritically, for there are various phases in its development.
In one phase progressive aspirations prevail; in another reactionary
tendencies come to the surface. From the moment independence is
won or nearly won, nationalism tends to shed its revolutionary aspect
altogether and turns into a retrograde ideology. We have seen this happening in India, Indonesia, Israel, and to some extent even in China.
And even in the revolutionary phase each nationalism has its streak of
irrationality, an inclination to exclusiveness, national egoism and
racism. Arab nationalism, despite all its historic merits and progressive
functions, has also carried within itself these reactionary ingredients.

The June crisis has revealed some of the basic weaknesses of Arab
political thought and action: the lack of political strategy; a proneness
to emotional self-intoxication; and an excessive reliance on nationalist
demagogy. These weaknesses were among the decisive causes of the
Arab defeat. By indulging in threats of the destruction of Israel and
even of 'extermination'—and how empty these threats were has been
amply demonstrated by the Arabs' utter military unpreparedness—
some of Egypt's and Jordan's propagandists provided plenty of grist to
Israeli chauvinism, and enabled Israel's government to work up the
mass of its people into the paroxysm of fear and ferocious aggressiveness which then burst upon Arab heads.

It is a truism that war is a continuation of policy. The six days' war
has shown up the relative immaturity of the present Arab regimes. The
Israelis owe their triumph not merely to the pre-emptive blow, but
also to a more modern economic, political, and military organization.
To some extent the war drew a balance on the decade of Arab development since the Suez war and has revealed its grave inadequacies. The

modernization of the socio-economic structures of Egypt and the other Arab states and of Arab political thinking has proceeded far more slowly than people, inclined to idealize the present Arab regimes, have assumed.

The persisting backwardness is, of course, rooted in socio-economic conditions. But Arab ideology and methods of organization are in themselves factors of weakness. I have in mind the single party system, the cult of Nasserism, and the absence of free discussion. All this has greatly hampered the political education of the masses and the work of socialist enlightenment. The negative results have made themselves felt on various levels. When major decisions of policy depend on a more or less autocratic Leader, there is in normal times no genuine popular participation in the political processes, no vigilant and active consciousness, no initiative from below. This has had many consequences, even military ones. The Israeli pre-emptive blow, delivered with conventional weapons, would not have had such devastating impact if Egypt's armed forces had been accustomed to rely on the initiative of individual officers and soldiers. Local commanders would then have taken the elementary defensive precautions without waiting for orders from above. Military inefficiency reflected here a wider and deeper, social-political weakness. The military-bureaucratic methods of Nasserism also hamper the political integration of the Arab movement of liberation. Nationalist demagogy flourishes all too easily; but it is no substitute for a real impulse to national unity and for a real mobilization of popular forces against the divisive, feudal and reactionary elements. We have seen how, during the emergency, excessive reliance on a single Leader made the fate of the Arab states dependent in fact on Great Power intervention and accidents of diplomatic manoeuvre.

Paradoxically and grotesquely, the Israelis appear now in the role of the Prussians of the Middle East. They have now won three wars against their Arab neighbours. Just so did the Prussians a century ago defeat all their neighbours with—in a few years, the Danes, the Austrians, and the French. The succession of victories bred in them an absolute confidence in their own efficiency, a blind reliance on the force of their arms, chauvinistic arrogance, and contempt for other peoples. I fear that a similar degeneration—for degeneration it is— may be taking place in the political character of Israel. Yet as the

Prussia of the Middle East, Israel can be only a feeble parody of the original. The Prussians were at least able to use their victories for uniting in their Reich all German-speaking peoples living outside the Austro-Hungarian Empire. Germany's neighbours were divided among themselves by interest, history, religion, and language. Bismarck, Wilhelm II, and Hitler could play them off against one another. The Israelis are surrounded by Arabs only. Attempts to play off the Arab states against one another are bound to fail in the end. The Arabs were at loggerheads with one another in 1948, when Israel waged its first war; they were far less divided in 1956, during Israel's second war; and they formed a common front in 1967. They may prove far more firmly united in any future confrontation with Israel.

The Germans have summed up their own experience in the bitter phrase: *'Man kann sich totsiegen!'* 'You can drive yourself victoriously into your grave.' This is what the Israelis have been doing. They have bitten off much more than they can swallow. In the conquered territories and in Israel there are now nearly a million and a half Arabs, well over forty per cent of the total population. Will the Israelis expel this mass of Arabs in order to hold 'securely' the conquered lands? This would create a new refugee problem, more dangerous and larger than the old one. Will they give up the conquered territories? No, say most of their leaders. Ben Gurion, the evil spirit of Israeli chauvinism, urges the creation of an 'Arab Palestinian State' on the Jordan, that would be an Israeli Protectorate. Can Israel expect that the Arabs will accept such a Protectorate? That they will not fight it tooth and nail? None of the Israeli parties is prepared even to contemplate a bi-national Arab-Israeli state. Meanwhile great numbers of Arabs have been 'induced' to leave their homes on the Jordan, and the treatment of those who have stayed behind is far worse than that of the Arab minority in Israel that was kept under martial law for nineteen years. Yes, this victory is worse for Israel than a defeat. Far from giving Israel a higher degree of security, it has rendered it much more insecure. If Arab revenge and extermination is what the Israelis feared, they have behaved as if they were bent on turning a bogey into an actual menace.

There was a moment, at the cease-fire, when it looked as if Egypt's defeat had led to Nasser's downfall and to the undoing of the policy associated with his name. If that had happened, the Middle East would have almost certainly been brought back into the Western sphere of influence. Egypt might have become another Ghana or Indonesia. This did not happen, however. The Arab masses who came out in the streets and squares of Cairo, Damascus, and Beirut to demand that Nasser should stay in office, prevented it happening. This was one of those rare historic popular impulses that redress or upset a political balance within a few moments. This time, in the hour of defeat, the initiative from below worked with immediate impact. There are only very few cases in history when a people have stood by a defeated leader in this way. The situation is, of course, still fluid. Reactionary influences will go on working within the Arab states to achieve something like a Ghanaian or Indonesian coup. But for the time being neo-colonialism has been denied the fruit of Israel's 'victory'.

The Russians have let us down!' was the bitter cry that came from Cairo, Damascus, and Beirut in June. And when the Arabs saw the Soviet delegate at the United Nations voting, in unison with the Americans, for a cease-fire to which no condition for a withdrawal of the Israeli troops was attached, they felt utterly betrayed. 'The Soviet Union will now sink to the rank of a second- or fourth-rate power,' Nasser was reported to have told the Soviet Ambassador. The events appeared to justify the Chinese accusation of Soviet collusion with the United States. The débâcle aroused an alarm in Eastern Europe as well. 'If the Soviet Union could let Egypt down like this, may it not also let us down when we are once again confronted by German aggression?', the Poles and the Czechs wondered. The Yugoslavs, too, were outraged. Tito, Gomulka, and other leaders rushed to Moscow to demand an explanation and a rescue operation for the Arabs. This was all the more remarkable as the demand came from the 'moderates' and the 'revisionists' who normally stand for 'peaceful coexistence' and *rapprochement* with the U.S.A. It was they who now spoke of Soviet 'collusion with American imperialism'.

The Soviet leaders had to do something. The fact that the intervention of the Arab masses had saved the Nasser régime, unexpectedly provided Moscow with fresh scope for manoeuvre. After the great let down, the Soviet leaders again came to the fore as the friends and protectors of the Arab states. A few spectacular gestures, breaking off diplomatic relations with Israel, and speeches at the United Nations, cost them little. Even the White House showed 'understanding' for Moscow's 'predicament' and for the 'tactical necessity' which presently brought Kosygin to the United Nations Assembly.

However, something more than gestures was required to restore the Soviet position. The Arabs demanded that the Soviet Union should at once help them to re-build their military strength, the strength they had lost through compliance with Soviet advice. They asked for new planes, new tanks, new guns, new stocks of munitions. But apart from the cost this involved—the value of the military equipment lost by Egypt alone is put at a billion pounds—the reconstitution of the Arab armed forces carries, from Moscow's viewpoint, major political risks. The Arabs refuse to negotiate with Israel; they may well afford to leave Israel to choke on its victory. Rearmament is Cairo's top priority. Israel has taught the Egyptians a lesson: next time the Egyptian air force may strike the pre-emptive blow. And Moscow has had to decide whether it will supply the weapons for that blow.

Moscow cannot favour the idea of such an Arab retaliation, but neither can it refuse to rearm Egypt. Yet Arab rearmament will almost certainly tempt Israel to interrupt the process and strike another pre-emptive blow in which case the Soviet Union would once again be faced with the dilemma which has worsted it in May and June. If Egypt were to strike first, the United States would almost certainly intervene. Its Sixth Fleet would not look on from the Mediterranean if the Israeli air force were knocked out and the Arabs were about to march into Jerusalem or Tel Aviv. If the U.S.S.R. again kept out of the conflict, it would irretrievably destroy its international power position.

A week after the cease-fire the Soviet Chief of Staff was in Cairo; and Soviet advisers and experts crowded the hotels there, beginning to work on the reconstitution of Egypt's armed forces. Yet Moscow cannot face with equanimity the prospect of an Arab-Israeli competition in pre-emptive blows and its wider implications. Probably the Soviet experts in Cairo were making haste slowly, while Soviet diplomacy tried to 'win the peace' for the Arabs after it had lost them the war. But even the most clever playing for time cannot solve the central issue of Soviet policy. How much longer can the Soviet Union adapt itself to the American forward push? How far can it retreat before the American economic-political and military offensives across the Afro-Asian area?

Not for nothing did *Krasnaya Zvezda* already in June suggest that the current Soviet conception of peaceful coexistence might be in need of some revision. The military, and not they alone, fear that Soviet retreats are increasing the dynamic of the American forward push; and that if this goes on a direct Soviet-American clash may become inevitable. If Brezhnev and Kosygin do not manage to cope with this issue, changes in leadership are quite possible. The Cuban and Vietnamese crises contributed to Khrushchev's downfall. The full consequences of the Middle Eastern crisis have yet to unfold.

I do not believe that the conflict between Arabs and Israelis can be resolved by military means. To be sure, no one can deny the Arab states the right to reconstitute their armed forces to some extent. But what they need far more urgently is a social and political strategy and new methods in their struggle for emancipation. This cannot be a purely negative strategy dominated by the anti-Israeli obsession. They may refuse to parley with Israel as long as Israel has not given up its conquests. They will necessarily resist the occupation regime on the Jordan and in the Gaza strip. But this need not mean a renewal of war.

The strategy that can yield the Arabs far greater gain than those that can be obtained in any Holy War or through a pre-emptive blow, a strategy that would bring them real victory, a civilized victory, must be centred on the imperative and urgent need for an intensive modernization of the structure of the Arab economy and of Arab politics and on the need for a genuine integration of Arab national life, which is still broken up by the old, inherited and imperialist-sponsored frontiers and divisions. These aims can be promoted only if the revolutionary and socialist tendencies in Arab politics are strengthened and developed.

Finally, Arab nationalism will be incomparably more effective as a liberating force if it is disciplined and rationalized by an element of internationalism that will enable the Arabs to approach the problem of Israel more realistically than hitherto. They cannot go on denying Israel's right to exist and indulging in bloodthirsty rhetoric. Economic growth, industrialization, education, more efficient organization and more sober policies are bound to give the Arabs what sheer numbers and anti-Israeli fury have not been able to give them, namely an actual preponderance which should almost automatically reduce Israel to its modest proportions and its proper role in the Middle East.

This is not, of course, a short term programme. Yet its realization need not take too much time; and there is no shorter way to emancipation. The short cuts of demagogy, revenge, and war have proved disastrous enough. Meanwhile, Arab policy should be based on a direct appeal to the Israeli people over the heads of the Israeli government, on an appeal to the workers and the kibbutzim. The latter should be freed from their fears by clear assurances and pledges that Israel's legitimate interests are respected and that Israel may even be welcome as a member of a future Middle Eastern Federation. This would cause the orgy of Israeli chauvinism to subside and would stimulate opposition to Eshkol's and Dayan's policy of conquest and domination. The capacity of Israeli workers to respond to such an appeal should not be underrated.

More independence from the Great Power game is also necessary. That game has distorted the social-political development of the Middle East. I have shown how much American influence has done to give Israel's policy its present repulsive and reactionary character. But Russian influence has also done something to warp Arab minds by feeding them with arid slogans, by encouraging demagogy, while Moscow's egoism and opportunism have fostered disillusionment and cynicism. If Middle East policy continues to be merely a plaything of the Great Powers, the prospect will be bleak indeed. Neither Jews nor Arabs will be able to break out of their vicious spirals. This is what we, of the Left, should be telling both the Arabs and the Jews as clearly and bluntly as we can.

The confusion of the international Left has been undeniable and widespread. I shall not speak here of such 'friends of Israel' as M. Mollet and his company, who, like Lord Avon and Selwyn Lloyd, saw in this war a continuation of the Suez campaign and their revenge for their discomfiture in 1956. Nor shall I waste words on the right-wing Zionist lobby in the Labour Party. But even on the 'extreme Left' of that party men like Sidney Silverman behaved in a way that might have been designed to illustrate someone's saying: 'Scratch a Jewish left-winger and you find only a Zionist.'

But the confusion showed itself even further on the Left and affected people with an otherwise unimpeachable record of struggle against imperialism. A French writer known for his courageous stand against the wars in Algeria and Vietnam this time called for solidarity with Israel, declaring that, if Israel's survival demanded American intervention, he would favour it and even raise the cry 'Vive le Président Johnson.' Didn't it occur to him how incongruous it was to cry 'A bas Johnson' in Vietnam and 'Vive!' in Israel? Jean-Paul Sartre also called, though with reservations, for solidarity with Israel, but then spoke frankly of the confusion in his own mind and its reasons. During the second World War, he said, as a member of the Resistance he learned to look upon the Jew as upon a brother to be defended in all circumstances. During the Algerian war the Arabs were his brothers, and he stood by them. The present conflict was therefore for him a fratricidal struggle in which he was unable to exercise cool judgment and was overwhelmed by conflicting emotions.

Still, we must exercise our judgment and must not allow it to be clouded by emotions and memories, however deep or haunting. We should not allow even invocations of Auschwitz to blackmail us into supporting the wrong cause. I am speaking as a Marxist of Jewish origin, whose next-of-kin perished in Auschwitz and whose relatives live in Israel. To justify or condone Israel's wars against the Arabs is to render Israel a very bad service indeed and to harm its own long-term interest. Israel's security, let me repeat, was not enhanced by the wars of 1956 and 1967; it was undermined and compromised by them. The 'friends of Israel' have in fact abetted Israel in a ruinous course.

They have also, willy-nilly, abetted the reactionary mood that took hold of Israel during the crisis. It was only with disgust that I could watch on television the scenes from Israel in those days; the displays of the conquerors' pride and brutality; the outbursts of chauvinism; and the wild celebrations of the inglorious triumph, all contrasting sharply with the pictures of Arab suffering and desolation, the treks of Jordanian refugees and the bodies of Egyptian soldiers killed by thirst in the desert. I looked at the medieval figures of the rabbis and khassidim jumping with joy at the Wailing Wall; and I felt how the ghosts of Talmudic obscurantism—and I know these only too well—crowded in on the country, and how the reactionary atmosphere in Israel had grown dense and stifling. Then came the many interviews with General Dayan, the hero and saviour, with the political mind of a regimental sergeant-major, ranting about annexations and venting a raucous callousness about the fate of the Arabs in the conquered areas. ('What do they matter to me?' 'As far as I am concerned, they may stay or they may go.') Already wrapped in a phoney military legend— the legend is phoney for Dayan neither planned nor conducted the six days' campaign—he cut a rather sinister figure, suggesting a candidate for the dictator's post: the hint was conveyed that if the civilian parties get too 'soft' on the Arabs this new Joshua, this mini-de Gaulle, will teach them a lesson, himself take power, and raise Israel's 'glory' even higher. And behind Dayan there was Begin, Minister and leader of the extreme right-wing Zionists, who had long claimed even Trans-Jordania as part of 'historic' Israel. A reactionary war inevitably breeds the heroes, the moods, and the consequences in which its character and aims are faithfully mirrored.

On a deeper historical level the Jewish tragedy finds in Israel a dismal sequel. Israel's leaders exploit in self-justification, and over-exploit Auschwitz and Treblinka; but their actions mock the real meaning of the Jewish tragedy.

European Jews paid a horrible price for the role they had played in past ages, and not of their own choosing, as representatives of a market economy, of 'money', among peoples living in a natural, money-less, agricultural economy. They were the conspicuous carriers of early capitalism, traders and money lenders, in pre-capitalist society. The image of the rich Jewish merchant and usurer lived on in gentile folklore and remained engraved on the popular mind, stirring distrust and fear. The Nazis seized this image, magnified it to colossal dimensions', and constantly held it before the eyes of the masses.

August Bebel once said that anti-semitism is the 'socialism of the fools'. There was plenty of that kind of 'socialism' about, and all too little of the genuine socialism, in the era of the Great Slump, and of the mass unemployment and mass despair of the 1930s. The European working classes were unable to overthrow the bourgeois order; but the hatred of capitalism was intense and widespread enough to force an outlet for itself and focus on a scapegoat. Among the lower middle classes, the *lumpenbourgeoisie* and the *lumpenproletariat*, a frustrated anti-capitalism merged with fear of communism and neurotic xenophobia. The impact of Nazi Jew-baiting was so powerful in part because the image of the Jew as the alien and vicious 'blood-sucker' was to all too many people still an actuality. This accounted also for the relative indifference and the passivity with which so many non-Germans viewed the slaughter of the Jews. The socialism of the fools gleefully watched Shylock led to the gas chamber.

Israel promised not merely to give the survivors of the European-Jewish communities a 'National Home' but also to free them from the fatal stigma. This was the message of the kibbutzim, the Histadruth, and even of Zionism at large. The Jews were to cease to be unproductive elements, shopkeepers, economic and cultural interlopers, carriers of capitalism. They were to settle in 'their own land' as 'productive workers'.

Yet they now appear in the Middle East once again in the invidious role of agents not so much of their own, relatively feeble, capitalism, but of powerful western vested interests and as *protegés* of neo-colonialism. This is how the Arab world sees them, not without reason. Once again they arouse bitter emotions and hatreds in their neighbours, in all those who have ever been or still are victims of imperialism. What a fate it is for the Jewish people to be made to appear in this role! As agents of early capitalism they were still pioneers of progress in feudal society; as agents of the late, over-ripe, imperialist capitalism of our days, their role is altogether lamentable; and they are placed once again in the position of potential scapegoats. Is Jewish history to come full circle in such a way? This may well be the outcome of Israel's 'victories'; and of this Israel's real friends must warn it.

The Arabs, on the other hand, need to be put on guard against the socialism or the anti-imperialism of the fools. We trust that they will not succumb to it; and that they will learn from their defeat and recover to lay the foundations of a truly progressive, a socialist Middle East.

• • •

Notes

[1] From an interview given to the *New Left Review* on 23 June 1967.

[2] In recent years Israel has been receiving up to 250 million dollars annually
in grants and loans from the western powers, in aid from the United States,
and in contributions from Jews abroad. This amounts to nearly 125 dollars
a year per head of the Israeli population.

I. F. Stone (1907–1989) was one of America's greatest muckraking jour-nalists. Born Isadore Feinstein to a Russian-Jewish family in Philadelphia, Stone started up his first newspaper when he was 14 years old, and dropped out of the University of Pennsylvania in his junior year to pursue a career in journalism. The Washington editor of The Nation *from 1940 to 1946, he founded I.F. Stone's Weekly in 1953, a magazine that won a wide reader-ship for its scathing, and painstakingly documented critiques of the Wash-ington establishment on civil rights, domestic repression, and the wars in Korea and Vietnam. Renowned for his investigative acumen, he was living proof that, in the finest journalism, objectivity and passion, far from being mutually exclusive, go hand in hand. Stone, who called himself a "Jeffer-sonian Marxist," was famously asked how on earth he could admire Jefferson, a slaveholder. "Because history is a tragedy, not a melodrama," he replied. Stone brought this sense of the tragic to his writings on the clash between Arab and Jew in Palestine As a young man, he had rallied to the cause of Israeli independence, and in 1946 published a book,* Underground to Palestine, *a sympathetic account of the migration of Jews at the end of the Second World War. By the 1960s, however, he had begun to experience increasing doubts about the nature of the Jewish state, and about its willing-ness to make peace—a just peace, as distinct from a conqueror's peace—with the Palestinians it had dispossessed, and with the neighboring Arab states. In 1969 in* The New York Review of Books, *Stone published a review of a spe-cial issue of* Les Temps Modernes *on the Arab-Israeli conflict, edited just after the 1967 War by the journal's founder, Jean-Paul Sartre, who, as a friend to both peoples, felt painfully divided. Stone's essay, "Holy War," remains of the best pieces written on the conflict, wry, fair-minded and deeply humane. As Stone underscores, "the Arab problem is the No. 1 Jewish problem. How we act toward the Arabs will determine what kind of people we become: either oppressors and racists in our turn like those from whom we have suffered, or a nobler race able to transcend the tribal xenophobias that afflict mankind."*

HOLY WAR

I. F. Stone

From *Polemics and Prophecies* (1969)

Stripped of propaganda and sentiment, the Palestine problem is, simply, the struggle of two different peoples for the same strip of land. For the Jews, the establishment of Israel was a Return, with all the mystical significance the capital R implies. For the Arabs it was another invasion. This has led to three wars between them in twenty years. Each has been a victory for the Jews. With each victory the size of Israel has grown. So has the number of Arab homeless.

Now to find a solution which will satisfy both peoples is like trying to square a circle. In the language of mathematics, the aspirations of the Jews and the Arabs are incommensurable. Their conflicting ambitions cannot be fitted into the confines of any ethical system which transcends the tribalistic. This is what frustrates the benevolent outsider, anxious to satisfy both peoples. For two years Jean-Paul Sartre has been trying to draw Israelis and Arabs into a confrontation in a special number of his review, *Les Temps Modernes*. The third war between them broke out while it was on the press.

This long-awaited special issue on *Le conflit israélo-arabe* is the first confrontation in print of Arab and Israeli intellectuals. But it turns out to be 991 pages not so much of dialogue as of dual monologue. The two sets of contributors sit not just in separate rooms, like employers and strikers in a bitter labor dispute, but in separate universes where the simplest fact often turns out to have diametrically opposite meanings. Physics has begun to uncover a new conundrum in the worlds of matter and anti-matter, occupying the same space and time but locked off from each other by their obverse natures, forever twin yet forever sundered. The Israeli-Arab quarrel is the closest analogue in the realm of international politics.

The conditions exacted for the joint appearance of Israelis and Arabs in the same issue of *Les Temps Modernes* excluded not only collaboration but normal editorial mediation or midwifery. Claude Lanzmann, who edited this special issue, explains in his Introduction that the choice of authors and of subjects had to be left "in full sovereignty" *(en toute souveraineté)* to each of the two parties. The Arabs threatened to withdraw if an article was included by A. Razak Abdel-Kader, an Algerian who is an advocate of Israeli-Arab reconciliation. When the Israelis objected that *Les Temps Modernes* at least allow Abdel-Kader to express himself as an individual, the Arabs insisted on an absolute veto: there would be no issue if Abdel-Kader were in it.

In his Preface Jean-Paul Sartre lays bare the conflicting emotions which led him to embark on so difficult a task as to attempt the role—in some degree—of peacemaker between Arab and Israeli. They awaken the memories of his finest hours. One was that of the Resistance. "For all those who went through this experience," M. Sartre writes, "it is unbearable to imagine that another Jewish community, wherever it may be, whatever it may be, should endure this Calvary anew and furnish martyrs to a new massacre." The other was Sartre's aid to the Arabs in their struggle for Algerian independence. These memories bind him to both peoples, and give him the respect of both, as the welcome he received in both Egypt and Israel last year attests. His aim in presenting their views is, he says wistfully, merely to *inform*. His hope is that information in itself will prove pacifying "because it tends more or less slowly to replace passion by knowledge." But the roots of this struggle lie deeper than reason. It is not at all certain that information will replace passion with knowledge.

The experiences from which M. Sartre draws his emotional ties are irrelevant to this new struggle. Both sides draw from them conclusions which must horrify the man of rationalist tradition and universalist ideals. The bulk of the Jews and the Israelis draw from the Hitler period the conviction that, in this world, when threatened one must be prepared to kill or be killed. The Arabs draw from the Algerian conflict the conviction that, even in dealing with so rational and civilized a people as the French, liberation was made possible only by resorting to the gun and the knife. Both Israeli and Arabs in other words feel that only force can assure justice. In this they agree, and this sets them on a collision course. For the Jews believe justice requires the recognition of Israel as a fact; for the Arabs, to recognize the fact is to acquiesce in the wrong done them by the conquest of Palestine. If God as some now say is dead, He no doubt died of trying to find an equitable solution to the Arab-Jewish problem.

The argument between them begins with the Bible. "I give this country to your posterity," God said to Abraham (Gen. 15:18) "from the river of Egypt up to the great river, Euphrates." Among the Jews, whether religious or secular mystics, this is the origin of their right to the Promised Land. The opening article in the Arab section of *Les Temps Modernes* retorts that the "posterity" referred to in Genesis includes the descendants of Ishmael since he was the son of Abraham by his concubine Ketirah, and the ancestor of all the Arabs, Christian or Muslim.

All this may seem anachronistic nonsense, but this is an anachronistic quarrel. The Bible is still the best guide to it. Nowhere else can one find a parallel for its enthnocentric fury. Nowhere that I know of is there a word of pity in the Bible for the Canaanites whom the Hebrews slaughtered in taking possession. Of all the nonsense which marks the Jewish-Arab quarrel none is more nonsensical than the talk from both sides about the Holy Land as a symbol of peace. No bit of territory on earth has been soaked in the blood of more battles. Nowhere has religion been so zestful an excuse for fratricidal strife. The Hebrew *shalom* and the Arabic *salaam* are equally shams, relics of a common past as Bedouins. To this day inter-tribal war is the favorite sport of the Bedouins; to announce "peace" in the very first word is a necessity if any chance encounter is not to precipitate bloodshed.

In Biblical perspective the Jews have been going in and out of Palestine for 3,000 years. They came down from the Euphrates under Abraham; returned from Egypt under Moses and Joshua; came back again from the Babylonian captivity and were dispersed again after Jerusalem fell to the Romans in 70 A.D. This is the third return. The Arabs feel they have a superior claim because they stayed put. This appearance side by side in *Les Temps Modernes* provides less than the full and undiluted flavor of an ancient sibling rivalry. Both sides have put their better foot forward. The Arab section includes no sample of the bloodcurdling broadcasts in which the Arab radios indulge; the

Israeli, no contribution from the right-wing Zionists who dream of a greater Israel from the Nile to the Euphrates (as promised in Genesis) with complete indifference to the fate of the Arab inhabitants. On neither side is there a frank exposition of the *Realpolitik* which led Arab nationalists like Nasser to see war on Israel as the one way to achieve Arab unity, and leads Jewish nationalists like Ben-Gurion and Dayan to see Arab disunity and backwardness as essential elements for Israeli security and growth. No voice on the Arab side preaches a Holy War in which all Israel would be massacred, while no voice on the Israeli side expresses the cheerfully cynical view one may hear in private that Israel has no realistic alternative but to hand the Arabs a bloody nose every five or ten years until they accept the loss of Palestine as irreversible.

The picture, however, is not wholly symmetrical. There is first of all the asymmetry of the victorious and the defeated. The victor is ready to talk with the defeated if the latter will acquiesce in defeat. The defeated, naturally, is less inclined to this kind of objectivity. The editor, Claude Lanzmann, speaks of an "asymmetry between the two collections of articles which derives at one and the same time from a radical difference in their way of looking at the conflict and from the difference in the nature of the political regimes in the countries involved." Even if not expressly authorized by their governments or organizations to participate, M. Lanzmann explains, all the Arabs except the North Africans wrote only after consultation and defend a common position, while the Israelis, "as is normal in a Western-style democracy," speak either for themselves or for one of their numerous parties. But this diversity may be exaggerated. On the fundamental issue which divides the two sides, no Arab contributor is prepared to advocate recognition of the state of Israel, while only one Israeli contributor is prepared to advocate its transformation into something other than a basically Jewish state.

The depth of this nationalistic difference may be measured by what happened to Israel's Communist party. Elsewhere national centrifugal tendencies have made their appearance in the once monolithic world of communism. In Israel the same nationalist tendencies split the Communist party into two, one Jewish the other Arab. The days when Arab Communists faithfully followed Moscow's line straight into the jails of Egypt, Iraq, Syria, and Jordan by supporting the 1947 partition plan have long passed away. Today Arab and Jewish Communists no longer find common ground.[1] It would be hard to find an Arab who would agree with Moshe Sneh, head of the Jewish Communist party (Maki) in Israel, when he told *L'Express* (June 19–25), "Our war is just and legitimate. What united the 13 Arab States against us, irrespective of their regime, was not anti-imperialism but pan-Arabism and anti-Jewish chauvinism." He added boldly that Moscow in supporting the Arabs had "turned its back on the politics of the international left and on the spirit of Tashkent." But even Sneh's bitter rival, Mek Vilner, the Jewish leader of, and one of the few Jews left in, the Arab Communist party (Rakka) expresses himself in *Les Temps Modernes* in terms with which no Arab contributor to it agrees. M. Vilner is for the return of all the refugees who wish it, for full equality to Arabs in Israel and for a neutralist policy, but he defends the existence of Israel as a legitimate fact and denies that "one can in any way compare the people (of Israel) to Algerian colons or the Crusaders." The comparisons rejected by the leader of the Arab Communist party in Israel are the favorite comparisons of the Arabs outside Israel. The diversity of viewpoint on the Israeli side thus ends with the basic agreement on its right to exist, and to exist as a Jewish state. This is precisely where the Arab disagreement begins.

The gulf between Arab and Jewish views becomes even clearer when one reads two supplementary pieces contributed by two French Jews, Maxime Rodinson, a distinguished sociologist and Orientalist, and Robert Misrahi, a well-known writer of the left. The former takes the Arab and the latter the Zionist side. But while M. Misrahi's article appears with the Israelis, M. Rodinson's contribution—by far the most brilliant in the whole volume—appears alone. He refused, for reasons of principle, to appear in the Arab ensemble. It is not hard to see why. For while M. Rodinson gives strong support to every basic Arab historical contention, he is too much the humanist (and in the last analysis no doubt the Jew) to welcome an apocalyptic solution at the expense of Israel's existence. There is still a gulf between M. Rodinson's pro-Arab position and the most moderate view any Arab statesman has yet dared express, that of Tunisia's President Bourguiba. Bourguiba's famous speech in Jericho, March 3, 1965, is reprinted in an appendix by *Les Temps Modernes,* along with an interview he gave *Le Nouvel Observateur* (April 15) a month later. But Bourguiba's speech, though it created a sensation by its relative moderation, merely suggested that the Arabs proceed to regain Palestine as they did Tunisia, by a series of more or less peaceful compromises. When *Le Nouvel Observateur* asked him whether this did not imply the progressive disappearance of the State of Israel, he would not go beyond the cryptic reply, "That is not certain."

The Arab section of the symposium is nevertheless far from being uniform. A Moroccan, Abdallah Larouia, professor of literature in Rabat, not only ends by saying that the possibilities of peaceful settlement must be kept open because a war would settle nothing, but even goes so far as to express the hope that the time may come when a settlement is possible without making a new exile, i.e., of the Israelis, pay for the end of another exile, i.e., of the Arabs from Palestine. He even suggests that under certain conditions, a Jewish community "with or without political authority"—a most daring remark—may prove compatible with Arab progress and development.

When we examine these conditions, we come to the heart of the fears expressed by the Arabs in this symposium. The Palestinian Arabs, from the first beginnings of Zionism, foresaw the danger of being swamped and dislodged by Jewish immigration. Neighboring Arab states feared that this immigration would stimulate a continuous territorial expansion at their expense and create a Jewish state powerful enough to dominate the area. The relative size and population of Israel when compared to its Arab neighbors are deceptive and may make these fears seem foolish, but historically the Middle East has often been conquered and dominated by relatively small bands of determined intruders. Even now, as the recent fighting showed, tiny Israel could without difficulty have occupied Damascus, Amman, and Cairo, and—were it not for the big powers and the UN—dictated terms to its Arab neighbors.

It was the attempt of the British to allay Arab apprehension by setting limits on Jewish immigration that precipitated the struggle between the British and the Jews. The 1917 Balfour Declaration, when it promised a "Jewish National Home" in Palestine, also said—in a passage Zionists have always preferred to forget—"that nothing shall be done which may prejudice the civil and religious rights of the existing non-Jewish communities in Palestine." British White Papers in

1922, in 1930, and again in 1939 tried to fulfill this companion pledge by steps which would have kept the Jews a permanent minority. It is this persistent and—as events have shown—justifiable Arab fear which is reflected in M. Laroui's article. In calling the Palestine problem "A Problem of the Occident" his basic point is that if the Occident wipes out anti-Semitism, or keeps it within harmless proportions, making refuge in Israel unnecessary for the bulk of Jewry, and Israel divorces its politics from the Zionist dream of gathering in all the Jews from Exile, this will end the danger of an inexorable expansion in search of *"leben-sraum"* at the expense of the Palestinian Arabs, and finally make peace possible between the two peoples. Since immigration into Israel has dwindled in recent years, this Arab fear seems at the moment less a matter of reality than of Zionist theory and of a past experience which leads them to take it seriously.

The suggestion that Israel abandon its supra-nationalist dream finds its only echo on the other side of this collection of essays in Israel's No. 1 maverick and champion of Arab rights, Uri Avnery. Avnery was born in Germany in 1923 and went to Palestine at the age of ten, the year Hitler took power. He began his political career on the far nationalist right, as a member of the Irgun terrorist group in the struggle against the British, but has since swung over to the far left of Israeli opinion, to the point where he is considered anti-nationalist. In the wake of the first Suez war, he supported the Egyptian demand for evacuation of the Canal Zone and in 1959 he formed an Israeli committee to aid the Algerian rebels. At one time he organized a movement which asserted that the Israelis were no longer Jews but "Canaanites" and therefore one with the Arabs, forcibly converted remnants of the same indigenous stock. When this far-out conception attracted few Jews and even fewer Canaanites, he formed a "Semitic Action" movement which has now become "the Movement of New Forces." This polled 1.2 percent of the vote in the 1965 elections and by virtue of proportional representation put Avnery into Parliament. Avnery has been more successful as a publisher. He has made his weekly *Haolam Hazeh* ("This World") the largest in Israel by combining non-conformist politics with what the rather puritanical Israelis call pornography, though that weekly's girlie pictures would seem as old-fashioned as the *Police Gazette* in America.

Avnery writes in *Les Temps Modernes* that he would turn Israel into a secular, pluralist, and multi-national state. He would abolish the Law of Return which gives every Jew the right to enter Israel and automatically become a citizen. Avnery says this pan-Judaism of Zionism feeds the anti-Zionism of pan-Arabism by keeping alive "the myth of an Israel submerged by millions of immigrants who, finding no place to settle, would oblige the government to expand the country by force of arms."

Yet Avnery, who asks Israel to give up its Zionist essence, turns out to be a Jewish nationalist, too. After sketching out a plan, for an Arab Palestinian state west of the Jordan, Avnery writes, "The Arabic reader will justly ask at this point, 'And the return of Israel to the limits of the UN plan of 1947?' " Since Israel in the 1947–48 fighting seized about 23 percent more territory than was allotted to it in the 1947 partition plan, this implies a modification of frontiers in favor of the Arab state which was supposed to be linked with it in an economically united Palestine. But to this natural Arab question Avnery replies,[2] "Frankly we see no possibility of this kind. The Arab armies are already 15 kilometers from Israel's most populous city (Tel Aviv) and at Nathanya are even closer to the sea." The Arabs may feel that Avnery is as unwilling to give up the fruits of conquest as any non-"Canaanite." Avnery is as reluctant as any conventional Zionist to see his fellow Canaanite too close to Tel Aviv.

It is easy to understand why neither side trusts the other. In any case M. Sartre's symposium is a confrontation largely of moderates and leftists, and on neither side do these elements command majority support. Another complexity is that while in settled societies the left tends to be less nationalistic than the right, in colonial societies the revolutionary left is often more nationalistic than the native conservative and propertied classes.

The overwhelming majority opinion on both sides, even as expressed in a symposium as skewed leftward as this one, shows little tendency to compromise. The Arabs argue that Israel is a colonialist implantation in the Middle East, supported from the beginning by imperialist powers; that it is an enemy of Arab union and progress; that the sufferings of the Jews in the West were the consequence of an anti-Semitism the Arabs have never shared; and that there is no reason why the Arabs of Palestine should be displaced from their homes in recompense for wrongs committed by Hitler Germany. M. Laroui alone is sympathetic enough to say that if the Jewish National Home had been established in Uganda, the Arabs who felt compassion for the sufferings of the Jews of Europe would have shown themselves as uncomprehending of the rights of the Ugandans as the West has been in Palestine. At the other end of the Arab spectrum a fellow Moroccan, a journalist, Tahar Benziane, ends up in classic anti-Semitism, blaming the Jews themselves, their separatism and their sense of superiority, for the prejudice against them. Benziane sees the only solution not just in the liquidation of Israel but in the disappearance of world Jewry through assimilation. His would indeed be a Final Solution. This bitter and hateful opinion, widespread in the Arab world, explains why Nazism found so ready an echo before the war in the Middle East and Nazi criminals so welcome a refuge in Egypt. It also disposes of the semantic nonsense that Arabs being Semite cannot be anti-Semitic!

The Zionist argument is that the Jewish immigration was a return to the Jewish homeland. Robert Misrahi even goes so far as to argue that the Jews had an older claim to Palestine than the Arabs since, the Jews had lived there in the ancient kingdom of the Hebrews long before the Hegira of Mohammed! Misrahi argues the familiar Zionist thesis that their struggle against Britain proves them to be anti-imperialist, that their colonies are socialist, that their enemies are the feudal elements in the Arab world, and that the Arab refugees are the moral responsibility of the Arab leaders since it was on their urging that the Arabs ran away.

There is a good deal of simplistic sophistry in the Zionist case. The whole earth would have to be reshuffled if claims 2,000 years old to *irredenta* were suddenly to be allowed. Zionism from its beginning tried to gain its aims by offering to serve as outpost in the Arab world for one of the great empires. Herzl sought to win first the Sultan and then the Kaiser by such arguments. Considerations of imperial strategy finally won the Balfour Declaration from Britain. The fact that the Jewish community in Palestine afterward fought the British is no more evidence of its not being a colonial implantation than similar wars of British colonists against the mother country, from the American Revolution to Rhodesia. In the case of Palestine, as of other such struggles, the Mother Country was assailed because it showed more concern for the native majority than was palatable to the colonist minority. The argument that the refugees ran away "voluntarily" or because their leaders urged them to do so until after the fighting was over not only rests on a myth but is irrelevant. Have refugees no right to return? Have German Jews no right to recover their properties because they too fled?

The myth that the Arab refugees fled because the Arab radios urged them to do so was analyzed by Erskine B. Childers in the London *Spectator* May 12, 1961. An examination of British and U.S. radio monitoring records turned up no such appeals; on the contrary there were appeals and "even orders to the civilians of Palestine, *to stay put.*" The most balanced and humane discussion of the question may be found in Christopher Sykes's book *Crossroads to Israel: 1917–48* (at pages 350–5). "It can be said with, a high degree of certainty," Mr. Sykes wrote, "that most of the time in the first half of 1948 the mass exodus was the natural, thoughtless, pitiful movement of ignorant people who had been badly led and who in the day of trial found themselves forsaken by their leaders. . . . But if the exodus was by and large an accident of war in the first stage, in the later stages it was consciously and mercilessly helped on by Jewish threats and aggression toward Arab populations. . . . It is to be noted, however, that where the Arabs had leaders who refused to be stampeded into panic flight, the people came to no harm." Jewish terrorism, not only by the Irgun, in such savage massacres as Deir Yassin, but in milder form by the Haganah, itself "encouraged" Arabs to leave areas the Jews wished to take over for strategic or demographic reasons. They tried to make as much of Israel as free of Arabs as possible.

The effort to equate the expulsion of the Arabs from Palestine with the new Jewish immigration out of the Arab countries is not so simple nor so equitable as it is made to appear in Zionist propaganda. The Palestinian Arabs feel about this "swap" as German Jews would if denied restitution on the grounds that they had been "swapped" for German refugees from the Sudetenland. In a sanely conceived settlement, some allowance should equitably be made for Jewish properties left behind in Arab countries. What is objectionable in the simplified version of this question is the idea that Palestinian Arabs whom Israel didn't want should have no objection to being "exchanged" for Arabic Jews it did want. One uprooting cannot morally be equated with the other.

A certain moral imbecility marks all ethnocentric movements. The Others are always either less than human, and thus their interests may be ignored, or more than human, and therefore so dangerous that it is right to destroy them. The latter is the underlying pan-Arab attitude toward the Jews; the former is Zionism's basic attitude toward the Arabs. M. Avnery notes that Herzl in his book *The Jewish State*, which launched the modern Zionist movement, dealt with working hours, housing for workers, and even the national flag but had not one word to say about the Arabs! For the Zionists the Arab was the Invisible Man. Psychologically he was not there. Ahad Ha'am, the Russian Jew who became a great Hebrew philosopher, tried to draw attention as early as 1891 to the fact that Palestine was not an empty territory and that this posed problems. But as little attention was paid to him as was later accorded his successors in "spiritual Zionism," men like Buber and Judah Magnes, who tried to preach *Ichud*, "unity," i.e., with the Arabs. Of all the formulas with which Zionism comforted itself none was more false and more enduring than Israel Zangwill's phrase about "a land without people for a people without a land." Buber related that Max Nordau, hearing for the first time that there was an Arab population in Palestine, ran to Herzl crying, "I didn't know that—but then we are committing an injustice." R. J. Zwi Werblowsky, dean of the faculty of letters at the Hebrew University, in the first article of this anthology's Israeli section, writes with admirable objectivity, "There can be no doubt that if Nordau's reaction had been more general, it would seriously have paralyzed the *élan* of the Zionist movement." It took refuge, he writes, in "a moral myopia."

This moral myopia makes it possible for Zionists to dwell on the 1,900 years of Exile in which Jews have longed for Palestine but dismiss as nugatory the nineteen years in which Arab refugees have also longed for it. "Homelessness" is the major theme of Zionism, but this pathetic passion is denied to Arab refugees. Even Meir Yaari, the head of Mapam, the leader of the "Marxist" Zionists of Hashomer Hatzair, who long preached bi-nationalism, says Israel can only accept a minority of the Arab refugees because the essential reason for the creation of Israel was to "welcome the mass of immigrant Jews returning to their historic fatherland!" If there is not room enough for both, the Jews must have precedence. This is what leads Gabran Majdalany, a Baath Socialist, to write that Israel is "a racist state founded from its start on discrimination between Jew and non-Jew." He compares the Zionists to the Muslim Brotherhood who "dream of a Muslim Israel in which the non-Muslims will be the gentiles, second-class citizens sometimes tolerated but more often repressed." It is painful to hear his bitter reproach—

> Some people admit the inevitably racist character of Israel but justify it by the continual persecutions to which the Jews have been subjected during the history of Europe and by the massacres of the Second World War. We consider that, far from serving as justification, these facts constitute an aggravating circumstance; for those who have known the effects of racism and of discrimination in their own flesh and human dignity, are less excusably racist than those who can only imagine the negative effects of prejudice.

When Israel's Defense Minister, Moshe Dayan, was on *Face the Nation* June 11, after Israel's latest victories, this colloquy occurred:

Sydney Gruson (*New York Times*): Is there any possible way that Israel could absorb the huge number of Arabs whose territory it has gained control of now?

Gen. Dayan: Economically we can; but I think that is not in accord with our aims in the future. It would turn Israel into either a bi-national or poly-Arab-Jewish state instead of the Jewish state, and we want to have a Jewish state. We can absorb them, but then it won't be the same country.

Mr. Gruson: And it is necessary in your opinion to maintain this as a Jewish state and purely a Jewish state?

Gen. Dayan: Absolutely—absolutely. We want a Jewish state like the French have a French state.

This must deeply disturb the thoughtful Jewish reader. Ferdinand and Isabella in expelling the Jews and Moors from Spain were in the same way saying they wanted a Spain as "Spanish," (i.e., Christian) as France was French. It is not hard to recall more recent parallels.

It is a pity the editors of *Les Temps Modernes* didn't widen their symposium to include a Jewish as distinct from an Israeli point of view. For Israel is creating a kind of moral schizophrenia in world Jewry. In the outside world the welfare of Jewry depends on the maintenance of secular, non-racial, pluralistic societies. In Israel, Jewry finds itself defending a society in which mixed marriages cannot be legalized, in which non-Jews have a lesser status than Jews, and in which the ideal is racial and exclusionist. Jews must fight elsewhere for their very security and existence—against principles and practices they find themselves defending in Israel. Those from the outside world, even in their moments of greatest enthusiasm amid Israel's accomplishments, feel twinges of claustrophobia, not just geographical but spiritual. Those caught up in Prophetic fervor soon begin to feel that the light they hoped to see out of Zion is only that of another narrow nationalism.

Such moments lead to a reexamination of Zionist ideology. That longing for Zion on which it is predicated may be exaggerated. Its reality is indisputable but its strength can easily be overestimated. Not until after World War II was it ever strong enough to attract more than a trickle of Jews to the Holy Land. By the tragic dialectic of history, Israel would not have been born without Hitler. It took the murder of six million in his human ovens to awaken sufficient nationalist zeal in Jewry and sufficient humanitarian compassion in the West to bring a Jewish state to birth in Palestine. Even then humanitarian compassion was not strong enough to open the gates of the West to Jewish immigration in contrition. The capitalist West and the Communist East preferred to displace Arabs rather than to welcome the Jewish "displaced persons" in Europe's postwar refugee camps.

It must also be recognized, despite Zionist ideology, that the periods of greatest Jewish creative accomplishment have been associated with pluralistic civilizations in their time of expansion and tolerance: in the Hellenistic period, in the Arab civilization of North Africa and Spain, and in Western Europe and America. Universal values can only be the fruit of a universal vision; the greatness of the Prophets lay in their overcoming of ethnocentricity. A Lilliputian nationalism cannot distill truths for all mankind. Here lie the roots of a growing divergence between Jew and Israeli; the former with a sense of mission as a Witness in the human wilderness, the latter concerned only with his own tribe's welfare.

But Jewry can no more turn its back on Israel than Israel on Jewry. The ideal solution would allow the Jews to make their contributions as citizens in the diverse societies and nations which are their homes while Israel finds acceptance as a Jewish State in a renascent Arab civilization. This would end Arab fears of a huge inflow to Israel. The Jews have as much reason to be apprehensive about that prospect as the Arabs.

It can only come as the result of a sharp recrudescence in persecution elsewhere in the world. Zionism grows on Jewish catastrophe. Even now it casts longing eyes on Russian Jewry. But would it not be better, more humanizing, and more just, were the Soviet Union to wipe out anti-Semitism and to accord its Jews the same rights of cultural autonomy and expression it gives all its other nationalities? The Russian Jews have fought for Russia, bled for the Revolution, made no small contribution to Russian literature and thought; why should they be cast out? This would be a spiritual catastrophe for Russia as well as Jewry even though it would supply another flow of desperate refugees to an Israel already short of Jews if it is to expand as the Zionist militants hope to expand it.

Israel has deprived anti-Semitism of its mystique. For the visitor to Israel, anti-Semitism no longer seems a mysterious anomaly but only another variant of minority-majority friction. *Es is schwer zu sein eid Yid* ("It's hard to be a Jew") was the title of Sholom Aleichem's most famous story. Now we see that it's hard to be a goy in Tel Aviv, especially an Arab goy. Mohammad Watad, a Muslim Israeli, one of the five Arabic contributors to the Israeli side of this symposium, begins his essay with words which startingly resemble the hostile dialogue Jews encounter elsewhere. "I am often asked," he writes, "about my 'double' life which is at one and the same time that of an Arab and that of an Israeli citizen." Another Arab contributor from Israel, Ibrahim Shabath, a Christian who teaches Hebrew in Arabic schools and is editor-in-chief of *Al Mirsad*, the Mapam paper in Arabic, deplores the fact that nineteen years after the creation of Israel "the Arabs are still considered strangers by the Jews." He relates a recent conversation with Ben-Gurion. "You must know," Ben-Gurion told him, "that Israel is the country of the Jews and only of the Jews. Every Arab who lives here has the same rights as any minority citizen in any country of the world, but he must admit the fact that he lives in a Jewish country." The implications must chill Jews in the outside world.

The Arab citizen of Israel, Shabath complains, "is the victim today of the same prejudices and the same generalizations as the Jewish people elsewhere." The bitterest account of what they undergo may be found in an anonymous report sent to the United Nations in 1964 by a group of Arabs who tried unsuccessfully to found an independent Socialist Arab movement and publication. Military authorities, despite a Supreme Court order, refused to permit this, and the courts declined to overrule the military. Their petition is reprinted in the Israeli section of this symposium. Though the military rule complained of was abolished last year, and police regulations substituted, it is too soon—especially because of the new outbreak of warfare—to determine what the effect will be on Arab civil liberties. Israelis admit with pleasure that neither in the Christian villages of Central Galilee nor in the Muslim villages of the so-called "Triangle" was there the slightest evidence of any Fifth Column activity. Those Israelis who have fought for an end of all discrimination against the Arabs argue that they have demonstrated their loyalty and deserve fully to be trusted.

It is to Israel's credit that the Arab minority is given place in its section to voice these complaints while no similar place is opened for ethnic minority opinion in the Arabic section. Indeed except for Lebanon and to some degree Tunisia there is no place in the Arab world where the dissident of any kind enjoys freedom of the press. There is no frank discussion of this in the Arab section. One of the most vigorous and acute expositions of the Arab point of view, for example, is an article by an Egyptian writer, Lotfallah Soliman, who has played a distinguished role in bringing modern ideas to the young intellectuals of his country since World War II. His autobiographical sketch says cryptically, if discreetly, "He lives presently in Paris." I stumbled on a more candid explanation. In preparing for this review, I read an earlier article in *Les Temps Modernes* (August-September 1960) by

Adel Montasser *on La répression anti-démocratique en Egypte*. Appended
to it was a list of intellectuals imprisoned by Nasser. Among them was
Lotfallah Soliman. Obviously it's hard to be a free Egyptian intellectual
in Nasser's Egypt. Many of those then imprisoned have since been
freed, but it is significant that a writer as trenchant and devoted as
Soliman has to work in exile.

It is true that the full roster of Arab minority complaints in Israel
had to be presented anonymously for fear of the authorities. But in the
Arab section of this book no place was allowed even anonymously for
the Jewish and the various Christian minorities to voice their complaints. As a result the Arab contributors were able to write as if their
countries, unlike Europe, were models of tolerance. They hark back to
the great days of Arabic Spain where (except for certain interludes not
mentioned) Christian and Jew enjoyed full equality, religious, cultural,
and political, with the Muslim: Spain did not become synonymous
with intolerance, Inquisition, and obscurantism until the Christian
Reconquest. But today no Arab country except, precariously, Lebanon,
dimly resembles Moorish Spain. As a result the Jews from the Arabic
countries tend to hate the Arab far more than Jews from Europe who
have never lived under his rule, which often recalls medieval Chris-
tiandom. A glimpse of these realities may be found in the most
moving article in this whole symposium. This is by Attalah Mansour,
a young Christian Arabic Israeli novelist of peasant origin who has
published two novels, one in Arabic and the other in Hebrew, and
worked as a journalist on Avnery's paper *Haolam Hazeh* and on the
staff of *Haaretz*, Israel's best and most objective daily paper. M. Mansour knows doubly what it is to be a "Jew." He is as an Arab a "Jew"
to the Israelis and as a Christian a "Jew" to the Muslims. He tells a
touching story of an accidental encounter in (of all places) the Paris
Metro with a young man who turned out like him to be Greek-rite
Christian though from Egypt. They exchanged stories of their troubles,
like two Jews in the Diaspora. "We in Egypt," the young stranger told
him, "have the same feelings as you. There is no law discriminating
between us and the Muslims. But the governmental administration, at
least on the everyday level, prefers Mahmoud to Boulos and Achmed
to Samaan"—i.e., the man with the Muslim name to the man with the
Christian. "Omar Sharif, the well-known movie actor," the Egyptian

Christian added, "is Christian in origin. But he had to change his Christian name for a Muslim to please the public." In Israel, similarly, Ibrahim often becomes Abraham to pass as a Jew and to avoid widespread housing discrimination.

If in this account I have given more space to the Arab than the Israeli side it is because as a Jew, closely bound emotionally with the birth of Israel,[3] I feel honor bound to report the Arab side, especially since the U.S. press is so overwhelmingly pro-Zionist. For me, the Arab-Jewish struggle is a tragedy. The essence of tragedy is a struggle of right against right. Its catharsis is the cleansing pity of seeing how good men do evil despite themselves out of unavoidable circumstance and irresistible compulsion. When evil men do evil, their deeds belong to the realm of pathology. But when good men do evil, we confront the essence of human tragedy. In a tragic struggle, the victors become the guilty and must make amends to the defeated. For me the Arab problem is also the No. 1 Jewish problem. How we act toward the Arabs will determine what kind of people we become: either oppressors and racists in our turn like those from whom we have suffered, or a nobler race able to transcend the tribal xenophobias that afflict mankind.[4]

Israel's swift and extraordinary victories have suddenly transmuted this ideal from the realm of impractical sentiment to urgent necessity. The new frontiers of military conquest have gathered in most of the Arab refugees. Zionism's dream, the "in gathering of the exiles," has been achieved, though in an ironic form; it is the Arab exiles who are back. They cannot be gotten rid of as easily as in 1948. Something in the order of 100,000 have again been "encouraged" to leave, but the impact on public opinion abroad and in Israel has forced the state to declare that it will allow them to return. While the UN proves impotent to settle the conflict and the Arab powers are unwilling to negotiate from a situation of weakness, Israel can to some degree determine its future by the way in which it treats its new Arab subjects or citizens. The wrangles of the powers will go on for months, but these people must be fed, clothed, and housed. How they are treated will change the world's picture of Israel and of Jewry, soften or intensify Arab anger, build a bridge to peace or make new war certain. To establish an Arab state on the West Bank and to link it with Israel, perhaps also with Jordan, in a

Confederation would turn these Arab neighbors, if fraternally treated, from enemies into a buffer, and give Israel the protection of strategic frontiers. But it would be better to give the West Bank back to Jordan than to try to create a puppet state—a kind of Arab Bantustan—consigning the Arabs to second-class status under Israel's control. This would only foster Arab resentment. To avoid giving the Arabs first-class citizenship by putting them in the reservation of a second-class state is too transparently clever.

What is required in the treatment of the Arab refugees Israel has gathered in is the conquest both of Jewish exclusivism and the resentful hostility of the Arabs. Even the malarial marshes of the Emek and the sandy wastes of the Negev could not have looked more bleakly forbidding to earlier generations of Zionist pioneers than these steep and arid mountains of prejudice. But I for one have a glimmer of hope. Every year I have gone to Palestine and later Israel I have found situations which seemed impossible. Yet Zionist zeal and intelligence overcame them. Perhaps this extraordinarily dynamic, progressive, and devoted community can even if need be transcend its essential self.

I was encouraged to find in this volume that the most objective view of the Arab question on the Israeli side was written by Yehudah Harkabi, a Haifa-born professional soldier, a brigadier general, but a general who holds a diploma in philosophy and Arabic studies from the Hebrew University and from Harvard. He has written a book on *Nuclear War and Nuclear Peace.* His article "Hawks or Doves" is extraordinary in its ability to rise above prejudice and sentiment. He does not shut his eyes at all to the Arab case. He feels peace can come only if we have the strength to confront its full human reality. "Marx affirms," he concludes, "that knowledge of the truth frees man from the determinism of history." It is only, General Harkabi says, when Israel is prepared "to accept the truth in its entirety that it will find the new strength necessary to maintain and consolidate its existence." The path to safety and the path to greatness lies in reconciliation. The other route, now that the West Bank and Gaza are under Israeli jurisdiction, leads to two new perils. The Arab populations now in the conquered territories make guerrilla war possible within Israel's own boundaries. And externally, if enmity deepens and tension rises between Israel and the Arab states, both sides will by one means or another obtain nuclear weapons for the next round.

This will change the whole situation. No longer will Israeli and Arab be able to play the game of war in anachronistic fashion as an extension of politics by other means. Neither will they be able to depend on a mutual balance of terror like the great powers with their "second-strike" capacity. In this pygmy struggle the first strike will determine the outcome and leave nothing behind. Nor will the great powers be able to stand aside and let their satellites play out their little war, as in 1948, 1956, and 1967. I have not dwelt here on the responsibility of the great powers, because if they did not exist the essential differences in the Arab-Israeli quarrel would still remain, and because both sides use the great power question as an excuse to ignore their own responsibilities. The problem for the new generation of Arabs is the social reconstruction of their decayed societies; the problem will not go away if Israel disappears. Indeed their task is made more difficult by the failure to recognize Israel, since that means a continued emphasis on militarization, diversion of resources, and domination by military men. For Israel, the problem is reconciliation with the Arabs; the problem will not go away even if Moscow and Washington lie down together like the lion and the lamb or blow each other to bits. But the great powers for their part cannot continue the cynical game of arming both sides in a struggle for influence when the nuclear stage is reached. It is significant that the one place where the Israeli and Arab contributors to this symposium tend to common conclusions is in the essays discussing the common nuclear danger. To denuclearize the Middle East, to defuse it, will require some kind of neutralization. Otherwise the Arab-Israeli conflict may some day set off a wider final solution. That irascible Old Testament God of Vengeance is fully capable, if provoked, of turning the whole planet into a crematorium.

August 3, 1969
New York Review

• • •

Notes

[1] The relative strength of the two since the split may be seen from the fact

that the Jewish branch was able to elect only one deputy while the Arab branch, which draws the largest vote among the Arab minority, elected three, two Arabs and one Jew.

[2] Avnery was writing, of course, before the new outbreak of warfare had again changed these borders to Israel's advantage.

[3] I first arrived in Palestine on Balfour Day Nov. 2, 1945, the day the Haganah blew up bridges and watch towers to begin its struggle against the British and immigration restrictions. The following spring I was the first newspaperman to travel with illegal Jewish immigrants from the Polish-Czech border through the British blockade. In 1947 I celebrated Passover in the British detention camps in Cyprus and in 1948 I covered the Arab-Jewish war. See my *Underground to Palestine* (1946) and *This is Israel* (1948). I was back in 1949, 1950, 1951, 1956, and 1964.

[4] In September [1967], Black Star will publish a vigorous little book *The Aryanization of the Jewish State*, by Michael Selzer, a young Pakistani Jew who lived in Israel. It may help Jewry and Israel to understand that the way to a fraternal life with the Arabs inside and outside Israel must begin with the eradication of the prejudices that greet the Oriental and Arabic-speaking Jews in Israel who now make up over half the population of the country. The bias against the Arab extends to a bias against the Jews from the Arab countries. In this, as in so many other respects, Israel presents in miniature all the problems of the outside world. Were the rest of the planet to disappear, Israel could regenerate from itself—as from a new Ark—all the bigotries, follies, and feuds of a vanished mankind (as well as some of its most splended accomplishments).

*For nearly four decades, **Uri Avnery** has been one of Israel's most dynamic and courageous peace activists. Born in Germany to a Jewish banker and his wife, he was nine when Hitler came to power. The family fled immediately to France, then to Palestine. "Zionism saved our lives," he wrote, "I never forgot this when I later became a non-Zionist, perhaps an anti-Zionist." At the age of 15, however, Avnery was drawn into the ranks of rightwing Zionism, impressed by their militant opposition to the British mandate. "Since then," he writes, "I have never forgotten this lesson: a terrorist is a freedom fighter in his own eyes, a freedom fighter is a terrorist in the eyes of his enemy." As a soldier in the 1948 Arab-Israeli war, Avnery came to grasp the full dimensions of the Palestinian tragedy—and Israel's responsibility for it.*

After the war, Avnery set about trying to find a just solution to the refugee problem. In September 1958, Avnery and Semitic Action published a "Hebrew Manifesto" calling upon Israel to redefine itself as a secular democracy, and to support the emerging decolonization movements in the Third World. A charismatic writer and speaker with an unusual flair for publicity, Avnery won a seat in parliament in 1965 "to the surprise of everyone, perhaps even myself."

Two years later, the 1967 war broke out, and on the fifth day of that war, Avnery published an open letter to the Prime Minister, Levi Eshkol, calling for the creation of a free and independent state in the West Bank and Gaza. There was no reply from Eshkol, but moderates in the PLO were taking notice. By the mid-1970s, when contacts with the PLO were still illegal in Israel, Avnery began to meet secretly with Said Hammami and Issam Sartawi, two of Arafat's closest aids. (Both men were later assassinated by agents of the notorious international terrorist Abu Nidal.) In the September 27 1981 issue of Haolam Hazeh, *a weekly magazine he edited, he published the full plan of Israel's invasion of Lebanon, eight months before the invasion was launched. In 1984, he established the Arab-Jewish Progressive List for Peace, the first time in the history of Israel in which Jews and Arabs had formed a fully integrated political force. During the last two intifadas, Avnery has fought tirelessly for a just peace with his new group, Gush Shalom (Peace Bloc). At the age of eighty, at a moment when the prospects for peace have never looked so dark, he remains the living embodiment of Antonio Gramsci's motto, "pessimism of the intellect, optimism of the will."*

PAX SEMITICA

Uri Avnery

From *Israel Without Zionists: A Plea for Peace in the Middle East* (1968)

Some months before the outbreak of the Six-Day War, I met a high-ranking member of the Egyptian regime. The meeting took place in Paris through the auspices of a mutual friend. Throughout the years, I have met many leaders of the different Arab states, exchanging opinions and trading ideas for a settlement. But this meeting was different.

At the outset, I said to my newfound friend: "Let's make a list of all possible solutions to the Israeli-Arab conflict. Let's analyze every solution in turn and see where we get."

Taking a pen, we wrote the following list on the paper cloth on our table in the Paris restaurant:

(A) Annihilation by war
(B) The destruction of Israel by political and economic isolation
(C) Status quo
(D) A Semitic federation.

The easiest solution of the problem would have been, of course, a decisive military victory by either side. If Israel could achieve a military victory big enough to compel the Arabs to accept an Israeli *diktat,* this would be one answer. But Israel would have to conquer the whole Arab world, an impossible feat even with the unquestioned superiority of the Israeli Army; the brilliant victory in the Six-Day War has now proved that one cannot dictate peace by military means. As General Dayan said four months after the war, "If anyone thought the Arabs had learned a lesson, he was mistaken." If the Arabs could conquer and annihilate Israel, that certainly would be a clear-cut solution. But my

Arab partner at the dinner table readily agreed that no such possibility exists. The military superiority of Israel will remain for a long time, and new weapons systems eventually will be introduced in the Middle East which will make it virtually certain that the destruction of Israel will be accompanied by the destruction of the Arab centers of population, thus setting the Region back at least two thousand years (and probably causing a thermonuclear holocaust all over the world). Both of us agreed that we must discount a military solution. (I assume that my partner realized how right he was a few months later, when the Six-Day War proved the point.)

The second proposal is dear to the Arab heart. Drawing an interesting—but, as we have seen, incomplete—analogy with the history of the Crusaders, Arabs tend to delude themselves that Israel can be wished away by not recognizing its existence. An economic and political boycott, they believe, can go on for so long that Israel will eventually wither away.

"We waited two hundred years for the Crusader State to disappear," Arabs will often say, "and we shall wait another two hundred years for the disappearance of Israel."

I asked my partner quite frankly, "Do you really want to hold up the march of Arab nationalism for two hundred years, just waiting for us to disappear? As long as we are here, and there is no solution to our conflict, you will not get anywhere in the fulfillment of your real aspirations. The conflict opens the Region for foreign intervention, both Western and Soviet, turning us all into pawns of a foreign game. No Arab unity can be achieved as long as a hostile Israel cuts the southern part of the Arab world off from the northern part. And the money you need for industrialization and reform, in order to create a modern and developed Arab society, you now must spend on arms which will become more expensive from year to year.

"Furthermore," I asked, "do you know of one single instance, in modern times, in which a sovereign state has just disappeared because of an economic or political boycott? During the last twenty years, in spite of the boycott, Israel has expanded both politically and economically in many parts of the world." After some discussion, we agreed that no such solution is practical.

Continuing the status quo cannot be considered a solution even in theory. Things will not right themselves automatically. Time is not the great healer in such a situation, with mutual hatred and fear intensifying from generation to generation. Indeed, this attitude is dangerous, taking into account the probable introduction of nuclear weapons into the region in the not-far-distant future. Such introduction seems inevitable. As long as the vicious circle continues to dominate the scene, with Israel fearing attack at any minute, no one can seriously expect the Israeli leadership to abstain for long from producing the ultimate weapon, a feat which Israel could attain, many experts believe, in a matter of months. On the other hand, in the same circumstances, the Arab leadership, fearing Israeli expansion, cannot tolerate a situation in which Israel has the bomb and the Arabs don't. If Israel produces the bomb, one can expect Egypt or Syria, at least, to pay any price, including a part of national independence, to get the bomb from Soviet Russia or China. One must also consider the possibilities inherent in a French-Arab alliance. It was at the height of the French-Israeli alliance that Israel started to develop its nuclear potential. Some people believe that the possession of nuclear bombs by Israel and the Arabs would ensure peace as does the balance of terror between the United States and the Soviet Union. This is an extremely dangerous fallacy. If anything, the 1967 war has proved that in the explosive Middle Eastern situation, a war can break out any time without anyone wanting it. Moreover, in any Middle Eastern state, power may be usurped by a wreckless adventurer who, one hopes, could not come to power in Washington or Moscow. The status quo in our Region is a very fragile thing indeed.

We did not write down, on our tablecloth, another theoretical solution, alien to the Arabs but popular in Israel. This is the idea that the great powers would compel the Arabs to make peace—peace meaning, of course, a peace acceptable to the Israelis, obliging the Arabs to recognize the status quo. According to this wishful thinking often voiced by Ben-Gurion and most Israeli leaders, some day Americans and Russians will meet and decide that it is in their mutual interest to impose a peace in our Region. It is just a question of waiting for the two great powers to settle their little differences throughout the world. This is sheer nonsense. Not only is it highly unlikely for the two superpowers to put an end to their rivalry in the Middle East, but even if they did this would only change the character of the Israeli-Arab confrontation without ending it. The Arabs would get from China the weapons they now receive from the Soviet Union—and more dangerous ones.

Throughout the Middle East there persists the naive notion that the conflict was created in some devious way by British imperialism and American intervention, and that we otherwise would all have lived happily ever after. This is a superficial view; as we have seen, the vicious circle was created by the clash of two authentic historical movements. Foreign influences acted on this situation but did not create it. If these influences were removed tomorrow—by some Divine intervention—the confrontation between the two movements would still go on. The solution, then, has to be found between the two sides themselves.

The first part of the solution I propose is the setting up of a federation between Israel and a new Arab-Palestinian republic, as outlined earlier. This, together with the settlement of the refugees, can be done by Israel in cooperation with the Palestinian Arabs, independent of any official contact between Israel and the Arab states.

The second part of the solution is Semitic Union, a great confederacy of all the states in the Region.

The two parts are not contradictory. I do not view the Palestinian federation as a replacement for a general Israeli-Arab peace. On the contrary, such a peace will be much easier to achieve once the Palestinian problem is solved by common consent. The Palestinian problem is both the reason and the pretext for the belligerent attitude of the other Arab nations toward Israel. In all their statements, Arab leaders maintain that the only reason for their war against Israel is either to "liberate Palestine" or to "restore the rights of the Palestinian-Arab people." Once the Arabs of Palestine declare themselves liberated and agree that their rights have been restored, the main obstacle to peace will have been removed. Or, to put it another way, those Arab leaders who wish, deep in their hearts, to reach some settlement with Israel will be able to say so and act accordingly once the Palestinian problem has been solved. Before this, any such statement or action would be considered treason against the Palestinian Arabs. Thus, a solution in Palestine is almost a prerequisite to a general

Semitic peace settlement, and at the same time, a Semitic peace is necessary to make the Palestinian solution meaningful and enduring.

I would like to explain here why I use the term *Semitic*. The reason has nothing to do with race; indeed, in the Middle East race is as uncertain as anywhere in the world. Both to Hebrews and to Arabs, race, today, means little. The term *Semitic* should, rather, be viewed as emphasizing an historical heritage, common to all peoples speaking languages of the Semitic family—Arabic, Hebrew, Amharic, and so forth. It also emphasizes the common cultural and spiritual background of all the peoples of our Region, so much influenced by their past. In this respect, the Semitic family of culture includes even the Turks, the Kurds, and the Persians, who are descended from different races and speak non-Semitic languages, but whose history is bound up with the culture of the Semitic world and the great religions of the Semites. Yet the main reason for the indispensability of this term is that it automatically includes Arabs and Hebrews, explains itself readily in the Region and throughout the world, and has the same meaning in all languages.

It is my deepest belief—and perhaps the point at which my friends and I differ from other people who aspire to peace in the Region—that such a peace cannot and must not contradict the national aspirations of both Hebrews and Arabs. Nationalism will reign supreme in our generation in all the countries of the Region, and nothing will stop it. Any idea, inspiring as it may be, which runs counter to the national feelings of the people concerned, will be by-passed by history.

I am a Hebrew nationalist, and I want to deal with Arab nationalists. I want to tell them: The last fifty years have shown that neither you nor we can achieve our national aspirations as long as we fight each other. Our two great national movements can neutralize each other, or they can be combined in one great regional movement of liberation and progress. This is what the Semitic idea means—an ideal combining the two nationalisms, an ideal with which nationalists on both sides can identify.

Joining a great Semitic confederacy would mean, for Israel, putting an end to the Zionist chapter in its history and starting a new one—the chapter of Israel as a state integrated in its Region, playing a part in the Region's struggle for progress and unity.

For the Arabs it would mean recognition of a post-Zionist Israel as a part of the Region, a part which could and should not be abolished because, in its new form, it is a factor in the struggle for the common good.

Let me be quite clear about this. A lot of nonsense has been written about solutions which do not recognize the existence of Israel as a sovereign state. Not one single Israeli, and certainly not I, would ever agree to any such solution. The existence of Israel as a sovereign state is the point of departure for any solution, as much as the rights and the aspirations of the Palestinian nation and any other Arab people.

Semitic Union not only provides a framework for mutual acceptance, but has many other advantages.

- First, it would end mutual fear and suspicion, the most dangerous elements in the present situation. Providing for common defense and coordinating the military affairs of all member states, it would make possible a gradual general disarmament and de-nuclearization with mutual inspection. By abolishing military secrecy, it would safeguard everyone from surprise attacks and surprise concentrations of troops—such as the Egyptian one which triggered the 1967 war, or the imaginary Israeli one on the Syrian front which led up to it.

- Union would also mean a pooling of political power. Joining the Union, Israel would, at long last, align itself with the prevalent trend in the Afro-Asian world and support those Arab struggles for liberation which are still unresolved. Israel's influence in the world would be put at the disposal of a Regional leadership, giving such leadership an impact which it lacked even at the height of Abdel-Nasser's successes as a leader of the "Third World."

- Economically, the potential advantages are enormous. For Israel, it would mean the end of Arab boycotts and the integration of its economy into the Region. For the Arabs it would mean the possibility of meaningful Regional planning, a Semitic common market which would harness the immense wealth of Arab oil to the cause of progress and industrialization of the Arab peoples, especially Egypt.

- A united Region, liberated from fear and foreign exploitation, could start at long last a rapid march toward the modernization of the whole Region, restoring it to the place it held both in ancient and Islamic times.

- It would mean breaking the vicious circle, which has embittered the lives of too many for too long, and starting a new cycle of mutual fertilization—a peaceful competition for the common good instead of a military competition, which can only end in mutual disaster.

All this sounds very optimistic. Indeed, it is.

I am an optimist. I believe that nothing in history is pre-determined. History in the making is composed of acts of human beings, their emotions and aspirations.

The depth of bitterness and hatred throughout our Semitic Region seems bottomless. Yet it is a comparatively new phenomenon, the outcome of the recent clash of our peoples. Nothing like European anti-Semitism ever existed in the Arab world prior to the events which created the vicious circle.

We have seen, in our times, Germans and Frenchmen cooperating, if not loving each other, after a war which lasted for many hundreds of years and whose bitter fruits are deeply embedded in both German and French culture. We are witnessing today the beginnings of an American-Soviet alliance which would have been unthinkable only a dozen years ago.

We are not dealing, therefore, with mystical phenomena, but with matters which can be changed by policy decisions, by new ideas, new leaders and new political forces—in short, by a new generation all over the Middle East disgusted with the mess their fathers have made and by the conventional lies of propaganda.

The first step has to be made by Israel. Throughout the last three generations, since the appearance of the first Zionist settlers in Palestine, it has been our side which has held the initiative, the Arabs reacting to our actions. It is up to us to change, by deliberate steps, the climate of hatred and suspicion in the Middle East.

We can start this by helping the Palestinian Arabs to set up their state and by settling the refugees. We can assume a completely new stance in the Region by supporting Arab nationalist aims in spirit and action, with a hundred small gestures, each insignificant by itself but contributing, in sum, to a gradual change in the atmosphere. By truly integrating the Israeli Arabs into the framework of our state and turning it into a pluralistic society, we can show the Arab world a new face—Israeli Arabs representing Israel, side by side with Hebrew Israelis, in all fields of endeavor, from the General Assembly of the United Nations to the playground of international soccer.

Nothing will change overnight. Each of our acts will be suspect in the beginning. Each will be denounced as a new Zionist plot. But slowly, by concerted action, suspicion will be dispelled and confidence gained, providing the psychological framework for new Arab policies.

Yet time is important.

An uneasy cease-fire prevails along the frozen fronts of the recent war, a cease-fire fraught with dangers, broken by intermittent shots.

The armies confronting each other across the cease-fire lines are arming quickly. A new war is assumed by all of them as a virtual certainty, with only the exact timing still in doubt. But the next war, or the one after it, will be quite different from the recent one, so different, in fact, that the *blitzkrieg* of June 1967, will look, in comparison, like a humanitarian exercise.

Nuclear weapons, missiles of all types, are nearing the Semitic scene. Their advent is inevitable. If the vicious circle is not broken, and broken soon, it will lead, with the preordained certainty of a Greek tragedy, toward a holocaust that will bury Tel Aviv and Cairo, Damascus and Jerusalem.

Semitic suicide is the only alternative to Semitic peace.

A different kind of tragedy is brewing in Palestine itself. If no just solution is found soon, the guerrilla war of organizations like *al-Fatah* will start a vicious circle of its own, a steep spiral of terror and counter-terror, killing and retaliation, sabotage and mass deportation, which will bring undreamt of miseries to the Palestinian people. It will poison the atmosphere and generate a nightmare that will make peace impossible in our lifetime, turning Israel into an armed and beleaguered camp forever, bringing the Arab march toward progress to a complete standstill, and perhaps spelling the end of the Palestinian-Arab people as a nation—the very people for whose freedom *al-Fatah* fights in vain.

Cease fire—this is not a passive imperative. In order to cease fire, acts of peace must be done. Peace must be waged—actively, imaginatively, incessantly. In the words of the psalmist: "Seek peace and pursue it." The search can be passive—the pursuit cannot.

One of the most beautiful books of the Bible, *Ecclesiastes*, contains a passage which has often disturbed me: "A time to kill, and a time to heal."

Did the Preacher really mean that there is a time to kill? Did he mean to advocate killing at any time?

I don't think so. I see the Preacher as a man full of wisdom and experience, who knew all human follies. He knew that, people being what they are, there are times when war cannot be averted. He wanted to say that after such a war, people must set about to build peace, to wage pace as they have waged war.

In these pages I have passed harsh judgment on both Zionists and Arabs, about their foolishness and shortsightedness. In theory, they could have acted differently, and thereby avoided untold suffering. But movements like theirs are children of their age, victims of its illusions and limitations; thus, Zionist and Arab could not really have behaved differently. Understanding this, we of a later time must set a new course.

It is thus that I understand the words of *Ecclesiastes*:

A time to be born, and a time to die;
A time to plant, and a time to pluck up what is planted;
A time to kill, and a time to heal;
A time to break down, and a time to build up;
A time to weep, and a time to laugh;
A time to mourn, and a time to dance;

A time to cast away stones, and a time to gather stones together;
A time to embrace, and a time to refrain from embracing;
A time to seek, and a time to lose;
A time to keep, and a time to cast away;
A time to rend, and a time to sew;
A time to keep silence, and a time to speak;
A time to love, and a time to hate;
A time for war, and a time for peace.

This chapter of *Ecclesiastes* starts with the sentence: "For everything there is a season, and a time for every matter under heaven."

The time for peace is now.

Noam Chomsky, a professor of linguistics at MIT, is America's best-known dissident intellectual. Born in 1928 to Russian-Jewish immigrants, Chomsky was raised in Philadelphia. While attending the University of Pennsylvania, he joined a left-wing Zionist group that favored the creation of a binational state in Palestine based on unity among Arab and Jewish workers. Since the 1960s, when he emerged as a leading opponent of the Vietnam War through his writings in The New York Review of Books, *Chomsky has established himself as a powerful critic of American foreign policy, and of Western imperialism. Never one to shy away from controversy, Chomsky has devoted several books, notably* The Fateful Triangle, *to the Israeli-Palestinian tragedy, cutting ferociously through the clichés that have permeated America's conversation about the Middle East. This essay, "Israel and the Palestinians," was written in 1975, at a time when many American liberals described Israel's occupation as "benign," and when the word "Palestinian" was itself taboo in some quarters. Infused with Chomsky's lifelong commitment to Arab-Jewish coexistence, "Israel and the Palestinians" offers a trenchant historical analysis of the origins of the conflict, of the dynamics of occupation, and of the contradictions of "Jewish democracy."*

ISRAEL AND THE PALESTINIANS

Noam Chomsky

From *Towards a New Cold War* (1975)

One land—two nations: That is the essence of the problem of Israel and the Palestinians. To be sure, the problem has always had regional and international dimensions. Given the strategic and economic importance of the region, great-power intervention has always been a decisive factor in determining the course of events. If the local problem of two claimants to the same territory is not amicably resolved, then a settlement will be imposed by external force, with no regard for the needs and interests of Israeli Jews or Palestinian Arabs. It is not out of the question that the present course will lead to the national destruction of both groups.

Proponents of each of the national movements are quick to dismiss the competing claims. I will not review the familar debate. It is a simple and pointless exercise to construct an argument to demonstrate the legitimacy of the claims of either side and the insignificance of the demands of its opponent. Each argument is convincing in its own terms. Each claim is, in a sense, absolute: a plea for national survival. Those who urge the demands of one or the other partner in this deadly dance, deaf to conflicting pleas, merely help pave the way to an eventual catastrophe. Such behavior is pathetic on the part of direct participants; disgraceful, on the part of those partisans from afar who will not have to pay the costs of their fanaticism. One may recall Chaim Weizmann's rebuke to American Zionists for urging "other people to the barricades to face tanks and guns"—"the speeches are made in New York," Weizmann added, "while the proposed resistance is to be made in Tel Aviv and Jerusalem." The same might be said—and probably has been—by Palestinians with regard to those who urge them on towards self-destruction.

Like it or not, there is little doubt that participants in the local conflict will continue to identify themselves as Jews and Arabs and to
demand self-government and national institutions. On this assumption, which surely seems realistic, any thought of a unitary democratic
secular state in Mandatory Palestine is an exercise in futility. It is
curious that this goal is advocated in some form by the most extreme
antagonists: the Palestine Liberation Organization (PLO) and expansionist elements within Israel. But the documents of the former indicate that what they have in mind is an Arab state that will grant civil
rights to Jews, and the pronouncements of the advocates of a Greater
Israel leave little doubt that their thoughts run along parallel lines,
interchanging "Jew" and "Arab." These are, in fact, charitable interpretations, in both cases.

The Current Situation
As I write (November 1974), prospects are gloomy. The conference of
Arab states at Rabat has designated the PLO as the sole legitimate representative of the Palestinians. The United Nations has in effect
endorsed this position. The government of Israel refuses adamantly to
deal with the PLO. As long as this impasse persists, the probability of
war is appreciable. As critics of Israeli government policy have been
warning, Israel has now backed itself into a corner, facing almost complete diplomatic isolation, committed to policies that can only be
implemented at the grave risk of war, hence the risk of eventual
destruction of a state that can lose only once and that can never finally
defeat its adversaries.

What is the likelihood of a change in the Israeli attitude towards the
Palestinians and their organizations? The official Israeli government
position, as presented in a "Decision of the Government of Israel," July
21, 1974, is the following:

> The Government will work towards negotiations for a peace
> agreement with Jordan. The peace will be founded on the exis-
> tence of two independent States only—Israel, with united
> Jerusalem as its capital, and a Jordanian-Palestinian Arab State,
> east of Israel, within borders to be determined in negotiations
> between Israel and Jordan. In this State, the independent identity

of the Jordanian and Palestinian Arabs can find expression in peace and good neighbourliness with Israel.

This position was reaffirmed by Foreign Minister Yigal Allon in October 1974 before the U.N. There is, he affirmed, a problem of "Palestinian identity," but it "can and should be solved in the context of the settlement of the dispute" between Israel and Jordan, which is "already the national home of the Palestinians." The PLO, Prime Minister Yitzhak Rabin asserts, is not the legitimate representative of the Palestinians, "since nobody has elected them." The government and American Zionists generally insist that the PLO cannot claim to speak for the Palestinians in the "administered territories" of the West Bank ("Judea and Samaria," in Israeli parlance) and the Gaza Strip. At the same time, Israel refuses to permit independent political organization or free political expression in the occupied territories, and the repression of the past years has been sharply intensified under the present Rabin government. The reason for the repression is simple: Any relaxation leads to the expression of pro-PLO sentiments. The contradiction is complete, and the impasse, total.

These policies have wide support within Israel. Thus, a leading dove, Arie Eliav, publicly opposes a Palestinian state "in the administered areas separate from the state of Jordan," and advocates instead some kind of partition of the West Bank and Gaza Strip between Israel and Jordan, optimally with "Israeli supervision or joint supervision by the two states" over these territories.

Meanwhile, Israeli settlement in the occupied territories continues, again with substantial popular support. In a recent poll, 71 percent approved of settlement in "Judea and Samaria" if initiated by the government, with less than 14 percent opposed. Every move in this direction is a step towards war.

Only marginal political groups in Israel have been calling for withdrawal from the occupied territories, which now plainly entails recognition of the PLO. State policy, particularly since 1970, has been moving towards integration of the territories. A program of virtual annexation was presented by the governing Labor party in its August 1973 electoral program. After the October war, the program was modified, but these plans will be reinstituted if the only alternative is to deal with the Palestinians.

Of course, these policies can be pursued only with U.S. backing. As of mid-1970, American policy was expressed in the Rogers Plan, which called for Israeli withdrawal in the context of a peace settlement. This proposal was abandoned by the United States as Henry Kissinger took over control of American policy towards the Middle East in 1970, instituting what should no doubt be called the "Kissinger Plan": tacit support for *de facto* Israeli annexation of the territories. Given the widely held belief that Israel's military and technological predominance was unchallengeable in the foreseeable future, the Kissinger Plan made a certain amount of sense, putting aside its characteristic cynicism and the equally characteristic blindness to longer-term historical tendencies, even though it did maximize the risk of war. The assumptions, however, were proven false by the October 1973 war. With the collapse of Kissinger's policies in October, the United States began a slow return towards something like the abandoned Rogers Plan, but this process depends on developments within the Arab world that are presently quite difficult to assess.

The program of *de facto* annexation raised with particular urgency what is called in Israel the "demographic problem," that is, the problem posed by the existence of Arabs in a Jewish state. There are only two ways for a Jewish state to become a functioning democracy: by restricting the "Jewishness" of the state to mere symbolism, or by guaranteeing that all citizens are Jews. The prospects for the former seem slight, a matter to which I will return. Those who believe otherwise might well embrace the official PLO slogan of democratic secularism. The alternative policy, namely, guaranteeing that citizens are Jews, can be achieved only by a program of expulsion. Then, indeed, Israel will be Jewish in the way that England is English, in accordance with a traditional Zionist slogan. " Under the U.S.-Israeli program of *de facto* annexation, the demographic problem could no longer be swept under the rug, since the "Jewish state" would soon have a population of Arabs approaching 50 percent. The Gaza Strip alone would double the Arab population of Israel, and Israeli officials have repeatedly insisted that this region will remain part of Israel under any peace settlement, a position that provokes little dispute within the political mainstream. As for the future borders of the Jewish state, it is also agreed with near unanimity in Israel that the Golan Heights will be

retained under any settlement, and Rabin has stated that Jewish settlement in the Jordan Valley is based "on the premise that the settlements
being established will remain included within our rule." In the region
west of Gaza, "new settlement outposts [are] planned for settling the
Rafah approaches between Yamit and Beersheva," and it is generally
agreed that the border with Egypt must be removed from the Gaza
Strip. Hence the "demographic problem" is severe.

Various solutions to the dilemma have been proposed. The current
(1974) premier, Yitzhak Rabin of the Labor party, has occasionally
been quoted in the press on this issue:

> I would like to create in the course of the next 10 to 20 years
> conditions which would attract natural and voluntary migration
> of the refugees from the Gaza Strip and the West Bank to East
> Jordan. To achieve this we have to come to agreement with King
> Hussein and not with Yasser Arafat.

Elsewhere, Rabin has explained his current views as follows:

> We must solve the problem in a form that will permit the Pales-
> tinians, if such is their wish, to have a voice—but only in the
> framework of a Jordanian-Palestinian state. I do not believe that
> there is a place for a third state between Israel and Jordan. *There
> is a need for a place to which it will be possible to transfer the quarter-
> million refugees who live in crowded conditions in the Gaza Strip.*
> This place cannot be other than Jordan, the one state in which
> Palestinians were absorbed in the society, to such a degree that
> they constitute half the government officials in Jordan.

Rabin had expressed similar ideas before he became prime minister.
In a symposium of Israeli ex-chiefs of staff, he proposed "to make such
conditions that during the next ten years, there would be a natural
shifting of population to the East Bank" of the Jordan. There should be
"a minimum of refugees in the West Bank" and "the problem of the
refugees of the Gaza Strip should not be solved in Gaza or in El-Arish,
but mainly in the East Bank."

Rabin is regarded as a dove. When his government was formed,

Moshe Dayan was appalled, saying that "not in my worst dreams" could he have imagined such a cabinet. Actually, Dayan's view of the matter is not very different. He urges that Israel should not annex the occupied territories but should nevertheless encourage Jewish settlement freely in them and maintain military control over them. In his view, "Judea and Samaria" are part of the Jewish homeland and Israel should insist on the right of permanent Jewish settlement everywhere on the West Bank and the right to maintain military bases as required throughout this region. In the same Knesset speech in which he outlined this program, Dayan went on to say that as for the refugees, "the Arab states now have land and water and also funds and Arab nationhood, and with all of this they can solve the refugee problem in their lands." With minor variations, this is in fact the standard position, and is commonly expressed in the United States as well. Though American Zionists are naturally displeased with the analogy, the fact remains that this position is analogous to that of extremist Arab nationalists who urge that European Jews should be resettled in Europe, where there are many European states and ample resources.

The long-range hope that somehow the Arabs will move away is no doubt one factor in the refusal by the government or much of the left-liberal opposition to contemplate a Palestinian state. A West Bank mini-state could not absorb the Arabs of Gaza along with refugees elsewhere. A Jordan-Palestine of the Rabin-Eliav variety might well absorb the Palestinians of most of the West Bank and elsewhere, under the guise of settlement in their former homeland of Palestine, leaving the occupied territories effectively under Israeli control.

It appears that the Golda Meir government actually made concrete proposals to Jordan in secret meetings, offering to permit Jordanian officials to conduct civil administration in parts of the West Bank under Israeli military occupation. The West Bank Palestinians would have become Jordanian citizens, though the area would have remained under Israeli military control, and, presumably, Jewish settlement could also proceed. Hussein's rule could only be imposed by force, as is generally recognized. Commenting on these secret proposals, Reserve-General Mattityahu Peled remarks that "even the worst of the European imperialist powers never reached such a degree of cynicism," namely, to abandon any responsibility for subject populations while maintaining military control over them—and in this case, we may add, guaranteeing the right of settlement by civilians of the dominant military power who claim "historic rights" to the territory in question. Peled's comments are overly harsh; European imperialism is guilty of far worse. But his dismay over these plans is understandable. He adds, realistically, that Egypt will not accept such an outcome, so that this policy, apart from its moral premises, increases the likelihood of future war.

The idea of inducing Palestinian Arabs to leave has often been expressed, in one or another form, in internal Zionist discussion over the years; it is, indeed, implicit in the concept of a democratic Jewish state. One of the founders of the socialist movement in the Palestinian *Yishuv*, Berl Katznelson—who elsewhere advocated binationalism and warned that Jews would betray the Zionist ideal if they sought a Jewish state in which they would be the Poles and Arabs would be the Jews— had this to say on one occasion:

> The matter of transfer of population raises a dispute among us: permitted or forbidden. My conscience is completely silent on this matter: a distant neighbor is better than a nearby enemy. They will not lose by their transfer and we will surely not. In the final analysis, this is a political resettlement reform for the benefit of the two sides. For a long time I have thought that this is the best solution, and in the days of the riots I was confirmed in my recognition that this result must come about some day. However, it did not occur to me that the transfer "outside of the Land of Israel" means to the neighborhood of Shechem [on the West Bank]. I believed, and I still believe that they must ultimately move to Syria and Iraq.

Similar thoughts were harbored privately by other socialist Zionists. Joseph Weitz, who was director of the Jewish National Fund Land and Afforestation Division and one of those responsible for the "outpost settlements" that helped determine the partition boundaries," wrote recently in *Davar* that in his diaries of 1940 he had recognized that "there is no room in this country for both peoples" so that the only solution is complete "transfer" of all Arabs at least from west of the

Jordan. American Zionists also view this prospect with equanimity, while insisting that the historical injustice resulting from the population transfer undertaken by imperial Rome two thousand years ago must be rectified. Thus, democratic socialist Michael Walzer observes with reference to Israel that "nation building in new states is sure to be rough on groups marginal to the nation," and sometimes "the roughness can only be smoothed . . . by helping people to leave who have to leave" even if these groups "marginal to the nation" have been deeply rooted in the country for hundreds of years, and constituted the overwhelming majority not many years ago. Walzer's point must surely be conceded, though he does not formulate it with sufficient clarity. If Israel is to be both a democratic state and a Jewish state, then non-Jews must be expelled, unless there is an evolution towards democratic secularism for which, at the moment, there are no indications and no substantial support.

Similar concepts are implicit, occasionally, even in the writings of Israeli civil libertarians. In an eloquent condemnation of the new tendency in Israel to dismiss "the humanist philosophy of the Gentiles" in favor of an allegedly "Jewish" commitment to the superior rights of the nation, Knesset member Shulamit Aloni protested against those who settled illegally in "Judea and Samaria," pretending that they will grant equal rights to a million Arabs in Greater Israel. She argues that equal rights cannot be granted "in the framework of a binational state," offering recent events in Cyprus as a proof:

> The failure in Cyprus is not that of the United Nations. It is a failure of the binational state idea. We should remember that the proportion of Turks in Cyprus compared to the Greeks is smaller than that of the Arabs in the Land of Israel compared to the Jews.

Accepting, for the sake of argument, Aloni's interpretation of the facts, consider the implications of these remarks. Note first that Cyprus could hardly be called a binational state. Rather, it resembled Israel today more than a hypothetical binational state, with a Turkish minority of about the same proportions as the Arabs of pre-1967 Israel. If this idea has failed, as Aloni argues, and the only alternative is the *de facto* partition and "population exchange" that took place in Cyprus after the Greek officers' coup and the Turkish invasion, then it would seem to follow that the Arabs of Israel should be expelled (or "exchanged") after the establishment of an Arab state "East of Israel," including "parts of Judea and Samaria," as Aloni proposes. While she nowhere advocates such "population transfer," it would appear to be implicit in her analysis.

Others are more explicit. Hagi Eshed, writing in the Labor party journal *Davar*, describes the establishment of a Palestinian state organized by the PLO as such a grave danger that "we cannot disqualify in advance nor reject outright any means or feasible solutions aimed at preventing this danger." He adds:

> In this context the idea of a population transfer has emerged, an idea that had not been totally rejected by Berl Katznelson nor even the British Labor Party. . . . Perhaps we cannot avoid raising anew the feasibility of transferring part of the refugees and even the permanent settlers of Judea, Samaria and Gaza to Jordan. Such a possibility will certainly arise if Jordan joins a war against Israel. It may be one of the possible outcomes of the renewal of war.

Israel will, very likely, now attempt to create a Quisling leadership on the West Bank and to hold on to what territories it can, in the hope that sooner or later the occupation will be accepted, or, at worst, the failure of other methods for recovering the occupied territories will impel the Arab states to accept the Israeli-Jordanian solution. At the Rabat conference, Hussein "complained that the United States plan called for the reestablishment of Jordanian administration in certain parts of the West Bank with the area remaining under Israeli military control"—the Israeli plan mentioned earlier. While the Rabat conference has undercut such plans for the moment, the longer-term possibility cannot be completely discounted. Again it must be stressed that even if successfully implemented, such a program could only delay the next major war, and would maintain the situation of economic crisis in an Israel that is forced to devote enormous resources to military preparation against adversaries of limitless wealth.

These are the likely prospects as long as U.S. support for Israeli annexation continues. This support will probably continue, if the Arab oil producers do not pressure the United States to compel Israel to withdraw to its pre-June 1967 borders. Whether they will do so depends on nationalist forces within the Arab world: the threat of "Qaddafist" coups by nationalist officers, popular unrest, and other obscure factors. The situation is complex, since Saudi Arabia, always the central concern of U.S. policy in the region, has an indirect stake in Israeli power, which stands as a barrier to radical Arab nationalism and Russian influence. There are strange alliances in the Middle East. Saudi Arabia has no love for Iran, but is happy to have Iranian forces engaged in counterinsurgency on its borders in Dhofar. A tacit alliance between Israel, Iran, and Saudi Arabia—overt, between Israel and Iran—with Turkey in the background, is a real possibility, in the framework of a Pax Americana.

Despite this possibility, pressure on the United States is likely, and despite much saber-rattling in the American press, it will probably be effective. At this point, Israel would have two options: to yield, or to go to war in the hope of achieving a quick victory and perhaps provoking a superpower confrontation that would again cement the Israeli-American alliance. The latter option might be chosen, despite the enormous risks, if Israel senses that there is some support for it in the United States. A respectful hearing is given in Israel to American political analysts who strongly imply that Israel will receive American backing if it takes a hard line. While such urgings are the height of irresponsibility, they may have their effect.

Suppose that the United States does impose a settlement by force, compelling Israel to return to the pre-1967 borders with the safeguards, such as they are, outlined in the U.N. resolutions and the Rogers Plan. If Israel accepts this outcome, a Palestinian entity of some sort will be established, organized by the PLO. The result will probably be a kind of "Latin Americanization" of the region, with a network of hostile states, dependent on the United States, and highly susceptible to reactionary forces within under conditions of tension and resentment.

For Israel, this arrangement is surely far less dangerous than the annexationist programs advocated by both major political groupings and supported virtually without question by American Zionists. Though these groups base their public opposition to a Palestinian entity on grounds of security, this argument can hardly be taken seriously. The problems for Israel lie elsewhere. For one thing, it would be necessary to abandon the hope for integration of substantial parts of the occupied territories within Israel, with the concomitant program of "population transfer" discussed earlier. Furthermore, Israel would suffer a severe loss of élan and the situation might revert to the depressed conditions of 1966. A further consequence might well be an increase in emigration, as in 1966, and redirection of the Russian Jewish emigration, if it continues, towards the West, which is not likely to be delighted with the prospect. All of this stirs ugly memories from the 1930s and the war years, when the United States was pleased to have Jewish refugees from Nazism go to Palestine, but was unwilling to absorb them here, even preventing refugees from landing in the United States, in one notorious case, though they had postdated U.S. visas.

A Two-State Solution
Two states west of the Jordan, one Jewish, one Palestinian: That would be a possible outcome of the conflict of claims to the same territory. The original General Assembly resolution of 1947 was based on this principle, but much has changed since, including the potential boundaries of the two states. The Palestinian state would be a pale reflection of what was contemplated at Lake Success. It is possible to build a case, as is commonly done in the United States, that these changes result solely from Arab intransigence, but the essential facts are in reality considerably more complex. Putting interpretation of the history aside, it is possible to imagine a stable two-state settlement west of the Jordan, essentially with the pre-1967 borders.

Such an arrangement would very likely satisfy the Arab oil producers, since the threat of radical Palestinian nationalism would be contained. It is unlikely that Syria or Egypt would raise problems once their territories are recovered. The arrangement would also satisfy the primary concerns of U.S. foreign policy: to ensure that other industrial societies do not gain independent access to the vast energy resources of the Middle East. The Soviet Union understands very well that the United States will not tolerate a challenge to its domination of the region. And the other potential rivals of the United States are in no position to undertake a challenge to American hegemony.

For Israel, it would be preferable for a settlement of this sort to be achieved through negotiations, but that is impossible as long as Israel refuses to deal with the PLO and regards its primary negotiating partner as the United States, and as long as the PLO takes its minimal negotiating position to be the elimination of Israel. A solution imposed by imperial force is hardly to be welcomed, but it is not easy to conjure up a preferable and feasible alternative. It appears that some segments of the Israeli left privately hope for such an outcome, as the least intolerable, under present circumstances.

A Palestinian state will be subordinated to Israel and Jordan, which will be allied to ensure that it has limited scope for development or independence. It can expect little assistance from the wealthy Arab states. The PLO should be no less able than other national movements to produce a group of leaders who can adapt themselves to this situation. The West Bank and Gaza Strip might continue to provide Israel with a reservoir of cheap labor, as has been the case since 1967. It is likely that a Palestinian state will be a mirror-image of Israel: an Arab state, based on discriminatory principles much like those of its counterpart, possibly exaggerated in a state founded on despair and subservience to its neighbors. Both states, one must expect, will be based on the principle of denial of rights to citizens of the wrong category. One can expect nothing else of a Jewish state or an Arab state, just as we would know what to expect of a white state or a Catholic state. The seeds of conflict will remain. This kind of Balkanization might well satisfy American imperial interests as well as the interests of the Arab states, which will be happy to have an end to Palestinian revolutionary rhetoric. The most important long-term consequence of the Rabat decision, from the point of view of the Arab states, may be that Palestinian energy will be directed towards a little region contained within a Jordanian-Israeli alliance, posing no further threat to ruling circles elsewhere. The outcome will be a painful one for Jews and Palestinians, but, as noted at the outset, it has always been likely that if they are unable to settle their local conflict, external force will sooner or later be applied to resolve it for them in a way that has little relation to their needs and interests.

Myths and Reality
Conceivably, if tensions reduce in the region, the Jewish and Palestinian

states might begin to dismantle discriminatory structures. Moves in this direction would require changes in popular attitudes and aspirations; not to speak of institutional structures, that would be virtually revolutionary. This may seem a harsh and unfair judgment, but I think that recent history tends to support it. The PLO exercises sovereignty nowhere. Thus one can only speculate about the meaning of its programs and their likely realization. But the State of Israel has existed for more than twenty-five years. From its experience, we can learn a good deal about the problems of a multinational society committed in theory to democracy. At least this is so, if we are willing to attend to the facts.

One fact is that for Israeli Jews, standards of freedom and democratic rights are easily on a par with those realized elsewhere. At the same time, Israel is a Jewish state with non-Jewish residents, some of them citizens, others stateless. Israel regards itself and is generally described as a Western-style democracy, but this characterization is misleading. In fact, the state is based on a fundamental and so far irresoluble contradiction. There is a commitment to democracy, but it is unrealizable, because the "Jewishness" of the Jewish state is no mere matter of symbolism but is built into the institutional structure and ideology in a fundamental manner and is subject to little internal challenge or debate. Only confusion can result from failure to perceive that Israel is not based on the model (however imperfectly realized) of the Western democracies.

Illusions about this question are most striking in the writings of left-liberal American Zionists. Michael Walzer, a Harvard University historian and political scientist, is one of the few to have tried to deal with, the issue. He writes that a democratic secular state "already exists in substance" in the former Palestine, namely, the State of Israel. Hence there is no merit in the propaganda of the Palestinian organizations that demand the establishment of a democratic secular state. True, the "power of Orthodox Jews" is greater than it should be. But apart from this, Walzer perceives no departure from democratic principle in the State of Israel. No problems of principle arise, in his view, as a result of the fact that the state is a Jewish state.

Walzer's efforts to evade the obvious give a certain insight into the intellectual level of left-liberal American Zionism. Evidently, if Israel is a Jewish state with non-Jewish citizens, then the respects in which the state is "Jewish" will be respects in which non-Jews are denied equal rights. Evidently, democratic principle is violated when a state discriminates between two categories of citizens, the severity of the violation depending on the nature of the discrimination (insignificant, in this case, if the "Jewishness" of the state is a matter of symbolism, and correspondingly important if it is not). Walzer claims to find these truisms "unintelligible." He counters with the following analogy. Suppose that Indonesia discriminates against Chinese. Then, he asks, would it be proper to say that Indonesia "is Indonesian in that respect, and therefore undemocratic"? Obviously, he continues, this would be an absurd conclusion; we would say that Indonesia is undemocratic in these respects, but not by virtue of its being an "Indonesian state." Therefore, Walzer concludes, my observations on the discriminatory character of a Jewish state must reflect an opposition to "the nationhood of the Jews (but of no one else)."

Walzer's reasoning is remarkable. Evidently, the appropriate analogy would pair Israel-Indonesia, Jewish-Malayan, Arab-Chinese. Correcting for Walzer's gross error in reasoning, suppose that Indonesia were to define itself as a "Malayan state," and were then to subject non-Malayans to repression or otherwise discriminate between Malayans and Chinese to the advantage of the former. Would we then say that *Indonesia is Malayan in these respects and therefore undemocratic,* by virtue of its being a "Malayan state" (the italicized phrase being the corrected version of Walzer's analogy)? The answer is obviously: Yes, we would, and we would sharply criticize the notion of a "Malayan state" with non-Malayan citizens as violating fundamental principles of democracy. These points are so elementary that it is quite remarkable that it is necessary to spell them out in such detail. These truisms are intolerable to left-liberal American Zionists such as Walzer, who therefore seek to create a complex web of error and falsification in an effort to obscure the plain facts and crucial principles.

To take another case, consider the discussion of Israeli democracy by Carl Cohen, a philosopher who has dealt extensively with problems of democracy. He arrives at conclusions quite similar to Walzer's. He sees the Israeli record as "remarkably good," despite the trying circumstances. In his view, in Israel all citizens are full participants with equal rights regardless of national affiliation:

Ugly terrorism, in the very bosom of daily life, has not resulted in the deprivation of rights to non-Jewish minorities. Indeed the continuing participation of Arab and other minorities in the life of the Israeli community—in local and national government, in economic and cultural activities—is a tribute not only to the self-control of the Israeli Jews but to the evident loyalty of Israelis of all religions and backgrounds. That loyalty has rendered suppression unthinkable.

There have been certain abuses of due process, Cohen notes, and instances of discrimination "in some social circles, in some fields of employment, in some housing developments." And "handling of suspected or known terrorists, infiltrators" has sometimes not been above reproach. But the "pluralistic ideal" is remarkably close to achievement. As for the Israeli Arabs, the largest ethnic minority, "Full civil rights—personal, political and economic—are theirs. . . . With respect to *rights*, in theory and in practice, the Arab minority is well protected." The ideal of democracy, with equal rights for all, "is an ideal seriously pursued, and it is, in fact, realized to a degree of which we Americans, who befriend and support Israel, may be proud."

Such observations can easily be multiplied. Like many other commentators, Walzer and Cohen never ask how it is possible for a state founded on the principle of Jewish dominance to be a democracy with equal rights for all regardless of national affiliation. They merely avoid the contradiction, following the traditional pattern of self-deception of those Zionists who spoke of a state that would be as Jewish as England is English. That sounds fair enough, until we realize that citizens of England and their offspring are English, whereas citizens of the Jewish state (or children born there) are not Jewish, unless the Orthodox rabbinate so determines.

Israeli liberals also tend to ignore the dilemma. The dean of the Tel Aviv University Law School, Amnon Rubinstein, describing the program of his new political grouping *Shinui* (Change), states that: "We want to bridge the gap between the two communities in Israel—the Ashkenazim [European Jews] and the Eastern Jews." There is, however, a third community in Israel: non-Jews, approximately 15 percent of the population apart from the occupied territories. It is striking, and characteristic, that their status is simply ignored.

Walzer and Cohen present no serious supporting evidence; thus it is impossible to know how they arrive at their conclusions. To test these, conclusions, it would be necessary to consider factual analyses or to hear what the Arabs have to say—their testimony on the matter of Arab rights is likely to be more illuminating than the unsupported opinions of American Zionists. Neither course is very easy to pursue. As one liberal American Zionist points out in a study of Israeli society, "Unhappily, social scientists have devoted little attention to the Arabs in Israel." He goes on to point out, correctly, that this is a symptom of a more general problem, that there is really no place for Arabs in the Jewish state: "The very powerful ethic of equal opportunity and full political equality must compete against the equally powerful ethic of a Jewish State." And the fact is that the latter wins, hands down. Critical Zionist analysts of Israeli society who are not social scientists also tend to ignore the Arab minority. It is, again, characteristic that a highly regarded study entitled *The Israelis* should have nothing to say about those Israelis who belong to the one-seventh of the population that is not Jewish. There are a few studies of the Israeli Arabs by Zionist scholars, but they are of little value, and largely ignore the serious issues that dominate the reports and studies produced by Israeli Arabs themselves.

As for writings by Arabs in Israel or expressions of popular opinion, these too are scanty. Contrary to the claims of American Zionists, these voices have been effectively stilled. Arab intellectuals have been heavily censored, repressed, subjected to "administrative detention" or house arrest, or compelled to leave the country. It is remarkable that American civil libertarians have defended these practices, or denied the facts. The most extensive discussion to date of the status of Arabs in Israel is in the work of Sabri Jiryis, an Israeli Arab lawyer who was confined under detention and house arrest for over a year without charge and now lives in Beirut. The picture he presents differs radically from the commentaries by left-liberal American Zionists. He gives a detailed analysis of the suppression of civil rights of Arabs, their dispossession through expropriation in the 1950S, the blocking of efforts at independent political expression, the tight controls exercised over the Israeli Arab intelligentsia, the continued application of the British

Mandatory laws, and so on. Jiryis relies primarily on Israeli sources, including court records. As far as I can determine, his account is quite accurate. Similarly, Fouzi el-Asmar, the "terrorist commander" of Dershowitz's inflamed imagination, now residing in the United States, has given a detailed account of the means used to expropriate Arabs, again relying on Israeli sources. But one would have some difficulty in locating his work or the sources on which it is based, or in fact any serious treatment of the issue, in the extensive English language literature on this subject.

Reports by Israeli Arab intellectuals who are sympathetic to Israel are not entirely lacking. After a visit to Arab villages and towns in 1966, Elias Tuma, an Arab citizen of Israel until 1969, wrote that the Arabs live "in a state of disorganization, distrust, and despair," particularly the younger generation. Arabs have given up farming and taken up wage-labor in Jewish enterprises, not from choice, but because of government land policies. "The grievances I heard against the land policy had no end." The general feeling was "that the government was pursuing policies that would ultimately lead to their destruction as farmers." Charges included expropriation, refusal to grant building permits on land reserved for future Jewish settlement, state-imposed price differentials for agricultural products that support Jewish production while barely covering production costs for Arabs, and so on. "The people are convinced that the government had bad intentions toward their land and was doing all it could to expropriate them by what might seem like legal procedures." Most of Tuma's information comes from discussions with workers and the self-employed. "Teachers, social workers, and white-collar employees refrained from talking unless I managed to see each one separately." They sympathized with the complaints, but were afraid to talk for fear that the numerous government informers would report what they say to the military authorities. "Those who held salaried jobs thought it wiser to be silent if they wanted to keep their jobs."

Jewish friends, Tuma reports, have little reaction to these facts. He quotes one "high-ranking official": "This is the way things are. We are in a democracy, and the minority must obey the majority. They are living better than do the Arabs under Nasser. If they do not like us, let them get out." Since assimilation is ruled out—intermarriage is illegal, and reportedly Arabs are not even permitted to take Jewish names—Tuma expects either demoralization of the Arab community or, conceivably, a violent insurrection. I stress again that these are the views of an Arab intellectual who is by no means hostile towards Israel.

Jerusalem is often put forth as the prime example of how Arabs thrive under Israeli rule. The few reports available in the West raise numerous questions about this success, even apart from the recent rioting in East Jerusalem in support of the PLO. Government programs make explicit the goal of preserving the "Jewish character" of Jerusalem through segregated housing development, overwhelmingly for Jews. In the latest elections (December 1973), most Arabs refused to participate. Reporting from Jerusalem, Henry Kamm observed that "many here feel that Arabs who vote are either municipal employees protecting their jobs or merchants requiring licenses or permits, or poor people responding to political bribes." Others reacted on the principle that the election "is not ours. It's against our will." The election was denounced in the Jerusalem Arab press, but editorials taking this position were blocked by Israeli censorship.

Another American reporter observes that "there is little social interaction" and "feelings of resentment can be heard." One Arab commented: "The problem is that Jews do not treat us as equals. I cannot go and stay overnight in the new part of Jerusalem, for instance," because of the official segregation. An Arab shopkeeper added:

> The Jews are still my friends and they are good to me. But the main thing is to have equality. I can't sell my business to an Arab—only to a Jew. An Arab can't go into the new town and buy a business there but a Jewish merchant can buy here. There should be equality and we should be friends. Then if old Jerusalem is under Israel that's fine.

Unfortunately, there is to be no equality. Opposition within Israel to the discriminatory structures that guarantee Jewish dominance is minimal. There is no tendency in this direction, so far as I can discern.

Recall again Cohen's report of the intense loyalty of Israeli Arabs to the state, which "has rendered suppression unthinkable," and which results from the fact that "full civil rights . . . are theirs."

There are a few relevant studies in Israeli sources. In one analysis, based on actual research, not mere impression or faith, Ian Lustick argues that "the widening socio-economic gaps between Arabs and Jews" result from the "separation of Arabs from the institutions of power in Israeli society"; since the roots of the problem "lie in the parochial character of Israel's most basic institutions and the differential consequences of their operation for the Jewish and Arab sectors," the problem will not be resolved and may only be aggravated by a peace settlement. In his factual analysis of the issues, he describes "the anger which flows from these perceptions" of the lack of "the full rights that should accrue to [Arabs] as law-abiding Israeli citizens." These rights are defined "in terms of land expropriated for use by Jewish settlements, electricity, roads, and water supplied free to Jews and at enormous expense to Arabs, the failure of the government to establish industry in the Arab sector, and the inability of Arab university graduates to secure employment outside of the teaching profession."

While Cohen's description is far closer to the norm, such facts as are available indicate that Lustick's is far closer to the truth. It is because they comprehend very well the fundamental discriminatory institutions and practices of the Jewish state, Lustick argues plausibly, that Arabs have flocked to the Communist party (Rakah)—a phenomenon that would be difficult to explain if Cohen's account had any relation to the facts.

Lustick's study is particularly valuable in that it exhibits some of the means by which Jewish dominance is maintained. He studied one device that has proven very effective, namely, reliance on the Jewish Agency for agricultural development. This quasi-governmental body supplies electricity, paves roads, and "assumes responsibility for the supply of all basic services and housing as well as the capital base for whatever industry or agricultural development is to take place." More than $1.2 billion has been spent by the Jewish Agency on the development of Jewish agricultural settlements since 1948. Through this device, a "tremendous gap in capital inflow" exists between the Arab and Jewish sectors, which "helps explain not only the gap in living standards between Jews and Arabs . . . but also the gap in means of production." While all Jewish villages have electricity, only about half of the Arab villages do. Economic development in the Arab sector is so low that "nearly 90% of Arab village working men must travel each day to and from Jewish towns and cities in order to find employment." Furthermore, "Arabs are concentrated in low paying, low skilled jobs, whereas Jews occupy the higher status and higher paid administrative and white collar positions," and it seems that "these developmental gaps, in terms of job distribution, are widening rather than closing." What is important, in the present connection, is "the role which Israel's major political, economic, and governmental institutions play in maintaining this fundamental inequality"—exactly as a rational observer would expect in a Jewish state with non-Jewish citizens. No doubt this lies behind the anger of Israeli Arabs described by objective Zionist observers, and the demoralization reported by Arab intellectuals.

Official statistics naturally require interpretation, but *prima facie*, they appear to reflect the policy of fostering inequality. Thus in 1973, of 1,815 dunams of cultivated area under irrigation, 1,753 were "Jewish farms" and 62 "non-Jewish farms." The Arab population doubled from 1960 to—1972, but cultivated area of "non-Jewish farms" dropped by about 12 percent from the near-peak year 1960–61 to 1972–73, as Arab farmers moved—hardly by choice, it appears—to other occupations, primarily construction labor.

The grievances against the land policies noted by Tuma and others are easy to understand. In the first decade after the establishment of the state, about 1 million dunams of land were expropriated for Jewish use, through a complicated series of legal and extralegal maneuvers. The process continued in the 1960s under such programs as the "Judaization of the Galilee," the most notorious example being the expropriation of lands of Arab villages for establishment of the all-Jewish city of Karmiel; the land was originally set aside for a military reservation, and local Arabs, who sensed what was coming, were officially assured at that time that there was "no basis" for their fears that this—was a preliminary step towards confiscation. After the 1967 war, similar operations were conducted in the occupied territories. They continue now. According to a document submitted to the government by the Mapam party, written largely by members of kibbutzim in the western Negev, in the region southwest of the Gaza Strip about 30,000 dunams were expropriated in 1969 from "Bedouins" (who, incidentally, describe themselves as farmers), and another 120,000 in January

1972, with 6,000 Bedouins evacuated. So far, there has been no new land or housing provided for those evacuated, and the document reports a plan to extend the program to an area of a million to a million and a half dunams entailing the deportation of about 20,000 farmers from all the agricultural land. Again, the alleged grounds are "security."

In the absence of comprehensive studies utilizing official documents and interviews with those directly involved, only parts of the story can be pieced together from reports that have appeared randomly and accidentally, as in the case just mentioned, where neighboring kibbutzim protested. The legal basis for the various programs is often obscure. The example that Lustick discusses—namely, reliance on a quasi-governmental body that carries out development and settlement programs only for Jews—is perhaps typical.

An interesting case is the system of land laws of the state. Prior to the establishment of the State of Israel, land was purchased on behalf of the Jewish people by the Keren Kayemeth Leisrael (Jewish National Fund; henceforth, JNF). The JNF was established "for the purpose of settling Jews on such lands" as were acquired, "to make any donations . . . likely to promote the interests of Jews," "to make advances to any Jews in the prescribed region," to use charitable funds in ways which "shall in the opinion of the Association be directly or indirectly beneficial to persons of Jewish religion, race or origin." The JNF is now "a public institution recognized by the Government of Israel and the World Zionist organization as the exclusive instrument for the development of Israel lands." Its earlier principles remain in force, under this new official status. The JNF is "a Company under Jewish control . . . engaged in the settlement of Jews" and promoting such settlement. Lands owned by the JNF are exclusively for Jewish use, in perpetuity. These lands "shall not be transferred either by sale or in any other manner." Furthermore, non-Jewish labor cannot be employed on these lands.

Prior to 1948, the JNF was a private self-help organization of a national group. It is now an official agency of the state. Its exclusivist principles have simply been absorbed as one element of the official policy of Jewish dominance in a Jewish state.

Under a covenant signed between the State of Israel and the JNF in 1961, the JNF undertook to establish a Land Development Administration and to appoint its director, "who shall be subordinate" to the JNF. This Development Administration is responsible for the "scheme for the development and afforestation of Israel lands," and "shall engage in operations of reclamation, development, and afforestation of Israel lands as the agent of the registered owners." Furthermore, "The Board for Land Reclamation and Development attached to the Keren Kayemeth Leisrael [JNF] shall lay down the development policy in accordance with the agricultural development scheme of the Minister of Agriculture," and "shall supervise the activities of the Development Administration and the manner in which it carries this Covenant into effect." This board is headed by the chairman of the board of directors of the JNF or "a person appointed in that behalf" by the JNF. The JNF itself "shall continue to operate, as an independent agency of the World Zionist Organization, among the Jewish public in Israel and the Diaspora . . . ," while continuing to function as the exclusive instrument for the development of Israel lands, with no change in the discriminatory principles cited earlier, which are natural enough in an agency of the World Zionist Organization.

The phrase "Israel lands" refers to state-owned lands. Official figures give these as over 75 percent of the land area within the pre-June 1967 borders, with another 14 percent owned by the JNF. The law permits state land to be transferred to the JNF; otherwise, it is inalienable, with minor exceptions. For over 90 percent of the land of the Israeli state (pre-June 1967), the Development Authority is under the control of a company that represents not the citizens of Israel but the Jewish people, in Israel and the Diaspora, and that is committed to the principle that it shall use charitable donations in such ways as are "beneficial to persons of Jewish religion, race or origin."

Given its status as "the exclusive instrument for the development of Israel lands," it is important to determine how the JNF interprets the state's land laws in its official publications. In the 1973 *Report*, we read:

> Following an agreement between the Government of Israel and Keren Kayemeth Leisrael [JNF], the Knesset in 1960 enacted the *Basic Law: Israel Lands* which gives legal effect to the ancient tradition of ownership of the land in perpetuity by the Jewish people—the principle on which the Keren Kayemeth Leisrael

was founded. The same law extended that principle to the bulk
of Israel's State domains.

These laws "extended the Keren Kayemeth principles of inalienability
of the soil and its use in terms of hereditary leaseholdship to all public
holdings in Israel, i.e., to 92% of the State's surface prior to June, *1967.*"
There appears to be no explicit basis in law for the conclusion in the
official JNF *Report* that the JNF principle of ownership of land by the
Jewish people was extended to state lands by the 1960 law. Nevertheless,
one will not, of course, lightly disregard the interpretation of the law by
the authority that has exclusive responsibility for land development. We
see here another example of the tendency noted earlier to shift, virtually
unconsciously, from the notion "Israeli" to the notion "Jewish"—again,
as one would expect in a Jewish state. This tendency not only appears in
commentary and discussion and in the interpretation of the law by
responsible agencies, but also in judgments by the courts on the question of who is a Jew—a critical question, in a Jewish state. In the case of
Dr. George Tamarin, a lecturer at Tel Aviv University who requested
alteration of his nationality identification from "Jew" to "Israeli," the
High Court ruled that "there is no Israeli nation apart from the Jewish
people, and the Jewish people consists not only of the people residing
in Israel but also of the Jews in the Diaspora." Thus the Court rejected
the appellant's contention that Israel was something other than the
Jewish people, holding that "no man can create a new nation with his
own breath and say I belong to it."

If, indeed, the principle on which the JNF was founded is now interpreted by the Development Authority as applying to all state lands as
well as JNF lands, it follows that non-Jewish citizens are effectively
excluded from nine-tenths of the land area of the country (pre-1967).
To determine whether the JNF interpretation of the law applies in practice, one would have to examine the record of leasehold contracts
given by the Land Authority since 1961. I do not know whether this is
possible; secondary sources give little information. Orni's JNF mono-
graphs states that "the leasehold contracts issued by the Land
Authority in general follow in their wording those used by the Jewish
National Fund in the decades preceding the Agreement." In that
period, the contracts certainly excluded non-Jews. Non-Jews could not

lease JNF lands, and furthermore, the JNF lease reads, "The lessee undertakes to execute all works connected with the cultivation of the holding only with Jewish labour." Orni gives several examples of lease-hold contracts: for moshavim, kibbutzim, moshavim shittufiyim, and "a registered Company functioning as lessee." The first three categories are solely Jewish. The latter need not be, but it would be interesting to determine whether (and if so, when and where) Arab companies have been able to lease state lands. Surveying the array of laws, principles, and institutions, it would seem reasonable to speculate that since 1961, it has been general policy to settle Jews on state lands (and surely, on JNF lands), perhaps apart from cases where expropriated Arabs were transferred to state lands. But in all of the abundant litera-ture on Israeli society, I can find no information whatsoever about this crucial subject.

Orni's interpretation of the impact of the laws in his quasi-official monograph is rather similar to that of the JNF *Report*. He writes that "in 1960, the State of Israel adopted the JNF guidelines for all publicly-owned lands, i.e., for over 90% of the State's area at that date"; by these laws "over 90% of the country's surface had by then become public property to which the JNF's agrarian principles could be applied." Dis-cussing the work of Dr. Abraham Granott, who headed the JNF, Orni explains that he "from 1948 onward worked systematically for the incorporation of JNF principles into Israel's legislation and their exten-sion so as to cover all public property. . . . Thanks to Dr. Granott's per-sistent efforts, the final and decisive stage was reached with the signing of the 1960 Agreement between the Government and the JNF and the simultaneous adoption by the Knesset of the Land Laws." He notes that the "most important" of the founding principles of the JNF was the "demand that the land purchased should forever remain the property of the Jewish people." One may tentatively conclude from these and other comments that the law is being interpreted by those responsible for land development as generally restricting it to Jewish use. The matter seems similar to the earlier system of expropriation described by Jiryis. There was no particular law that stated that lands could be taken from Arabs for exclusive use by Jews, but there was a network of con-ditions, interpretations, bureaucratic structures for making determina-tions, etc., that had just this effect. Similarly, there is no law that states that Jewish farms receive priority for electrification, etc., but resort to quasi-governmental institutions achieves this result, as noted earlier.

Again, it is important to stress, first, that in the absence of any comprehensive study, judgments can only be tentative; and second, that as Fein points out in the comments cited above (see note 35), the absence of such studies in part reflects the nature of the problem. Still, it is fair to conclude tentatively that the system of land laws operates much in the manner of the other programs discussed, namely, as a complex device for guaranteeing Jewish dominance. Hence the grievances among dispossessed Arab peasants.

Examples of application of the laws and discriminatory practices are occasionally reported. In one recent incident, a Druze mason, a twenty-year veteran of the Israeli Border Patrol, was not allowed to open a business in the all-Jewish town of Karmiel (see above, p. 243). In 1971, the Agricultural Ministry brought legal action against Jewish settlements that had leased land to non-members, mostly Arabs, "in violation of the law which prohibits the lease of national land." The practice was stopped. The incident was regarded as particularly serious because "in certain cases it was even revealed that the [Jewish] settlers leased lands to Arabs who had lived there prior to the war of independence [1948] and a situation began to develop in which Arabs were returning in an indirect way to their lands." The experience of several Arab villages is reported by David Caploe. Lands were taken from villages "for security reasons" and later turned over to the JNF. Villagers who refuse to sell land to the JNF are harassed until they find it difficult to refuse. In one case, villagers report that a neighboring Mapam kibbutz erected barbed-wire fences to separate the village from its grazing lands so as to contribute to the JNF pressures on the villagers. Compensation, they allege, is far below land values. Caploe's figures indicate that the villages in question were deprived of much of their land by such measures, and that as a result most villagers must seek wage labor elsewhere. Comprehensive documentation is lacking, but the sporadic reports available give ample basis for understanding the grievances of the Arab citizens of Israel.

Two facts are particularly worthy of notice with regard to the system of discrimination that has just been briefly reviewed. The first is that one has no inkling of any of this in the encomiums to Israeli democracy that appear regularly in left-liberal publications in the United States. The second is that this system of principles is presented to "progressive opinion" in the West with considerable pride. Thus, Orni's JNF monograph is directed to "alert opinion in the free world, with collegiate youth in the forefront," which "is in a turmoil of soul-searching" and critical examination of "social, economic and political relationships." "What is hoped . . . is that people abroad who wish to form an opinion on Israel—be it on the political, social or cultural plane—will see need to include in their study also the subject of its achievements in the agrarian sphere"—in particular, the achievements under settlement and development programs conducted by quasi-governmental agencies that use charitable contributions for the benefit of "persons of Jewish religion, race or origin" and based on the "ancient tradition of ownership of the land in perpetuity by the Jewish people."

The achievements in the agrarian sphere, Orni explains, are based ultimately on Biblical precept, with its "deeply-rooted sense of social justice and a consciousness of the duty to protect the community's poorer and weaker strata." Orni notes, with some justice, that "to a surprising degree, it is possible to deduce the form and spirit of a government or a society . . . from the laws, customs and arrangements it applies to immovable property." Looking at those laws, customs, and arrangements, we discover that they embody a remarkable and perhaps unconscious system of severe discrimination. Orni reports that the London Zionist Conference of 1920 established that "the guiding principle of Zionist land policy is to transfer into the common possession of the Jewish people those areas in which Jewish settlement is to take place," with the JNF as "the instrument of Jewish land policy" which will act to "transfer the land into Jewish possession" and "make Jewish labor secure." But he never asks what all of this implies, as this "guiding principle" is worked into the "laws, customs and arrangements" of a state that assigns responsibility for development of over 90 percent of its land to a company that represents not the citizens of the state but rather the Jewish majority and the Jewish people in the Diaspora.

Orni's point is that the system governing immovable property in effect socializes such property, a testimony to the egalitarian and just character of the Israeli state. The conclusion may be legitimate, insofar as we restrict attention to the Jewish majority. But there is a typical oversight: There are non-Jews in the Jewish state. Correcting for the oversight, we reach rather different conclusions.

State ownership in itself guarantees no human rights. Thus King Leopold of Belgium made the state owner of 90 percent of the Congo territory, so that "native rights in nine-tenths of the Congo territory being thus declared non-existent, it followed that the native population had no proprietary right in the plants and trees growing upon that territory." More generally, white settlement was established in Africa by:

> The adopting by a white ruling race of legal measures designed expressly to compel the individual natives to whom they apply to quit land, which they occupy and by which they can live, in order to work in white service for the private gain of the white man.

To be sure, Israel is not white Africa. Far from it. But the principle of exclusive rights for the settlers who displaced the native population, with its predictable consequences, is deeply embedded in the institutional structures of the state, almost to the point of lack of awareness. This is a serious matter. The actual record, and the failure to comprehend it, indicate that far-reaching and quite radical changes will be necessary if the system of discrimination is to be dismantled.

In his study, Orni points out that the 1948 war "brought in its wake a revolutionary reversal in land ownership" and that "the situation created by the Six Day War [June 1967] made land redemption through purchase again a vital task." It is quite true that after 1948, substantial territories were expropriated from Arabs, including those who remained—in Israel. JNF holdings increased from 936,000 dunams in May 1948 to almost 3,400,000 in 1950. And after the 1967 war, the JNF began to work in the occupied territories as well. Orni alleges that "today, as in the past, transfers are entirely voluntary." That is far from true. In the occupied territories, the villagers of Aqraba were forced to evacuate their fields after defoliation by the Israeli Air Force; the lands were then "transferred" to Jewish settlement. The Bedouin farmers of Pithat Rafiah were expelled, their wells closed, and their lands fenced in and then converted to Jewish use, their homes, mosques, cemeteries bulldozed. Reports from within

Israel, some cited earlier, indicate that all sorts of pressures have been applied to coerce (or, if one prefers cynicism, "induce") Arabs to sell land, and that in many cases, lands were simply expropriated by the state and then turned over to Jewish settlement.

As for the "voluntary transfers" in the pre-state years, it may be true that the absentee landlords and feudal proprietors were willing to sell their land, but there is no lack of evidence that peasants were forcibly displaced. This was always understood by the Zionist leadership. Arthur Ruppin, who was in charge of land purchase and who played a major role in founding the binationalist Brith Shalom, wrote in 1930 that it was illusory to believe that Jewish settlement could be carried out without damaging Arab interests, if only because "there is hardly any land which is worth cultivating which is not already being culti-vated, [so that] it is found that wherever we purchase land and settle it, by necessity its present cultivators are turned away, whether they are owners or tenants. . . . The advice we tend to give the Arabs—to work their land more intensively, in order to manage with a smaller allot-ment of land—may appear to the Arabs as a joke at the expense of the poor" since the peasants have neither the requisite capital nor agricul-tural knowledge. Ruppin wrote that until that time, most purchases had been of sparsely settled land, though this would no longer be pos-sible. That is not the whole story, however. According to a Zionist paci-fist who was one of the early settlers of Nahallal:

> When the land of Nahallal was purchased there was an Arab vil-lage on the hill, Mahllul. The Jewish National Fund left the Arabs some of the land so that they could subsist under the stip-ulation that if within six years they could refund the Jewish National Fund they could hold the land. They could not raise the money and were forcefully removed from the land.

Thousands of tenants were evicted in the land purchases of the early 1920S, and in fact, years before, Zionist commentators had objected to the forcible displacement of local inhabitants.

Perhaps this is enough to underscore the obvious: The Zionist movement, from the start, could not help but injure and impinge on the rights of the people who lived in the country. Furthermore, the belief that a Jewish state with non-Jewish citizens can be a democracy guaranteeing equal rights to all is not tenable, and the practice of a quarter-century simply demonstrates that what was to be expected did in fact occur.

In the light of the factual record, the reports and analyses by American Zionist intellectuals make depressing reading. One can perhaps offer a rationale for the historical development on grounds of conflict of rights and greater need, and in terms of the perceived need to create a Jewish proletariat rather than a Jewish planter-aristocracy ruling the native Arab population. The problems that arose were not trivial, and if we grant the right of Jewish settlement, the policies of the JNF and the *Yishuv* in general until the establishment of the state can perhaps be justified as the least unjust option under unfortunate circumstances—though it is worthy of note that the system of discrimination against Arab labor and boycott of Arab produce was criticized from the left at the time, within the Palestinian *Yishuv*. Since the establishment of the state, no such justification is possible. It is presumably for this reason that the facts are simply ignored or denied. Thus we read that Israel is already a democratic secular state with full equality of rights for all, or that "major victories" have been won on matters of civil liberties which "still leave the Arabs cut off from whatever sense of Jewishness is fostered by the Israeli state," but nothing more; thus their situation is no different from that of minorities throughout the world, for example, Arab citizens of France who may have little interest in Bastille Day. As so often in the past, many left-liberal intellectuals are quick to deny injustice and repression in states that claim their loyalty. Until these illusions are recognized and dispelled, there can be no serious discussion of the dangerous and explosive problems of the Middle East.

Israeli Jews also suffer from the commitment to Jewish dominance. The severe religious controls over personal life, deplored by liberal American Zionists as well as Israeli civil libertarians, are in part a result of the need to enforce a second-class status for non-Jews, and are therefore likely to persist irrespective of the problems of coalition politics. Some basis must be established to distinguish the privileged majority from the remainder of the population. Thus, even if the majority of Jews have little interest in Judaism as a religion, it is natural that the rabbinate is given a major role in the affairs of state and that theocratic patterns that are foreign to traditional Judaism develop. It will not be an easy matter for the Jewish majority in a Jewish state to free itself from religious intrusion into personal life.

A further concomitant of life in a society based on discrimination is the rise of all kinds of racial mythology. In the long run, this will prove damaging to a society that survives by virtue of its technical rationality, just as it is harmful to cultural and intellectual life, and, of course, to the oppressed minority. Such mysticism has been on the rise since 1967. The issue of "historic rights" is a case in point. The first official commitment to the principle that the "historic right of the Jewish people to the land of Israel is beyond question" was in 1972, in a parliamentary motion responding to Hussein's plan for a Jordanian federation. Although Israel will surely not impress many people by founding its case on Biblical authority, it is remarkable that a belief to the contrary is often expressed. Thus, in a mass circulation daily, Michael Deshe explains that the root problem in the Arab-Jewish conflict is that the Arabs have made a "terrible error," and "if only we can succeed in convincing our enemy-neighbors that their point of view is based on a false premise, lacking foundation," then perhaps a settlement is in sight. Their error is their failure to understand that "the original people of this land, its legal owners," have now returned to it, and that "no temporary inhabitant, even if he lives here for 1000 years," can claim superseding rights. Just as the Arab conquerors in Spain were finally driven out by its native inhabitants, so the land of Israel, which "was never an Arab land," must return to "the legal owners of the land." The Arabs must be persuaded to understand this "historical and legal fact." Even in 1967, the territories they lost were "Jewish territories," which "had been conquered in Arab hands for generations." The Arabs have "no national rights in this land," but its "true and legal owner, the Jewish people," should nevertheless graciously arrive at some compromise with the temporary Arab residents. We must explain these facts to the Arabs, thus laying the basis for a peaceful settlement, he argues, with apparent seriousness.

The Ministry of Education and Culture is not far behind on the matter of "historic rights." A new textbook distinguishes between "the State of Israel," which has defined geographical borders, and "the historic land of Israel, to which the [Jewish] people was bound in all generations by prayer, customs, attempts to immigrate, and the struggles of the Messianic movements." The latter concept, which is "a significant concept from the geo-historical point of view," refers to a region that extended to parts of Syria, most of Transjordan, and parts of what is now Iraq, during the period of the First Temple, so the new texts explain. In the same report, the minister of education explains that:

> It is important that the youth should know that when we returned to this country we did not find here any other nation, and certainly no nation that lived here for hundreds of years. Such Arab inhabitants as we found here arrived only some tens of years before us, in the thirties and the forties of the nineteenth century, as refugees from the oppression of Muhammad Ali in Egypt.

This new page of history is designed to contribute to:

> The effort to reestablish Zionism, both with regard to the moral and humane character of the return to Zion, and also in the matter of the foundation of our rights to the Land of Israel. It is important that the young Israeli will be ready to debate with an educated young Arab or with the New Left that calls him an imperialist mercenary.

Even among critics of chauvinist tendencies one finds such arguments in an extraordinary muddle. Thus Arie Eliav asserts that there can be no doubt as to the "historic right of the Jewish people to the Land of the Twelve Tribes," though "part of those historic rights" should be waived, in the interest of peace. In successive paragraphs, he writes that Jews are almost unique among the nations of the world in that they "are the direct descendants of their forefathers in the land of Israel, and that their genealogy was never severed, from the time of the destruction of the Temple to this very day"—yet "on returning to our country we brought with us pigments from all the countries of the Diaspora: the mahogany black of the Cochin Jews, the burnished copper of the Jews of Yemen, and the white skin of the Jews of

Ashkenaz (Germany) and the north." As for the Palestinians, "It is very likely that these Arabs, were the descendants of ancient settlers: Jews, Samaritans," etc., but Israeli Jews should nevertheless not deny the national rights of the Palestinians merely because the Palestinians "came here as conquerors."

While some Israelis may be able to convince themselves of the force of these arguments about "historic rights" and racial origins, the belief that others will find them compelling indicates a severe case of irrationality. Israel can ill afford to sink into a system of mystical beliefs. In its present precarious position, a loss of the capacity for clear-headed and objective analysis can be extremely dangerous. But since 1967, there has been a dangerous drift in this direction. One example is the "vision of our own omnipotence and of total Arab ineptitude" that was surely a factor leading to the "earthquake" of October 1973. I think it is not surprising that these striking changes in the mentality of the Israeli public should have come about during a period when a policy of creeping annexation; raised to the fore the problem of how a Jewish state, with a commitment to democracy and equality of rights, would deal with a substantial population that cannot be granted these rights, consistent with the founding principle of the state.

Some Possible Alternatives
It is difficult to see how Israel and the Palestinians can extricate themselves from the dynamics outlined earlier, leading either to war, or to continued Israeli domination of most of the occupied territories with war always threatening, or to a two-state solution west of the Jordan imposed by imperial force. But that is not to say that the Israeli or Palestinian left, or those who sympathize with their aspirations, should adopt any such program. The prospects for libertarian socialism in the United States, at the moment, are perhaps no greater than the apparent prospects for capitalist democracy in the eighteenth century. But that is plainly no reason to abandon hope. Correspondingly, in the Middle East there have always been, and remain, alternatives that are much to be preferred to the system that is evolving. In the face of current tendencies, the left may still try to work towards a very different resolution of the complex problems of Israel and Palestine.

Of course, the initiative lies elsewhere. In situations of national conflict, the initiative lies generally in the hands of chauvinistic and violent elements whose task is to embitter relations among people who must someday live in harmony if they are to survive in any decent manner at all, with such tactics as shooting up apartments with sub-machine guns or bombarding refugee camps with planes and gun-boats. The goal may be to vanquish the enemy by force, but neither party will achieve that end, though either may succeed in creating a sit-uation in which both national groups will be demolished, each firm in its own rectitude, marching towards destruction to the applause of blind and fanatic partisans a safe distance removed.

One possibility that might be imagined if a two-state settlement is reached is the dismantling of the discriminatory structure of the Jewish and (it is safe to assume) Palestinian states. For reasons discussed above, such moves will require radical changes within Israel and, pre-sumably, the new Palestinian state as well. But it is possible to work for such changes. A second possibility, which might be pursued along with the first, is to move towards integration of the two states, first through some federal structure (perhaps sooner or later including Jordan as well), and later, with the growth of trust and mutual interest, towards a binational arrangement of the sort that was advocated by much of the Zionist movement prior to the Second World War, based on the prin-ciple that "whatever the number of the two peoples may be, no people shall dominate the other or be subject to the government of the other."

It is useful to recall, in this connection, that in the period before the Second World War, Zionist leaders, particularly those associated with the labor movement that dominated the Palestinian *Yishuv*, forcefully opposed the idea of a Jewish state, "which would eventually mean Jewish domination of Arabs in Palestine," on grounds that "the rule of one national group over the other" is illegitimate and that the Arabs of Palestine "have the right not to be at the mercy of the Jews." It has been argued that opposition to a Jewish state within the Zionist movement was merely a cynical tactic. Thus, some Arab initiatives towards bina-tionalism were in fact rebuffed by Zionist leaders who, a few years ear-lier, had advocated similar positions themselves in a period of complete Arab rejection of such attempts. Some Zionist leaders have argued quite explicitly that official denial of the goal of a Jewish state was merely a tactic, a matter of waiting for the "propitious moment."

In his autobiography, Nahum Goldmann condemns the chauvinist spokesman Ze'ev Jabotinsky for expressing "his political ideas at the wrong moment":

The rightness of a political idea is never absolute; it always has a lot to do with the propitious moment. When Jabotinsky demanded, at the exciting Seventeenth Zionist Congress in 1931, that the official Zionist program include the establishment of a Jewish state, this demand, which was rejected by the vast majority, was at that time politically absurd. If the congress had accepted this plank, continued resettlement and the peaceful conquest of Palestine would have been impossible. All of us who voted against it desired a Jewish state just as fervently as Jabotinsky did, but we knew that the time was not ripe. Not until the time seemed to have come, at the Biltmore Conference during the Second World War, did we proclaim the establishment of the Jewish state as a political demand.

If Goldmann is correct, then it was pure hypocrisy for Ben-Gurion, Katznelson, and other labor Zionist leaders to expound on the injustice of the concept of a Jewish state, to "declare before world opinion, before the workers' movement, and before the Arab world, that we shall not agree, either now or in the future, to the rule of one national group over the other"; or for Chaim Weizmann to state, in his opening speech at the 1931 congress, that "we, on our part, contemplate no political domination" but rather "would welcome an agreement between the two kindred races on the basis of political parity."

I doubt the accuracy of Goldmann's interpretation, many years after the event and after a Jewish state had in fact been established. Views such as those just cited were commonly expressed in internal memoranda and discussions, and in a context that suggests that the commitment to non-domination was undertaken with extreme seriousness. It should be recalled that this was a period of intense class struggle as well as national conflict in Palestine, a period when a labor leader like Ben-Gurion could not only oppose Jabotinsky's call for a Jewish state, but also his advocacy of fascist-style organization and strike-breaking, and could in fact write an article entitled "Jabotinsky in the Footsteps of Hitler." Socialist and humanist forces within the Zionist movement, particularly in the *Yishuv*, were very powerful. Given the historical circumstances and the social context, one must, I think, reject Goldmann's cynical assessment and accept rather the conclusion of Susan Lee Hattis in her recent study that "there is no doubt that during this phase [1931] MAPAI was advocating a bi-national state in Palestine," as were workers' groups to its left, and also liberal currents within the World Zionist Organization. Katznelson defined the general concept, rather vaguely to be sure, in the following way at the time:

> What then constitutes a bi-national state? It is a state whose two nationalities enjoy an equal measure of freedom, independence, participation in government, and rights of representation. Neither nationality encroaches upon the other. The term "bi-nationalism" as a whole is of import only if it is expressed in political-judicial norms securing the principle of the political parity of the nationalities. This it is that converts the state into a State of nationalities, differing fundamentally from the national State. . . . What it signifies is that a bi-national political order does not recognize the population at large but takes cognizance of its two national segments to both of which the right to share in shaping the country's regime is secured in equal measure and both of which are equally entitled to guide its destinies.

This is not to deny that socialist Zionists would have preferred a situation in which there were no Arabs to concern themselves about. But they also recognized that in the real world the Arabs did exist and lived on the land, and constituted a large majority of the population. Similarly nonsocialist groups such as Brith Shalom observed that binationalism "is not the ideal but the reality, and if this reality is not grasped Zionism will fail"—at least, Zionism as understood generally by left and liberal Zionists.

A great deal happened in subsequent years to undermine these convictions and reverse the direction of the Zionist movement. The bitter conflict in Palestine between 1936 and 1939 was one such factor, but dominating everything was the rise of Nazism and the growing awareness that it implied the physical destruction of European Jewry. Particularly after the British White Paper of 1939, limiting Jewish immigration to Palestine, other and more urgent demands displaced the ideals of left and liberal Zionism, and in 1942 the demand for a Jewish state was adopted as official policy. To use Goldmann's phrase, "the time was not ripe" for advocacy of binationalism, or so it might be argued. But history moves on, and it may be that the time is now ripe to resurrect the basic principles of the Zionism of a different era. The general principle that neither of the two national groups should dominate or be subservient to the other was a valid one when it was enunciated, and it might once again be adopted by the left, within Israel and among the Palestinians. It can, of course, only serve now as a general principle under which left-wing movements might conceivably unite. As an editorial statement in an Israeli journal puts it, "binationalism could . . . be a banner or a long-range program on which Jews and Arabs could unite and which could make them readier to yield the short-range concessions that more immediate agreements will demand."

If each of the national movements presents to the other a face of stony intransigence, short-term accommodation is excluded. Within the framework of a broader long-term program that might satisfy the just demands of both groups for national institutions, equal rights, social justice, and access in principle to all of the territory of the former Palestine, short-term accommodation might well be facilitated. While it is natural to suppose that one's ends can only be attained through the use of force and armed struggle, the conclusion is not necessarily correct. I think, in fact, that it is far from correct, and that it is, furthermore, suicidal as a guide to policy, both for Israeli Jews and Palestinians.

Assuming that two states will be established—under present circumstances, probably by imperial force—moves towards internal democratization and towards federal arrangements might well be contemplated. Such programs are not without support within Israel. The president of the Council of the Sephardic Community in Israel, Elie Eliachar, has sharply criticized the refusal of the Europe-oriented Israeli leadership to recognize Palestinian nationalism, to seek good relations with the local Arab population, or to bring authentic voices of the Oriental Jewish community into the "establishment" for fear of "levantinization" and "Arabization" of the society. He expresses his hope that if these policies change, there will eventually be "some form of federal arrangement" between Israel and a "future Palestinian entity," with Jerusalem as the shared capital. Other proposals along similar lines have also occasionally appeared. In the 1967–73 period, Israel had a real opportunity to move in this direction. Such moves might have made a good deal of sense had they been based on the traditional Zionist principle of equality and non-domination. The barrier was never security; on the contrary, such programs would have substantially reduced the security risk by offering an acceptable long-term political solution to the Palestinians. Again, it must be stressed that security for Israel lies in political accommodation and creation of bonds of unity and solidarity with the Palestinian population, not in military dominance, which will at best only delay an eventual catastrophe, given the historical, political, and economic realities. The problem was not security but rather the commitment to Jewish—in fact, European Jewish—dominance in the Jewish state. While the opportunities of the 1967–73 period have now been lost, nevertheless, under the changed circumstances, certain possibilities still exist.

Either of the possibilities mentioned—democratization or moves towards further integration—require substantial, if not revolutionary, changes in popular attitudes and aspirations. It seems to me reasonable to suppose that such changes could only come about as part of a broader movement of the left seeking social justice and, ultimately, radical reform or social revolution. Within such a context, the common needs of Jews and Palestinians could find expression, even granting the stability of national ties. I emphasize again that within the framework of a long-term program of reconciliation, it is possible to imagine short-term steps that would otherwise be difficult to initiate. It is unrealistic to dismiss long-range proposals as "Utopian." They may provide the only basis for the simpler and more immediate steps that will reduce tension and permit the growth of mutual trust and the expression of common interests that cross national lines—specifically, class interests—and thus lay the groundwork for an eventual just and peaceful settlement.

By their very nature, programs of democratization, federation, or socialist binationalism cannot be advanced by armed struggle, military force, or outside intervention. They must arise from forces within each

of the national movements that are now engaged in a bitter and suicidal struggle, forces that will never be able to crystallize or progress
under conditions of conflict. Even taking at face value the PLO program, one must surely conclude that the commitment in principle to
armed struggle aimed at the destruction of Israeli social and political
institutions is a hopelessly irrational strategy, which can only make the
stated goals even more difficult of attainment than they presently are,
quite apart from the question of whether these are the proper goals.
And the more recent tactic of directing murderous attacks precisely
against the poor Oriental segment of the Israeli community can only
be described as insane, quite apart from its moral level, given the professed goals. Authentic libertarian movements, if they develop, will
follow a very different course.

With the collapse of pre-October 1973 exuberance, it is to be
expected that the Israeli government will also put forth some version
of a federal solution as the only means for maintaining control of the
occupied territories in coordination with an imposed Quisling leadership. According to a recent report, Israeli Defense Minister Shimon
Peres announced in a talk in Tel Aviv "that he favors a federation
between Israel and the Arabs of the west bank, excluding the PLO."
Such proposals are meaningless at best, deeply cynical at worst. The
condition that the PLO must be excluded means that the State of Israel
will determine what is "acceptable political expression" within the
West Bank, which will therefore remain nothing but a colony of a
Greater Israel. Peres's proposal fails on three counts: (1) It does not
arise from each of the two communities that are to enter into federation, but is to be imposed on one by the other; (2) it is not based on
the principle of equality and non-domination; (3) it is too late. That is,
a proposal of this sort, despite its fundamental defects of principle,
might have had some meaning prior to October 1973, when it could
have been interpreted as a gesture by Israel, perhaps ultimately meaningful, towards political accommodation. Now, its meaning is all too
plain. The fact that the proposal is made at all signifies a belated recognition that the policy of reliance on force was a grave error. Unfortunately, the error cannot be rectified by the means proposed.

Let us suppose, as a point of departure, that a two-state solution is
imposed by the great powers in cis-Jordan. Add further the reasonable

supposition that the Palestinian state will mimic the Jewish state in its discriminatory institutions and in the ties of the dominant majority to an external "nation." Libertarian socialist elements within the two states, should they exist and survive an imperial settlement, ought then to turn their attention to combating discriminatory institutions and practices as well as the structures of exploitation and oppression within each state. Right-wing elements will have their own reasons for maintaining tensions and hostility, if only to suppress class struggle. Correspondingly, socialist movements will seek to reduce inter-state tension and will search for allies across national and state lines. They should, I believe, place on the agenda, within each society, a program for federalism worked out by cooperating forces within the two states and coupled with a program for social change. The inevitable tendency towards discrimination against the national minority might be alleviated somewhat within a federal structure. Furthermore, the very existence of such a joint program, even if its realization is only a future possibility, should facilitate moves towards relaxing hostilities.

A federal system would involve a sharing of political power between a centralized authority and two regions. It is then possible to envision further steps, natural for libertarian socialists at least, towards distribution of political power among municipalities or cantons with a varied mixture of Jews and Arabs. Socialists will work for democratization of the economy through workers' councils, with higher economic integration of production and regional units through federation. Two parliaments might be established—one Jewish, one Arab—each with veto power over decisions affecting international relations or state policy. National institutions might exist side by side for the organization of cultural and social life. Options should also exist for individuals who choose to identify themselves not as Jews or as Arabs but in different terms. Thus, there should be a possibility to live one's life simply as an individual. Workers' organizations will develop joint interests, along class rather than national lines, and might in the course of time discover that their fundamental interests will be realized only through common programs to create a socialist society that might well preserve parallel national institutions, either throughout the common territory or through a cantonal federal arrangement. Immigration should give priority to Jews and Palestinians. Depending on events elsewhere, there might be moves towards a broader Middle East federation, or closer relations with socialist movements in Europe and elsewhere.

In earlier periods, some detailed programs were developed for a binational state. In many parts of the world, socialist movements must seek a way to combine a commitment to an end to domination and exploitation with a recognition of national and ethnic bonds within complex multinational societies. In the advanced industrial societies as well, ethnic and racial conflicts stand in the way of movements working for social justice, and are often manipulated and exacerbated for the purpose of preserving privilege and oppression. Ultimately, socialist movements must be internationalist in their orientation, but "internationalism" does not imply opposition in principle to national ties or to other forms of voluntary association among individuals.

Developments within the industrial societies will naturally set certain bounds on what can be achieved elsewhere. Socialist internationalism is the only force that can prevent imperialist intervention in the long run, or that can come to terms with the critical problems of the global economy, so it seems to me. There are certain steps that can be taken by the left in particular regions such as the Middle East, with the support of sympathetic groups outside. Such steps might, perhaps, lead towards a more peaceful and just resolution of local conflicts, and even contribute to the growth of an international movement that may be able to face and overcome the much more far-reaching problems that arise in a world of authoritarian states and oppressive institutions and practices.

In October 1953, after an Israeli mother and her two children were killed by Palestinian guerillas who crossed the Jordanian border into Israel, Ariel Sharon, then a young major in the Israeli army, led a commando unit in a raid on the Jordanian border town of Qibya. Forty-five houses were blown up, and sixty-nine civilians, mostly women and children, were killed, triggering an international outcry. For **Yeshayahu Leibowitz**, a member of the chemistry department at Hebrew University and a deeply pious Jew, the lessons of Qibya were disturbingly clear. Although a committed Zionist, Leibowitz argued that nationalism had become a religion for young Israelis. With their blind worship of the state, Israelis could justify any action conducted in the name of national security—even massacres like Qibya.

Leibowitz (1903–1994), often described as the "conscience of Israel," was born in Riga, Latvia. In 1935 he arrived in Jerusalem, where he emerged as a leading scientist and a writer on Judaism, ethics, and politics. A maverick opponent of Israel's nuclear program, Leibowitz condemned the occupation from the day it began, highlighting the corrupting effects it would have on Israeli society, and praised conscientious objectors who refused to serve in the Occupied Territories and in Lebanon. He was a fearless, uncompromising humanist, and his voice is sorely missed today.

OCCUPATION AND TERROR

Yeshayahu Leibowitz

From *Judaism, Human Values, and the Jewish State* (1976)

In our times of worldwide decolonization, a colonial regime necessarily gives birth to terrorism. Conditions and circumstances today, both material and psychological, are no longer those of earlier generations, when "primitive" (compared to the power centers of Western civilization) populations accepted the rule of "developed" states, or at any rate refrained from active, violent opposition to this rule. The nature of colonial rule does not matter. Whether it treats the subjects with a light or a heavy hand, whether it grants them material or cultural benefits or exploits them to its own advantage—such rule is not tolerated. The subjects rise up, or will rise up, against it and will employ any means they consider effective. The type of "means" used has also changed. Previously, when the material and military superiority of the Western world was clearly acknowledged, this recognition was accompanied by the conscious or unconscious conviction that the methods of political action prevalent in the Western world—or at least recognized as the acceptable means of political struggle—were best. Asian and African national liberation movements in the pre-World War II era imposed great restraints upon themselves. They evinced tremendous patience, seeking to attain their goals by methods of persistent political opposition, protracted and exhaustive negotiation, reliance on accepted and agreed principles, and mobilization of public opinion. Confusion and difficulties for colonial authorities were effected by passive resistance to its acts in the hope of finally reaching a recognized agreement. To the extent the nationalists envisioned active rebellion, it was in terms of an officially declared war conducted by regular armies, as in the national liberation wars of Poland against the Russians in 1830–31, the Hungarians and Italians against the Habsburgs in 1848–49, Garibaldi's march against the Bourbons of Naples in 1860, and the like.

All this has completely changed. Not only has deference to the West's (or more accurately—the North's) power to rule over the East (more accurately—the South) been undermined, but the psychological factors making the colonial regimes possible have vanished, both for the former rulers, who call themselves "the developed world" or "the free world" (of which the state of Israel is also a part), and for the former colonial lands, called "the developing world" or "the third world." At the same time, the Western world itself, since 1914, has violated all accepted—or at least nominally accepted—restrictions on the means of violence in international conflict, as well as in struggles for liberation. Already in the years following the First World War the conditions for continued stability of colonial rule were being undermined. Light years separated the type of war fought by the Sinn Fein against the Black-and-Tans in the 1920s from the nineteenth-century version of national wars of liberation! After World War II the possibility of gradual, step-by-step progress toward independence disappeared. Patience and restraint were gone, and any delay necessarily led to terrorist activity, followed by counterterror in vicious sequence (Kenya, Algeria, and elsewhere).

In a world from which colonialism has been eliminated, Israel, since 1967, is endeavoring to impose colonial rule on the territory of a foreign people. Two aspects of Israeli rule over the West Bank and Gaza ought to be considered.

First is the question of the internal implications of including one and a quarter million Arabs of the West Bank and Gaza under the rule of the state of Israel. It will cease to be a state of the Jewish people, for whose history such a state cannot be a continuation. The colonizing situation will lead to the establishment of a political structure combining the horrors of Lebanon with those of Rhodesia—the state of a people possessing a common national heritage will turn into a system of imposed rule over two peoples, one ruling and the other ruled. In such circumstances, national conflicts become social conflicts. The Arabs will be the nation of workers and the Jews will be foremen, clerks, and police in a state dominated by security police. It is unlikely that human rights and civil freedoms can exist even in the Jewish sector.

The second problem involves the implications for Jewish-Arab relations. The occupation rule in the West Bank and Gaza will bring about solidarity of the half a million Israeli Arab citizens with their brothers in the occupied territories. This will lead to a radical change in their state of mind. Inevitably, they will no longer regard themselves as Arab citizens of the state of Israel, but rather as members of a people exploited by that state. In such a situation, one must expect the constant incidence of terror and counterterror.

Israeli policy in the occupied territories is one of self-destruction of the Jewish state, and of relations with the Arabs based on perpetual terror. There is no way out of this situation except withdrawal from the territories. "Withdrawal" is presented here as the antithesis to the slogan common among "dovish" circles in Israel: "territories in exchange for peace." This slogan means holding on to the territories indefinitely. There is no chance of "peace"—meaning an agreed solution—between us and the Arabs today or in the foreseeable future. It is a vision for the distant future. Only a solution imposed upon both sides by the superpowers, which will probably include withdrawal from the territories, offers an escape from a struggle threatening to escalate into an out-and-out war, which is likely to result in catastrophic for one side, perhaps for both. In any case, not only real peace (involving very extensive preliminaries), but any solution, including an imposed one, is conditioned on withdrawal. There is every reason for us to be prepared to accept such an imposed solution. We are obliged to strive toward this, though we do not know if peace or agreement will come, and if it comes—when.

The slogan "peace for territories" is a program for continuing the Israeli occupation "for the time being." But meanwhile, every day of continued occupation increases the tension and the hatred along with their inevitable consequences. New obstacles will impede the road to agreement. Corruption of state, society, and people is continually exacerbated. Neither decent treatment of the population by the occupying power (if the term "decency" can be used at all for colonial occupation), nor even the prospect of terminating the occupation upon achievement of an agreement, will relax the tension. They will not prevent terrorism, which inevitably flows from impatience and leads to repressive countermeasures. There is, moreover, no psychological possibility of preventing

Jewish settlement in territories administered by Israeli rule. Such settlement will add fuel to the flames and make amelioration more and more difficult. Dialogue with the Palestinians is not likely to take place on the sole basis of the explicit intention to return the territories after reaching an agreement. Honest dialogue is not possible between rulers and ruled: it is possible only between equals.

Thus a program of "peace (or agreement) in return for territories" does not seem feasible. Evacuation of the territories necessarily precedes any serious effort toward peace (or any agreed arrangement). This is stated without illusions: while evacuation of the territories is a necessary condition for peace (or an agreement under pressure of the superpowers), it is not certain that it is also a sufficient condition. After withdrawal, a dialogue with the Arabs will perhaps become possible with the help of the superpowers. It is impossible before evacuation. Yet there is no guarantee that evacuation will bring us real peace, or even an agreement granting reasonable security. But "security" is not guaranteed even with an Israeli army of occupation on the Jordan River. If, as citizens of our Jewish state as it was, we were determined to maintain our political independence and defend it with all our resources, we—and the Jewish people and the whole world—would know what we were fighting for. The monstrosity known as "the undivided land of Israel" is ruinous from the human, Jewish, and Zionist perspectives. It could neither evoke the determination, dedication, and perseverance in ourselves, nor the understanding on the part of others, without which our independence will always be precarious.

Yehudi Menuhin (1916–1999) was one of the finest violinists of the twentieth century. Born of Russian-Jewish parents who had immigrated to New York, Menuhin made his public debut at age seven with the San Francisco Orchestra, the beginning of a long and distinguished career. But Menuhin also made his mark as a humanitarian, founding a school in England for musically gifted children, and speaking out against injustice, whether it was anti-Semitism in Soviet Russia or anti-Arab racism in Israel. Although Mehuhin had strong links to Israel and to his Jewish identity, he was reviled by right-wing Jews because of his opposition to the occupation and his insistence that Israel would never be secure until its Arab citizens were granted absolute equality. His belief in Arab-Jewish coexistence was no idle one: Menuhin gave many concerts in Palestinian refugee camps, hoping art could help bridge the divide between the two communities.

In 1991, toward the end of the first intifada, he received Israel's prestigious Wolf prize for his contribution to music. In his acceptance speech on the Knesset floor, excerpted below, he condemned Israel's "steady asphyxiation of a dependent people." Not only was this morally repugnant; it was "unworthy of my great people . . . who themselves know all too well the unforgettable suffering of such an existence." At such moments, Menuhin's voice was as powerful as his violin.

MERCY AND TRUTH (1991)

Yehudi Menuhin

A ll around us we see pain, anguish and horror. Is this not the very moment when we, as Jews gathered together in Israel, should recognize our supreme destiny—to heal and help?

Reciprocity is the pragmatic rule of all societies. Those who live by the sword shall die by the sword and terror and fear provoke terror and fear. Hatred and contempt are fatally infectious, so by the same token, you must love if you yearn to be loved: You must trust to be trusted, serve in return to be served.

My friends, Israel has come of age. The moment is ripe. The challenge is yours. Do not calculate your actions out of the darkness of fear or you will continue to let yourselves be governed by this fear and violence, remaining a bitter armed camp as long as you survive.

Whatever the choice of solutions, that of two separate states or the one federated state (which latter would seem preferable and less likely to carry the endemic danger of war)—or again a humiliating conference of other powers sitting in judgment upon Israel—one factor surely must remain prime: there must be absolute reciprocity, absolute equality, mutual recognition of the dignity of life, respect for each others' traditions and background. These are the *sine qua non* of peace, not peace as a hiatus in which to prepare further wars, but peace in its integral sense, which must remain and will remain a constant and high minded struggle.

This offer can only come from the stronger. Thus will this land ever become stronger, confident in the forging of new and worthy friends when it will face the ineluctable fact that, living amongst them, are people equally dedicated to the land, equally ready to die for their loyalties and who are ultimately destined to become each others' friends.

One fact is surely abundantly clear, namely this wasteful governing by fear, by contempt for the basic dignities of life, this steady asphyxiation of a dependent people should be the very last means to be adopted by those who themselves know too well the awful significance, the unforgettable suffering, of such an existence.

It is unworthy of my great people, the Jews, who have striven to abide by a code of moral rectitude for some 5,000 years, who can create and achieve a land and a society for themselves such as we see around, but can yet deny the sharing of its great qualities and benefits to those others dwelling amongst them.

6 | ZIONISM'S INTERNAL COLONY

Ella Habiba Shohat, *a professor of Cultural Studies and Women's Studies at the City University of New York, was born and raised in Israel, by Iraqi Jews who fled their native country in the early 1950s. "As an Arab Jew," she has written, "I am often obliged to explain the 'mysteries' of this oxymoronic entity. That we have spoken Arabic, not Yiddish; that for millennia our cultural creativity, secular and religious, had been largely articulated in Arabic." About half of Israel's Jewish inhabitants are Mizrahis like Shohat; i.e., Sephardic Jews who trace their roots back to North Africa and the Middle East, rather than Europe. Zionism, a product of Europe, a German-Jewish invention appropriated by Eastern European Jews, never spoke to their condition; indeed, from the perspective of Zionism's Ashkenazi founders, the Mizrahi were a backward people, different from "the Arabs" only in their religion. When they arrived in Israel, the Mizrahis were encouraged, in ways both blatant and subtle, to abandon their language and heritage, and to adopt the ways of the Ashkenazi who had established the new state. By the 1970s, Ashknenazi hegemony had engendered a Mizrahi resistance movement, known as the Black Panthers.*

Shohat's self-description as an "Arab Jew" is not an uncontroversial one, perhaps especially among Mizrahis who despise the Arabs, the closest of strangers, and vote for right-wing parties. For these Mizrahis, Israel is seen as a sanctuary from anti-Semitism, which grew sharper with the rise of Arab nationalism and still sharper following the Arab defeat in 1948. Yet a significant minority of Mizrahi activists and intellectuals, of which Shohat is an eloquent spokeswoman, has forged a radical critique of Israeli society, one that links the fate of the Mizrahi to that of the Palestinians. As Shohat has argued, "the same historical process that dispossessed Palestinians of their property, lands and national-political rights, was linked to the dispossession of Middle Eastern and North African Jews of their property, lands, and rootedness in Muslim countries." In the following essay, Shohat makes a provocative case for seeing the Mizrahi—Israel's future majority—as a "semi-colonized nation-within-a-nation."

SEPHARDIM IN ISRAEL: ZIONISM FROM THE STANDPOINT OF ITS JEWISH VICTIMS

Ella Shohat

From *Social Text* (1988)

Alternative critical discourse concerning Israel and Zionism has until now largely focused on the Jewish/Arab conflict, viewing Israel as a constituted state, allied with the West against the East, whose very foundation was premised on the denial of the Orient and of the legitimate rights of the Palestinian people. I would like to extend the terms of the debate beyond earlier dichotomies (East versus West, Arab versus Jew, Palestinian versus Israeli) to incorporate an issue elided by previous formulations, to wit, the presence of a mediating entity, that of the Arab Jews or Mizrahi/Oriental Jews, those Sephardi Jews coming largely from the Arab and Muslim countries. A more complete analysis, I will argue, must consider the negative consequences of Zionism not only for the Palestinian people but also for the Sephardim who now form the majority of the Jewish population in Israel. For Zionism not only undertakes to speak for Palestine and the Palestinians, thus "blocking" all Palestinian self-representation, but also presumes to speak for Oriental Jews. The Zionist denial of the Arab-Muslim and Palestinian East, then, has as its corollary the denial of the Jewish "Mizrahim" (the "Eastern Ones"), who, like the Palestinians, but by more subtle and less obviously brutal mechanisms, have *also* been stripped of the right of self-representation. Within Israel, and on the stage of world opinion, the hegemonic voice of Israel has almost invariably been that of European Jews, the Ashkenazim, while the Sephardi/Mizrahi voice has been largely muffled or silenced.

Zionism claims to be a liberation movement for *all* Jews, and Zionist ideologists have spared no effort in their attempt to make the two terms "Jewish" and "Zionist" virtually synonymous. In fact, however, Zionism has been primarily a liberation movement for European Jews (and that, as we know, problematically) and more precisely for that tiny minority of European Jews actually settled in Israel. Although Zionism claims to provide a homeland for *all* Jews, that homeland was not offered to all with the same largess. Sephardi Jews were first brought to Israel for specific European-Zionist reasons, and once there they were systematically discriminated against by a Zionism that deployed its energies and material resources differentially, to the consistent advantage of European Jews and to the consistent detriment of Oriental Jews. In this essay, I would like to delineate the situation of structural oppression experienced by Sephardi Jews in Israel, to trace briefly the historical origins of that oppression, and to propose a symptomatic analysis of the discourses—historiographic, sociological, political, and journalistic—that sublimate, mask, and perpetuate that oppression.

Superimposed on the East/West problematic will be another issue, related but hardly identical, namely, that of the relation between the "First" and the "Third" Worlds. Although Israel is not a Third World country by any simple or conventional definition, it does have affinities and structural analogies to the Third World, analogies that often go unrecognized even, and perhaps especially, within Israel itself. In what sense, then, can Israel, despite the views of it offered by official spokesmen, be seen as partaking in "Third Worldness"? To begin, in purely demographic terms, a majority of the Israeli population can be seen as Third World or at least as originating in the Third World. The Palestinians make up about 20 percent of the population while the Sephardim, the majority of whom have come, within very recent memory, from countries such as Morocco, Algeria, Egypt, Iraq, Iran, and India, countries generally regarded as forming part of the Third World, constitute another 50 percent of the population, thus giving us a total of about 70 percent of the population as Third World or Third World-derived (and almost 90 percent if one includes the West Bank and Gaza). European hegemony in Israel, in this rereading of the demographic map, is the product of a distinct numerical minority, a minority in whose interest it is to downplay Israel's "Easternness" as well as its "Third Worldness."

Within Israel, European Jews constitute a First World elite dominating not only the Palestinians but also the Oriental Jews. The
Sephardim, as a Jewish Third World people, form a semicolonized
nation-within-a-nation. My analysis here is indebted to anticolonialist
discourse generally (Frantz Fanon, Aimé Césaire) and specifically to
Edward Said's indispensable contribution to that discourse, his
genealogical critique of Orientalism as the discursive formation by
which European culture was able to manage—and even produce—the
Orient during the post-Enlightenment period.[1] The Orientalist attitude
posits the Orient as a constellation of traits, assigning generalized
values to real or imaginary differences, largely to the advantage of the
West and the disadvantage of the East, so as to justify the former privileges and aggressions. Orientalism tends to maintain what Said calls a
"flexible positional superiority," which puts the Westerner in a whole
series of possible relations with the Oriental, but without the Westerner ever losing the relative upper hand. My essay concerns, then, the
process by which one pole of the East/West dichotomy is produced and
reproduced as rational, developed, superior, and human, and the other
as aberrant, underdeveloped, and inferior, but in this case as it affects
Oriental Jews.

The Zionist Master Narrative

The view of the Sephardim as oppressed Third World people goes
directly against the grain of the dominant discourse within Israel and
disseminated by the Western media outside of Israel. According to
that discourse, European Zionism "saved" Sephardi Jews from the
harsh rule of their Arab "captors." It took them out of "primitive conditions" of poverty and superstition and ushered them gently into a
modern Western society characterized by tolerance, democracy, and
"humane values," values with which they were but vaguely and errati-
cally familiar due to the "Levantine environments" from which they
came. Within Israel, of course, they have suffered not simply from the
problem of "the gap," that between their standard of living and that of
European Jews, but also from the problem of their "incomplete integration" into Israeli liberalism and prosperity, handicapped as they
have been by their Oriental, illiterate, despotic, sexist, and generally
premodern formation in their lands of origin, as well as by their

propensity for generating large families. Fortunately, however, the political establishment, the welfare institutions, and the educational system have done all in their power to "reduce this gap" by initiating the Oriental Jews into the ways of a civilized, modern society. Fortunately as well, intermarriage is proceeding apace, and the Sephardim have won new appreciation for their "traditional cultural values," their folkloric music, their rich cuisine and warm hospitality. A serious problem persists, however. Due to their inadequate education and "lack of experience with democracy," the Jews of Asia and Africa tend to be extremely conservative, even reactionary, and religiously fanatic, in contrast to the liberal, secular, and educated European Jews. Antisocialist, they form the base of support for the right-wing parties. Given their "cruel experience in Arab lands," furthermore, they tend to be "Arab-haters," and in this sense they have been an "obstacle to peace," preventing the efforts of the "peace camp" to make a "reasonable settlement" with the Arabs.

I will speak in a moment of the fundamental falsity of this discourse, but I would like first to speak of its wide dissemination, for this discourse is shared by right and "left," and it has its early and late versions as well as its religious and secular variants. An ideology that blames the Sephardim (and their Third World countries of origin) has been elaborated by the Israeli elite, expressed by politicians, social scientists, educators, writers, and the mass media. This ideology orchestrates an interlocking series of prejudicial discourses possessing clear colonialist overtones. It is not surprising, in this context, to find the Sephardim compared, by the elite, to other "lower" colonized peoples. Reporting on the Sephardim in a 1949 article, during the mass immigration from Arab and Muslim countries, the journalist Arye Gelblum wrote:

This is immigration of a race we have not yet known in the country . . . We are dealing with people whose primitivism is at a peak, whose level of knowledge is one of virtually absolute ignorance, and worse, who have little talent for understanding anything intellectual. Generally, they are only slightly better than the general level of the Arabs, Negroes, and Berbers in the same regions. In any case, they are at an even lower level than what we knew with regard to the former Arabs of Eretz Israel . . .

These Jews also lack roots in Judaism, as they are totally subordinated to the play of savage and primitive instincts . . . As with
the Africans you will find card games for money, drunkenness
and prostitution. Most of them have serious eye, skin and sexual
diseases, without mentioning robberies and thefts. Chronic
laziness and hatred for work, there is nothing safe about this
asocial element. . . . "Aliyat HaNoar" [the official organization
dealing with young immigrants] refuses to receive Moroccan
children and the Kibbutzim will not hear of their absorption
among them.[2]

Sympathetically citing the friendly advice of a French diplomat and
sociologist the conclusion of the article makes clear the colonial parallel operative in Ashkenazi attitudes toward Sephardim. Basing his
comments on the French experience with its African colonies, the
diplomat warns:

You are making in Israel the same fatal mistake we French
made. . . . You open your gates too wide to Africans. . . . [T]he
immigration of a certain kind of human material will debase
you and make you a levantine state, and then your fate will
be sealed. You will deteriorate and be lost.[3]

Lest one imagine this discourse to be the product of the delirium of an
isolated retrograde journalist, we have only to quote then prime minister
David Ben-Gurion, who described the Sephardi immigrants as lacking
even "the most elementary knowledge" and "without a trace of Jewish or
human education."[4] Ben-Gurion repeatedly expressed contempt for the
culture of the Oriental Jews: "We do not want Israelis to become Arabs. We
are in duty bound to fight against the spirit of the Levant, which corrupts
individuals and societies, and preserve the authentic Jewish values as they
crystallized in the Diaspora."[5] Over the years Israeli leaders constantly
reinforced and legitimized these Eurocentric ideas, which encompassed
both Arabs and Oriental Jews. For Abba Eban, the "object should be to
infuse [the Sephardim] with an Occidental spirit, rather than allow them
to drag us into an unnatural Orientalism."[6] Or again: "One of the great
apprehensions which afflict us . . . is the danger lest the predominance of

immigrants of Oriental origin force Israel to equalize its cultural level with that of the neighboring world."[7] Golda Meir projected the Sephardim, in typical colonialist fashion, as coming from another, less developed time, for her, the sixteenth century (and for others, a vaguely defined "Middle Ages"): "Shall we be able," she asked, "to elevate these immigrants to a suitable level of civilization?"[8] Ben-Gurion, who called the Moroccan Jews "savages" at a session of a Knesset committee and who compared Sephardim, pejoratively (and revealingly), to the blacks brought to the United States as slaves, at times went so far as to question the spiritual capacity and even the Jewishness of the Sephardim.[9] In an article entitled "The Glory of Israel," published in the government's annual, the prime minister lamented that "the divine presence has disappeared from the Oriental Jewish ethnic groups," while he praised European Jews for having "led our people in both quantitative and qualitative terms."[10] Zionist writings and speeches frequently advance the historiographically suspect idea that Jews of the Orient, prior to their "ingathering" into Israel, were somehow "outside of history, thus ironically echoing nine-teenth-century assessments, such as those of Hegel, that Jews, like blacks, lived outside of the progress of Western civilization. European Zionists in this sense resemble Fanon's colonizer who always "makes history"; whose life is "an epoch," "an Odyssey" against which the natives form an "almost inorganic background."[11]

Again in the early 1950s, some of Israel's most celebrated intellectuals from Hebrew University in Jerusalem wrote essays addressing the "ethnic problem." "We have to recognize," wrote Karl Frankenstein, "the primitive mentality of many of the immigrants from backward countries," suggesting that this mentality might be profitably compared to "the primitive expression of children, the retarded, or the mentally disturbed." Another scholar, Yosef Gross, saw the immigrants as suffering from "mental regression" and a "lack of development of the ego." The extended symposium concerning the "Sephardi problem" was framed as a debate concerning the "essence of primitivism." Only a strong infusion of European cultural values, the scholars concluded, would rescue the Arab Jews from their "backwardness."[12] And in 1964, Kalman Katznelson published his frankly racist *The Ashkenazi Revolution*, where he protested the dangerous admission into Israel of large numbers of Oriental Jews and where he argued the essential, irreversible genetic inferiority of the Sephardim, fearing the tainting of the Ashkenazi race by mixed marriage and calling for the Ashkenazim to protect their interests in the face of a burgeoning Sephardi majority.

Such attitudes have not disappeared; they are still prevalent, expressed by Euro-Israelis of the most diverse political orientations. The "liberal" Shulamit Aloni, head of the Citizen's Rights Party and a member of the Knesset, in 1983 denounced Sephardi demonstrators as "barbarous tribal forces" that were "driven like a flock with tom-toms" and chanting like "a savage tribe."[13] The implicit trope comparing Sephardim to black Africans recalls, ironically, one of the favored topics of European anti-Semitism, that of the "black Jew." (In European-Jewish conversations, Sephardim are sometimes referred to as *schwartze chaies* or "black animals.") Amnon Dankner, a columnist for the "liberal" daily *Ha'aretz*, favored by Ashkenazi intellectuals and known for its presumably high journalistic standards, meanwhile, excoriated Sephardi traits as linked to an Islamic culture clearly inferior to the Western culture "we are trying to adopt here." Presenting himself as the anguished victim of an alleged official "tolerance," the journalist bemoans his forced cohabitation with Oriental subhumans:

This war [between Ashkenazim and Sephardim] is not going to be between brothers, not because there is not going to be war but because it won't be between brothers. Because if I am a partner in this war, which is imposed on me, I refuse to name the other side as my "brother." These are not my brothers, these are not my sisters, leave me alone, I have no sister. . . . They put the sticky blanket of the love of Israel over my head, and they ask me to be considerate of the cultural deficiencies of the authentic feelings of discrimination. . . . [T]hey put me in the same cage with a hysterical baboon, and they tell me "OK, now you are together, so begin the dialogue." And I have no choice; the baboon is against me, and the guard is against me, and the prophets of the love of Israel stand aside and wink at me with a wise eye and tell me: "Speak to him nicely. Throw him a banana. After all, you people are brothers."[14]

Once again we are reminded of Fanon's colonizer, unable to speak of the colonized without resorting to the bestiary, the colonizer whose terms are zoological terms.

The racist discourse concerning Oriental Jews is not always so over-wrought or violent, however; elsewhere it takes a "humane" and rela-tively "benign" form. Read, for example, Dr. Dvora and Rabbi Menachem Hacohen's *One People: The Story of the Eastern Jews*, an "affectionate" text thoroughly imbued with Eurocentric prejudice.[15] In his foreword, Abba Eban speaks of the "exotic quality" of Jewish communities on the outer margins of the Jewish world." The text proper, and its accompanying photographs, convey a clear ideological agenda. The stress throughout is on "traditional garb," on "charming folkways," on premodern "crafts-manship," on cobblers and coppersmiths, on women "weaving on prim-itive looms." We learn of a "shortage of textbooks in Yemen," and the photographic evidence shows only sacred writings on the *ktuba* or on Torah cases, never secular writing. Repeatedly, we are reminded that some North African Jews inhabited caves (intellectuals such as Alberit Memmi and Jacques Derrida apparently escaped this condition), and an entire chapter is devoted to "the Jewish cave-dwellers."

The actual historical record, however, shows that Oriental Jews were overwhelmingly urban. There is, of course, no intrinsic merit in being urban or even any intrinsic fault in living in "cave-like dwellings." What is striking, on the part of the commentator, is a kind of "desire for prim-itivism," a miserabilism that feels compelled to paint the Asian and African Jews as innocent of technology and modernity. The pictures of Oriental misery are then contrasted with the luminous faces of the Ori-entals in Israel itself, learning to read and mastering the modern tech-nology of tractors and combines. The book forms part of a broader national export industry of Sephardi "folklore," an industry that circu-lates (the often expropriated) goods—dresses, jewelry, liturgical objects, books, photos, and films—among Western Jewish institutions eager for Jewish exotica. In this sense, the Israeli Ashkenazi glosses the enigma of the Eastern Jews for the West—a pattern common as well in academic studies. Ora Gloria Jacob-Arzooni's *The Israeli Film: Social and Cultural Influences, 1912–1973*, for example, describes Israel's "exotic" Sephardi community as having been plagued by "almost unknown tropical diseases"—the geography here is somewhat fanciful—and as "virtually destitute." The North African Jews, we are told—in language that surprises so long after the demise of the Third Reich—were hardly "racially pure," and among them one finds "witchcraft and other superstitions far removed from any Judaic law."[16] We are reminded of Fanon's ironic account of the colonialist description of the natives: "torpid creatures, wasted by fevers, obsessed by ancestral customs."[17]

The Theft of History

An essential feature of colonialism is the distortion and even the denial of the history of the colonized. The projection of Sephardim as coming from backward rural societies lacking all contact with technological civilization is at best a simplistic caricature and at worst a complete misrepresentation. Metropolises such as Alexandria, Baghdad, and Istanbul, in the period of Sephardi emigration, were hardly the desolate backwaters without electricity or automobiles implied by the official Zionist account, nor were these lands somehow miraculously cut off from the universal dynamism of historical processes. Yet Sephardi and Palestinian children, in Israeli schools, are condemned to study a history of the world that privileges the achievements of the West, while effacing the civilizations of the East. The political dynamics of the Middle East, furthermore, are presented only in relation to the fecundating influence of Zionism on the preexisting desert. The Zionist master narrative has little place for either Palestinians or Sephardim, but while Palestinians possess a clear counternarrative, the Sephardi story is a fractured one embedded in the history of both groups. Distinguishing the "evil" East (the Muslim Arab) from the "good" East (the Jewish Arab), Israel has taken upon itself to "cleanse" the Sephardim of their Arabness and redeem them from their "primal sin" of belonging to the Orient. Israeli historiography absorbs the Jews of Asia and Africa into the monolithic official memory of European Jews. Sephardi students learn virtually nothing of value about their particular history as Jews in the Orient. Much as Senegalese and Vietnamese children learned that their "ancestors the Gauls had blue eyes and blond hair," Sephardi children are inculcated with the historical memory of "our ancestors, the residents of the shtetls of Poland and Russia," as well as with a pride in the Zionist founding fathers for establishing pioneer outposts in a savage area. Jewish history is conceived as primordially European, and the silence of historical texts concerning the Sephardim forms a genteel way of hiding the discomfiting presence of an Oriental "other," here subsumed under a European-Jewish "we."

From the perspective of official Zionism, Jews from Arab and Muslim countries appear on the world stage only when they are seen on the map of the Hebrew state, just as the modern history of Palestine is seen as beginning with the Zionist renewal of the biblical mandate. Modern Sephardi history, in this sense, is presumed to begin with the coming of Sephardi Jews to Israel, and more precisely with the "Magic Carpet" or "Ali Baba" operations (the latter refers to the bringing to Israel of the Jews of Iraq in 1950–51, while the former refers to that of Yemeni Jews in 1949–50). The names themselves, borrowed from *A Thousand and One Nights*, evoke Orientalist discourses by fore-grounding the naive religiosity and the technological backwardness of the Sephardim, for whom modern airplanes were "magic carpets" transporting them to the promised land. The Zionist gloss on the Exodus allegory, then, emphasized the "Egyptian" slavery (Egypt here being a synecdoche for all the Arab lands) and the beneficent death of the (Sephardi) "desert generation." European Zionism took on the patriarchal role in the Jewish oral tradition of fathers passing to sons the experiences of their peoples (*vehigadeta lebinkha bayom hahu* . . .). And the stories of the Zionist pater drowned out those of the Sephardi fathers and mothers whose tales thus became unavailable to the sons and daughters.

Filtered through a Eurocentric grid, Zionist discourse presents culture as the monopoly of the West, denuding the peoples of Asia and Africa, including Jewish peoples, of all cultural expression. The multi-layered culture of Jews from Arab and Muslim countries is scarcely studied in Israeli schools and academic institutions. While Yiddish is prized and officially subsidized, Ladino and Judeo-Arabic dialects are neglected ("Those who do not speak Yiddish," Golda Meir once said, "are not Jews"). Yiddish, through an ironic turn of history, became for Sephardim the language of the oppressor, a coded speech linked to privilege.[18] While the works of Sholem Aleichem, Y. D. Berkowitz, and Mendle Mocher Sfarim are examined in great detail, the works of

Anwar Shaul, Murad Michael, and Salim Darwish are ignored, and when Sephardi figures are discussed, their Arabness is downplayed. Maimonides, Yehuda Halevi, and Iben Gabirol are viewed as the product of a decontextualized Jewish tradition, or of Spain, that is, Europe, rather than of what even the Orientalist Bernard Lewis recognizes as the "Judeo-Islamic symbiosis." Everything conspires to cultivate the impression that Sephardi culture prior to Zionism was static and passive and, like the fallow land of Palestine, lying in wait for the impregnating infusion of European dynamism. Although Zionist historiography concerning Sephardim consists of a morbidly selective "tracing of the dots" from pogrom to pogrom (often separated by centuries), part of a picture of a life of relentless oppression and humiliation, in fact the Sephardim lived, on the whole, quite comfortably within Arab-Muslim society. Sephardi history can simply not be discussed in European-Jewish terminology; even the word "pogrom" derives from and is reflective of the specificities of the European-Jewish experience. At the same time, we should not idealize the Jewish-Muslim relationship as idyllic. While it is true that Zionist propaganda exaggerated the negative aspects of the Jewish situation in Muslim countries, and while the situation of these Jews over fifteen centuries was undeniably better than in the Christian countries, the fact remains that the status of *dhimmi*, applied to both Jews and Christians as "tolerated" and "protected" minorities, was intrinsically inegalitarian. But this fact, as Maxime Rodinson points out, was quite explicable by the sociological and historical conditions of the time and was not the product of a pathological European-style anti-Semitism.[19] The Sephardi communities, while retaining a strong collective identity, were generally well integrated and indigenous to their countries of origin, forming an inseparable part of their social and cultural life. Thoroughly Arabized in their traditions, the Iraqi Jews, for example, used Arabic even in their hymns and religious ceremonies. The liberal and secular trends of the twentieth century engendered an even stronger association of Iraqi Jews and Arab culture, allowing Jews to achieve a prominent place in public and cultural life. Jewish writers, poets, and scholars played a vital role in Arab culture, translating, for example, books from other languages into Arabic. Jews distinguished themselves in Iraqi Arabic-speaking theater, in music, as singers, as composers, and as players of traditional instruments. In Egypt, Syria, Lebanon, Iraq, and Tunisia, Jews became members of legislatures, of municipal councils, of the judiciary, and even occupied high economic positions; the finance minister of Iraq, in the 1940s, was Ishak Sasson, and in Egypt, Jamas Sanua—higher positions, ironically, than those usually achieved by Sephardim within the Jewish state.

The Lure of Zion

Zionist historiography presents the emigration of Arab Jews as the result of a long history of anti-Semitism, as well as of religious devotion, while Zionist activists from the Arab-Jewish communities stress the importance of Zionist ideological commitment as a motivation for the exodus. Both versions neglect crucial elements: the Zionist economic interest in bringing Sephardim to Palestine/Israel, the financial interest of specific Arab regimes in their departure, historical developments in the wake of the Arab/Israeli conflict, as well as the fundamental connection between the destiny of the Arab Jews and that of the Palestinians. Arab historians, as Abbas Shiblak points out in *The Lure of Zion*, have also underestimated the extent to which the policies of Arab governments in encouraging Jews to leave were self-defeating and ironically helpful to the Zionist cause and harmful both to Arab Jews and to Palestinians.[20] It is important to remember that Sephardim, who had lived in the Middle East and North Africa for millennia (often even before the Arab conquest), cannot be seen as simply eager to settle in Palestine and in many ways had to be "lured" to Zion. Despite the messianic mystique of the Land of Zion, which formed an integral part of Sephardi religious culture, they did not exactly share the European-Zionist desire to "end the diaspora" by creating an independent state peopled by a new archetype of Jew. Sephardim had always been in contact with the promised land, but this contact formed a "natural" part of a general circulation within the countries of the Ottoman Empire. Up through the 1930s, it was not uncommon for Sephardim to make purely religious pilgrimages or business trips to Palestine, at times with the help of Jewish-owned transportation companies. (Although the Zionist geographical mindset projected the Sephardi lands of origin as remote and distant, in fact they were, obviously, closer to Eretz Israel than Poland, Russia, and Germany.)

Before the Holocaust and the foundation of Israel, Zionism had been a minority movement among world Jewry. Although both enthusiasm and hostility were expressed toward the Zionist project, the majority of Sephardi Jews were quite indifferent to it. The Iraqi-Jewish leadership, for its part, cooperated with the Iraqi government to stop Zionist activity in Iraq; the chief rabbi of Iraq even published an "open letter" in 1929 denouncing Zionism and the Balfour Declaration.[21] In Palestine, some of the leaders of the local (Sephardi) Jewish community made formal protests against Zionist plans. In 1920, they signed an anti-Zionist petition organized by Palestinian Arabs, and in 1923 some Palestinian Jews met in a synagogue to denounce Ashkenazi-Zionist rule (some even cheered the Muslim-Christian Committee and its leader Mussa Hassam al-Husseini), an event that the National Jewish Committee managed to prevent from being discussed in the newspapers.[22] Zionism, in this period, created wrenching ideological dilemmas for the Palestinian Jewish, Muslim, and Christian communities alike. The national Arab movement in Palestine and Syria carefully distinguished, in the early phases, between the Zionist immigrants and the local Jewish inhabitants (largely Sephardim) "who live peacefully among the Arabs."[23] The first petition of protest against Zionism by the Jerusalem Palestinian Arabs stated in November 1918: "We want to live . . . in equality with our Israelite brothers, long-standing natives of this country; their rights are our rights and their duties are our duties."[24] The all-Syrian convention of July 1919, attended by a Sephardi Arab-Jewish representative, even claimed to represent all Arab Syrians, Muslims, Christians, and Jews. The manifesto of the first Palestinian convention in February 1919 also insisted on the local Jewish/Zionist distinction, and in March 1920, during the massive demonstrations against the Balfour Declaration, the Nazareth area petition spoke only against Zionist immigration and not against Jews in general: "The Jews are people of our country who lived with us before the occupation, they are our brothers, people of our country, and all the Jews of the world are our brothers."[25]

At the same time, however, there were real ambivalences and fears on the part of both Arab Jews and Arab Muslims and Christians. While some Muslim and Christian Arabs rigorously maintained the Zionist/Jewish distinction, others were less cautious. The Palestinian

Anglican priest of Nazareth deployed anti-Semitic theological arguments against "the Jews" in general, while Arab demonstrators, in bloody rebellions both in 1920 and in 1929, did not distinguish between Zionist targets per se and the traditional communities quite uninvolved in the Zionist project.[26] Zionism, then, brought a painful binarism into the formerly relatively peaceful relationship between diverse Palestinian religious communities. The Sephardi Jew was prodded to choose between anti-Zionist "Arabness" and a pro-Zionist "Jewishness." For the first time in Arab-Jewish history, Arabness and Jewishness were posed as antonyms. The situation led the Palestinian Muslims and Christians, meanwhile, to see all Jews as at least potential Zionists. With the pressure of waves of Ashkenazi-Zionist immigration and the swelling power of its institutions, the Jewish/Zionist distinction was becoming more and more precarious, much to the advantage of European Zionism. Had the Arab nationalist movement maintained this distinction, as even the Zionist historian Yehoshua Porath has recognized, it would have had significant chances for enlisting Sephardi support in the anti-Zionist cause.[27]

Outside of Palestine, meanwhile, it was not an easy task for Zionism to uproot the Arab-Jewish communities. In Iraq, for example, despite the Balfour Declaration in 1917, despite the tensions generated by Palestinian/Zionist clashes in Palestine, despite Zionist propaganda among Sephardi Jews in Arab-Muslim lands, despite the historically atypical attacks on Iraqi Jews in 1941 (attacks inseparable from the geopolitical conflicts of the time), and even after the proclamation of Israeli statehood, most Arab Jews were not Zionist and remained reluctant to emigrate. Even subsequent to the foundation of the state, the Jewish community in Iraq was constructing new schools and founding new enterprises, clear evidence of an institutionalized intention to stay. When the Iraqi government announced in 1950 that any Jews who wanted to leave were free to do so contingent upon relinquishing their citizenship and property, and set a time limit for the exodus, only a few families applied for exit permits. Since the carrot was insufficient, therefore, a stick was necessary. A Jewish underground cell, commanded by secret agents sent from Israel, planted bombs in Jewish centers so as to create hysteria among Iraqi Jews and thus catalyze a mass exodus to Israel.[28] In one case, on January 14, 1951, a bomb was thrown into the courtyard of the Mas'ouda Shemtob Synagogue in Baghdad, at a time when hundreds were gathered.[29] Four people, including a boy of twelve, were killed, and a score were wounded. These actions appear to have been the product of a collusion between two groups—Israeli Zionists (including a small group of Iraqi Zionists) and factions in the Iraqi government (largely those around the British-oriented ruler Nuri Said) who were pressured by the international Zionist-led campaign of denunciation and who had an immediate financial interest in the expulsion of the Iraqi Jews.[30] Caught in the vice of Iraqi government-Zionist collaboration, the Sephardi community panicked and was virtually forced to leave. What its proponents themselves called "cruel Zionism"—namely, the idea that Zionists had to use violent means to dislodge Jews from exile—had achieved its ends.

The same historical process that dispossessed Palestinians of their property, lands, and national-political rights was linked to the process that dispossessed Sephardim of their property, lands and rootedness in Arab countries (and within Israel itself, of their history and culture). This overall process has been cynically idealized in Israel's diplomatic pronouncements as a kind of "spontaneous population exchange" and a justification for expelling Palestinians, but the symmetry is factitious, for the so-called "return from exile" of the Arab Jews was far from spontaneous and in any case cannot be equated with the condition of the Palestinians, who have been exiled from their homeland and wish to return there. In Israel itself, as the Palestinians were being forced to leave, the Sephardim underwent a complementary trauma, a kind of image in negative, as it were, of the Palestinian experience. The vulnerable new immigrants were ordered around by arrogant officials, who called them "human dust," and crowded into *ma'abarot* (transient camps), hastily constructed out of corrugated tin. Many were stripped of their "unpronounceable" Arab, Persian, and Turkish names and outfitted with "Jewish" names by Godlike Israeli bureaucrats. The process by which millennial pride and collective self-confidence and creativity were to be destroyed was inaugurated here. This was a kind of Sephardi "middle passage" where the appearance of a voluntary "return from exile" masked a subtle series of coercions. But while Palestinians have been authorized to foster the collective militancy of nostalgia in exile (be it under an Israeli, Syrian, or Kuwaiti passport or on the basis of *laissez-passer)*, Sephardim have been forced by their no-exit situation to repress their communal nostalgia. The pervasive notion of "one people" reunited in their ancient homeland actively disauthorizes any affectionate memory of life before the state of Israel.

"Hebrew Work": Myth and Reality

The Zionist "ingathering from the four corners of the earth" was never the beneficent enterprise portrayed by official discourse. From the early days of Zionism, Sephardim were perceived as a source of cheap labor that had to be maneuvered into immigrating to Palestine. The economic structure that oppresses Sephardim in Israel was set in place in the early days of the *yishuv* (prestate Zionist settlement in Palestine). Among the orienting principles of the dominant socialist Zionism, for example, were the twin notions of *avoda ivrit* (Hebrew work) and *avoda atzmit* (self-labor), suggesting that a person, and a community, should earn from their own, not from hired, labor, an idea whose origins trace back to the Haskalah, or eighteenth-century Hebrew Enlightenment. Many Jewish thinkers, writers, and poets, such as Mapu, Brenner, Borochov, Gordon, and Katznelson, highlighted the necessity of transforming Jews by "productive labor," especially agricultural labor. Such thinkers advanced *avoda ivrit* as a necessary precondition for Jewish recuperation. The policy and practice of *avoda ivrit* deeply affected the historically positive self-image of the Hebrew pioneers and later of Israeli as involved in a noncolonial enterprise, which unlike colonialist Europe did not exploit the "natives" and was, therefore, perceived as morally superior in its aspirations.

In its actual historical implication, however, *avoda ivrit* had tragic consequences, engendering political tensions not only between Arabs and Jews but also between Sephardim and Ashkenazim as well as between Sephardim and Palestinians. At first, the European-Jewish settlers tried to compete with Arab workers for jobs with previously settled Jewish employers; "Hebrew work" then meant in reality the boycotting of Arab work. The immigrants' demands for relatively high salaries precluded their employment, however, thus leading to the emigration of a substantial proportion. At a time when even the poorest of Russian Jews were heading toward the Americas, it was difficult to convince European Jews to come to Palestine. It was only after the failure of Ashkenazi immigration that the Zionist institutions decided to bring in Sephardim. Ya'acov Tehon, from the Eretz Israel Office, wrote in 1908 about this problem of "Hebrew workers." After detailing the economic and psychological obstacles to the goal of *avoda ivrit* as well as the dangers posed by employing masses of Arabs, he proposed, along with other official Zionists, the importation of Sephardim to "replace" the Arab agricultural workers. Since "it is doubtful whether the Ashkenazi Jews are talented for work other than in the city," he argued, "there is a place for the Jews of the Orient, and particularly for the Yemenites and Persians, in the profession of agriculture." Like the Arabs, Tehon goes on, they "are satisfied with very little" and "in this sense they can compete with them."[31] Similarly, in 1910, Shmuel Yavne'eli published in *HaPoel HaTzair* (The young worker, the official organ of the Zionist Party of the Workers in Eretz Israel, later part of the Labor Party) a two-part article entitled "The Renaissance of Work and the Jews of the Orient" in which he called for an Oriental-Jewish solution for the "problem" of the Arab workers. *HaTzvi*, a newspaper, gave expression to this increasingly disseminated position:

> This is the simple, natural worker capable of doing any kind of work, without shame, without philosophy, and also without poetry. And Mr. Marx is of course absent both from his pocket and from his mind. It is not my contention that the Yemenite element should remain in its present state, that is, in his barbarian, wild present state. . . . [T]he Yemenite of today still exists at the same backward level as the *Fellahins*. . . . [T]hey can take the place of the Arabs.[32]

Zionist historiographers have recycled these colonialist myths, applied both to Arabs and to Arab Jews, as a means of justifying the class positioning into which Sephardim were projected. Yemeni workers have been presented as "merely workers," socially "primeval matter," while Ashkenazi workers have been described as "creative" and "idealists, able to be devoted to the ideal, to create new moulds and new content of life."[33]

Regarded by European Zionists as capable of competing with Arabs but refractory to more lofty socialist and nationalist ideals, the

Sephardim seemed ideal imported laborers. Thus the concept of "natural workers" with "minimal needs," exploited by such figures as Ben-Gurion and Arthur Ruppin, came to play a crucial ideological role, a concept subtextually linked to color; to quote Ruppin: "Recognizable in them [Yemeni Jews] is the touch of Arab blood. . . . [T]hey have a very dark color."[34] The Sephardim offered the further advantage of generally being Ottoman subjects, and thus, unlike most Ashkenazim, without legal difficulties in entering the country, partially thanks to Jewish (Sephardi) representation in the Ottoman parliament.[35]

Tempted by the idea of recruiting "Jews in the form of Arabs," Zionist strategists agreed to act on "the Sephardi option." The bald economic-political interest motivating this selective "ingathering" is clearly discernible in emissary Yavne'eli's letters from Yemen, where he states his intention of selecting only "young and healthy people" for immigration.[36] His reports about potential Yemeni laborers go into great detail about the physical characteristics of the different Yemeni regional groups, describing the Jews of Dal'a, for example, as "healthy" with "strong legs," in contrast with the Jews of Ka'ataba, with their "shrunken faces and skinny hands."[37] These policies of a quasi-eugenic selection were repeated during the 1950s in Morocco, where young men were chosen for aliya on the basis of physical and gymnastic tests.

Often deluding Sephardim about realities in the "land of milk and honey," Zionist emissaries engineered the immigration of over ten thousand Sephardim (largely Yemenis) before World War I. They were put to work mainly as agricultural day laborers in extremely harsh conditions to which, despite Zionist mythology, they were *decidedly not* accustomed. Yemeni families were crowded together in stables, pastures, windowless cellars (for which they had to pay) or simply obliged to live in the fields. Unsanitary conditions and malnutrition caused widespread disease and death, especially of infants. The Zionist Association employers and the Ashkenazi landowners and their overseers treated the Yemeni Jews brutally, at times abusing even the women and children who labored over ten hours a day.[38] The ethnic division of labor, in this early stage of Zionism, had as its corollary the sexual division of labor. Tehon wrote in 1907 of the advantages of having "Yemenite families living permanently in the settlements," so that "we could also have women and adolescent girls work in the households instead of the Arab women who now work at high salaries as servants in almost every family of the colonists."[39] Indeed, the "fortunate" women and girls worked as maids; the rest worked in the fields. Economic and political exploitation went hand in hand with habitual European feelings of superiority. Any treatment accorded to the Sephardim was thought to be legitimate, since they were bereft, it was assumed, of all culture, history, or material achievement. Sephardim were excluded, furthermore, from the socialist benefits accorded European workers.[40] Labor Zionism, through the Histadrut (the General Federation of Labor), managed to prevent Yemenis from owning land or joining cooperatives, thus limiting them to the role of wage earners. As with the Arab workers, the dominant "socialist" ideology within Zionism thus provided no guarantee against ethnocentrism. While presenting Palestine as an empty land to be transformed by Jewish labor, the founding fathers presented Sephardim as passive vessels to be shaped by the revivifying spirit of Promethean Zionism.

At the same time, the European Zionists were not enthralled by the prospect of "tainting" the settlements in Palestine with an infusion of Sephardi Jews. The very idea was opposed at the first Zionist Congress.[41] In their texts and congresses, European Zionists consistently addressed their remarks to Ashkenazi Jews and to the colonizing empires that might provide support for a national homeland; the visionary dreams of a Zionist Jewish state were not designed for the Sephardim. But the actual realization of the Zionist project in Palestine, with its concomitant aggressive attitude toward all the local peoples, brought with it the possibility of the exploitation of Sephardi Jews as part of an economic and political base. The strategy of promoting a Jewish majority in Palestine in order to create a Jewish national homeland entailed at first the purchase and later the expropriation of Arab land. The policy, favored by *tzionut ma'asit* (practical Zionism), of creating de facto Jewish occupation of Arab land formed a crucial element in Zionist claims on Palestine. Some Zionists were afraid that Arab workers on Jewish lands might someday declare that "the land belongs to those who work it," whence the need for Jewish (Sephardi) workers. This skewed version of *avoda ivrit* generated a long-term structural competition between Arab workers and the majoritarian group of Jewish (Sephardi) workers, now reduced to the status of a subproletariat.

It was only after the failure of European immigration—even in the post-Holocaust era most European Jews chose to immigrate elsewhere—that the Zionist establishment decided to bring Sephardi immigrants *en masse*. The European-Zionist rescue fantasy concerning the Jews of the Orient, in sum, masked the need to rescue European Zionism from possible economic and political collapse. In the 1950s, similarly, Zionist officials continued to show ambivalence about the mass importation of Sephardi Jews, But once again demographic and economic necessities—settling the country with Jews, securing the borders, and having laborers to work and soldiers to fight—forced the European-Zionist hand. Given this subtext, it is instructive to read the sanitized versions promoted even by those most directly involved in the exploitation of Sephardi labor. Yavne'eli's famous *shlihut* (Zionist mission promoting aliya) to Yemen, for example, has always been idealized by Zionist texts. The gap between the "private" and the more public discourse is particularly striking in the case of Yavne'eli himself: his letters to Zionist institutions stress the search for cheap labor, but his memoirs present his activity in quasi-religious language, as bringing "to our brothers Bnei-Israel [Sons of Israel], far away in the land of Yemen, tidings from Eretz Israel, the good tidings of Renaissance, of the Land and of Work."[42]

The Dialectics of Dependency

These problems, present in embryonic form in the time of the prestate era, came to their bitter "fruition" after the establishment of Israel, but now explained away by a more sophisticated set of rationalizations and idealizations. Israel's rapid economic development during the 1950s and 1960s was achieved on the basis of a systematically unequal distribution of advantages. The socioeconomic structure was thus formed contrary to the egalitarian myths characterizing Israel's self-representation until the last decade. The discriminatory decisions of Israeli officials against Sephardim began even before Sephardi arrival in Israel and were consciously premised on the assumption that the Ashkenazim, as the self-declared "salt of the earth," deserved better conditions and "special privileges."[43]

In contrast with Ashkenazi immigrants, Sephardim were treated inhumanely already in the camps constructed by the Zionists in their lands of origin as well as during transit. A Jewish Agency report on a camp in Algiers speaks of a situation in which "more than fifty people were living in a room of four or five square meters."[44] A doctor working in a Marseilles transit camp for North African Jewish immigrants noted that as a result of the bad housing and the recent decline in nutrition, children had died, adding that "I can't understand why in all the European countries the immigrants are provided with clothes while the North African immigrants are provided with nothing."[45] When information about anti-Sephardi discrimination in Israel filtered back to North Africa, emigration from North Africa declined. Some left the transit camps in order to return to Morocco, while others, to quote a Jewish Agency emissary, had virtually "to be taken aboard the ships by force."[46] In Yemen, the journey across the desert, exacerbated by the inhuman conditions in the Zionist transit camps, led to hunger, disease, and massive death, resulting in a brutal kind of natural selection. Worrying about the burden of caring for sick Yemenis, Jewish Agency members were reassured by their colleague Itzhak Refael (of the Nationalist Religious Party) that "there is no need to fear the arrival of a large number of chronically ill, as they have to walk by foot for about two weeks. The gravely ill will not be able to walk."[47]

The European-Jewish scorn for Eastern-Jewish lives and sensibilities— at times projected onto the Sephardim by Ashkenazi Orientalizing "experts," who claimed that death for Sephardim was a "common and natural thing"—was evident as well in the notorious incident of "the kidnapped children of Yemen."[48] Traumatized by the reality of life in Israel, some Sephardim, most of them Yemenis, fell prey to a ring of unscrupulous doctors, nurses, and social workers who provided, according to some estimations, several thousand Sephardi babies for adoption by Ashkenazi families (some of them outside of Israel, largely in the United States), while telling the natural parents that the children had died. The conspiracy was extensive enough to include the systematic issuance of fraudulent death certificates for the adopted children and to ensure that over several decades Sephardi demands for investigation were silenced and information was hidden and manipulated by government bureaus.[49] On June 30, 1986, the Public Committee for the Discovery of the Missing Yemenite Children held a massive protest rally. The rally, like many Sephardi protests and demonstrations, was almost completely ignored by the media, but a few months later Israeli television produced a documentary on the subject, blaming the bureaucratic chaos of the period for unfortunate "rumors" and perpetuating the myth of Sephardi parents as careless breeders with little sense of responsibility toward their own children.

Ethnic discrimination against Sephardim began with their initial settling. Upon arrival in Israel the various Sephardi communities, despite their will to stay together, were dispersed across the country. Families were separated; old communities disintegrated; and traditional leaders were shorn of their positions. Oriental Jews were largely settled in *ma'abarot*, remote villages, agricultural settlements, and city neighborhoods, some of them only recently emptied of Palestinians. As the absorption facilities became exhausted, the settlement authorities constructed *ayarot pituha* (development towns) largely in rural areas and frontier regions, which became, predictably, the object of Arab attack. The declared policy was to "strengthen the borders," implying not only against Arab military attacks but also against any attempt by Palestinian refugees to return to their homeland. Although Israeli propaganda lauded the better-protected Ashkenazi kibbutzim for their courage in living on the frontiers, in fact their small number (about 3 percent of the Jewish population, and half that if one considers only border settlements) hardly enabled them to secure long borders, while the settlement of the more numerous Sephardim on the borders did ensure a certain security. Sephardi border settlements lacked, furthermore, the strong infrastructure of military protection provided to Ashkenazi settlements, thus leading to Sephardi loss of life. The ethnic segregation that tends to characterize Israeli urban housing also dates from this period. While Ashkenazim tend to live in the more prosperous "northern" zones, Sephardim are concentrated in the less wealthy "southern" zones. Despite this quasi-segregation, the two communities are generally linked in a relation of dependency, whereby the poor neighborhoods serve the privileged neighborhoods, a relational structure that mirrors that between the "socialist" kibbutzim and the neighboring development towns.

In cases where Sephardim were moved into preexisting housing—and in Israel preexisting housing means Palestinian housing—the Sephardim often ended up by living in promiscuous conditions because the Orientalist attitudes of the Israeli authorities found it normal to crowd many Sephardi families into the same house, on the assumption that they were "accustomed" to such conditions. These poor Sephardi neighborhoods were then systematically discriminated against in terms of infrastructural needs, educational and cultural advantages, and political self-representation. Later, when some of these neighborhoods became obstacles to urban gentrification, the Sephardim were forced, against their will and despite violent demonstrations, to other "modern" poor neighborhoods. In Jaffa, for example, the authorities, after the removal of the Sephardim, renovated the very same houses that they had refused to renovate for their Sephardi dwellers, thus facilitating the transition by which sections of "Oriental" Jaffa became a "bohemian" touristic locale dotted with art galleries. More recently, the Sephardi neighborhood of Musrara in Jerusalem has been undergoing a similar process. Now that the neighborhood is no longer near the pre-1967 border, the authorities have been trying to remove its Sephardi residents and force them to relocate to settlements on the West Bank, again under the pretense of improving their material conditions. The pattern is clear and systematic. The areas forcibly vacated by the Sephardim soon become the object of major investments, leading to Ashkenazi gentrification; in these areas the elite enjoy living within a "Mediterranean" *mise-en-scène* but without the inconvenience of a Palestinian or Sephardi presence, while the newly adopted Sephardi neighborhoods become decapitalized slums.

As a cheap, mobile, and manipulable labor-force, Sephardim were indispensable to the economic development of the state of Israel. Given the need for mass housing in the 1950s, many Sephardim became ill-paid construction workers. The high profits generated by the cheap labor led to the rapid expansion of construction firms, managed or owned by Ashkenazim. Recruited especially into the mechanized and nonskilled sectors of agricultural production within large-scale government projects, Sephardim provided much of the labor force for settling the land. In the case of agricultural settlements, they received less and poorer lands than the various Ashkenazi settlements such as the kibbutzim and much less adequate means of production, resulting in lower production, lower income, and gradually the economic collapse of many of the Sephardi settlements.[50] After agricultural development and construction work reached a saturation point in the late 1950s and early 1960s, the government acted to industrialize the country, and Sephardi workers once again were crucial to Israel's rapid development. A large section of the Sephardim came to form, in this period, an industrial proletariat. (In recent years, the monthly wage of production-line workers in textile factories has hovered around $150–200, roughly equivalent to that earned by many Third World workers.)[51] In fact, Israel's appeals for foreign (largely Jewish) investment were partially based on the "attraction" of local cheap labor. The low wages of workers led to a widening gap between the upper and lower salary ranges in the industry. Development towns, essential to industrial production, became virtual "company towns" in which a single factory became the major single provider of employment for a whole town, whose future became inextricably linked to the future of the company.[52]

While the system relegated Sephardim to a futureless bottom, it propelled Ashkenazim up the social scale, creating mobility in management, marketing, banking, and technical jobs. Recent published documents reveal the extent to which discrimination was a calculated policy that knowingly privileged the European immigrants, at times creating anomalous situations in which educated Sephardim became unskilled laborers, while much less educated Ashkenazim came to occupy high administrative positions.[53] Unlike the classical paradigm where immigration is linked to a desire for individual, familial, and community improvement, in Israel this process, for Sephardim, was largely reversed. What for Ashkenazi immigrants from Russia or Poland was a social *aliya* (literally "ascent") was for Sephardi immigrants from Iraq or Egypt a *yerida* (a "descent"). What was for persecuted Ashkenazi minorities a certain solution and a quasi-redemption of a culture was for Sephardim the complete annihilation of a cultural heritage, a loss of identity, and a social and economic degradation.

The Facade of Egalitarianism
These discriminatory policies were executed under the aegis of the Labor Party and its affiliates, whose empire included a tentacular set of institutions, the most important of which was the General Federation

of Labor (Histadrut). The Histadrut controls the agricultural sector, the kibbutzim, and the largest labor unions in the industrial sector. With its own industries, marketing cooperatives, transportation systems, financial institutions, and social-service network, it exercises immense power. (Solleh Boneh, a Histadrut construction company, for example, could easily "freeze out" private builders from the Likud Party.) As a kind of caricature of trade unionism, the Histadrut, despite its professed socialist ideology, generally wields its vast power for the benefit of the elite, consistently favoring Ashkenazim for white-collar management positions and Sephardim for blue-collar skilled and unskilled labor, leaving the latter most vulnerable in situations where factories are closed or workers are laid off. The same relational structure of oppression operates in the process whereby regional factories (even government-owned regional factories) tend to be managed by the largely Ashkenazi kibbutzim while the workers are largely Sephardi or Palestinian. The dominant institutions, and more specifically the "socialist"-Zionist elite, have thus virtually forced the Sephardim into underdevelopment, and this contrary both to Ashkenazi denials that such processes have been taking place and to the claims that those processes were unconscious and uncalculated.

The dominant socialist-humanist discourse in Israel hides this negative dialectic of wealth and poverty behind a mystifying facade of egalitarianism. The Histadrut and the Labor Party, claiming to represent the workers, monopolize socialist language. Their May Day celebrations, the flying of red flags alongside the blue and white, and their speeches in the name of the "working class" mask the fact that the Labor network really represents only the interests of the Euro-Israeli elite, whose members nevertheless still refer to themselves nostalgically as *Eretz Israel HaOvedet* (working Eretz Israel). The Sephardim and the Palestinians, the majority of workers in Israel, have been represented by special Histadrut departments called, respectively, the Oriental Department and the Minority Department. (The Histadrut is not preoccupied, it goes without saying, with the economic exploitation of West Bank and Gaza Strip workers). The manipulation of syndicalist language and the co-optation of socialist slogans have thus served as a smoke screen for classed, racialized, and gendered inequalities. As a consequence, Sephardi militants have had to confront a kind of visceral aversion, on the part of working-class Sephardim, to the very word "socialist," associated, for them, with oppression rather than liberation.

Although the official meliorative discourse suggests a gradual lessening of the "gap" between Sephardim and Ashkenazim, in fact the inequalities are more glaring now than they were two generations ago.[54] The system continues to reproduce itself, for example, in the differential treatment accorded to present-day European immigrants versus that accorded to "veteran" Mizrahim. While second-generation Sephardim stagnate in substandard housing in poor neighborhoods, newly arrived Russian immigrants (with the exception of Asian-Soviets, such as Georgian Jews) are settled by the government into comfortable housing in central areas. (I do not examine here the racism suffered by the Ethiopian Jews, now undergoing what the Sephardim experienced in the 1950s, supplemented by the added humiliation of religious harassment.) Indeed, the ethnic allegiances of the establishment become especially clear with regard to immigration policy. While supposedly promoting universal aliya and the end to the Diaspora, the establishment, given its (unnamed) fear of a Sephardi demographic advantage, energetically promotes immigration by Soviet Jews—a majority of whom would prefer to go elsewhere—while dragging its feet in response to the Ethiopian Jews (Falashas), who wish to go and whose very lives have been endangered.

The largely segregated and unequal educational system in Israel also reproduces the ethnic division of labor through a tracking system that consistently orients Ashkenazi pupils toward prestigious white-collar positions requiring a strong academic preparation while pointing Sephardi pupils toward low-status blue-collar jobs. Euro-Israelis have double the representation in white-collar occupations. The schools in Ashkenazi neighborhoods have better facilities, better teachers, and higher status. Ashkenazim have on the average three more years of schooling than Sephardim. Their attendance rate in academic high school is 2.4 times as high, and it is 5 times as high in universities.[55] Most Mizrahi children, furthermore, study in schools designated by the Ministry of Education as schools for the *teunei tipuah* (literally, "those who need nurture," or "the culturally deprived"), a designation premised on the equation of cultural difference with inferiority. The educational system functions, as Shlomo Swirski puts it, as "a huge labelling mechanism that has, among other things, the effect of lowering the achievement and expectations of Oriental children and their parents."[56]

On whatever level—immigration policy, urban development, labor policy, or government subsidies—we find the same pattern of a racialized discrimination that touches even the details of daily life. The government, for example, subsidizes certain basic dietary staples, one of them being European-style bread; the pita favored as a staple by both Sephardim and Palestinians, meanwhile, is not subsidized. These discriminatory processes, which were shaped in the earliest period of Zionism, are reproduced every day and on every level, reaching into the very interstices of the Israeli social system. As a result, the Sephardim, despite their majority status, are underrepresented in the national centers of power—in the government, in the Knesset, in the higher echelons of the military, in the diplomatic corps, in the media, and in the academic world—and they are overrepresented in the marginal, stigmatized regions of professional and social life.

The dominant sociological accounts of Israel's "ethnic problem" have attributed the inferior status of Oriental Jews not to the classed and raced structure of Israeli society but rather to their origins in "premodern," "culturally backward" societies. Borrowing heavily from the intellectual arsenal of American functionalist studies of development and modernization, Shumuel Eisenstadt and his many social-scientist disciples gave ideological subterfuge the aura of scientific rationality. The influential role of this "modernization" theory derived from its perfect match with the needs of the establishment.[57] Eisenstadt borrowed from American structural functionalism (Parsons) its teleological view of a "progress" that takes us from "traditional" societies, with their less complex social structures, to "modernization" and "development." Since the Israeli social formation was seen as that entity collectively created during the *Yishuv* period, the immigrants were perceived as integrating themselves into the preexisting dynamic whole of a modern society patterned on the Western model. The underlying premise of Zionism, the "ingathering of the exiles," was thus translated into the sociological jargon of structural functionalism. The "absorption" *(klita)* of Sephardi immigrants into Israeli society entailed the acceptance of the established consensus of the "host" society and the abandonment of "premodern" traditions. While European immigrants required only "absorption," the immigrants from Africa and Asia required "absorption through modernization." For the Eisenstadt tradition, the Oriental Jews had to undergo a process of "deserialization" (i.e., erasure of their cultural heritage) and of "resocialization" (i.e., assimilation to the Ashkenazi way of life). Thus cultural difference was posited as the cause of maladjustment. (The theory would have trouble explaining why other Sephardim, coming from the same "premodern" countries, at times from the very same families, suffered no particular maladjustment in such "postmodern" metropolises as Paris, London, New York, and Montreal.) At times the victim is even blamed for blaming an oppressive system. Here is sociologist Yosef Ben David: "In such cases ethnic difficulties will render yet more acute the immigration crisis. . . . The immigrant will tend to rationalize the failure by putting the blame openly or implicitly on ethnic discrimination."[58]

The Ashkenazim, however, hid behind the flattening term "Israeli society," an entity presumed to embody the values of modernity, industry, science, and democracy. As Swirski points out, this presentation camouflaged the actual historical processes by obscuring a number of facts: first, that the Ashkenazim, not unlike the Sephardim, had also come from countries on the periphery of the world capitalist system, countries that entered the process of industrialization and technological-scientific development roughly at the same time as the Sephardi countries of origin; second, that a peripheral *Yishuv* society had *also* not reached a level of development comparable to that of the societies of the "center"; and, third, that Ashkenazi "modernity" was made possible thanks to the labor force provided by Oriental mass immigration.[59] The ethnic/racial basis of this process is often elided even by most Marxist analysts who speak generically of "Jewish workers," a simplification roughly parallel to speaking of the exploitation of "American" workers in Southern cotton plantations.

The Ordeals of Civility
The Oriental Jew clearly represents a problematic entity for European hegemony in Israel. Although Zionism collapses the Sephardim and the Ashkenazim into the single category of "one people," at the same time the Sephardi's Oriental "difference" threatens the European

ideal-ego that fantasizes Israel as a prolongation of Europe "in" the Middle East but not "of" it. Ben-Gurion, we may recall, formulated his visionary Utopia for Israel as that of a "Switzerland of the Middle East," while Herzl called for a Western-style capitalist-democratic miniature state, to be made possible by the grace of imperial patrons such as England or even Germany. The leitmotif of Zionist texts is the cry to form a "normal civilized nation," without the myriad "distortions" and forms of pariahdom typical of the Diaspora. (Zionist revulsion for shtetl "abnormalities," as some commentators have pointed out, is often strangely reminiscent of the very anti-Semitism it presumably so abhors.) The Ostjuden, perennially marginalized by Europe, realized their desire of becoming Europe, ironically, in the Middle East, this time on the back of their own "Ostjuden," the Eastern Jews. Having passed through their own "ordeal of civility," as the "blacks" of Europe, they now imposed their civilizing tests on "their own" blacks.[60]

The paradox of secular Zionism is that it attempted to end the Diaspora, during which Jews suffered intensely in the West and presumably had their heart in the East—a feeling encapsulated in the almost daily repetition of the phrase "next year in Jerusalem"—only to found a state whose ideological and geopolitical orientation has been almost exclusively turned toward the West. It is in this same context that we must understand the oppression of Sephardi not only as Middle Eastern people but also as embodying, for the Sabra-Zionist mind, what it erroneously perceived as a reminiscence of an "inferior" shtetl Jewishness. (This attitude was at times expressed toward Ashkenazi newcomers as well.) The immigrants or refugees from the Third World, and especially from Arab-Muslim countries, provoked "anti-Jewish" feelings in the secularly oriented Sabra culture both because of the implicitly threatening idea of the heterogeneity of Jewish cultures and because of the discomforting amalgam of "Jewishness" and what was perceived as "backwardness." This latter combination was seen as a malignancy to be eradicated, and this ideological impulse was manifested in measures taken to strip Sephardi Jews of their heritage: religious Yemenis shorn of their sidelocks, children virtually forced into Euro-Zionist schools, and so forth. The openness toward Western culture, then, must be understood within the relational context of a menacing heteroglossia, as a reaction against the vestiges of shtetl culture as well as against a projected penetration of "alien" Oriental Jews. The Sephardi cultural difference was especially disturbing to a secular Zionism whose claims for representing a single Jewish people were premised not only on common religious background but also on common nationality. The strong cultural and historical links that Sephardim shared with the Arab-Muslim world, stronger in many respects than those they shared with the Ashkenazim, threatened the conception of a homogeneous nation akin to those on which European nationalist movements were based.

Those Sephardim who came under the control of Ashkenazi religious authorities, meanwhile, were obliged to send their children to Ashkenazi religious schools, where they learned the "correct" Ashkenazi forms of practicing Judaism, including Yiddish-accented praying, liturgical-gestural norms, and sartorial codes favoring the dark colors of centuries-ago Poland. Some Oriental Jews, then, were forced into the Orthodox mold. The caricatural portrayal of Sephardim as religious fanatics, when not the product of *mauvaise foi*, is linked to a Eurocentric confusion between religiousness and Orthodoxy. In fact, however, the wrenching dechirement of the secular-Orthodox split, so characteristic of the European-Jewish experience, has been historically quite alien to Sephardi culture. Among Sephardim, Jewishness has generally been lived in an atmosphere of flexibility and tolerance, downplaying both abstract laws and rabbinical hierarchy. It is not uncommon, among Sephardim, to find coexisting within the same family diverse ways of being Jewish without this diversity entailing conflict. In Israel, the clash that pits secular against Orthodox Jews largely divides Ashkenazim rather than Sephardim, the majority of whom, whether religious or secular, feel repelled by the rigidity of both camps while being mindful of the ways both camps have oppressed them, albeit in different ways.

As an integral part of the topography, language, culture, and history of the Middle East, Sephardim were necessarily close to those who were posited as the common enemy for all Jews—the Arabs. Fearing an encroachment of the East upon the West, the establishment repressed the Middle Easternness of Sephardim as part of an attempt to separate and create hostility between the two groups. Arabness and Orientalness were consistently stigmatized as evils to be uprooted. For the Arab

Jew, existence under Zionism has meant a profound and visceral schizophrenia, mingling stubborn self-pride with an imposed self-rejection,
typical products of a situation of colonial ambivalence. The ideological
dilemmas of Sephardim derive from the contradictions inherent in a
situation where they are urged to see Judaism and Zionism as syn-
onyms and Jewishness and Arabness as antonyms (for the first time in
their history), when in fact they are both Arab and Jewish, and less
historically, materially, and emotionally invested in Zionist ideology
than the Ashkenazim.

Sephardim in Israel were made to feel ashamed of their dark olive
skin, of their guttural language, of the winding quarter tones of their
music, and even of their traditions of hospitality. Children, trying desperately to conform to an elusive Sabra norm, were made to feel
ashamed of their parents and their Arab countries of origins. At times
the Semitic physiognomies of the Sephardim led to situations in which
they were mistaken for Palestinians and therefore arrested or beaten.
Since Arabness led only to rejection, many Sephardim internalized the
Euro-Israeli perspective and turned into self-hating Sephardim. Thus
not only did the "West" come to represent the "East," but also, in a
classic play of colonial specularity, the East came to view itself
through the West's distorting mirror. Indeed, if it is true, as Malcolm
X said, that the white man's worst crime was to make the black man
hate himself, then the establishment in Israel has much to answer for.
In fact, Arab-hatred when it occurs among Oriental Jews is almost
always a disguised form of self-hatred. As research from 1978 indicates,
Sephardi respect for Arabs rises with their own self-esteem.[61]

Sephardi hostility to Arabs, to the extent that it does exist, is very
much "made in Israel."[62] Oriental Jews had to be taught to see the
Arabs, and themselves, as other. The kind of *selbst-hass* that sometimes marked the post-Enlightenment Ashkenazi community had
never been a part of Sephardi existence in the Muslim world; for the
Sephardim, *selbst-hass* (of themselves as Orientals) had to be
"learned" from the Ashkenazim, who themselves had "learned" self-
hatred at the feet and among the ranks of the Europeans. Here too we
are confronted with problematic antonyms, in this case that
opposing the words "Zionism" and "anti-Semitism." (But that subject merits separate discussion.)

The Demonization of Sephardim

The "divide and conquer" approach to Sephardi/Palestinian relations operated, as we have seen, by turning Sephardim into the most accessible targets for Arab attacks as well as in the deformation of the ideal of "Hebrew work." But the everyday power mechanisms in Israeli society also foster concrete economic pressures that generate tension between the two communities. Those Sephardim who continue to constitute the majority of the Jewish blue-collar workers are constantly placed in competition with the Palestinians for jobs and salaries, a situation that allows the elite to exploit both groups more or less at will. The considerable government expenditures for West Bank settlements, similarly, prod some Sephardim to move there for economic reasons—rather than ideological reasons that motivate many Ashkenazi settlers—and thus provoke Palestinians. Finally, because of the segregation between the two, Sephardim and Palestinians in Israel tend to learn about each other through the Euro-Israeli-dominated media, with little direct contact. Thus the Sephardim learn to see the Palestinians as "terrorists," while the Palestinians learn to see Sephardim as "Kahanist fanatics," a situation that hardly facilitates mutual understanding and recognition.

Although liberal left discourse in Israel has in recent years taken a small step toward recognizing the "Palestinian entity," it continues to hermetically seal off the Sephardi issue as an internal social problem to be solved once peace is achieved. Just as this discourse elides the historical origins of the Palestinian struggle and thus nostalgically looks back to an imagined prelapsarian past of "beautiful Israel," so it also elides the historical origins of Sephardi resentment and thus constructs the myth of "reactionaries." One problem is compartmentalized as political and foreign and the other as social and internal; the mutual implication of the two issues and their common relation to Ashkenazi domination are ignored. In fact the Sephardi movement constitutes a more immediate threat to Ashkenazi privilege and status than the abstract, perpetually deferred, future solution to the Palestinian question. Whereas the "Palestinian problem" can be still presented as the inevitable clash of two nationalities, acknowledgment of the exploitation and deculturalization of Sephardim in a putatively egalitarian Jewish state implies the indictment of the Israeli system itself as incorrigibly oppressive toward all peoples of the Orient.

Peace Now leaders such as General Mordechai Bar-On attribute the lack of Sephardi enthusiasm for Peace Now to "strong rightist tendencies" and "excited loyalty to the personal leadership of Menahem Begin," symptomatic of the Sephardim's "natural and traditional tendency . . . to follow a charismatic leader," all compounded with a "deep-rooted distrust in the Arabs."[63] The Sephardi other is portrayed as uncritical, instinctual, and, in accord with Oriental-despotic traditions, easily manipulated by patriarchal demagogues. The Sephardim, when not ignored by the Israeli "left," appear only to be scapegoated for everything that is wrong with Israel: "they" have destroyed beautiful Israel; "they" are turning Israel into a right-wing, antidemocratic state; "they" support the occupation; "they" are an obstacle to peace. These prejudices are then disseminated by Israeli "leftists" in international conferences, lectures, and publications. The caricatural presentation of Sephardim is a way for the Israeli left to enjoy a self-celebratory we-of-the-liberal-West image before international public opinion (at a time when Israel has undeniably lost its progressive allure and past unquestioned status) while continuing to enjoy, in Israel itself, a comfortable position as an integral part of the establishment. This facile scapegoating of Sephardim for a situation generated by Ashkenazi Zionists elides the reality of significant Sephardi pro-Palestinian activities as well as the lack of Sephardi access to the media and the consequent inability to counter such charges, which are then taken seriously by Palestinians and public opinion around the world. The demonization of Sephardim also has the advantage of placing the elite protesters in the narcissistic posture of perpetual seekers after peace who must bear the hostility of the government, the right wing, the Sephardim, and recalcitrant Palestinians. This martyrdom of the "shoot-and-cry" public-relations left contributes almost nothing to peace, but it does create the optical illusion of a viable oppositional peace force. Even the progressive forces in the peace camp that support a Palestinian state alongside Israel seldom abandon the idea of a Jewish Western state whose subtext inevitably is the ethnic/racial and class oppression of Sephardim. Within such a context, it is hardly surprising that the membership of Peace Now is almost exclusively Ashkenazi, with almost no Sephardi, or for that matter, Palestinian, participation.

Sephardi hostility toward Peace Now, rather than being discussed in class and racial terms, is conveniently displaced by Ashkenazi liberals onto the decoy-issue of a presumed general Sephardi animosity toward Arabs. This formulation ignores a number of crucial points. First, anti-Arabism forms an integral part of Zionist practice and ideology; Sephardim should not be scapegoated for what the Ashkenazi establishment itself has promoted. Second, Ashkenazim form the leadership of the right-wing parties, and many Euro-Israelis vote for these parties. (Polls taken during the 1981 elections showed that 36 percent of foreign-born Ashkenazim and 45 percent of Israeli-born Ashkenazim opted for Likud.[64] Sephardim, for their part, have also voted for Labor and other liberal parties, including the Communist Party.) In fact, however, the relatively high Sephardi vote for Likud has little to do with the latter's policies toward the Arabs; it is, rather, a minimal and even misplaced expression of Sephardi revolt against decades of Labor oppression. Since Sephardim cannot really represent themselves within the Israeli political system, a vote for the opposition interests within the ruling class becomes a way, as some Sephardi militants put it, of "strengthening the hyena in order to weaken the bear." Some independent leftist Sephardi activists viewed Likud, for example, as "an overnight shelter" where Oriental Jews could find temporary refuge while beginning to forge a powerful Sephardi revolt. The difference between Likud and Labor with regard to the Palestinians, in any case, has not been one of practice but rather one of discourse, one aggressive-nationalist and the other humanist-liberal. The difference between the two parties with regard to Sephardim, similarly, is less one of policy than one of a contrast between populist appeals (Likud) and elitist condescension (Labor).

From Kahane to the Communists, the ideologies of the Israeli parties—from non-Zionist religious Orthodoxy dating back to Eastern European anti-Zionist opposition, through religious nationalism that foregrounds the "holiness of the land" (a religious variant on a common topos of European nationalism), to the dominant secular-humanist Zionism, based on European Enlightenment ideals—"translate" on a political register the various Jewish-European identity dilemmas. Founded, led, and controlled by Ashkenazim, these parties are the locus of struggle over the share of power among the various Ashkenazi groups. Within this structure there is little place for Sephardi aspirations. The

Jewish-Sephardi majority has been politically marginalized, in other words, in a Jewish state, and in what is ritually and erroneously referred to as the "only democracy in the Middle East." The historical reasons for this marginalization are complex and can hardly be detailed here, but they include the following: the historical legacy of the Ashkenazi domination of the institutional party apparati prior to the arrival en masse of the Sephardim; the inertia of a hierarchical top-down structure that leaves little room for major shifts in direction; the delegitimization of the traditional Sephardi leadership; objectively harsh conditions, in the 1950s and 1960s, which left little time and energy for effective political and communal reorganization; and the repression as well as the co-optation of Sephardi revolts.

Political manipulation of Sephardi immigrants began virtually on their arrival, and at times even before, when Israeli party recruiters competed for Sephardi allegiance in the diverse countries of origins of Sephardim. In Israel, the immigrants or refugees were met in the airports not only by the officials in charge of arrival procedures but also by representatives of the various parties, who parceled out the Sephardim along the existing political spectrum. In the *ma'abarot*, as in Palestinian villages, the government controlled the populace through the intermediary of "notables" authorized to dispense favors in exchange for votes. At the time of the foundation of the state, there was some discussion of having a token Sephardi among the first twelve cabinet members, and considerable energy was expended on finding a sufficiently insignificant post ("The Sephardi minister," said David Remez of the Labor Party, "cannot have any grandiose pretensions").[65] At the same time, the Ashkenazi institutional apparatus has always claimed to represent the interests of all Jewish people, including Sephardim, as demonstrated by the proliferation of "Oriental departments." Unlike Palestinians, Sephardim were never denied official access to any Israeli institutions, and they were allowed, even encouraged, to find refuge in existing organizations. Class resentments could thus be exorcised through "socialist" organizations, while traditional Jewish activities could be entertained through religious institutions.

Signs of Sephardi Rebellion
Despite these obstacles, Sephardi revolt and resistance have been

constant. Already in the transient camps there were "bread-and-jobs" demonstrations. David Horowitz, then general director of the Ministry of Finance, during a political consultation with Ben-Gurion, described the Sephardi population in the camps as "rebellious" and the situation as "incendiary" and "dynamite."[66] Another major revolt against misery and discrimination began in Haifa, in the neighborhood of Wadi-Salib, in 1959. Israeli authorities suppressed the rebellion with military and police terror. The Labor Party (Mapai), furthermore, tried to undermine the political organization that emerged from the riots by obliging slum residents to join the party if they hoped for a job. Another large-scale rebellion broke out again in the 1970s, when the Israeli Black Panthers called for the destruction of the regime and for the legitimate rights of all the oppressed without regard to religion, origin, or nationality. This alarmed the establishment, and the movement's leaders were arrested and placed under administrative detention. At that moment, the Black Panthers launched demonstrations that shook the entire country. In a demonstration that has since become famous (May 1971), tens of thousands, in response to police repression, went into the streets and threw Molotov cocktails against police and government targets. The same evening, 170 activists were arrested; 35 were hospitalized; and more than 70 policemen and officers were wounded. Taking their name from the American movement, the Black Panther revolt was led by the children of the Arab-Jewish immigrants, many of them having passed through rehabilitation centers or prisons. Gradually becoming aware of the political nature of their "inferiority," they sabotaged the myth of the melting pot by showing that there is in Jewish Israel not one but two peoples. They often used the term *dfukim veshehorim* (screwed and blacks) to express the racial/class positioning of Sephardim and viewed the American black revolt as a source of inspiration. (The choice of the name "Black Panthers" also ironically reverses the Ashkenazi reference to Sephardim as "black animals.") More recently, in December 1982, riots broke out in response to the police murder of a Mizrahi slum resident whose only crime was to build an illegal extension to his overcrowded house.

The establishment, meanwhile, has consistently tried to explain away all manifestations of Sephardi revolt. The "bread-and-jobs" demonstrations in the transient camps were dismissed as the result of the agitational work of leftist Iraqi immigrants; the demonstrations of Wadi-Salib and the Black Panthers were the expression of "violence-prone Moroccans"; individual acts of resistance were the symptoms of "neurosis" or "maladjustment." Golda Meir, prime minister during the Black Panther revolts, complained maternalistically that "they are not nice kids." Demonstrators were described in the press and in academic studies as lumpen proletarian deviants, and the movements were caricatured in the media as "ethnic organizing" and an attempt to "divide the nation." Class and ethnic antagonisms were often suppressed in the name of a supposedly imminent national-security disaster. In any case, all attempts at independent Sephardi political activity have faced the carrot-and-stick countermeasures of the establishment, measures that range on a spectrum from symbolic gestures toward token "change" channeled via the welfare infrastructure, through systematic co-optation of Sephardi activists (offering jobs and privilege is a major source of power in a small centralized country), to harassment, character assassination, imprisonment, torture, and, at times, pressures to leave the country.

The orchestrated attacks on Sephardi independent political activities—including by the "left"—were executed in the name of national unity in the face of the Arab threat. The assumption throughout was that the dominant parties were *not* "ethnic"—the very word, here as often, reflects a marginalizing strategy premised on the implicit contrast of "norm" and "other"—when in fact the existing Israeli institutions were *already* ethnically based according to countries of origins, a reality masked by a linguistic facade that made the Ashkenazim "Israelis" and the Sephardim *Bnei Edot haMizrah* (sons of the Oriental ethnic communities). The plural here covered the fact of the Sephardi numerical superiority, emphasizing plurality of origin, in contrast with a presumed preexisting (Ashkenazi) Israeli unity, and disguised the fact that the Sephardim, whatever their country of origin, have come in Israel to form a collective entity based both on cultural affinities and on the shared experience of oppression. Like many other ethnically/racially based dominating groups, the Israeli Ashkenazim have a kind of *pudeur* about being named; they rarely refer to themselves, or their power, as Ashkenazi; they do not see themselves as an ethnic group (partially because "Ashkenazi" evokes the "unflattering" memory of shtetl Jews).

The Sephardim, however, do not share this *pudeur*. Sephardim, whatever their superficial political allegiance, often refer to the "Ashkenazi state," "the Ashkenazi newspapers," "the Ashkenazi television," "the Ashkenazi parties," "the Ashkenazi court," and at times even "the Ashkenazi army." The overwhelming majority of army deserters is to be found in the Sephardi community, particularly among the very working class, whose behavior reveals a reluctance to "give anything to this Ashkenazi state," and this in a society whose very structure sends the subliminal message: "Fight the Arabs and then we will accept you." A recent editorial in a Sephardi-neighborhood newspaper, entitled "Forty Years of the Ashkenazi State," summed up Sephardi feelings after four decades of statehood:

> This is the 40th year of independence for the Ashkenazi state called Israel, but who is going to celebrate? Our Oriental brothers who sit in jails? Our prostitute sisters from Tel Baruch? Our sons in schools, will they be celebrating the decline in the level of education? Will we celebrate the Ashkenazi theater of Kishon's Sallah? Or the rising fanaticism in our society? The flight from peace? The Oriental music broadcast only in the ghettoes of the media? The unemployment in development towns? It seems that the Orientals have no reason to celebrate. The joy and light are only for the Ashkenazim, and for the glory of the Ashkenazi state.[67]

Although effaced or overshadowed by the Israeli/Arab conflict, and despite official harassment, Sephardi resistance is always present, going through transformations, changing organizational forms. Despite the attempts to engender hostility between Sephardim and Palestinians, there have always been Sephardi activities in favor of justice for the Palestinians. Many members of the older Sephardi generation, both inside and outside of Israel, were eager to serve as a bridge of peace to the Arabs and to the Palestinians, but their efforts were consistently refused or undercut by the establishment.[68] The Black Panthers, seeing themselves as a "natural bridge" for peace, called in the 1970s for a "real dialogue" with the Palestinians, who are "an integral part of the political landscape of the Middle East" and whose "representatives must be allowed to take part in all meetings and discussions which seek a solution to the conflict."[69] The Panthers were also among the first Israeli groups to meet with the PLO. In the 1980s, movements such as East for Peace and the Oriental Front in Israel and Perspectives Judeo-Arabes in France—the names themselves point to the shedding of self-shame and the vision of integration into the political and cultural East—have called for an independent Palestinian state led by the PLO. The Oriental Front stresses that Sephardim are not Zionists in the conventional sense, but rather "in the Biblical meaning of Zion,' of a Jewish life in the birthplace of the Jewish people." It stresses as well the "debt of respect to Arab countries that gave [us] protection during centuries" and the strong Sephardi love and respect for Arab culture, since "there is no alienation between the Arab existence and the Oriental [Jewish] one."[70]

Epilogue

In many respects, European Zionism has been an immense confidence trick played on Sephardim, a cultural massacre of immense proportions, an attempt, partially successful, to wipe out, in a generation or two, millennia of rooted Oriental civilization, unified even in its diversity. *My argument here, I hasten to clarify, is not an essentialist one. I am not positing a new binarism of eternal hostility between Ashkenazim and Sephardim. In many countries and situations, the two groups, despite cultural and religious differences, have coexisted in relative peace; it is only in Israel that they exist in a relation of dependency and oppression. (In any case, only 10 percent of Ashkenazi Jews are in Israel.) Obviously, Ashkenazi Jews have been the prime victims of the most violent kinds of European anti-Semitism, a fact that makes it more delicate to articulate not only a pro-Palestinian point of view but also a pro-Sephardi point of view. A Sephardi critique is expected to be suppressed in the name of the menaced "unity of the Jewish people" in the post-Holocaust era (as if within all unities, especially those of recent construction, there were not also differences and dissonances). My argument is also not a moralistic or characterological one, positing a Manichaean schematism contrasting good Oriental Jews with evil Ashkenazi oppressors. My argument is structural, an attempt to account theoretically for the "structure of feeling," the deep current of rage against the Israeli establishment that unites most Sephardim independent of their declared party affiliation. My argument is situational and analytical; it claims that the Israeli sociopolitical formation continually generates the underdevelopment of the Mizrahim.

A specter haunts European Zionism, the specter that all of its victims—Palestinians, Sephardim (as well as critical Ashkenazim, in and outside Israel, stigmatized as "self-hating" malcontents)—will perceive the linked analogies between their oppressions. To conjure this specter, the Zionist establishment in Israel has done everything in its power: the fomenting of war and the cult of national security, the simplistic portrayal of Palestinian resistance as terrorism; the fostering of situations that catalyze Sephardi-Palestinian tension; the caricaturing of Sephardim as Arab-haters and religious fanatics; the promotion, through the educational system and the media, of Arab-hatred and Sephardi self-rejection; the repression or co-optation of all those who might promote a progressive Palestinian-Sephardi alliance. I in no way mean to equate Palestinian and Sephardi suffering—obviously Palestinians are those most egregiously wronged by Zionism—or to compare the long lists of crimes against both. The point is one of affinity and analogy rather than perfect identity of interests or experience. I am not asking Palestinians to feel sorry for the Sephardi soldiers who might be among those shooting at them. It is not Sephardim, obviously, who are being killed, time after time, in the streets of Gaza or in the refugee camps of Lebanon. What is at stake, in any case, is not a competition for sympathy but a search for alternatives. Until now both Palestinians and Sephardim have been the objects and not the subjects of Zionist ideology and policies, and until now they have been played against each other. But it was not the Sephardim who made the crucial decisions leading to the brutal displacement and oppression of the Palestinians—even if the Sephardim were enlisted as cannon fodder after the fact—just as it was not the Palestinians who uprooted, exploited, and humiliated the Sephardim. The present regime in Israel inherited from Europe a strong aversion to respecting the right of self-determination of non-European peoples; whence the quaint vestigial, out-of-step quality of its discourse, its atavistic talk of the "civilized nations" and "the civilized world." As much as it is impossible to imagine peace between Israel and the Arabs without recognizing and affirming the historical rights of the Palestinian people, so a real peace must not overlook the collective rights of Mizrahim. It would be short-sighted to negotiate only with those in power or embraced by it, dis-missing the subjection of Jews from Arab and Muslim countries as an "internal Jewish" problem; that position would be analogous to taking the Zionist attitude that the Palestinian question is an "internal" Arab problem. I am not suggesting, obviously, that all Sephardim would ascribe to my analysis, although most would endorse much of it. I am suggesting, rather, that only such an analysis can account for the com-plexities of the present situation and the depth and extent of Sephardi rage. My analysis hopes, finally, to open up a long-range perspective that might aid in a larger effort to move beyond the present intolerable impasse.

• • •

Notes

Throughout this essay, all translations from the Hebrew are mine.

[1]·Edward Said, *Orientalism* (New York: Vintage, 1978), 31.

[2]·Arye Gelblum, *HaAretz*, April 22, 1949.

[3]·Ibid.

[4]·David Ben-Gurion, *Eternal Israel* (Tel Aviv: Ayanot, 1964), 34.

[5]·Quoted in Sammy Smooha, *Israel: Pluralism and Conflict* (Berkeley: Univer-sity of California Press, 1978), 88.

[6]·Abba Eban, *Voice of Israel* (New York, 1957), 76, as quoted in Smooha, *Israel*

[7]·Quoted in Smooha, *Israel*, 44

[8]·Quoted in ibid., 88–89.

[9]·Quoted in Tom Segev, *1949: The First Israelis* (New York: Free Press, 1986), 156–57.

[10]·Quoted in Tom Segev, *1949: The First Israelis* (Jerusalem: Domino Press, 1984), 156 (in Hebrew).

[11]·See Frantz Fanon, *The Wretched of the Earth* (New York: Grove Press, 1964), 51.

[12]·Quotations taken from Segev, 1949, 157 (Hebrew).

[13]·Quoted in David K. Shipler, *Arab and Jew* (New York: Times Books, 1986), 24.

[14]·Amnon Dankner, "I Have No Sister," *HaAretz*, February 18, 1983.

[15]·Dr. Devora and Rabbi Menachem Hacohen, *One People: The Story of the Eastern Jews* (New York: Adama Books, 1986).

[16]·Ora Gloria Jacob-Arzooni, *The Israeli Film: Social and Cultural Influences, 1912–1973* (New York: Garland, 1983), 22, 23, 25. For a critique of Israeli colonial discourse, see Ella Shohat, *Israeli Cinema: East/West and the Politics of Representation* (Austin: University of Texas Press, 1989).

[17]·See Fanon, *Wretched of the Earth*, 51.

[18]·On the various forms of encouragement given to Yiddish in Israel, see Itzhak Koren (of the World Council for Yiddish and Jewish Culture), "Letter to the Editor," *Ma'ariv*, December 4, 1987.

[19]·See Maxime Rodinson, "A Few Simple Thoughts on Anti-Semitism" in *Cult, Ghetto, and State* (London: Al Saqi, 1983).

[20]·See Abbas Shiblak, *The Lure of Zion* (London: Al Saqi, 1986).

[21]·Yosef Meir, *Beyond the Desert* (Israel: Ministry of Defence, 1973), 19, 20 (in Hebrew).

[22]·Yehoshua Porath, *The Emergence of the Palestinian-Arab National Movement, 1919–1929* (Tel Aviv: Am Oved, 1976), 49 (in Hebrew).

[23]·Ibid., 48.

[24]·Ibid.

[25]·Ibid., 48–49.

[26]·Ibid., 49.

[27]·Ibid., 22, 23, 24.

[28]·See *Haolam Haze*, April 20, 1966 (Hebrew); *The Black Panther*, November 9, 1972 (Hebrew); Wilbur Crane Eveland, *Ropes of Sands: America's Failure in the Middle East* (New York: Norton, 1980), 48–49; Shiblak, *Lure of Zion;*

Uri Avnery, *My Friend, the Enemy* (Westport, Conn.: Lawrence Hill, 1986), 133–40.

[29]·Segev, *1949*, 167 (Hebrew).

[30]·See "Denaturalization" and "Exodus," in Shiblak, *Lure of Zion*, 78–127.

[31]·Quoted in Yosef Meir, *The Zionist Movement and the Jews of Yemen* (Tel Aviv: Afikim Library, 1983), 43 (Hebrew).

[32]·Quoted in ibid., 48.

[33]·See Yaakov Zerubavel, *Alei-haim* (Tel Aviv: Y. L. Peretz Library Publication, 1960) (Hebrew).

[34]·Arthur Ruppin, *Chapters of My Life* (Tel Aviv: Am Oved, 1968), pt. 2, p. 27 (Hebrew).

[35]·Yaakov Rabinovitz, *HaPoel HaTzair*, July 6, 1910.

[36]·Shmuel Yavne'eli, *A Journey to Yemen* (Tel Aviv: Ayanot, 1963), 106 (Hebrew).

[37]·Ibid., 83–90.

[38]·Meir, *Zionist Movement*, 97–98.

[39]·Quoted in ibid., 44.

[40]·See Meir, *Zionist Movement*, esp. 113–21. Cf. Niza Droyan, *And Not with a Magic Carpet* (Jerusalem: Ben-Tzvi Institute for Research into the Communities of Israel in the East 134–48 (in Hebrew).

[41]·Meir, *Zionist Movement*, 58.

[42]·Quoted in ibid., 65.

[43]·Segev, *1949*, 171–74 (Hebrew).

[44]·Quoted in Segev, *1949*, 169 (English).

[45]·Quoted in ibid., 166 (Hebrew).

[46]·Ibid., 167, 328.

[47]·Ibid., 330.

[48]·Ibid., 178.

[49]·See Dov Levitan, "The *Aliya* of the 'Magic Carpet' as a Historical Continuation of the Earlier Yemenite *Aliyas*" (M.A. thesis, Bar Ilan University [Israel], 1983) (Hebrew); Segev, *1949*, 185–87, 331 (Hebrew).

[50]·Segev, *1949*, 172–73 (Hebrew).

[51]·Shlomo Swirski and Menahem Shoushan, *Development Towns in Israel* (Haifa: Breirot Publishers, 1986), 7.

[52]·See ibid.

[53]·For citations from some of the documents, see Segev, *1949* (English) particularly pt. 2: Between Veterans and Newcomers," 93–194.

[54]·Ya'acov Nahon, *Patterns of Education Expansion and the Structure of Occupation Opportunies: the Ethnic Dimension* (Jerusalem: Jerusalem Institute for the Research of Israel, 1987).

[55]·Smooha, *Israel*, 178–79.

[56]·Shlomo Swirski, "The Oriental Jews in Israel," *Dissent* 31, no. 1 (winter 1984): 84.

[57]·Shlomo Swirski, *Orientals and Ashkenazim in Israel* (Haifa: Mahbarot LeMehkar UleBikoret, (Hebrew).

[58]·Yosef Ben David, "Integration and Development," in S. N. Eisenstadt, Rivkah Bar Yosef, and Haim Adler, eds., *Integration and Development in Israel* (Jerusalem: Israel Universities Press, 1970), 374.

[59]·Swirski, *Orientals*, 53–54.

[60]·For a discussion of the secular European-Jewish encounter with Protestant culture, see John Murray Cuddihy, *The Ordeal of Civility* (Boston: Beacon Press, 1974).

[61]·See *The Sephardic Community in Israel and the Peace Process* (New York: Institute for Middle East Peace and Development, CUNY, 1986), directed by Harriet Arnone and Ammiel Alcalay.

[62]·See Hashem Mahameed and Yosef Gottman, "Autostereotypes and Heterostereotypes of Jews and Arabs under Various Conditions of Contact," *Israeli Journal of Psychology and Counseling in Education* (Jerusalem: Ministry of Education and Culture) 16 (September 1983).

[63]·Mordechai Bar-On, *Peace Now: The Portrait of a Movement* (Tel Aviv: HaKibbutz HaMeuchad, 1985), 89–90 (Hebrew).

[64]·Swirski, "Oriental Jews," 89–90.

[65]·Segev, *1949*, 174 (Hebrew).

[66]·Ibid., *1949*, 161.

[67]·Beni Zada, "Forty Years of the Ashkenazim State," *Pa'amon* 16 (December 1987).

[68]·Abba Eban, for example, opposed "regarding our immigrants from Oriental countries as a bridge toward our integration with the Arabic-speaking world" (quoted in Smooha, *Israel*, 88).

[69]·Cited from a Black Panther press conference held in Paris, March 1975.

[70]·Quotations are taken from several speeches of the Oriental Front delivered in their meeting with the PLO in Vienna, July 1986.

7

THE USE AND MISUSE OF HOLOCAUST MEMORY

In December 1987, an Israeli truck driver accidentally ran over four residents of a refugee camp in the Gaza Strip, detonating the first Palestinian intifada. Within days, tens of thousands of Palestinians in Gaza and the West Bank had taken to the streets, in a popular revolt aimed at ending the Israeli occupation and achieving self-determination. To the shock of many Israelis, the Arab residents of the West Bank and Gaza revealed themselves to be Palestinians, waving the banned Palestinian flag and declaring their support for the Palestine Liberation Organization and their desire for an independent and sovereign state of their own. "Break their bones," Minister of Defense Yitzhak Rabin reportedly instructed his troops, on their way to confront protestors armed only with stones. By "might, force, and beatings," Rabin said, Israel would crush the uprising. Instead, these punitive measures only strengthened the determination of Palestinians to resist the Israeli army—and starkly exposed, in the eyes of the world, the reality of Israel's "benign occupation."

When the intifada began, five years had passed since Ariel Sharon's invasion of Lebanon, which culminated in the Sabra and Shatila massacres and shattered the myth that Israel only acted in self-defense. Yet, in large part because of the Holocaust, many Jews were still accustomed to seeing themselves as victims, and Israel as a weak country permanently under siege, an image painstakingly cultivated by Israel's leaders and by their advocates abroad. The intifada was a watershed not only in the history of the Israeli-Palestinian conflict, but in the history, and moral imagination, of the Jewish people. As the uprising generated a steady flow of images of Israeli soldiers brutalizing young Palestinians, what **Marc Ellis** calls "Holocaust theology" began to crumble among Jews of conscience, giving way to a sober reckoning with the nature of Israel and with their own position in the world. "Holocaust theology speaks eloquently about the struggle for human dignity in the death camps, and radically about the question of God and Jewish survival," writes Ellis, the author of several books on Jewish theology and politics, "but [it] has virtually nothing to say about the ethics of a Jewish state possessing nuclear weapons, supplying military arms and assistance to authoritarian regimes, expropriating land and torturing resisters to occupation."

THE PALESTINIAN UPRISING AND THE FUTURE OF THE JEWISH PEOPLE

Marc Ellis

From *Towards a Jewish Theology of Liberation: The Uprising and the Future* (1988)

Afterword

Since December 1987, as the twenty-year occupation of the West Bank and Gaza erupted into a veritable civil war, the Jewish community in North America and Israel awakened with a start. An outpouring of anger ensued over the betrayal of our ethical witness and a commitment arose to end the occupation. Michael Lerner, editor of the progressive Jewish journal *Tikkun*, summed up these feelings with an editorial titled, "The Occupation: Immoral and Stupid." In passionate and unequivocal language he called on Israel to "Stop the beatings, stop the breaking of bones, stop the late night raids on people's homes, stop the use of food as a weapon of war, stop pretending that you can respond to an entire people's agony with guns and blows and power. Publicly acknowledge that the Palestinians have the same right to national self-determination that we Jews have and negotiate a solution with representatives of the Palestinians!"[1]

In a sense, Lerner and many other Jews are moving toward a position almost unthinkable before the Palestinian uprising: solidarity with the Palestinian people. For the uprising brings again to mind Johann Baptist Metz's reflection, previously quoted, on the Christian and Jewish journey after the Holocaust. The statement bears repetition: "We Christians can never go back behind Auschwitz: to go beyond Auschwitz, if we see clearly, is impossible for us by ourselves. It is possible only together with the victims of Auschwitz." In light of the uprising, these words assume a new meaning, relating to the common journey of Jew and Palestinian. For Jews the challenge might be stated thusly: "We Jews can never go back behind empowerment: to go beyond empowerment, if we see clearly, is impossible for us by ourselves. It is possible only with the victims of our empowerment."[2]

Thus the question facing the Jewish people in Israel and around the world involves, and yet moves far beyond, negotiation of borders, recognition of the P.L.O., the cessation of the expropriation of human, land and water resources in the occupied territories, and even the public confession of Israeli torture and murder. For in the end the Israeli-Palestinian conflict involves the political, military and economic spheres of Jewish life while at the same time addressing the deepest theological presuppositions of post-Holocaust Jewry. Without addressing the implicit and explicit theology of our community, any adjustment of political, military, or economic borders will represent superficial moments to be transgressed when the opportunity presents itself. Surely political settlement of any significance in Israel and Palestine without a movement toward solidarity is, by the very nature of the conflict, impossible.

As the uprising has made clear, the normative theology of the Jewish community today—Holocaust theology—is unable to articulate this path of solidarity. Nor can the most well known of Jewish spokespersons, some of whom helped to create this theology and others who operate within it, speak clearly on this most important issue. There are many reasons for this inability to address concisely the subject of solidarity. Holocaust theology, emerging out of reflection on the death camps, represents the Jewish people as we were, helpless and suffering; it does not and cannot speak of the people we are today and who we are becoming—powerful and often oppressive. Holocaust theology argues correctly for the Jewish need to be empowered; it lacks the framework and the skills of analysis to investigate the cost of that empowerment. Holocaust theology speaks eloquently about the struggle for human dignity in the death camps, and radically about the question of God and Jewish survival, but has virtually nothing to say about the ethics of a Jewish state possessing nuclear weapons, supplying military arms and assistance to authoritarian regimes, expropriating land and torturing resisters to Israeli occupation.[3]

Although this information is readily available and accepted as documented by the world community, written about or even discovered by Jews in Israel and in the United States, Holocaust theologians often refuse to accept it, as if the suggestion that Jews could support such policies, rather than the policies themselves, is treasonable and grounds for excommunication from the community. Because of the power of Holocaust theology in mainstream Jewish institutions, media and organized Jewish religious life, these "facts" are deemed outside of Jewish discourse *as if they are not happening, because it is impossible that Jews would do such things.* Thus a community which prides itself on its intelligence and knowledge is on its most crucial issue—the behavior of our people—profoundly ignorant.[4]

That is why the dialectic of Holocaust and empowerment, surfaced in Holocaust theology, needs, more than ever, to be confronted by the dynamic and dangerous element of solidarity. Solidarity, often seen as a reaching out to other communities in a gesture of good will, at the same time necessitates a probing of one's own community. To come into solidarity, knowledge of the other is needed; soon, though, we understand a deeper knowledge of self is called for as well. If we recognize the national aspirations of the Palestinian people, that is only a step toward the more difficult and critical question of how Israeli policy has interacted with those aspirations. If we support the struggle of South African blacks, the relationship of Israel and the South African government needs a thorough and continuing investigation. What we find today is a powerful and flawed Jewish community which has become something other than that innocent victim abandoned by the world.[5]

Because of the Palestinian uprising, increasing numbers of Jews are beginning to understand that our historical situation has changed radically in the last two decades and that something terrible, almost tragic, is happening to us. With what words do we speak such anguished sentiments? Do we feel alone with these feelings so that they are better left unspoken? Do such words, once spoken, condemn us as traitors or with the epithet, self-hating Jew? Or does articulating the unspeakable challenge the community to break through the silence and paralysis which threatens to engulf us? And those of us who know and empathize with the Palestinians, can we speak without being accused of creating the context for another holocaust? Can we be seen as emissaries of an option to halt the cycle of destruction and death?[6]

This is the challenge which faces the Jewish people. And with it is the task of creating a new Jewish theology consonant with the history we are creating and the history we want to bequeath to our children. When all is said and done, should it be that we are powerful where once we were weak, that we are invincible where once we were vulnerable? Or would we rather be able to say that the power we created, necessary and flawed, was simply a tool to move beyond empowerment to a liberation that encompassed all those struggling for justice, including those we once knew as enemy? And that our power, used in solidarity with others, brought forth a healing in the world which ultimately began to heal us of our wounds from over the millennia?

New movements of renewal within the Jewish community which have developed or expanded during the uprising point the way to this theology. In Israel, the Committee Confronting the Iron Fist, made up of Israelis and Palestinians whose first publication carried the provocative title "We Will Be Free In Our Own Homeland!" creates dialogue situations and stages demonstrations to end the occupation. Members of the anti-war movement *Yesh Gvul*, or There Is A Limit, made up of Israelis who refused to serve in the Lebanese War and today refuse to serve in the West Bank and Gaza, are courageous in their willingness to say "no" to the oppression of others, even at the expense of imprisonment. Women in Black, made up of Israelis who vigil in mourning dress, and Women Against Occupation, who adopt Palestinian women political prisoners and detainees, are just two more of many Jewish groups protesting the occupation and expressing solidarity with the Palestinian uprising.[7]

Since the uprising North American Jews are increasingly vocal in relation to the pursuit of justice in the Middle East. New Jewish Agenda, a movement of secular and religious Jews, continues to argue for Israeli security and the just demands of Palestinian nationhood. *Tikkun*, the progressive Jewish magazine, is in the forefront of vocal argument and organizing for a new understanding of the Israeli-Palestinian situation. And now with the recent crisis, Jewish intellectuals, such as Arthur Hertzberg and Irving Howe, and institutions, including the Union of American Hebrew Congregations, have voiced their horror at Israeli policies in the occupied territories.[8]

What these individuals and movements represent is a groping toward a theological framework which nurtures rather than hinders expressions of solidarity. It is almost as if a long-repressed unease is coming to the surface, breaking through the language and symbol once deemed appropriate. Of course the risk is that if the crisis passes without fundamental change, the language of solidarity will recede and the more familiar patterns will reassert themselves. And it is true to state that even the movements cited are often limited in their scope and vision, equivocating where necessary to retain some credibility within the Jewish community.

Still the drift is unmistakable and the task clear. The theological framework we need to create is hardly a departure, but a renewal of the themes which lie at the heart of our tradition, the exodus and the prophetic, interpreted in the contemporary world. A Jewish theology of liberation is our oldest theology, our great gift to the world, which has atrophied time and again only to be rediscovered by our own community and other communities around the world. A Jewish theology of liberation confronts Holocaust and empowerment with the dynamic of solidarity, providing a bridge to others as it critiques our own abuses of power. By linking us to all those who struggle for justice, a Jewish theology of liberation will, in the long run, decrease our sense of isolation and abandonment and thus begin a process of healing so necessary to the future of the Jewish community.

If it is true that we cannot go back behind empowerment, we now know that we cannot go forward alone. Could it be that the faces which confront us are those of the Palestinian people and that somehow in these faces lies the future of the Jewish people? This is why a two state solution is only the beginning of a long and involved process that demands political compromise and a theological transformation which is difficult to envision. For if our theology is not confronted and transformed, then the political solutions will be superficial and transitory. A political solution may give impetus to this theological task; a theological movement may nurture a political solution. However, a political solution without a theological transformation simply enshrines the tragedy to be repeated again.

Here we enter the most difficult of arenas; for the presupposition is that in the faces of the Palestinians lies the future of what it means to be Jewish, that at the center of the struggle to be faithful as a Jew today is the suffering and liberation of the Palestinian people. Despite the uprising, such a thought is still *hardly considered in Jewish theological circles*. At some point, though, an essential integration of Jew and Palestinian in a larger arena of political, cultural and religious life is integral to a Jewish future. But this assumes that a fundamental confession and repentance of past and present transgressions is possible and a critical understanding of our history uncovered.

The Occupation is Over

Since the beginning of the uprising we have awakened to reports of beatings and the deaths of Palestinian people, mostly youth, in the occupied territories. But this raises a strange and disturbing question: if Palestinians cease to die, will the uprising—at least for North American Jews and Christians—cease to matter? A horrible thought follows: for the Palestinian cause it is crucial that they continue to die in ever increasing numbers if we are to understand that *the occupation, as we have known it, is over*. Unable to accept this conclusion, I approached Palestinians and church workers who have returned from the West Bank and Gaza. All have the same thoughts. It is true, and the Palestinian leadership—as well as the Palestinian villagers—understand this tragic fact: the uprising is dependent on the continuing death of children.

But can Jewish Israelis continue to beat and kill Palestinian children *ad infinitum*? Can North American Jews continue to support these horrible acts? And can Christians, especially those who have chosen to repent the anti-Jewishness of the Christian past and who have accepted Israel as an integral part of the contemporary Jewish experience, remain silent on the uprising and Israeli brutality? Or, are we all hoping that somehow the situation will dissipate, go unreported, or better still, disappear? This much seems clear: the willingness of Palestinians to endure torture and death, and the willingness of Israel to inflict such acts of brutality, point to the most difficult of situations which many would choose to ignore—that some basic themes of post-Holocaust Jewish and Christian life are being exposed in a radical and unrelenting way.

If it is true that the occupation of the territories is in fact over, that it has moved beyond occupation to uprising and civil war, then the theological support for the occupation in Jewish and Christian theology must end as well. The focus of both theologies in their uncritical support of

Israel has been shattered. The uprising, therefore, is a crisis on many fronts and is at its deepest level a theological crisis. Of course, like any crisis the uprising presents us with both tragedy and possibility. By uplifting the truth at the price of broken bones and lives, the children of Palestine force us to think again and to break through ignorance, half-truths, and lies. But will we have the tenacity and courage in safe and comfortable North America that the Palestinian children have on the streets of Gaza and the West Bank? Or, will the inevitable allegations of Jewish self-hate and Christian anti-Jewishness deter us? Are we willing to reexamine our theological presuppositions as particular communities and in dialogue with each other, or will we attempt to pass over the question in silence?

It is not too much to say that the uprising poses the future of Judaism in stark and unremitting terms. The tragedy of the Holocaust is well documented and indelibly ingrained in our consciousness: we know who we were. But do we know who we have become? Contemporary Jewish theology helps us come to grips with our suffering; it hardly recognizes that today we are powerful. A theology that holds in tension Holocaust and empowerment speaks eloquently for the victims of Treblinka and Auschwitz yet ignores Sabra and Shatila. It pays tribute to the Warsaw Ghetto uprising but has no place for the uprising of ghetto dwellers on the other side of Israeli power. Jewish theologians insist that the torture and murders of Jewish children be lamented and commemorated in Jewish ritual and belief. It has yet to imagine, though, the possibility that Jews have in turn tortured and murdered Palestinian children. Holocaust theology relates the story of the Jewish people in its beauty and suffering. Yet it fails to integrate the contemporary history of the Palestinian people as integral to our own. Thus, this theology articulates who we were but no longer helps us understand who we have become.

So Jews who are trying to understand the present become a contradiction to themselves while others simply refuse to acknowledge the facts of contemporary Jewish life. A dilemma arises: awareness of Jewish transgressions has no framework to be articulated and acted upon; ignorance (albeit preferred rather than absolute) insists that what is occurring is impossible, that torture and murder are not in fact happening at all, that Jews could not do such things. Jews who become aware have few places to turn theologically, and the ignorant become more and more bellicose in their insistence and in their anger. Meanwhile, despite increasing dissent, Holocaust theology continues as normative in the Jewish community, warning dissident Jews that they approach the terrain of excommunication and continuing to reenforce the ignorance of many Jews as a theological prerequisite to community membership.

As we become more and more powerful, the neoconservative trend is buttressed by fear, anger, and by a deepening sense of isolation. Anyone who works in the Jewish community recognizes this immediately, the almost uncontrollable emotional level that criticism of Israel engenders. To be accused of creating the context for another holocaust is almost commonplace, as are the charges of treason and self-hate. Yet on a deeper level one senses a community which, having emerged from the death camps, sees little option but to fight to the bitter end. It is as if the entire world is still against us, as if the next trains depart for Eastern Europe, as if the death camps remain ready to receive us after an interval of almost half a century. This is why though the entire world understands Yasir Arafat to be a moderate, there is no other name linked by the Jewish community so closely to Adolf Hitler. This is why Prime Minister Shamir spoke of the plans to launch a ship of Palestinian refugees to Israel as an attempt to undermine the state of Israel, as an act of war.[9]

Years after the liberation of the camps, Elie Wiesel wrote, "Were hatred a solution, the survivors, when they came out of the camps, would have had to burn down the whole world." Surely with the nuclear capacity of Israel, coupled with the sense of isolation and anger, Wiesel's statement remains a hope rather than a concluded option. Is it too much to say that any theology which does not understand the absolute difference between the Warsaw Ghetto and Tel Aviv, between Hitler and Arafat, is a theology which may legitimate that which Wiesel cautioned against?

Christians who have entered into solidarity with the Jewish people are similarly in a dilemma. The road to solidarity has been paved both by Christian renewal, especially with regard to the Hebrew scriptures, and by Holocaust theology. Understanding the beauty and suffering of the Jewish people as a call to Christian repentance and transformation hardly prepares the community for a confrontation with Israeli power. How do Christians respond now when, over the years, the centrality of Israel has been stressed as necessary to Christian confession in the arena of dialogue, and no words of criticism against Israel are countenanced as anything but anti-Jewish? Too, Christian Zionism, fundamentalist and liberal, is ever present. What framework do Christians have to probe the history of the state of Israel, to understand the uprising—to question the cost of Jewish empowerment? Can Christian theologians articulate a solidarity with the Jewish people which is a critical solidarity, one that recognizes the suffering *and* the power of the Jewish people? Can Christian theologies in the spirit of a critical solidarity open themselves to the suffering of the Palestinian people as a legitimate imperative of what it means to be Christian today?

The uprising continues to push Christian theologians to rethink their theology and move beyond frightened silence or paternalistic embrace. A critical solidarity is increasingly called for, especially in the works of feminist theologian Rosemary Radford Ruether. As a friend of the Jewish people, Ruether is calling attention to attitudes and behavior which can only lead to disaster. Repentance of Christian anti-Jewishness and the promotion of Jewish empowerment can only be authentic today within the context of a recognition of the legitimate rights of the Palestinian people.[10]

Clearly the Palestinian struggle for nationhood poses more than the prospect of political negotiation and compromise. For Jews and Christians it presents fundamental theological material which lends depth to the inevitable (though long suffering) political solutions. Without this theological component a political solution may or may not appear. However, the lessons of the conflict would surely be lost and thus the political solution would tend toward superficiality and immediacy rather than depth and longevity. A political solution without a theological transformation would simply enshrine the tragedy to be repeated again. An important opportunity to move beyond our present theologies toward theologies of solidarity, which may usher in a new age of ecumenical cooperation, would be lost. Could it be that the struggle of the Palestinian people—their struggle to be faithful—is a key to the Jewish and Christian struggle to be faithful in the contemporary world?

The torture and death of Palestinian children calls us to a theology which recognizes empowerment as a necessary and flawed journey toward liberation. It reminds us that power in and of itself, even for survival, ends in tragedy without the guidance of ethics and a strong sense of solidarity with all those who are struggling for justice. Today, the Palestinian people ask the fundamental question relating to Jewish empowerment: can the Jewish people in Israel, indeed Jews around the world, be liberated without the liberation of the Palestinian people? Once having understood the question posed by the Palestinian people, the occupation can no longer continue. What remains is to build a theological framework which delegitimates the torture and the killing—a theology of liberation which sees solidarity as the essence of what it means to be Jewish and Christian.

A New Theological Framework

The development of a theological framework is crucial to delegitimate torture and murder—that is, to end theologies which promote a myriad of occupations including, though not limited to, that of the Palestinian people. In this case we focus on the Israeli occupation as the breakthrough point for Jewish theology. The theological framework which legitimates occupation also, if we look closely, forces Jews to take positions on other issues which would be questioned, even abhorred, if the framework were different. If our theology did not support the occupation, its vision of justice and peace would be transformed. Thus we turn again to the prospect that the uprising represents a culmination and a possibility, if we will only seize the moment.

An essential task of Jewish theology is to deabsolutize the state of Israel. To see Israel as an important Jewish community among other Jewish communities, with an historical founding and evolution, is to legitimate theologically what the Jewish people have acted out with their lives: the continuation of diverse Jewish communities outside the state. Thus the redemptive aspect of Jewish survival after the Holocaust is found in a much broader arena than the state of Israel, and must be critically addressed rather than simply asserted in unquestioning allegiance to a state where most Jews do not live. Deabsolutizing Israel hardly means its abandonment. Instead it calls forth a new, more mature relationship. Jews cannot bilocate forever and the strain of defending policies implemented by others, of criticizing without being able to influence directly, of supporting financially and being made to feel guilty for not living in Israel, is impossible to continue over a long period of time. With this new understanding responsibilities between Jewish communities assume a mutuality which includes a critical awareness of the centrality of our ethical tradition as the future of our community. Therefore, the present crisis and any future crisis moves beyond the call for unquestioned allegiance or disassociation from Israel to a critical solidarity with responsibilities and obligations on all sides.[11]

A second parallel task is to deal with the Holocaust in its historical context and to cease its application as a possible future outcome to issues of contemporary Jewish life. The constant use of the Holocaust with reference to Israel is to misjudge and therefore refuse to understand the totally different situation of pre-and post-Holocaust Jewry. Pre-Holocaust European Jewry had no state or military; it was truly defenseless before the Nazi onslaught. Israel is a state with superior military ability. Pre-Holocaust European Jewry lived among populations whose attitudes toward Jews varied from tolerance to hatred. Post-Holocaust Jewry, with its population concentrations in France, England, Canada, and the United States, resides in countries where anti-Jewishness is sporadic and politically inconsequential. Pre-Holocaust Jewry lived among Christians who had as a group little reason to question Christian anti-Jewishness. Post-Holocaust Jewry lives among Christians who have made repeated public statements, writings, even ritual affirmations of the centrality of the Jewish people and Christian culpability for an anti-Jewish past. The differences between pre-and post-Holocaust Jewry can be listed on many other levels as well, which is not to deny that anti-Jewishness continues to exist. As many Jewish writers have pointed out, the paradox is that the most dangerous place for Jews to live today is in the state of Israel rather than the Jewish centers of Europe and North America.

Even in relation to Israel the application of Holocaust language is clearly inappropriate. Israel has been involved in two wars since 1967 and can claim victory in neither; no civilian life was lost outside the battlefield. The great fear, repeated over and over again, is that one day Israel will lose a war and that the civilian population will be annihilated, i.e., another holocaust. It is important to note here that if the situation continues as it is today it is inevitable that one day Israel will lose a war and face the possibility of annihilation. No nation is invincible forever, no empire exists that is not destined to disappear, no country that does not, at some point in its history, lose badly and suffer immensely. Can our present theology exempt Israel from the reality of shifting alliances, military strategies, and political life? *The only way to prevent military defeat is to make peace when you are powerful.* Of course, even here there is never any absolute protection from military defeat, as there is never any absolute protection from persecution. But if military defeat does come and if the civilian population is attacked, the result, though tragic, will not by any meaningful definition be another holocaust. And it would not, by any means, signal the end of the Jewish people, as many Holocaust theologians continue to speculate. It would be a terrible event, too horrible to mention. And perhaps the differences between the Holocaust and any future military defeat of Israel are too obvious to explore, and would hardly need exploration if our present theology was not confused on this most important point.

To deabsolutize the state of Israel and distinguish the historical event of the Holocaust from the situation of contemporary Jewish life is imperative to the third task of Jewish theology: the redefinition of Jewish identity. This is an incredibly difficult and complex task whose parameters can only be touched upon here. Yet it is the most crucial of areas raising the essential question that each generation faces: what does it mean to be Jewish in the contemporary world?

There is little question that Holocaust theology is the normative theology of the Jewish community today and that at the center of this theology is the Holocaust and the state of Israel. Rabbinic theology, the normative Jewish theology for almost two millennia, initially sought to continue as if neither the Holocaust nor the state of Israel were central to the Jewish people, and Reform Judaism, the interesting, sometimes shallow nineteenth-century attempt to come to grips with modern life, also sought to bypass the formative events of our time. Yet after the Holocaust, and especially since the 1967 Six Day War, both theological structures have been transformed with an underlying Holocaust theology. Secular Jews, as well, often affiliated with progressive politics and economics, have likewise experienced a shifting framework of interpretation.

Though not explicitly religious, their aid has been solicited by Holocaust theologians to build the state of Israel as the essential aspect of belonging to the Jewish people. In sum, both those who believed in Jewish particularity and those who sought a more universal identification have increasingly derived their Jewish identity from the framework of Holocaust and Israel. And there is little reason to believe that any of these frameworks—Orthodox, Reform, or secular humanism—can ever again return to their pre-Holocaust, pre-Israel positions.

We can only move ahead by affirming the place of Holocaust and Israel as important parts of Jewish identity while insisting that they are not and cannot become the sum total of what it means to be Jewish. The point here is to take the dynamic of Holocaust and Israel and understand it in new ways. In both events there is, among other things, an underlying theme of solidarity which has been buried in our anger and isolation. This includes solidarity with our own people as well as others who have come into solidarity with us. As importantly, if we recover our own history, there is a theme of Jewish solidarity with others even in times of great danger. The latter include some of the early settlers and intellectuals involved in the renewal of the Jewish community in Palestine, well-known figures like Albert Einstein, Hannah Arendt, and many others.[12]

Even during the Holocaust there were voices, Etty Hillesum, for one, who argued that their suffering should give birth to a world of mutuality and solidarity so that no people should ever suffer again. As she voluntarily accompanied her people to Auschwitz, Hillesum was hardly a person who went like a lamb to her slaughter. Rather, she chose a destiny as an act of solidarity with her own people and the world. Is it possible that those who affirmed human dignity where it was most difficult—and those who argued, and continue to argue today, for reconciliation with the Palestinian people even with the risks involved—represent the only future worth bequeathing to our children? By emphasizing our dignity and solidarity we appropriate the event of Holocaust and Israel as formative in a positive and critical way. Thus they ask us to once again embrace the world with the hope that our survival is transformative for our own people and the world.

The key to a new Jewish identity remains problematic unless we understand that deabsolutizing Israel, differentiating Holocaust and the contemporary Jewish situation, and recovering the history of solidarity within our tradition and with those outside it, leads us to a critical confrontation with our own empowerment. To celebrate our survival is important; to realize that our empowerment has come at a great cost is another thing altogether. Can we, at the fortieth anniversary of the state of Israel, realize that the present political and religious sensibilities can only lead to disaster? Can we argue openly that the issue of empowerment is much broader than an exclusive Jewish state and that other options, including autonomy with confederation, may be important to contemplate for the fiftieth anniversary of Israel? Can we openly articulate that as American Jews we can no longer ask American foreign policy to support policies which contradict the ethical heart of what it means to be Jewish? Can we, in good conscience and faith, appeal to Christians, Palestinians, and people of good will around the world to help us end the occupation and if we do not heed the call, to force us to stop for our own sake?

For this is the place we have arrived, well beyond the pledge of loyalty and the private criticism that has abounded for so many years. The uprising challenges the power of the Israeli government and the heart of the Jewish people. But the power to inflict injury and death remains. And therefore the power to change our history, to redefine our inheritance, to alter what it means to be Jewish remains in the hands of those who would see the occupation continue. And with the occupation come a myriad of policies around the world which bring only shame to those who invoke the victims of the Holocaust to legitimate terror.

With the uprising we have lost our innocence; a Jewish theology of liberation must begin with this loss. A weak and helpless people has arisen with a power that surprises and now saddens us. A people set apart returns to the history of nations less as a beacon than as a fellow warrior, living at the expense of others, almost forfeiting its sense of purpose. The commanding voice of Sinai and of Auschwitz beckons us to struggle to reclaim the ethical witness of the Jewish people.

• • •

Notes

[1] Michael Lerner, "The Occupation: Immoral and Stupid," *Tikkun* 3 (March/April 1988): 8. Lerner continues: "The crisis in Israel is a moment of truth for all of us. It should be responded to with the deepest seriousness and with the full understanding that the choices we make now may have consequences that reverberate for centuries to come." (p. 12).

[2] Johann Baptist Metz, *The Emergent Church: The Future of Christianity in a Postbourgeois World*, trans. Peter Mann (New York: Crossroad, 1981), p. 19. This is *not* an attempt to compare the Nazi period with the Israeli-Palestinian conflict or to create a scenario of evil Israelis and innocent Palestinians. Neither do I want to suggest that Palestinians have only been victimized by Israelis. It is to suggest that Israel, at this point in history, is powerful and thus the responsibility is clear. Further, it is to suggest that even justice is not enough. We can only move forward *with* the Palestinian people.

[3] For a discussion of dissent and Israel's nuclear capability see Rudolf Peierls, "The Case of Mordechai Vanunu," *New York Review of Books* 35 (June 16, 1988): 56. Also see Jane Hunter, "Vanunu and Israel's Nuclear Crimes," *Israeli Foreign Affairs* 4 (February 1988): 3. For the fate of the young during the uprising see *Palestinians Killed by Israeli Occupation Forces, Settlers, and Civilians During Uprising, December 9, 1987, through April 18, 1988*, (Chicago: Database Project on Palestinian Human Rights, 1988), and *Children of the Stones*, (Jerusalem: Palestinian Center for the Study of Nonviolence, 1988). For the response of Irving Greenberg to the uprising see his "The Ethics of Jewish Power," *Perspectives* (New York: National Jewish Center for Learning and Leadership, 1988). For the response of Elie Wiesel see his "A Mideast Peace—Is it Impossible?" *New York Times*, June 23,1988, p. 22.

[4] A major task of theology is to nurture the questions a people need to ask about the future they are creating. In its time Holocaust theology did this and thus reoriented most of Jewish theology and Jewish secular thought. But today Holocaust theology is distant from the history we are creating and therefore applies past categories to present realities. Our behavior is filtered through this framework: that which cannot happen within this framework thus by definition is not happening. Two options appear. Either we lose touch with the history we are creating, producing dissonance, a sense of isolation, paralysis, or even cynicism; or if we understand the history we are creating, we do so uncritically. Hence the neoconservative drift in Jewish theology. When theology ceases to nurture the questions a people need to ask about the history they are creating, critical thought atrophies. In the case of the Jewish people more than thought is at stake: We are in danger of becoming everything we loathed about our oppressors.

[5] For an important historical understanding of the interaction of Israel and Palestine see Simha Flapan, *The Birth of Israel: Myths and Realities* (New York: Pantheon, 1987). Flapan, a life-long Zionist and resident of Israel/Palestine from 1930 until his death in 1987, writes that Israel's myths, "forged during the formation of the state have hardened into this impenetrable, and dangerous, ideological shield" (p. 8). To understand the contemporary scene, Flapan reassesses the birth of Israel and in a sense his own birth as a Zionist. On the subject of the Israel-South Africa relationship after its announced termination in 1987, see Jane Hunter, "South Africa Hurls Israeli Technology Against Angola, May Build Lavi Aircraft," *Israeli Foreign Affairs* 3 (December 1987): 1,5, and ibid., "Israelis Help South African Air Force," *Israeli Foreign Affairs* 4 (April 1988): 1,8.

[6] One such attempt to break through the silence is found in David Grossman's *The Yellow Wind*, trans. Haim Watzman (New York: Farrar, Straus and Giroux, 1988). In the wake of the uprising it became a bestseller in Israel and the United States.

[7] For the first publication of the Committee Confronting the Iron Fist, see *We Will Be Free in Our Own Homeland: A Collection of Readings for International Day of Fast and Solidarity with Palestinian Prisoners,* (Jerusalem, 1986). A report on *Yesh Gvul* can be found in "Israeli Doves Arousing Little Response," *New York Times*, March 1,1988. See also "A Captain's Ideals Lead Him to Jail," ibid., March 20, 1988 and Gideon Spiro, "The Israeli Soldiers Who Say 'There is a Limit,' " *Middle East International No.* 333 (September 9,1988): 18–20.

[8] For New Jewish Agenda's response to the uprising see Ezra Goldstein and Deena Hurwitz, "No Status Quo Ante" *New Jewish Agenda* 24 (Spring 1988): 1–3. Arthur Hertzberg is probably the most articulate and widely read Jewish intellectual on the uprising. See his "The Uprising" *New York Review of Books* 35 (February 4,1988): 30–32, and "The Illusion of Jewish Unity," *New York Review of Books,* 35 (June 16,1988): 6,8,10–12. Also see the cable sent to the President of Israel by Rabbi Alexander M. Schindler, President of the Union of American Hebrew Congregations, found in *AS Briefings: Commission on Social Action of Reform Judaism*, March, 1988, Appendix A. He begins the cable, "I am deeply troubled and pained in sending you this message, but I cannot be silent. The indiscriminate beating of Arabs, enunciated and implemented as Israel's new policy to quell the riots in Judea, Samaria and Gaza, is an offense to the Jewish spirit. It violates every principle of human decency. And it betrays the Zionist dream." Also see Albert Vorspan, "Soul Searching," *New York Times Magazine*, May 8,1988, pp. 40–41,51, 54.

[9] Shamir's response is a prime lesson in Holocaust theology. At a news conference in Jerusalem, Shamir said: "It is the height of temerity and hypocrisy that members of the terrorist organization speak of returning. This boat

which loads its decks with murderers, terrorists who sought to murder us—all of us, each of us. They wish to bring them to the land of Israel, and demonstrate that they are returning to the same place in which they wished to slay us. We will and do view this as a hostile act, an act which endangers the state of Israel." Quoted in "Israel's Furious Over a Palestinian Plan to 'Return' to Haifa by Sail," *New York Times*, February 11, 1988, p. 15.

[10] See Rosemary Radford Ruether and Herman J. Ruether, *The Wrath of Jonah: The Crisis of Religious Nationalism in the Israeli-Palestinian Conflict* (San Francisco: Harper and Row, 1988). For a fascinating Jewish response to Christian critical solidarity with the Jewish people see *Interreligious Currents*, ed. Annette Daum, 7 (Winter/Spring 1988): 1–8.

[11] The strains of this highly problematic and emotional relationship have increasingly come to the surface in recent years. Witness the upheavals in North American Jewish life relating to the Lebanese War, the massacres at Sabra and Shatila, the Pollard spy case, and now the uprising. My point is simply that the relationship between Jews in Israel and Jews outside of Israel cannot remain as it is without ultimately dividing the community at its very roots.

[12] For Hannah Arendt's prophetic understanding of the choices facing the Jewish settlers in Palestine, see a collection of her essays *Hannah Arendt; the Jew as Pariah: Jewish Identity and Politics in the Modern Age*, ed. Ron H. Feldman (New York: Grove Press, 1978).

The words "never again" mean different things to different people. For the self-appointed leaders of the Jewish community, it means every effort should be made to ensure that the Jewish people never again suffer a comparable horror—and that any policy directed toward that end is thereby justified. Unconditional support for Israel flows from this line of reasoning. **Sara Roy,** the daughter of Holocaust survivors, draws a strikingly different lesson from the Holocaust, one that underscores the importance of human solidarity against oppression, particularly when the oppressors are one's own people. Roy, a research scholar at Harvard University's Center for Middle Eastern Studies, is best known for her study of what she calls the political and economic "de-development" of the Gaza Strip. She first traveled to the Occupied Territories in 1985, and there witnessed treatment of ordinary Palestinians that reminded her of stories her parents had told her. "Israel's occupation of the Palestinians is not the moral equivalent of the Nazi genocide of the Jews," she writes in this moving essay. "But it does not have to be. No, this is not genocide, but it is repression, and it is brutal . . . And just as there is no moral equivalence or symmetry between the Holocaust and the occupation, so there is no moral equivalence or symmetry between the occupier and the occupied, no matter how much we as Jews regard ourselves as victims." By her exemplary, courageous work among Palestinians, Roy has shown that there is another way to honor the memory of Hitler's victims.

LIVING WITH THE HOLOCAUST: THE JOURNEY OF A CHILD OF HOLOCAUST SURVIVORS

Sara Roy

From *The Journal of Palestine Studies* (2003)

Some months ago I was invited to reflect on my journey as a child of Holocaust survivors. This journey continues and shall continue until the day I die. Though I cannot possibly say everything, it seems especially poignant that I should be addressing this topic at a time when the conflict between Israelis and Palestinians is descending so tragically into a moral abyss and when, for me at least, the very essence of Judaism, of what it means to be a Jew, seems to be descending with it.

The Holocaust has been the defining feature of my life. It could not have been otherwise. I lost over 100 members of my family and extended family in the Nazi ghettos and death camps in Poland—grandparents, aunts, uncles, cousins, a sibling not yet born—people about whom I have heard so much throughout my life, people I never knew. They lived in Poland in Jewish communities called shtetls.

In thinking about what I wanted to say about this journey, I tried to remember my very first conscious encounter with the Holocaust. Although I cannot be certain, I think it was the first time I noticed the number the Nazis had imprinted on my father's arm. To his oppressors, my father, Abraham, had no name, no history, and no identity other than that blue-inked number, which I never wrote down. As a young child of four or five, I remember asking my father why he had that number on his arm. He answered that he had once painted it on but then found it would not wash off, so was left with it.

My father was one of six children, and he was the only one in his family to survive the Holocaust. I know very little about his family because he could not speak about them without breaking down. I know little about my paternal grandmother, after whom I am named, and even less about my father's sisters and brother. I know only their names. It caused me such pain to see him suffer with his memories that I stopped asking him to share them.

My father's name was recognized in Holocaust circles because he was one of two known survivors of the death camp at Chelmno, in Poland, where 350,000 Jews were murdered, among them the majority of my family on my father's and mother's sides. They were taken there and gassed to death in January 1942. Through my father's cousin I learned that there is now a plaque at the entrance to what is left of the Chelmno death camp with my father's name on it—something I hope one day to see. My father also survived the concentration camps at Auschwitz and Buchenwald and because of it was called to testify at the Eichmann trial in Jerusalem in 1961.

My mother, Taube, was one of nine children—seven girls and two boys. Her father, Herschel, was a rabbi and *shohet*—a ritual slaughterer—and deeply loved and respected by all who knew him. Herschel was a learned man who had studied with some of the great rabbis of Poland. The stories both my mother and aunt have told me also indicate that he was a feminist of sorts, getting down on his hands and knees to help his wife or daughters scrub the floor, treating the women in his life with the same respect and reverence he gave the men. My grandmother, Miriam, whose name I also have, was a kind and gentle soul but the disciplinarian of the family since Hershel could never raise his voice to his children. My mother came from a deeply religious and loving family. My aunts and uncles were as devoted to their parents as they were to them. As a family they lived very modestly, but every Sabbath my grandfather would bring home a poor or homeless person who was seated at the head of the table to share the Sabbath meal.

My mother and her sister Frania were the only two in their family to survive the war. Everyone else perished, except for one other sister, Shoshana, who had emigrated to Palestine in 1936. My mother and Frania had managed to stay together throughout the war—seven years in the Pabanice and Lodz ghettos, followed by the Auschwitz and

Halbstadt concentration camps. The only time in seven years they were separated was at Auschwitz. They were in a selection line, where Jews were lined up and their fate sealed by the Nazi doctor Joseph Mengele, who alone would determine who would live and who would die. When my aunt had approached him, Mengele sent her to the right, to labor (a temporary reprieve). When my mother approached him, he sent her to the left, to death, which meant she would be gassed. Miraculously, my mother managed to sneak back into the selection line, and when she approached Mengele again, he sent her to labor.

A defining moment in my life and journey as a child of Holocaust survivors occurred even before I was born. It involved decisions taken by my mother and her sister, two very remarkable women, that would change their lives and mine.

After the war ended, my aunt Frania desperately wanted to go to Palestine to join their sister, who had been there for ten years. The creation of a Jewish state was imminent, and Frania felt it was the only safe place for Jews after living with the holocaust the Holocaust. My mother disagreed and adamantly refused to go. She told me many times during my life that her decision not to live in Israel was based on a belief, learned and reinforced by her experiences during the war, that tolerance, compassion, and justice cannot be practiced or extended when one lives only among one's own. "I could not live as a Jew among Jews alone," she said. "For me, it wasn't possible and it wasn't what I wanted. I wanted to live as a Jew in a pluralist society, where my group remained important to me but where others were important to me, too."

Frania emigrated to Israel and my parents went to America. It was extremely painful for my mother to leave her sister, but she felt she had no alternative. (They have remained very close and have seen each other often, both in this country and in Israel.) I have always found my mother's choice and the context from which it emanated remarkable.

I grew up in a home where Judaism was defined and practiced not as a religion but as a system of ethics and culture. God was present but not central. My first language was Yiddish, which I still speak with my family. My home was filled with joy and optimism although punctuated at times by grief and loss. Israel and the notion of a Jewish homeland were very important to my parents. After all, the remnants of our family were there. But unlike many of their friends, my parents were not uncritical of Israel, insofar as they felt they could be. Obedience to a state was not an ultimate Jewish value, not for them, not after the Holocaust. Judaism provided the context for our life and for values and beliefs that were not dependent upon national boundaries, but transcended them. For my mother and father, Judaism meant bearing witness, railing against injustice and foregoing silence. It meant compassion, tolerance, and rescue. It meant, as Ammiel Alcalay has written, ensuring to the extent possible that the memories of the past do not become the memories of the future. These were the ultimate Jewish values. My parents were not saints; they had their faults and they made mistakes. But they cared profoundly about issues of justice and fairness, and they cared profoundly about people—all people, not just their own.

The lessons of the Holocaust were always presented to me as both particular (i.e., Jewish) and universal. Perhaps most importantly, they were presented as indivisible. To divide them would diminish the meaning of both.

Looking back over my life, I realize that through their actions and words, my mother and father never tried to shield me from self-knowledge; instead, they insisted that I confront what I did not know or understand. Noam Chomsky speaks of the "parameters of thinkable thought." My mother and father constantly pushed those parameters as far as they could, which was not far enough for me, but they taught me how to push them and the importance of doing so.

It was perhaps inevitable that I would follow a path that would lead me to the Arab-Israeli issue. I visited Israel many times while growing up. As a child, I found it a beautiful, romantic, and peaceful place. As a teenager and young adult I began to feel certain contradictions that I could not fully explain but which centered on what seemed to be the almost complete absence in Israeli life and discourse of Jewish life in Eastern Europe before the Holocaust, and even of the Holocaust itself. I would ask my aunt why these subjects were not discussed, and why Israelis didn't learn to speak Yiddish. My questions were often met with grim silence.

Most painful to me was the denigration of the Holocaust and pre-state Jewish life by many of my Israeli friends. For them, those were times of shame, when Jews were weak and passive, inferior and unworthy, deserving not of our respect but of our disdain. "We will never allow our-selves to be slaughtered again or go so willingly to our slaughter," they would say. There was little need to understand those millions who per-ished or the lives they lived. There was even less need to honor them. Yet at the same time, the Holocaust was used by the state as a defense against others, as a justification for political and military acts.

I could not comprehend nor make sense of what I was hearing. I remember fearing for my aunt. In my confusion, I also remember pro-found anger. It was at that moment, perhaps, that I began thinking about the Palestinians and their conflict with the Jews. If so many among us could negate our own and so pervert the truth, why not with the Pales-tinians? Was there a link of some sort between the murdered Jews of Europe and the Palestinians? I did not know, but so my search began.

The journey has been a painful one but among the most meaningful of my life. At my side, always, was my mother, constant in her support, although ambivalent and conflicted at times. My father had died a young man; I do not know what he would have thought, but I have always felt his presence. My Israeli family opposed what I was doing and has always remained steadfast in their opposition. In fact, I have not spoken with them about my work in over fifteen years.

Despite many visits to Israel during my youth, I first went to the West Bank and Gaza in the summer of 1985, two and a half years before the first Palestinian uprising, to conduct fieldwork for my doctoral disser-tation, which examined American economic assistance to the West Bank and Gaza Strip. My research focused on whether it was possible to promote economic development under conditions of military occu-pation. That summer changed my life because it was then that I came to understand and experience what occupation was and what it meant I learned how occupation works, its impact on the economy, on daily life, and its grinding impact on people. I learned what it meant to have little control over one's life and, more importantly, over the lives of one's children.

As with the Holocaust, I tried to remember my very first encounter with the occupation. One of my earliest encounters involved a group of Israeli soldiers, an old Palestinian man, and his donkey. Standing on a street with some Palestinian friends, I noticed an elderly Palestinian walking down the street, leading his donkey. A small child no more than three or four years old, clearly his grandson, was with him. Some Israeli soldiers standing nearby went up to the old man and stopped him. One soldier ambled over to the donkey and pried open its mouth. "Old man," he asked, "why are your donkey's teeth so yellow? Why aren't they white? Don't you brush your donkey's teeth?" The old Palestinian was mortified, the little boy visibly upset. The soldier repeated his question, yelling this time, while the other soldiers laughed. The child began to cry and the old man just stood there silently, humiliated. This scene repeated itself while a crowd gathered. The soldier then ordered the old man to stand behind the donkey and demanded that he kiss the animal's behind. At first, the old man refused but as the soldier screamed at him and his grandson became hysterical, he bent down and did it. The soldiers laughed and walked away. They had achieved their goal to humiliate him and those around him. We all stood there in silence, ashamed to look at each other, hearing nothing but the uncontrollable sobs of the little boy. The old man did not move for what seemed a very long time. He just stood there, demeaned and destroyed.

I stood there too, in stunned disbelief. I immediately thought of the stories my parents had told me of how Jews had been treated by the Nazis in the 1930s, before the ghettos and death camps, of how Jews would be forced to clean sidewalks with toothbrushes and have their beards cut off in public. What happened to the old man was absolutely equivalent in principle, intent, and impact to humiliate and dehumanize. In this instance, there was no difference between the German soldier and the Israeli one. Throughout that summer of 1985, I saw similar incidents: young Palestinian men being forced by Israeli soldiers to bark like dogs on their hands and knees or dance in the streets.

In this critical respect, my first encounter with the occupation was the same as my first encounter with the Holocaust, with the number on my father's arm. It spoke the same message: the denial of one's humanity. It is important to understand the very real differences in volume, scale, and horror between the Holocaust and the occupation and to be careful about comparing the two, but it is also important to recognize parallels where they do exist.

As a child of Holocaust survivors I always wanted to be able in some way to experience and feel some aspect of what my parents endured, which, of course, was impossible. I listened to their stories, always wanting more, and shared their tears. I often would ask myself, what does sheer terror feel like? What does it look like? What does it mean to lose one's whole family so horrifically and so immediately, or to have an entire way of life extinguished so irrevocably? I would try to imagine myself in their place, but it was impossible. It was beyond my reach, too unfathomable.

It was not until I lived with Palestinians under occupation that I found at least part of the answers to some of these questions. I was not searching for the answers; they were thrust upon me. I learned, for example, what sheer terror looked like from my friend Rabia, eighteen years old, who, frozen by fear and uncontrollable shaking, stood glued in the middle of a room we shared in a refugee camp, unable to move, while Israeli soldiers were trying to break down the front door to our shelter. I experienced terror while watching Israeli soldiers beat a pregnant women in her belly because she flashed a V-sign at them, and I was too paralyzed by fear to help her. I could more concretely understand the meaning of loss and displacement when I watched grown men sob and women scream as Israeli army bulldozers destroyed their home and everything in it because they built their house without a permit, which the Israeli authorities had refused to give them.

It is perhaps in the concept of home and shelter that I find the most profound link between the Jews and the Palestinians and, perhaps, the most painful illustration of the meaning of occupation. I cannot begin to describe how horrible and obscene it is to watch the deliberate destruction of a family's home while that family watches, powerless to stop it. For Jews as for Palestinians, a house represents far more than a roof over one's head; it represents life itself. Speaking about the demolition of Palestinian homes, Meron Benvenisti, an Israeli historian and scholar, writes:

> It would be hard to overstate the symbolic value of a house to an individual for whom the culture of wandering and of becoming rooted to the land is so deeply engrained in tradition, for an individual whose national mythos is based on the tragedy of being uprooted from a stolen homeland. The arrival of a first-born son and the building of a home are the central events in

such an individual's life because they symbolize continuity in time and physical space. And with the demolition of the individual's home comes the destruction of the world.

Israel's occupation of the Palestinians is the crux of the problem between the two peoples, and it will remain so until it ends. For the last thirty-five years, occupation has meant dislocation and dispersion; the separation of families; the denial of human, civil, legal, political, and economic rights imposed by a system of military rule; the torture of thousands; the confiscation of tens of thousands of acres of land and the uprooting of tens of thousands of trees; the destruction of more than 7,000 Palestinian homes; the building of illegal Israeli settlements on Palestinian lands and the doubling of the settler population over the last ten years; first the undermining of the Palestinian economy and now its destruction; closure; curfew; geographic fragmentation; demographic isolation; and collective punishment.

Israel's occupation of the Palestinians is not the moral equivalent of the Nazi genocide of the Jews. But it does not have to be. No, this is not genocide, but it is repression, and it is brutal. And it has become frighteningly natural. Occupation is about the domination and dispossession of one people by another. It is about the destruction of their property and the destruction of their soul. Occupation aims, at its core, to deny Palestinians their humanity by denying them the right to determine their existence, to live normal lives in their own homes. Occupation is humiliation. It is despair and desperation. And just as there is no moral equivalence or symmetry between the Holocaust and the occupation, so there is no moral equivalence or symmetry between the occupier and the occupied, no matter how much we as Jews regard ourselves as victims.

And it is from this context of deprivation and suffocation, now largely forgotten, that the horrific and despicable suicide bombings have emerged and taken the lives of more innocents. Why should innocent Israelis, among them my aunt and her grandchildren, pay the price of occupation? Like the settlements, razed homes, and barricades that preceded them, the suicide bombers have not always been there.

Memory in Judaism—like all memory—is dynamic, not static,

embracing a multiplicity of voices and shunning the hegemony of one. But in the post-Holocaust world, Jewish memory has faltered—even failed—in one critical respect: it has excluded the reality of Palestinian suffering and Jewish culpability therein. As a people, we have been unable to link the creation of Israel with the displacement of the Palestinians. We have been unwilling to see, let alone remember, that finding our place meant the loss of theirs. Perhaps one reason for the ferocity of the conflict today is that Palestinians are insisting on their voice despite our continued and desperate efforts to subdue it.

Within the Jewish community it has always been considered a form of heresy to compare Israeli actions or policies with those of the Nazis, and certainly one must be very careful in doing so. But what does it mean when Israeli soldiers paint identification numbers on Palestinian arms; when young Palestinian men and boys of a certain age are told through Israeli loudspeakers to gather in the town square; when Israeli soldiers openly admit to shooting Palestinian children for sport; when some of the Palestinian dead must be buried in mass graves while the bodies of others are left in city streets and camp alleyways because the army will not allow proper burial; when certain Israeli officials and Jewish intellectuals publicly call for the destruction of Palestinian villages in retaliation for suicide bombings or for the transfer of the Palestinian population out of the West Bank and Gaza; when 46 percent of the Israeli public favors such transfers and when transfer or expulsion becomes a legitimate part of popular discourse; when government officials speak of the "cleansing of the refugee camps"; and when a leading Israeli intellectual calls for hermetic separation between Israelis and Palestinians in the form of a Berlin Wall, caring not whether the Palestinians on the other side of the wall may starve to death as a result.

What are we supposed to think when we hear this? What is my mother supposed to think?

In the context of Jewish existence today, what does it mean to preserve the Jewish character of the State of Israel? Does it mean preserving a Jewish demographic majority through any means and continued Jewish domination of the Palestinian people and their land? What is the narrative that we as a people are creating, and what kind of voice are we seeking? What sort of meaning do we as Jews derive from the debasement and humiliation of Palestinians? What is at the center of our moral and ethical discourse? What is the source of our moral and spiritual legacy? What is the source of our redemption? Has the process of creating and rebuilding ended for us?

I want to end this essay with a quote from Irena Klepfisz, a writer and child survivor of the Warsaw ghetto, whose father spirited her and her mother out of the ghetto and then himself died in the ghetto uprising.

> I have concluded that one way to pay tribute to those we loved who struggled, resisted and died is to hold on to their vision and their fierce outrage at the destruction of the ordinary life of their people. It is this outrage we need to keep alive in our daily life and apply it to all situations, whether they involve Jews or non-Jews. It is this outrage we must use to fuel our actions and vision whenever we see any signs of the disruptions of common life: the hysteria of a mother grieving for the teenager who has been shot; a family stunned in front of a vandalized or demolished home; a family separated, displaced; arbitrary and unjust laws that demand the dosing or opening of shops and schools; humiliation of a people whose culture is alien and deemed inferior; a people left homeless without citizenship; a people living under military rule. Because of our experience, we recognize these evils as obstacles to peace. At those moments of recognition, we remember the past, feel the outrage that inspired the Jews of the Warsaw Ghetto and allow it to guide us in present struggles.

For me, these words define the true meaning of Judaism and the lessons my parents sought to impart.

8 TALKING ABOUT ANTI-SEMITISM

Is it anti-Semitic to criticize Israel? "Not necessarily," says Abraham Foxman, the national director of the Anti-Defamation League. But the implication in that "not necessarily" is that it usually is. The charge of anti-Semitism is perhaps the most powerful weapon in the arsenal of Israel's knee-jerk supporters who have used it to silence critics of Israeli policy. According to Foxman, criticism of Israel is, more often than not, merely a camouflage for anti-Semitism. Indeed, anti-Zionism constitutes a "new" anti-Semitism, which has shifted its irrational hatred of Jews from the Jewish individual to the collective state. Never mind that many of Israel's most eloquent critics are themselves Jews; this apparently cuts no ice with Foxman, for whom no doubt it is evidence of the "self-hatred" from which dissident Jews suffer. He would rather make common cause with anti-Semitic Evangelical Christians who share his vision of an Israel cleansed of Palestinians.

All of which is not to diminish the problem of anti-Semitism. Some criticisms of Israel do cross the line, and anyone who has done any Web research on the Middle East knows that the volatile subject of Israel and Palestine is a magnet for raving bigots and Holocaust deniers, some of whom do disguise their Jew-hatred in the garb of principled anti-Zionism. What is more, anti-Semitism with a distinctly fascist odor has been on the rise throughout the Arab world, where people widely believe rumors about the Mossad's involvement in September 11 and television shows feature scripts based on the Protocols of the Elders of Zion. Ariel Sharon, meanwhile, is all too happy to benefit from the spread of the anti-Semitic virus, of which his government is, as Uri Avnery recently observed, a veritable laboratory.

Last year, Lawrence Summers, the president of Harvard University, publicly characterized campus protests against the Israeli occupation as "actions that are anti-Semitic in their effect, if not their intent." In the pages of the New York Times, The New Yorker and other less hallowed forums of opinion Summers' speech was hailed as an example of moral leadership. In this powerful rejoinder, **Judith Butler**, a professor of literature at the University of California and a pioneering theorist of gender, offers an incisive critique of Summers' logic, arguing that it is based on a misleading equation of anti-Zionism and anti-Semitism, and that its principal effect is to stifle genuine debate.

THE CHARGE OF ANTI-SEMITISM: THE RISKS OF PUBLIC CRITIQUE

Judith Butler

From the *London Review of Books* (2003)

Profoundly anti-Israel views are increasingly finding support in progressive intellectual communities. Serious and thoughtful people are advocating and taking actions that are anti-Semitic in their effect if not their intent.
                    —Lawrence Summers, 17 September 2002

When the president of Harvard University declared that to criticise Israel at this time and to call on universities to divest from Israel are 'actions that are anti-Semitic in their effect, if not their intent', he introduced a distinction between effective and intentional anti-Semitism that is controversial at best. The counter-charge has been that in making his statement, Summers has struck a blow against academic freedom, in effect, if not in intent. Although he insisted that he meant nothing censorious by his remarks, and that he is in favour of Israeli policy being 'debated freely and civilly', his words have had a chilling effect on political discourse. Among those actions which he called 'effectively anti-Semitic' were European boycotts of Israel, anti-globalisation rallies at which criticisms of Israel were voiced, and fund-raising efforts for organisations of 'questionable political provenance'. Of local concern to him, however, was a divestment petition drafted by MIT and Harvard faculty members who oppose Israel's current occupation and its treatment of Palestinians. Summers asked why Israel was being 'singled out— among all nations' for a divestment campaign, suggesting that the singling out was evidence of anti-Semitic intentions. And though he claimed that aspects of Israel's 'foreign and defence policy can be and should be vigorously challenged', it was unclear how such challenges could or would take place without being construed as anti-Israel, and why these policy issues, which include occupation, ought not to be vigorously challenged through a divestment campaign. It would seem that calling for divestment is something other than a legitimately 'vigorous challenge', but we are not given any criteria by which to adjudicate between vigorous challenges that should be articulated, and those which carry the 'effective' force of anti-Semitism.

Summers is right to voice concern about rising anti-Semitism, and every progressive person ought to challenge anti-Semitism vigorously wherever it occurs. It seems, though, that historically we have now reached a position in which Jews cannot legitimately be understood always and only as presumptive victims. Sometimes we surely are, but sometimes we surely are not. No political ethics can start from the assumption that Jews monopolise the position of victim. 'Victim' is a quickly transposable term: it can shift from minute to minute, from the Jew killed by suicide bombers on a bus to the Palestinian child killed by Israeli gunfire. The public sphere needs to be one in which both kinds of violence are challenged insistently and in the name of justice.

If we think that to criticise Israeli violence, or to call for economic pressure to be put on the Israeli state to change its policies, is to be 'effectively anti-Semitic', we will fail to voice our opposition for fear of being named as part of an anti-Semitic enterprise. No label could be worse for a Jew, who knows that, ethically and politically, the position with which it would be unbearable to identify is that of the anti-Semite. The ethical framework within which most progressive Jews operate takes the form of the following question: will we be silent (and thereby collaborate with illegitimately violent power), or will we make our voices heard (and be counted among those who did what they could to stop that violence), even if speaking poses a risk? The current Jewish critique of Israel is often portrayed as insensitive to Jewish suffering, past as well as present, yet its ethic is based on the experience of suffering, in order that suffering might stop.

Summers uses the 'anti-Semitic' charge to quell public criticism of Israel, even as he explicitly distances himself from the overt operations of censorship. He writes, for instance, that 'the only antidote to dangerous ideas is strong alternatives vigorously advocated.' But how does one vigorously advocate the idea that the Israeli occupation is brutal and wrong, and Palestinian self-determination a necessary good, if the voicing of those views calls down the charge of anti-Semitism?

To understand Summers's claim, we have to be able to conceive of an effective anti-Semitism, one that pertains to certain speech acts. Either it follows on certain utterances, or it structures them, even if that is not the conscious intention of those making them. His view assumes that such utterances will be taken by others as anti-Semitic, or received within a given context as anti-Semitic. So we have to ask what context Summers has in mind when he makes his claim; in what context is it the case that any criticism of Israel will be taken to be anti-Semitic?

It may be that what Summers was effectively saying is that the only way a criticism of Israel can be heard is through a certain acoustic frame, such that the criticism, whether it is of the West Bank settlements, the closing of Birzeit and Bethlehem University, the demolition of homes in Ramallah or Jenin, or the killing of numerous children and civilians, can only be interpreted as showing hatred for Jews. We are asked to conjure a listener who attributes an intention to the speaker: so-and-so has made a public statement against the Israeli occupation, and this must mean that so-and-so hates Jews or is willing to fuel those who do. The criticism is thus given a hidden meaning, one that is at odds with its explicit claim. The criticism of Israel is nothing more than a cloak for that hatred, or a cover for a call for discriminatory action against Jews. In other words, the only way to understand effective anti-Semitism is to presuppose *intentional* anti-Semitism; the effective anti-Semitism of any criticism turns out to reside in the intention of the speaker as retrospectively attributed by the listener.

It may be that Summers has something else in mind; namely, that the criticism will be exploited by those who want to see not only the destruction of Israel but the degradation or devaluation of Jewish people in general. There is always that risk, but to claim that such criticism of Israel can be taken only as criticism of Jews is to attribute to that particular interpretation the power to monopolise the field of reception. The argument against letting criticism of Israel into the public sphere would be that it gives fodder to those with anti-Semitic intentions, who will successfully co-opt the criticism. Here again, a statement can become effectively anti-Semitic only if there is, somewhere, an intention to use it for anti-Semitic purposes. Indeed, even if one believed that criticisms of Israel are by and large heard as anti-Semitic (by Jews, anti-Semites, or people who could be described as neither), it would become the responsibility of all of us to change the conditions of reception so that the public might begin to distinguish between criticism of Israel and a hatred of Jews.

Summers made his statement as president of an institution which is a symbol of academic prestige in the United States, and although he claimed he was speaking not as president of the university but as a 'member of our community', his speech carried weight in the press precisely because he was exercising the authority of his office. If the president of Harvard is letting the public know that he will take any criticism of Israel to be effectively anti-Semitic, then he is saying that public discourse itself ought to be so constrained that such statements are not uttered, and that those who utter them will be understood as engaging in anti-Semitic speech, even hate speech.

Here, it is important to distinguish between anti-Semitic speech which, say, produces a hostile and threatening environment for Jewish students—racist speech which any university administrator would be obliged to oppose and regulate—and speech which makes a student uncomfortable because it opposes a particular state or set of state policies that he or she may defend. The latter is a political debate, and if we say that the case of Israel is different, that any criticism of it is considered as an attack on Israelis, or Jews in general, then we have singled out this political allegiance from all other allegiances that are open to public debate. We have engaged in the most outrageous form of 'effective' censorship.

The point is not only that Summers's distinction between effective and intentional anti-Semitism cannot hold, but that the way it collapses in his formulation is precisely what produces the conditions under which certain public views are taken to be hate speech, in effect if not in intent. Summers didn't say that anything that Israel does in the name of self-defence is legitimate and ought not to be questioned. I don't know whether he approves of all Israeli policies, but let's imagine, for the sake of argument, that he doesn't. And I don't know whether he has views about, for instance, the destruction of homes and the killings of children in Jenin which attracted the attention of the United Nations last year but was not investigated as a human rights violation because Israel refused to open its borders to an investigative team. If he objects to those actions, and they are among the 'foreign policy' issues he believes ought to be 'vigorously challenged', he would be compelled, under his formulation, not to voice his disapproval, believing, as he does, that that would be construed, effectively, as anti-Semitism. And if he thinks it possible to voice disapproval, he hasn't shown us how to do it in such a way as to avert the allegation of anti-Semitism.

Summers's logic suggests that certain actions of the Israeli state must be allowed to go on unimpeded by public protest, for fear that any protest would be tantamount to anti-Semitism, if not anti-Semitism itself. Now, all forms of anti-Semitism must be opposed, but we have here a set of serious confusions about the forms anti-Semitism takes. Indeed, if the charge of anti-Semitism is used to defend Israel at all costs, then its power when used against those who do discriminate against Jews—who do violence to synagogues in Europe, wave Nazi flags or support anti-Semitic organisations—is radically diluted. Many critics of Israel now dismiss all claims of anti-Semitism as 'trumped up', having been exposed to their use as a way of censoring political speech.

Summers doesn't tell us why divestment campaigns or other forms of public protest are anti-Semitic. According to him, some forms of anti-Semitism are characterised as such retroactively, which means that nothing should be said or done that will then be taken to be anti-Semitic by others. But what if those others are wrong? If we take one form of anti-Semitism to be defined retroactively, what is left of the possibility of legitimate protest against a state, either by its own population or anyone else? If we say that every time the word 'Israel' is spoken, the speaker really means 'Jews', then we have foreclosed in advance the possibility that the speaker really means 'Israel'. If, on the other hand, we distinguish between anti-Semitism and forms of protest against the Israeli state (or right-wing settlers who sometimes act independently of the state), acknowledging that sometimes they do, disturbingly, work together, then we stand a chance of understanding that world Jewry does not see itself as one with Israel in its present form and practice, and that Jews in Israel do not necessarily see themselves as one with the state. In other words, the possibility of a substantive Jewish peace movement depends on our observing a productive and critical distance from the state of Israel (which can be coupled with a profound investment in its future course).

Summers's view seems to imply that criticism of Israel is 'anti-Israel' in the sense that it is understood to challenge the right of Israel to exist. A criticism of Israel is not the same, however, as a challenge to Israel's existence, even if there are conditions under which it would be possible to say that one leads to the other. A challenge to the right of Israel to exist can be construed as a challenge to the existence of the Jewish people only if one believes that Israel alone keeps the Jewish people alive or that all Jews invest their sense of perpetuity in the state of Israel in its current or traditional forms. One could argue, however, that those polities which safeguard the right to criticise them stand a better chance of surviving than those that don't. For a criticism of Israel to be taken as a challenge to the survival of the Jews, we would have to assume not only that 'Israel' cannot change in response to legitimate criticism, but that a more radically democratic Israel would be bad for Jews. This would be to suppose that criticism is not a Jewish value, which clearly flies in the face not only of long traditions of Talmudic disputation, but of all the religious and cultural sources that have been part of Jewish life for centuries.

What are we to make of Jews who *dis*identify with Israel or, at least, with the Israeli state? Or Jews who identify with Israel, but do not condone some of its practices? There is a wide range here: those who are silently ambivalent about the way Israel handles itself; those who only half articulate their doubts about the occupation; those who are strongly opposed to the occupation, but within a Zionist framework; those who would like to see Zionism rethought or, indeed, abandoned. Jews may hold any of these opinions, but voice them only to their family, or only to their friends; or voice them in public but then face an angry reception at home. Given this Jewish ambivalence, ought we not to be suspicious of any effort to equate Jews with Israel? The argument that all Jews have a heartfelt investment in the state of Israel is untrue. Some have a heartfelt investment in corned beef sandwiches or in certain Talmudic tales, religious rituals and liturgy, in memories of their grandmother, the taste of borscht or the sounds of the old Yiddish theatre. Others have an investment in historical and cultural archives from Eastern Europe or from the Holocaust, or in forms of labour activism, civil rights struggles and social justice that are thoroughly secular, and exist in relative independence from the question of Israel.

What do we make of Jews such as myself, who are emotionally invested in the state of Israel, critical of its current form, and call for a radical restructuring of its economic and juridical basis precisely because we are invested in it? It is always possible to say that such Jews have turned against their own Jewishness. But what if one criticises Israel in the name of one's Jewishness, in the name of justice, precisely because such criticisms seem 'best for the Jews'? Why wouldn't it always be 'best for the Jews' to embrace forms of democracy that extend what is 'best' to everyone, Jewish or not? I signed a petition framed in these terms, an 'Open Letter from American Jews', in which 3700 American Jews opposed the Israeli occupation, though in my view it was not nearly strong enough: it did not call for the end of Zionism, or for the reallocation of arable land, for rethinking the Jewish right of return or for the fair distribution of water and medicine to Palestinians, and it did not call for the reorganisation of the Israeli state on a more radically egalitarian basis. It was, nevertheless, an overt criticism of Israel.

Many of those who signed that petition will have felt what might reasonably be called heartache at taking a public stand against Israeli policy, at the thought that Israel, by subjecting 3.5 million Palestinians to military occupation, represents the Jews in a way that these petitioners find not only objectionable, but terrible to endure, as Jews; it is as Jews that they assert their disidentification with that policy, that they seek to widen the rift between the state of Israel and the Jewish people in order to produce an alternative vision of the future. The petitioners exercised a democratic right to voice criticism, and sought to get economic pressure put on Israel by the US and other countries, to implement rights for Palestinians otherwise deprived of basic conditions of self-determination, to end the occupation, to secure an independent Palestinian state or to re-establish the basis of the Israeli state without regard to religion so that Jewishness would constitute only one cultural and religious reality, and be protected by the same laws that protect the rights of others.

Identifying Israel with Jewry obscures the existence of the small but important post-Zionist movement in Israel, including the philosophers

Adi Ophir and Anat Biletzki, the sociologist Uri Ram, the professor of theatre Avraham Oz and the poet Yitzhak Laor. Are we to say that Israelis who are critical of Israeli policy are self-hating Jews, or insensitive to the ways in which criticism may fan the flames of anti-Semitism? What of the new Brit Tzedek organisation in the US, numbering close to 20,000 members at the last count, which seeks to offer a critical alternative to the American Israel Political Action Committee, opposing the current occupation and working for a two-state solution? What of Jewish Voices for Peace, Jews against the Occupation, Jews for Peace in the Middle East, the Faculty for Israeli-Palestinian Peace, Tikkun, Jews for Racial and Economic Justice, Women in Black or, indeed, Neve Shalom-Wahat al-Salam, the only village collectively governed by both Jews and Arabs in the state of Israel? What do we make of B'Tselem, the Israeli organisation that monitors human rights abuses in the West Bank and Gaza, or Gush Shalom, an Israeli organisation opposing the occupation, or Yesh Gvul, which represents the Israeli soldiers who refuse to serve in the Occupied Territories? And what of Ta'ayush, a Jewish-Arab coalition against policies that lead to isolation, poor medical care, house arrest, the destruction of educational institutions, and lack of water and food for Palestinians?

It will not do to equate Jews with Zionists or Jewishness with Zionism. There were debates among Jews throughout the 19th and early 20th centuries as to whether Zionism ought to become the basis of a state, whether the Jews had any right to lay claim to land inhabited by Palestinians for centuries, and as to the future for a Jewish political project based on a violent expropriation of land. There were those who sought to make Zionism compatible with peaceful co-existence with Arabs, and those who used it as an excuse for military aggression, and continue to do so. There were those who thought, and still think, that Zionism is not a legitimate basis for a democratic state in a situation where a diverse population must be assumed to practise different religions, and that no group ought to be excluded from any right accorded to citizens in general on the basis of their ethnic or religious views. And there are those who maintain that the violent appropriation of Palestinian land, and the dislocation of 700,000 Palestinians, was an unsuitable foundation on which to build a state. Yet Israel is now repeating its founding gesture in the containment and dehumanisation of Palestinians in the Occupied Territories. Indeed, the wall now being built threatens to leave 95,000 Palestinians homeless. These are questions about Zionism that should and must be asked in a public domain, and universities are surely one place where we might expect critical reflections on Zionism to take place. Instead, we are being asked, by Summers and others, to treat any critical approach to Zionism as effective anti-Semitism and, hence, to rule it out as a topic for legitimate disagreement.

Many important distinctions are elided by the mainstream press when it assumes that there are only two possible positions on the Middle East, the 'pro-Israel' and the 'pro-Palestinian'. The assumption is that these are discrete views, internally homogeneous, non-overlapping, that if one is 'pro-Israel' then anything Israel does is all right, or if 'pro-Palestinian' then anything Palestinians do is all right. But few people's political views occupy such extremes. One can, for instance, be in favour of Palestinian self-determination, but condemn suicide bombings, and find others who share both those views but differ on the form self-determination ought to take. One can be in favour of Israel's right to exist, but still ask what is the most legitimate and democratic form that existence ought to take. If one questions the present form, is one anti-Israel? If one holds out for a truly democratic Israel-Palestine, is one anti-Israel? Or is one trying to find a better form for this polity, one that may well involve any number of possibilities: a revised version of Zionism, a post-Zionist Israel, a self-determining Palestine, or an amalgamation of Israel into a greater Israel-Palestine where all racially and religiously based qualifications on rights and entitlements would be eliminated?

What is ironic is that in equating Zionism with Jewishness, Summers is adopting the very tactic favoured by anti-Semites. At the time of his speech, I found myself on a listserve on which a number of individuals opposed to the current policies of the state of Israel, and sometimes to Zionism, started to engage in this same slippage, sometimes opposing what they called 'Zionism' and at other times what they called 'Jewish' interests. Whenever this occurred, there were objections, and several people withdrew from the group. Mona Baker, the academic in Manchester who dismissed two Israeli colleagues from the board of her academic journal in an effort to boycott Israeli institutions, argued that there was no way to distinguish between individuals and institutions. In dismissing these individuals, she claimed, she was treating them as emblematic of the Israeli state, since they were citizens of that country. But citizens are not the same as states: the very possibility of significant dissent depends on recognising the difference between them. Baker's response to subsequent criticism was to submit e-mails to the 'academicsforjustice' listserve complaining about 'Jewish' newspapers and labelling as 'pressure' the opportunity that some of these newspapers offered to discuss the issue in print with the colleagues she had dismissed. She refused to do this and seemed now to be fighting against 'Jews', identified as a lobby that pressures people, a lobby that had put pressure on her. The criticism that I made of Summers's view thus applies to Baker as well: it is one thing to oppose Israel in its current form and practices or, indeed, to have critical questions about Zionism itself, but it is quite another to oppose 'Jews' or assume that all 'Jews' have the same view, that they are all in favour of Israel, identified with Israel or represented by Israel. Oddly, and painfully, it has to be said that on this point Mona Baker and Lawrence Summers agree: Jews are the same as Israel. In the one instance, the premise works in the service of an argument against anti-Semitism; in the second, it works as the effect of anti-Semitism itself. One aspect of anti-Semitism or, indeed, of any form of racism is that an entire people is falsely and summarily equated with a particular position, view or disposition. To say that all Jews hold a given view on Israel or are adequately represented by Israel or, conversely, that the acts of Israel, the state, adequately stand for the acts of all Jews, is to conflate Jews with Israel and, thereby, to commit an anti-Semitic reduction of Jewishness.

In holding out for a distinction to be made between Israel and Jews, I am calling for a space for dissent for Jews, and non-Jews, who have criticisms of Israel to articulate; but I am also opposing anti-Semitic reductions of Jewishness to Israeli interests. The 'Jew' is no more defined by Israel than by anti-Semitism. The 'Jew' exceeds both determinations, and is to be found, substantively, as a historically and culturally changing identity that takes no single form and has no single telos. Once the distinction is made, discussion of both Zionism and anti-Semitism can begin, since it will be as important to understand the legacy of Zionism and to debate its future as to oppose anti-Semitism wherever we find it.

What is needed is a public space in which such issues might be thoughtfully debated, and to prevent that space being defined by certain kinds of exclusion and censorship. If one can't voice an objection to violence done by Israel without attracting a charge of anti-Semitism, then that charge works to circumscribe the publicly acceptable domain of speech, and to immunise Israeli violence against criticism. One is threatened with the label 'anti-Semitic' in the same way that one is threatened with being called a 'traitor' if one opposes the most recent US war. Such threats aim to define the limits of the public sphere by setting limits on the speakable. The world of public discourse would then be one from which critical perspectives would be excluded, and the public would come to understand itself as one that does not speak out in the face of obvious and illegitimate violence.

9

IN PRAISE
OF
RESISTANCE

Michel Warschawski was born in 1948 into a deeply religious family in Strasbourg, France. His father, who had fought with the Jewish underground in the southeast of France, was the Grand Rabbi of Strasbourg. At the age of 16, Michel Warschawski moved to Jerusalem to study the Talmud. He never left. But instead of devoting his life to religious study, he became one of the leading figures of the radical left in Israel, helping to found Matzpen, a small anti-Zionist party that joined forces with the Palestinian opposition to occupation and championed the cause of Arab-Jewish equality within Israel. In 1984 Warschawski (affectionately known as "Mikado") established the Alternative Information Center, along with a group of Palestinian and Israeli activists. As Mikado explains in his 2002 memoir, Sur La Frontière (On the Border), the Center has two objectives: to "provide information on Israel in Arabic, and to provide information in Hebrew on Palestinian reality," and to "make visible the activities and positions of the new organizations of Palestinian resistance, as well as the diverse currents of the left-wing and pacifist forces in Israel." With the outbreak of the first intifada in December 1987, the Center played an increasingly important role in mobilizing public opinion against the occupation, leading to Mikado's arrest in 1989 for providing aid to illegal Palestinian organizations. He was sentenced to twenty months of prison. In Sur La Frontière, Warschawski writes of his sentence; of his concept of the border as it pertains not only to Jews and Palestinians, but to Ashkenazi and Mizrahi Jews; and of his vision of an Israel beyond occupation and, indeed, beyond Zionism itself.

A DISCOURSE ON THE BORDER (1989)

Michel Warschawski

This speech was delivered at a public meeting held in October 1989, a few days after Warschawski had been sentenced to twenty months in prison for aiding and abetting illegal organizations.

From *Sur La Frontière* (2002). Translated by Randall Cherry

T he concept of the border is central to the lives of all Israelis: it exerts a formative influence on all our lives, frames our horizons, and acts as a line of demarcation between the sense of fear and security, between enemies and brothers. In a country that is at once a ghetto and a bunker under siege, the border is omnipresent, and at every step we collide with it. Yes, the border is not only in the heart of each soldier, as the words of the song go, but in the heart of each citizen of Israel, and it is an integral part of his very being.

The border is also present there where the majority of my fellow countrymen spend several weeks a year, as members of the military reserve, and it is from that border that they can catch a glimpse of the other side, gazing upon the Other, the other world. I have served on the border with Jordan longer than any other reservist, not only because my battalion is regularly assigned there, but also because I'm sent there every time I refuse to rejoin my unit whenever it's ordered to serve in the midst of the Arab population of the West Bank and Gaza. And from the observation post where I've often been stationed, one hundred meters from the banks of the Jordan River, I like to peer at the other side, looking toward Jordan, and dream about what that region might be like if there were no war or conflicts.

And there were also other boundaries which, like my comrades at

"Yesh Gvul," I am not willing to overstep: the border with Lebanon, for example, which I refused to cross on three occasions; and I drew the line at repression in the occupied territories. Three times I paid for my refusal to obey orders in the form of sentences in military prison. I felt my refusal had to be proclaimed and not uttered timidly, in retreat. One must be willing to pay the price for making that choice. To refuse to cross the border, to refuse to participate in a war of lies and injustice, to refuse to take part in repression, is to make a political statement. As such, it is a stance that must be assumed in public, head held high.

The law, too, is a border, separating what is permitted from what is prohibited. With my fellow comrades in struggle, I chose to respect that particular boundary. I am not a resistance fighter in the sense that my father was when he armed himself to fight against the Nazis. I am not a *porteur de valise* in the manner of my French friends, who risked their freedom by actively supporting Algerian fighters and some of whom paid dearly for their solidarity.[1] They had all chosen to defy authority by engaging in an illegal activity. We did not make such a choice. We comply with the law, as imperfect as it is, because we live under a political system that guarantees us Israeli Jews not only freedom to act according to our own discretion, but also democratic rights and the means—however limited—to seek support for our political cause by arguing that there is a need for radical change in the existing regime. The State and I are bound by a kind of contract: as long as it honors its obligations toward citizens, that is, human rights and liberties, I will play by the rules of the game, and will not transgress the limits set by the law. Honoring this contract serves more than merely pragmatic ends: it safeguards the democratic framework, as imperfect as it may be, so that it is less susceptible to being replaced by a regime that would deny freedom in any form.

We pushed the boundary a little more each time; we were ready to be arrested; we were sentenced by the courts; we appealed to the Supreme Court. But we refused to renounce what, for us, was the underpinning of our freedom. That is why we were able to assert rights that many democratic countries would envy. It is by testing the limits that one expands one's freedom; by becoming lax, less vigilant, there is the risk one's freedom will be lost entirely. For that very reason, I refuse to quit the border and will not be content to snuggle up to the warm glow of legality. I have nothing but contempt for those who are reticent to act because they are not sure it is allowed. My judges criticized me for drawing so close to the border. I am sorry they saw it that way, because that is where I decided to defend our rights and broaden them.

There is still another border, the most important one perhaps, which separates the two peoples who live on this land: the border between Israel and Palestine. It is a border built from disputes, wars and bloodshed. It is on that border that the conflict transpires and where hatred and fear are vented. But it is also there that our two peoples come together, and there, too, that hands must reach out, to be greeted by other, outstretched hands. I have never believed in a peace that was only the absence of war, along the lines of "You stay in your place, we'll stay in ours, now leave us in peace!" The Israeli–Palestinian peace will be a peace of cooperation, coexistence—or else, it simply will not be! The construction of that coexistence must begin now, through dialogue, cooperation and solidarity. These objectives cannot be met by seeking a consensus within the safe confines of our community, or by turning to our *bien-pensant* left. Israeli–Palestinian cooperation can be built on the border and only on the border. In 1968 I decided to take up a place there, based within my own clan but getting as close as possible to the other group. If we helped contribute, even in a small way, toward the prospect of an Israeli–Palestinian peace, we did so thanks to taking up this position on the border, which facilitated the first steps toward dialogue and Israeli–Palestinian cooperation. I refuse to be a border guard. I want to continue being a frontier runner, passing through the walls of hate and the barriers of segregation . . .

This verdict has actually been pronounced against all of you militants for peace. It is no accident that Judge Tal went to such lengths to stress that the sentence was not at all severe, stating that the court had decided to take into account the arguments for the defense and that it had been favorably impressed by my closing statement, so that they eventually agreed to hand down a sentence of only . . . thirty months' imprisonment, twenty months firm. A twenty–month firm prison sentence for having, in their words, closed my eyes! I cannot agree with those who view Judge Tal's statement as cynical. He honestly believes what he said, and his call for clemency is addressed to you, my friends, even if you do not entirely share my position on the border—you who are approaching the border, step by step, helping to build a new rapport between Israelis and Palestinians. They are saying to you, "Watch out, border ahead!" and warning that the border is a danger zone. Stay back. The toll exacted: twenty months, to ensure that you'll keep your eyes closed. A veritable bargain. Next time it will be much higher. Keep away from the border.

• • •

Notes

[1] Editors's note: The *porteurs de valises*, literally "baggage carriers," were French sympathizers of the Algerian National Liberation Front who smuggled funds for the guerillas during the Algerian War of Liberation of 1954–1962.

Criticizing one's own people is always a tricky business. It is especially tricky when they have suffered a calamity that brought them to the verge of extinction. There is, of course, a distinction between Israel and the Jewish people— a distinction that Jewish critics of Israel rightly insist upon. But this, again, is not easy, since Israel defines itself not as a Jewish state, but as the Jewish state, and since it continues to command the (largely unquestioning) support of the majority of Jews. As a result, to publicly criticize Israel as a Jew is invariably to stand accused of "self-hatred," as if loyalty to an occupying power were a form of love, rather than idolatry. The ethnocentric rhetoric of "solidarity with Israel," with its appeal to the logic of blood and tradition, is hardly a monopoly of the Jews; it exists in other diaspora communities, from Serbs to Hindu nationalists. Nevertheless, narrow allegiance to the tribe must be combated, in the name of a higher form of love. For if solidarity means "defending the indefensible," writes **Brian Klug,** *it can "only lead to moral blindness." A British-Jewish philosopher who has published widely on Jewish affairs, Klug asks: "Holding to the standards Judaism affirms, and believing as I do that Israel has gone off the rails: how can I not speak out?"*

A TIME TO SPEAK OUT: RETHINKING JEWISH IDENTITY AND SOLIDARITY WITH ISRAEL

Brian Klug

From *The Jewish Quarterly* No 188, Winter 2002–2003

On 27 August 2002, the *Guardian* published an interview with Chief Rabbi Professor Jonathan Sacks. In the course of the interview, the Chief Rabbi made certain comments about Israel that sparked a fierce controversy within the Jewish community in the UK and abroad. Some praised his courage for speaking out about Israel. Many denounced him. A typical accusation was that he was 'giving comfort to Israel's enemies'. And yet, as he himself was at pains to emphasize later, he did not criticize Israel at all; he merely lamented the fact that the prolonged conflict with the Palestinians is having a corrupting effect on the nation and its culture. The real significance of his comments lies less in their content than in the scale of the public reaction. Both the praise and the denunciation—especially the latter—were out of all proportion to what he actually said. This raises the question: Why were his remarks received this way? Why the exaggerated reaction? It points to something that lies beneath the surface of the controversy.

The deeper issue is a tendency among Jews to define Jewish identity in terms of the State of Israel, and the ethos of 'solidarity' to which this gives rise. This ethos has led to an environment within the Jewish community in the UK and elsewhere that is intolerant of all criticism of Israel, mild or strong, actual or—as in the case of the Chief Rabbi's comments in the *Guardian* interview—merely perceived.

In this essay I shall critically discuss this ethos and the place Israel has come to occupy in Jewish self-understanding. I shall argue that the spirit in which Jews are bonding together in the name of solidarity with Israel is misguided and unhealthy. In the first place, it distorts Jewish identity, whether secular or religious, to collapse the distinction between being Jewish and owing allegiance to the State of Israel. In the second place, it prevents Jews who do feel a tie to Israel from thinking clearly about what genuine solidarity means. After making certain distinctions that form the basis of the argument, I focus on the Israel Solidarity Rally that took place in Trafalgar Square, London, on Bank Holiday Monday, 6 May 2002, in which tens of thousands of people took part. *The Jewish Chronicle* (10 May) observed that 'more British Jews turned out, in response to a call for public solidarity, than ever before'. Everything that is wrong with the whole ethos of solidarity was concentrated in this landmark event. I conclude by drawing out some implications for the future.

I

The subject of Jewish identity, not least in relation to Israel, is complex, confusing and fraught with emotion. It is difficult to differentiate between the various elements (cultural, religious, ethnic and so on) that enter into someone's sense of being Jewish and their tie—or lack of a tie—to Israel. It varies from person to person. It would, therefore, be rash to try to speak across the board: anyone who tries to define what it means to be Jewish is taking their life in their hands! Consequently, although the subject is a general one, I am not sure how to tackle it except in the first person singular, which is the tack I shall take. I shall speak for myself and leave it to readers to judge to what extent, and with what adjustments or qualifications, the following reflection speaks for them too.

There is a song—and a question—that haunts me from childhood: 'Vi Ahin Soll Ich Geh'n?' ('Where Can I Go?'). Some time in the 1940s (probably around 1948 when the State of Israel came into existence) Leo Fuld, the 'King of Yiddish Music', recorded the song in Yiddish and English. We frequently played the record, an old 78 rpm, at our North London home. My mother would sing it with feeling, as if its questions were hers and its answer an answer to her prayers. To the best of my (and her) recollection, the English version of the first verse was as follows:

Tell me, Where can I go?

There's no place I can see.
Where to go, where to go?
Every door is closed to me.
To the left, to the right,
It's the same in every land.
There is nowhere to go
And it's me who should know,
Won't you please understand?

Even without the soulful melody, these despairing words ring in my ears; when sung they go straight to the heart. As a young child, the first verse seemed to me as melancholy as Kol Nidre—the solemn supplication that opens the evening service on Yom Kippur, the Day of Atonement—but less obscure. Here was a person in a nightmare: lost, shut out, cut off, set apart, a voice crying in the wilderness. I was a child and I understood crying. I understood lost as well. 'Won't you please understand?' Oh, but I did, to the core. But where to go, where to go? The song itself supplies the answer, expressed in the jubilant second verse:

Now I know where to go,
Where my folk proudly stand.
Let me go, let me go
To that precious promised land.
No more left no more right.
Lift your head and see the light.
I am proud, can't you see,
For at last I am free:
No more wandering for me.
No more wandering, no more questions. Unless it's the question
'Can't you see?'

But I could see. I saw a nightmare ending. I saw the person in the song approaching a light at the end of the tunnel. This was my first glimpse of Israel. I was a child and so was the state. However, 50 years later we have both lost our innocence; I have learned that light can be deceptive and that it can also be blinding. The song comes back to haunt me, but I see a different nightmare now, one that has the whole of 'that precious promised land' and all its inhabitants, Jewish and other, in its grip. And the question I hear, subtly altered, is a cry of bewilderment rather than despair: 'Tell me, now that I'm here, where am I going?'

Given the ethos of 'solidarity with Israel', it is difficult to make this question audible, let alone offer an answer. Calls for solidarity rain down from the pulpit. While this varies from congregation to congregation, and although there are notable exceptions,[1] rabbis of every stripe (including the Chief Rabbi) tell their congregations to rally round in support of the Jewish state. Leaders of community organizations proclaim the same message. Some hasten to add that Israel is not beyond reproach. They acknowledge that Jews of goodwill may hold views about Israel that depart from the mainstream. But God forbid if anyone does. And if they do, this is taken to indicate that they are clearly not Jews of goodwill. They are branded as either naïve or ignorant or cowards or self-hating traitors or some strange behemoth that is a hybrid of all these things. Now is not the time, we are told, for Jews in the 'Diaspora' to criticize the government of Israel.[2] Loyalty is what is expected of us now. But why now, especially? And why of me, exactly? And what is loyalty, anyway? Or is it disloyal to ask?

The fact of the matter is that, above the din of sermons and admonitions, I hear the question the song puts to me in the here and now: 'Where am I going?' ('Am I going wrong? Where am I going wrong?') So of one thing I am positive: now, especially now, is not the time for closing ranks and keeping quiet, nor for vociferous expressions of blind support for Israel in the name of unity. It is a time for clarity rather than unity: for making distinctions, for questioning certitudes, for thinking through; a time, ultimately, to speak out.

Clarity begins at home. Accordingly, I shall try to clarify why the song haunts me. What chord in me does it strike? To put it another way, what does Israel have to do with me? Well, when I am asked (or expected) to show solidarity, at least two separate claims are made, though they are so fused together that it is hard to pick them apart. On the one hand, there is the claim based on the idea that Israel, being a Jewish state, is my state, and that its people, the Jewish people, are my people. This is the point of view of Zionism, the movement to establish a home for the Jewish people in the land of Israel on the model of a nation-state. Zionism, a modern political idea, draws heavily on

Judaism, an ancient religious and ethical tradition whose roots lie in the Torah and the Talmud. The fact that Zionism uses the vocabulary of Judaism, but adapts it to the idiom of modern political theory, goes a long way towards explaining why this subject—Israel and Jewish identity—is so confusing. For at the heart of Judaism there is also the notion of the Jewish people, but it is a significantly different notion. This notion—the religious and ethical notion of the Jewish people—is the other basis on which I am asked to show solidarity with the State of Israel. I shall discuss this basis first, and then turn to the claim that derives from Zionism.

Zion, in the Bible, refers to Jerusalem. But it is not a city merely. In the biblical and religious context, Zion is the place of which Isaiah (2:2-3) speaks when he proclaims his vision of 'the last days', saying, 'out of Zion shall go forth the Torah, and the word of the Lord from Jerusalem'. Isaiah speaks as a prophet and 'Zion' is a term of his art. Now, if this is the Zion in whose name I am being asked to show solidarity with Israel, then it is appropriate to respond in kind—by invoking the prophetic ethic to which this idea of Zion belongs and judging Israel's actions by that standard; for that is the standard I am being asked to affirm. It is the standard I do affirm if I am in shul on shabbat for the opening of the Ark at the beginning of Kriat Hatorah (the Reading of the Torah) and join the congregation in the singing of the very verse from Isaiah that I have just quoted. To appeal to my Jewish identity, and at the same time tell me not to apply to Israel those standards of truth and justice which, along with peace, Judaism itself insists upon as fundamental[3]—this strikes me as inconsistent. It is certainly incongruous when, week in week out, in the Torah readings that are the focus of the shabbat service, the children or people of Israel are constantly being chastised and criticized for their failings. To take self-criticism out of Judaism would be like taking the light out of a candle or the heat out of a flame: it would mean taking the 'Jewish' out of the Jewish people. The whole point of this people, in the context of the Torah, is that they are constituted by commitment to an ethic— the covenant they accept at Sinai—in order to be (in the words of Isaiah 49:6) 'a light to the nations'. It is precisely this commitment that makes them, as it were, a people apart, 'a kingdom of priests and a holy nation' (Exodus 19:6), rather than an ethnic group as such. This is the concept of Am Yisrael, the people of Israel, the Jewish people, in the Torah: a people constituted by their commitment to the book or word of God. This commitment constitutes a way of life, not a modern political state. It cannot be the basis for unconditional solidarity with a country—any country, especially one called Israel.

If, on the other hand, I am expected to show solidarity on the basis that Israel, being a Jewish state, is my state, then my response is this. I do feel a tie to Israel insofar as Israel came into existence to provide a home for Jews fleeing persecution and seeking a place where they could live in peace and security. After the Second World War and the Holocaust, Israel was a state for the stateless, for Jews who had lost everything and had nowhere to go because, in the words of the song that still haunts me, every door was closed to them. It was the same in every land. Then suddenly, miraculously as it seems, there was one door that opened and they stepped through it into what they believed would be the safe haven of Israel. At last they were free. It was the end of a nightmare—or so they believed. But now their dream is shattered. They live in fear of their lives every day. Even when they go to the market, or eat at a pizzeria, or sit down to a Seder with family and friends to celebrate freedom: they are not free. At every turn their lives are at risk—just as before they came to this land. What can they do? Where can they go? I see their plight and my heart goes out to them. It goes out to them as fellow human beings. But on top of that I know that there but for the proverbial grace of God go I, for they are Jewish, and I am Jewish, and being Jewish is what brought them to these straits. This makes their predicament more poignant for me—not greater than the predicament of other human beings in similar circumstances but more pointed.

This is the tie that I feel, these are the chords that are struck by the song. They resonate with me deeply. But the tie is a tie of affection, not loyalty or allegiance. Israel is not my country and I am not its citizen. To put it another way, 'the people of Israel', in the modern political sense of that phrase, is not synonymous with 'the people of Israel' of which the Torah speaks. Many Jewish Israelis feel no affiliation whatsoever to Judaism and even repudiate it totally. They are Jewish people but they do not see themselves as part of 'the Jewish people', Am Yisrael, the People of the Book. Moreover, about one million Israeli citizens—

approximately one fifth of the total population—are not Jewish: they are ethnically Arab and profess either Islam or Christianity or feel as secular as some of their Jewish co-citizens. They also are part of the (modern) people of Israel. They are, I'm not. There are other minority groups within Israel too. In short, while in terms of dominant culture Israel is a Jewish state, the people of Israel, like the people of Britain, are a motley crew.

Moreover, if Israel were my country, I would not consider it my patriotic duty to support it right or wrong. If I thought its policies were foolish or shameful, unwise or unjust, I hope I would not hesitate to speak out, even in a time of crisis—all the more in a time of crisis because this is the part of a conscientious citizen. More to the point, it is what Israelis do. Israel is not a monolith. Its citizens are at odds over the issues of the day, and are hardly shy about saying what they think. In particular, on the subject of the future of the Occupied Territories, the question of land for peace, the two-state solution and the treatment of Palestinians in the interim: there are diametrically opposed camps. The divisions pit Israeli Jew against Israeli Jew. Consequently, not only do I not feel under an obligation, as a Jew, to show solidarity with Israel, but there is no such thing as 'solidarity with Israel': it is a sentimental illusion.

II

Some readers who have got this far will, I expect, be itching to tell me that I have completely missed the point about solidarity with Israel. In particular, they will want to put me right about the Trafalgar Square rally, to which I now turn. I imagine them giving me a little lecture, speaking, as it were, on behalf of the Jewish community. To draw on published sources, I would hear something like this: 'Of course there are diametrically opposed camps in Israel. What do you expect: it's a Jewish state. But there is something that transcends party politics: survival and the right to live in peace and security. This is why Jews were urged to attend the Israel Solidarity Rally: to stand shoulder-to-shoulder with the people of Israel and to say in one clear voice. 'We are with you. Yes to peace. No to terror.' Is this so wrong?'

Yes. Given the spin being put on it, it is so wrong that it is hard to know where to start. The lecture makes the claim that the Israel Solidarity Rally transcended party politics. I take it that this claim refers to domestic politics in Israel, and I assume for the sake of argument that the rally was genuinely intended to be non-partisan. No doubt, many people who took part saw it that way. The fact that there was some diversity of view on the speakers' platform might have seemed to give substance to that perception. However, what the onlooker saw was something else: a high profile public statement of support by British Jewry for the policies of Prime Minister Ariel Sharon. Consider the message proclaimed by the main official banner (and cited in the lecture): 'Yes to peace. No to terror.' What does this really mean? Saying 'yes to peace', in itself, means nothing. Who says no to peace? Everyone, unless they are insane, ultimately wants peace. The real issue is not peace per se but peace on whose terms and peace by what means. Here, for example, is Sharon on the subject of Israel's intentions: 'Israel will act, and with might. Israel will fight anyone who tries to wage fear [sic] through suicide terrorism. Israel will fight. Israel will triumph. And when victory comes, Israel will make peace' (*Ha'aretz*, 8 May 2002). So, if peace means triumph, Sharon is 'a man of peace', to use President Bush's sobriquet. But who isn't? 'Yes to peace' is an empty platitude, a well-meaning but meaningless gesture. 'No to terror', on the other hand, is telling. It determines the political sense of the rally—because of what it doesn't say. It doesn't say 'No to settlements'. Nor does it say no to curfews, closures, collective punishment, deportations, demolition of homes, destruction of vineyards, uprooting of olive groves, and all the other apparatus of Israel's occupation of the West Bank and Gaza Strip.

Thus, far from being apolitical, the rally could hardly have been more partisan. Within the Israeli political spectrum it came down, broadly speaking, on one side (say, Likud) over another (say, Meretz). This was compounded by the way the limelight fell on Binyamin Netanyahu, the former Prime Minister, whose hardline hawkish views are similar to Sharon's. When I told an Israeli friend that Netanyahu was going to be one of the main speakers, she e-mailed me emphatically, 'I'd agree that it would be far more supportive to stay away from such a rally!' So when the demonstrators waved their banners saying 'Israel, we're with you', who were they with exactly? Not with my friend, and not with those Israelis who feel as she does: who oppose the appropriation of Palestinian land and the spread of Jewish settlements in the Occupied Territories; who stand up against their own government's repeated violations of the international human rights conventions to which Israel is a signatory; who promote Jewish-Palestinian cooperation; and who seek a resolution of the conflict that will enable two long-suffering populations to have a future side by side; all of which happens to be in Israel's interest. These far-seeing Israelis want and need solidarity. They and their cause—which includes the peace and security of Israel—were betrayed by the Israel Solidarity Rally on 6 May.

Of course, there are those who attended the rally who take a different view of the conflict with the Palestinians and of Israel's long-term interests. In their opinion, the Israelis I am calling far-seeing are at best shortsighted. The last thing they would want is to give succour to Israelis like my friend. Some of these people think the Palestinians must be bludgeoned into submission; some believe in a 'Greater Israel' that incorporates the Occupied Territories; some went on the rally in the spirit of ethnic bonding, pure and simple. (As one letter to the *Jewish Chronicle* on 3 May 2002 put it, 'We cannot abandon our kith and kin'.) All such people are entitled to express their views. However, on the one hand, they should stand up and be recognized for who they are rather than hide behind the fuzzy veil of a vague 'solidarity with Israel'. On the other hand, for some Jews who took part in the rally nothing could have been further from their minds than the policy of brute force or the cause of expansionism or the values of ethnic bonding. These people went in a spirit of peace, a peace based on negotiation, not subjugation; on sharing the land, not appropriating the whole of it; on universal principles of justice and human rights, not on the racial or ethnic interest of one of the parties to the conflict. But a public rally makes a public statement. And the statement it actually makes is not necessarily the same as the one in the minds and hearts of people who take part.

What did the world see on 6 May? It saw a mass expression of jingoism in which Jews, as Jews, were siding with an established state occupying the land of a stateless people. True, the banners said 'Yes to peace'. But again: by what means and on whose terms? If this had genuinely been a peace rally, rather than a blatantly nationalistic one, then

Trafalgar Square would not have been awash with blue-and-white Israeli flags (plus the odd Union Jack). As it is, irrespective of intentions, and even without any overtly anti-Arab placards, the slogan 'Israel, we're with you' conveyed to the onlooker the message 'Palestinians, we're against you', as surely as tails is the opposite of heads. This is not the attitude of peace—unless for 'peace' read 'triumph'. Those people who took part in the rally and whose sympathies lie with the peace movement in Israel were either duped or self-deceived.

Yet, given the way the State of Israel and its institutions are written into Judaism and Jewish identity, it is almost impossible to keep one's head. For example, the new edition of the widely-used *Authorised Daily Prayer Book of the United Hebrew Congregations of the Commonwealth* (1998) includes the following prayer as part of the liturgy for the shabbat morning service: 'Heavenly Father: Remember the Israel Defence Forces, the guardians of our Holy Land. Protect them from all distress and anguish, and send blessing and prosperity upon all the work of their hands.' All the work? Including the destruction and havoc caused in Jenin and Ramallah and Nablus, the humiliation and indignities visited daily on Palestinians at checkpoints in the Occupied Territories, not to mention the violence sometimes meted out to Israeli Jews who protest against their government's violations of human rights? Note the poetic, biblical language—'all the work of their hands'—and the sacred epithet, 'the guardians of our Holy Land'. This makes Israel's military an institution of Judaism itself. The rabbi or chazan (cantor) recites this prayer in front of the open Ark, holding a Sefer Torah (Scroll of the Law), with the whole of the congregation standing united. United as what? As Am Yisrael before God? Or as the local weekly Israel Solidarity Rally? There is no room, in such a climate, to stop and think about the nature of your tie as a Jew to the State of Israel. How can you think, when your very identity is soldered to the state? (So where do you go if, as a Jew, you do not identify yourself in terms of Israel, but no longer feel you can ignore the community's definition? Or if you are alienated by a prayer that implicates you in military actions that you abhor? Where do you go if you wish to go to shul, whether regularly or for festivals and special occasions? More and more individuals are liable to feel that the doors of the synagogues are closed to Jews who either do not define themselves in terms of Israel or who repudiate the Israeli government of the day. Increasingly, they will feel excluded. Reform or orthodox, to the left to the right: there is nowhere to go.)

And yet, even as I protest, I myself feel a longing to believe the very thing I am repudiating. There is something in me that wants it to be true—that wants the modern State of Israel to be the salve that heals all the wounds of Jewish history. Those wounds go deep. Even if there were no external pressures brought to bear by the community to show 'solidarity with Israel', there would be those exerted from within: experiences, memories, stories stored at the back of the mind that seep into the heart, a song from childhood that resonates down to the present day. Unless I am mistaken, when Jews turned up in their tens of thousands to support Israel, they were simultaneously showing solidarity with the past, with all those Jewish communities, long gone, that came under attack and did not—could not—defend themselves. It feels like a debt to the dead: to stand up and fight for the living. It also seems like a duty to posterity: not to let history repeat itself, the history of discrimination, inquisition, expulsion, pogrom, and finally mass extermination. But who will discharge this debt and perform this duty? For many Jews, Israel came into the world for this very purpose. 'Never again' is the state's unofficial motto.

This gets to the crux of the relationship between Jews in the 'Diaspora' and Israel. It is something I grew up with: the sense that Jews must come to the defence of Israel so that Israel can come to the defence of Jews. Hence the prayer for the Israel Defence Forces; it is as if they defend not only Israel but Jews everywhere. Hence also Sharon, Prime Minister of Israel, calling himself in an interview with CNN 'the prime minister of the Jewish people' (*Ha'aretz*, 10 June 2002). And when he says, 'Israel is the only place in the world where Jews have the right and capability to defend themselves, by themselves', he hits a nerve with Jews around the globe. Significantly, he said this at Yad Vashem, Israel's memorial to the Holocaust, on 18 April 2001, the eve of Holocaust Remembrance Day. Speaking, as it were, in his dual capacity of (elected) Prime Minister of Israel and (self-appointed) Prime Minister of the Jewish people, Sharon has described the conflict with the Palestinians in epic terms: 'This is a battle for the survival of the Jewish people, for survival of the state of Israel' (televised address to the nation, reported on www.news.bbc.co.uk, 10 April 2002). The leaflet advertising the rally used the same word: survival. 'Survival', for Jews, is a buzzword. Once the conflict with the Palestinians is put in terms of survival, the floodgates of collective memory open and Jews are moved to rally round. To invert what I said earlier, it is as if a massive congregation assembled in the open-air synagogue of Trafalgar Square in order to affirm with one voice 'We will survive'. All distinction between religious and secular, Orthodox and Reform, was dropped for the purposes of this non-denominational 'service' so as to make it as inclusive as possible. Seen this way, the rally was less a demo than a love-in, a coming together for its own sake; which is why those words 'Yes to peace' seemed to signify something, even though they didn't. In the spirit of this love-in, the slogan 'Israel, we're with you' was not meant badly; it wasn't intended to imply 'Palestinians, we're against you'. It wasn't really aimed at them at all but at 'the world', a world that has always been against 'us', that has denied 'us' peace, and, in the words of a London Jewish lawyer quoted in *The Times* (11 April 2002), 'does not like to see Israel strong'.

I understand—from the inside—these perceptions and emotions and why they seem so compelling. Nonetheless, in fact, the Jewish people do not have a Prime Minister. Israel is not the only place in the world where Jews have the right—or the capability—to defend themselves. Israel's conflict with the Palestinians is not a battle for the survival of the Jewish people. And 'the world' is not a unified body that wants to see Israel weak. These ideas are not just false, they are crazy. Even to say that the survival of the state is at risk is to distort both reality and history. One correspondent to the *Jewish Chronicle* (3 May 2002) put it succinctly:

The suggestion that it is Israel, rather than the Palestinians, whose survival is currently threatened is not only nonsense, it also diminishes the very real dangers that the Israeli nation—and the Jewish people— have faced in the past.

Nonsense and craziness are all that can come from a state of mind that cannot distinguish fantasy from fact, Arafat from Hitler, the intifada from the Inquisition.

III

'Vi Ahin Soll Ich Geh'n?' 'Where Can I Go?' There were two echoes of this song in the reportage that followed the intense 10-day battle fought between the Israel Defence Forces and Palestinians in the Jenin refugee camp in April 2002. One was a message left on a wall of a house that the Israeli army had occupied and used as a base. A soldier had written 'in neat blue ink' the simple sentence, 'I don't have another land' (*Guardian*, 16 April 2002). The other was a remark attributed to an elderly Palestinian who refused to leave his home when soldiers were about to demolish it. This 'stubborn old man' is reported to have said, 'Fifty years ago you expelled me from Haifa. Now I have nowhere to go' (*Ha'aretz*, 19 April 2002). In a way, these two statements sum up the whole conflict. However, the appearance of parity is misleading. For when the dust settled on the battle, where did each of them go? The soldier to his barracks—and ultimately to his home in Israel. But the 'stubborn old man' was left in the dust. There is no equality between this Israeli and this Palestinian. The one has a state, the other is stateless. He has nowhere to go—and it's we who should know.

Jews should know, partly from their own historical experience, and partly because of the impact this had on Palestinians. The old man alluded to this when he said, 'Fifty years ago you expelled me from Haifa.' Like many Jews, I grew up believing that the Palestinian 'refugee problem' was not caused by Israel; that it was an artificial problem created by surrounding Arab nations who, promising to crush the new Jewish state, urged Palestinians to flee their homes temporarily. The whole truth of this story, however, is more complex and less comfortable, as Israeli historians such as Simha Flapan, Benny Morris and Avi Shlaim have shown. What cannot be denied is that, tragically, solving one refugee problem led to another. On the one hand, Jews who survived the Holocaust found a haven in Israel. On the other hand, the creation of the state displaced around 700,000 Palestinians. 15 May, which Israelis celebrate as Yom Ha'atzmaot, Independence Day, is remembered by Palestinians as the date of al-Nakba, the Catastrophe. This is not because they are anti-Semites who think that anything good that happens to Jews is ipso facto catastrophic. They are not Nazis actuated by hatred. They are people who suffered a great loss: their homes, their land, their livelihoods. The creation of the State of Israel was a catastrophe for them. This is fact, not anti-Israel propaganda.

It is time to face this fact and to stop insisting on the exclusive righteousness of Israel's cause. While Israel, despite the way it is sometimes portrayed, is not the wicked witch of the Middle East, nor is it a paragon of
virtue, with the Arabs as the villain of the piece. The conflict between Israel,
its Arab neighbours and the Palestinians is political. It is not a battle
between good and evil; thinking this way can only lead to moral blindness.
It is time to see the Palestinians in the light of the Jewish experience of state-
lessness; to recognize their predicament; to say 'Never again' and refuse to
subjugate them or force them out—as if they had somewhere to go.

The truth is that neither Israelis nor Palestinians have anywhere else
to go. Any solution to the conflict that is not based on this truth is
either doomed to fail or, if it were to succeed, would be abominable.
But as Abba Eban said, shortly after the first Camp David talks (which
led to a peace treaty between Israel and Egypt), 'We shall never construct a harmony in the Middle East unless we learn to separate ourselves from our past' (Address to the Toronto Leadership Conference,
13 September 1979). To separate itself from its past, Israel needs a new
understanding with Jewry worldwide. It needs to be taken off its
mythic pedestal and relieved of its impossible millennial role as the
defender and saviour of the Jewish people. Jews outside of Israel must
allow Israel to be its own state, not theirs, so that it can concentrate on
its own vital interest in the here and now—making its peace with the
region of which it is a part—rather than carrying the whole burden of
Jewish history on its shoulders. It needs to cure that corruption of its
culture of which the Chief Rabbi spoke in his *Guardian* interview. It
needs to do these things for the sake of its own people, the people of
Israel—all its people, Jewish and non-Jewish, equally and alike.

By the same token, Jewish communities in the so-called Diaspora need
to live in their here and now, 'constructing a harmony' within the world.
This implies the reverse of the ethos of 'solidarity with Israel'. Instead of
lumping everything together, it is time to make distinctions—between
Judaism and Zionism, Israeli and Jew, the biblical and the political. When
everything is lumped together, judgement goes to pieces. Why else do so
many Jews of goodwill and sound mind persist in defending the indefensible when it comes to Israel? Making distinctions allows those who care
about the state to offer something better than blind, unconditional support: cool, careful, measured, qualified, sustained, candid criticism—the

kind you cannot give unless you are at one remove. This is solidarity worth its salt. At the same time, it means making room within Jewry for all Jews, including those who feel no tie to Israel.

For my part, my tie with Israel goes back to the song that haunts me from childhood and the question it puts in the here and now: 'Tell me, Where am I going?' ('Am I going wrong? Where am I going wrong?') Hearing this question, holding to the standards Judaism affirms, and believing as I do that Israel has gone off the rails: how can I not speak out?

• • •

Notes

[1] The exceptions can be found across the various Jewish denominations, but apparently more among Liberal and Reform rabbis. At the other end of the religious spectrum there are ultra-Orthodox movements that are either luke-warm about Israel or, as in the case of the Neturei Karta, positively hostile to Zionism and the very existence of the Jewish state.

[2] The term 'Diaspora' is itself problematic. In terms of Judaism, it denotes the state of exile that will come to an end in the Messianic era. With the creation of the State of Israel, it has acquired a purely secular sense and simply means those Jews who do not live in Israel. Diaspora, as a religious concept, implies a longing to return, with all that this implies about restoring a relationship with God. The secular use of Diaspora has, as it were, borrowed the sense of longing, thus conveying the idea that Jewish life outside of Israel is not as complete—not as Jewish—as it is within Israel.

[3] In the words of Rabbi Shimon ben Gamliel, 'The world endures by three things (d'varim): truth, justice, and peace' (Mishnah, Tractate Avot, I:18). In a commentary on this mishnah, Rav Muna says, 'These three things are one. Where justice is done, truth is accomplished and peace is made (Tractate Derech Eretz Zuta, Perek Hashalom, 2).

I am grateful to several people, particularly Reva Klein, for their invaluable comments, suggestions and corrections based on reading earlier versions of this essay. My thinking on this subject has benefited greatly from conversation and correspondence with numerous friends over a long period.

10

THE
END OF OSLO
AND THE
RETURN OF
BINATIONALISM

Tony Judt is the director of the Remarque Institute at New York University, and the author of several influential books on the history of modern Europe. The child of East European Jews who made their way to England before the Second World War, Judt was born in London and educated there and at Cambridge University. During much of the mid-1960s Judt was active in the left-Zionist Kibbutz Hame'uhad movement and lived for some time on a kibbutz in the northern Galilee; at the outbreak of the 1967 war he organized a European-wide network of young volunteers to come to Israel and replace soldiers called up for the fighting. In a recent series of articles for The New York Review of Books, to which he has been a longstanding contributor, Judt has argued that Israel's current leadership is embarked on a road to nowhere, one that not only condemns the residents of the Occupied Territories to lives of misery and desperation, but jeopardizes the physical safety of Jews in Israel and the Diaspora.

ISRAEL: AN ALTERNATIVE FUTURE

Tony Judt

From *The New York Review of Books*, October 23, 2003

The Middle East peace process is finished. It did not die: it was killed. Mahmoud Abbas was undermined by the President of the Palestinian Authority and humiliated by the Prime Minister of Israel. His successor awaits a similar fate. Israel continues to mock its American patron, building illegal settlements in cynical disregard of the "road map." The President of the United States of America has been reduced to a ventriloquist's dummy, pitifully reciting the Israeli cabinet line: "It's all Arafat's fault." Israelis themselves grimly await the next bomber. Palestinian Arabs, corralled into shrinking Bantustans, subsist on EU handouts. On the corpse-strewn landscape of the Fertile Crescent, Ariel Sharon, Yasser Arafat, and a handful of terrorists can all claim victory, and they do. Have we reached the end of the road? What is to be done?

At the dawn of the twentieth century, in the twilight of the continental empires, Europe's subject peoples dreamed of forming "nation-states," territorial homelands where Poles, Czechs, Serbs, Armenians, and others might live free, masters of their own fate. When the Habsburg and Romanov empires collapsed after World War I, their leaders seized the opportunity. A flurry of new states emerged; and the first thing they did was set about privileging their national, "ethnic" majority—defined by language, or religion, or antiquity, or all three—at the expense of inconvenient local minorities, who were consigned to second-class status: permanently resident strangers in their own home.

But one nationalist movement, Zionism, was frustrated in its ambitions. The dream of an appropriately sited Jewish national home in the middle of the defunct Turkish Empire had to wait upon the retreat of imperial Britain: a process that took three more decades and a second world war. And thus it was only in 1948 that a Jewish nation-state was established in formerly Ottoman Palestine. But the founders of the Jewish state had been influenced by the same concepts and categories as their fin-de-siècle contemporaries back in Warsaw, or Odessa, or Bucharest; not surprisingly, Israel's ethno-religious self-definition, and its discrimination against internal "foreigners," has always had more in common with, say, the practices of post-Habsburg Romania than either party might care to acknowledge.

The problem with Israel, in short, is not—as is sometimes suggested—that it is a European "enclave" in the Arab world; but rather that it arrived too late. It has imported a characteristically late-nineteenth-century separatist project into a world that has moved on, a world of individual rights, open frontiers, and international law. The very idea of a "Jewish state"—a state in which Jews and the Jewish religion have exclusive privileges from which non-Jewish citizens are forever excluded—is rooted in another time and place. Israel, in short, is an anachronism.

In one vital attribute, however, Israel is quite different from previous insecure, defensive microstates born of imperial collapse: it is a democracy. Hence its present dilemma. Thanks to its occupation of the lands conquered in 1967, Israel today faces three unattractive choices. It can dismantle the Jewish settlements in the territories, return to the 1967 state borders within which Jews constitute a clear majority, and thus remain both a Jewish state and a democracy, albeit one with a constitutionally anomalous community of second-class Arab citizens.

Alternatively, Israel can continue to occupy "Samaria," "Judea," and Gaza, whose Arab population—added to that of present-day Israel—will become the demographic majority within five to eight years: in which case Israel will be either a Jewish state (with an ever-larger majority of unenfranchised non-Jews) or it will be a democracy. But logically it cannot be both.

Or else Israel can keep control of the Occupied Territories but get rid of the overwhelming majority of the Arab population: either by forcible expulsion or else by starving them of land and livelihood, leaving them no option but to go into exile. In this way Israel could indeed remain both Jewish and at least formally democratic: but at the cost of becoming the first modern democracy to conduct full-scale ethnic cleansing as a state project, something which would condemn Israel forever to the status of an outlaw state, an international pariah.

Anyone who supposes that this third option is unthinkable above all for a Jewish state has not been watching the steady accretion of settlements and land seizures in the West Bank over the past quarter-century, or listening to generals and politicians on the Israeli right, some of them currently in government. The middle ground of Israeli politics today is occupied by the Likud. Its major component is the late Menachem Begin's Herut Party. Herut is the successor to Vladimir Jabotinsky's interwar Revisionist Zionists, whose uncompromising indifference to legal and territorial niceties once attracted from left-leaning Zionists the epithet "fascist." When one hears Israel's deputy prime minister, Ehud Olmert, proudly insist that his country has not excluded the option of assassinating the elected president of the Palestinian Authority, it is clear that the label fits better than ever. Political murder is what fascists do.

The situation of Israel is not desperate, but it may be close to hopeless. Suicide bombers will never bring down the Israeli state, and the Palestinians have no other weapons. There are indeed Arab radicals who will not rest until every Jew is pushed into the Mediterranean, but they represent no strategic threat to Israel, and the Israeli military knows it. What sensible Israelis fear much more than Hamas or the al-Aqsa Brigade is the steady emergence of an Arab majority in "Greater Israel," and above all the erosion of the political culture and civic morale of their society. As the prominent Labor politician Avraham Burg recently wrote, "After two thousand years of struggle for survival, the reality of Israel is a colonial state, run by a corrupt clique which scorns and mocks law and civic morality."[1] Unless something changes, Israel in half a decade will be neither Jewish nor democratic.

This is where the US enters the picture. Israel's behavior has been a disaster for American foreign policy. With American support, Jerusalem has consistently and blatantly flouted UN resolutions requiring it to withdraw from land seized and occupied in war. Israel is the only Middle Eastern state known to possess genuine and lethal weapons of mass destruction. By turning a blind eye, the US has effectively scuttled its own increasingly frantic efforts to prevent such weapons from falling into the hands of other small and potentially belligerent states. Washington's unconditional support for Israel even in spite of (silent) misgivings is the main reason why most of the rest of the world no longer credits our good faith.

It is now tacitly conceded by those in a position to know that America's reasons for going to war in Iraq were not necessarily those advertised at the time.[2] For many in the current US administration, a major strategic consideration was the need to destabilize and then reconfigure the Middle East in a manner thought favorable to Israel. This story continues. We are now making belligerent noises toward Syria because Israeli intelligence has assured us that Iraqi weapons have been moved there—a claim for which there is no corroborating evidence from any other source. Syria backs Hezbollah and the Islamic Jihad: sworn foes of Israel, to be sure, but hardly a significant international threat. However, Damascus has hitherto been providing the US with critical data on al-Qaeda. Like Iran, another longstanding target of Israeli wrath whom we are actively alienating, Syria is more use to the United States as a friend than an enemy. Which war are we fighting?

On September 16, 2003, the US vetoed a UN Security Council resolution asking Israel to desist from its threat to deport Yasser Arafat. Even American officials themselves recognize, off the record, that the resolution was reasonable and prudent, and that the increasingly wild pronouncements of Israel's present leadership, by restoring Arafat's standing in the Arab world, are a major impediment to peace. But the US blocked the resolution all the same, further undermining our credibility as an honest broker in the region. America's friends and allies around the world are no longer surprised at such actions, but they are saddened and disappointed all the same.

Israeli politicians have been actively contributing to their own difficulties for many years; why do we continue to aid and abet them in their mistakes? The US has tentatively sought in the past to pressure Israel by threatening to withhold from its annual aid package some of the money that goes to subsidizing West Bank settlers. But the last time this was attempted, during the Clinton administration, Jerusalem got around it by taking the money as "security expenditure." Washington went along with the subterfuge, and of $10 billion of American aid over four years, between 1993 and 1997, less than $775 million was kept back. The settlement program went ahead unimpeded. Now we don't even try to stop it.

This reluctance to speak or act does no one any favors. It has also corroded American domestic debate. Rather than think straight about the Middle East, American politicians and pundits slander our European allies when they dissent, speak glibly and irresponsibly of resurgent anti-Semitism when Israel is criticized, and censoriously rebuke any public figure at home who tries to break from the consensus.

But the crisis in the Middle East won't go away. President Bush will probably be conspicuous by his absence from the fray for the coming year, having said just enough about the "road map" in June to placate Tony Blair. But sooner or later an American statesman is going to have to tell the truth to an Israeli prime minister and find a way to make him listen. Israeli liberals and moderate Palestinians have for two decades been thanklessly insisting that the only hope was for Israel to dismantle nearly all the settlements and return to the 1967 borders, in exchange for real Arab recognition of those frontiers and a stable, terrorist-free Palestinian state underwritten (and constrained) by Western and international agencies. This is still the conventional consensus, and it was once a just and possible solution.

But I suspect that we are already too late for that. There are too many settlements, too many Jewish settlers, and too many Palestinians, and they all live together, albeit separated by barbed wire and pass laws. Whatever the "road map" says, the real map is the one on the ground, and that, as Israelis say, reflects facts. It may be that over a quarter of a million heavily armed and subsidized Jewish settlers would leave Arab Palestine voluntarily; but no one I know believes it will happen. Many of those settlers will die—and kill—rather than move. The last Israeli politician to shoot Jews in pursuit of state policy was David Ben-Gurion, who forcibly disarmed Begin's illegal Irgun militia in 1948 and integrated it into the new Israel Defense Forces. Ariel Sharon is not Ben-Gurion.[3]

The time has come to think the unthinkable. The two-state solution— the core of the Oslo process and the present "road map"—is probably already doomed. With every passing year we are postponing an inevitable, harder choice that only the far right and far left have so far acknowledged, each for its own reasons. The true alternative facing the Middle East in coming years will be between an ethnically cleansed Greater Israel and a single, integrated, binational state of Jews and Arabs, Israelis and Palestinians. That is indeed how the hard-liners in Sharon's cabinet see the choice; and that is why they anticipate the removal of the Arabs as the ineluctable condition for the survival of a Jewish state.

But what if there were no place in the world today for a "Jewish state"? What if the binational solution were not just increasingly likely, but actually a desirable outcome? It is not such a very odd thought. Most of the readers of this essay live in pluralist states which have long since become multiethnic and multicultural. "Christian Europe," *pace* M. Valéry Giscard d'Estaing, is a dead letter; Western civilization today is a patchwork of colors and religions and languages, of Christians, Jews, Muslims, Arabs, Indians, and many others—as any visitor to London or Paris or Geneva will know.[4]

Israel itself is a multicultural society in all but name; yet it remains distinctive among democratic states in its resort to ethnoreligious criteria with which to denominate and rank its citizens. It is an oddity among modern nations not—as its more paranoid supporters assert—because it is a *Jewish* state and no one wants the Jews to have a state; but because it is a Jewish *state* in which one community—Jews—is set above others, in an age when that sort of state has no place.

For many years, Israel had a special meaning for the Jewish people. After 1948 it took in hundreds of thousands of helpless survivors who had nowhere else to go; without Israel their condition would have been desperate in the extreme. Israel needed Jews, and Jews needed Israel. The circumstances of its birth have thus bound Israel's identity inextricably to the *Shoah*, the German project to exterminate the Jews of Europe. As a result, all criticism of Israel is drawn ineluctably back to the memory of that project, something that Israel's American apologists are shamefully quick to exploit. To find fault with the Jewish state is to think ill of Jews; even to imagine an alternative configuration in the Middle East is to indulge the moral equivalent of genocide.

In the years after World War II, those many millions of Jews who did not live in Israel were often reassured by its very existence—whether they thought of it as an insurance policy against renascent anti-Semitism or simply a reminder to the world that Jews could and would fight back. Before there was a Jewish state, Jewish minorities in Christian societies would peer anxiously over their shoulders and keep a low profile; since 1948, they could walk tall. But in recent years, the situation has tragically reversed.

Today, non-Israeli Jews feel themselves once again exposed to criticism and vulnerable to attack for things they didn't do. But this time it is a Jewish state, not a Christian one, which is holding them hostage for its own actions. Diaspora Jews cannot influence Israeli policies, but they are implicitly identified with them, not least by Israel's own insistent claims upon their allegiance. The behavior of a self-described Jewish state affects the way everyone else looks at Jews. The increased incidence of attacks on Jews in Europe and elsewhere is primarily attributable to misdirected efforts, often by young Muslims, to get back at Israel. The depressing truth is that Israel's current behavior is not just bad for America, though it surely is. It is not even just bad for Israel itself, as many Israelis silently acknowledge. The depressing truth is that Israel today is bad for the Jews.

In a world where nations and peoples increasingly intermingle and intermarry at will; where cultural and national impediments to communication have all but collapsed; where more and more of us have multiple elective identities and would feel falsely constrained if we had to answer to just one of them; in such a world Israel is truly an anachronism. And not just an anachronism but a dysfunctional one. In today's "clash of cultures" between open, pluralist democracies and belligerently intolerant, faith-driven ethno-states, Israel actually risks falling into the wrong camp.

To convert Israel from a Jewish state to a binational one would not be easy, though not quite as impossible as it sounds: the process has already begun de facto. But it would cause far less disruption to most Jews and Arabs than its religious and nationalist foes will claim. In any case, no one I know of has a better idea: anyone who genuinely supposes that the controversial electronic fence now being built will resolve matters has missed the last fifty years of history. The "fence"—actually an armored zone of ditches, fences, sensors, dirt roads (for tracking footprints), and a wall up to twenty-eight feet tall in places—occupies, divides, and steals Arab farmland; it will destroy villages, livelihoods, and whatever remains of Arab-Jewish community. It costs approximately $1 million per mile and will bring nothing but humiliation and discomfort to both sides. Like the Berlin Wall, it confirms the moral and institutional bankruptcy of the regime it is intended to protect.

A binational state in the Middle East would require a brave and relentlessly engaged American leadership. The security of Jews and Arabs alike would need to be guaranteed by international force— though a legitimately constituted binational state would find it much easier policing militants of all kinds inside its borders than when they are free to infiltrate them from outside and can appeal to an angry, excluded constituency on both sides of the border.[5] A binational state in the Middle East would require the emergence, among Jews and Arabs alike, of a new political class. The very idea is an unpromising mix of realism and utopia, hardly an auspicious place to begin. But the alternatives are far, far worse.

—September 25, 2003

• • •

Notes

[1] See Burg's essay, *"La révolution sioniste est morte,"* Le Monde, September 11, 2003. A former head of the Jewish Agency, the writer was speaker of the Knesset, Israel's Parliament, between 1999 and 2003 and is currently a Labor Party member of the Knesset. His essay first appeared in the Israeli daily *Yediot Aharonot;* it has been widely republished, notably in the Forward (August 29, 2003) and the London *Guardian* (September 15, 2003).

[2] See the interview with Deputy Secretary of Defense Paul Wolfowitz in the July 2003 issue of *Vanity Fair.*

[3] In 1979, following the peace agreement with Anwar Sadat, Prime Minister Begin and Defense Minister Sharon did indeed instruct the army to close down Jewish settlements in the territory belonging to Egypt. The angry resistance of some of the settlers was overcome with force, though no one was killed. But then the army was facing three thousand extremists, not a quarter of a million, and the land in question was the Sinai Desert, not "biblical Samaria and Judea."

[4] Albanians in Italy, Arabs and black Africans in France, Asians in England all continue to encounter hostility. A minority of voters in France, or Belgium, or even Denmark and Norway, support political parties whose hostility to "immigration" is sometimes their only platform. But compared with thirty years ago, Europe is a multicolored patchwork of equal citizens, and that, without question, is the shape of its future.

[5] As Burg notes, Israel's current policies are the terrorists' best recruiting tool: "We are indifferent to the fate of Palestinian children, hungry and humiliated; so why are we surprised when they blow us up in our restaurants? Even if we killed 1000 terrorists a day it would change nothing." See Burg, *"La révolution sioniste est morte."*

ACKNOWLEDGMENTS

I have incurred numerous debts in editing this collection.

My wonderfully supportive editors at *Nation Books*, Carl Bromley and Ruth Baldwin, recognized the importance of this book and shepherded it to publication with passion for the subject and patience for the author. Roane Carey—whose political intelligence and moral sensitivity are nothing short of awe-inspiring—was an invaluable interlocutor every step of the way, and helped me to refine the book's conception. This project could not have succeeded without the help of three extraordinary recent Nation interns: Ibrahim Ahmad and Kate Levin, who provided indispensable research assistance, and Kevin McCarthy, who tracked down permissions. I would also like to thank my colleagues at The Nation: Victor Navasky, Katrina vanden Heuvel, Betsy Reed, Karen Rothmyer and Hillary Frey.

This book is, in large measure, the outgrowth of conversations over the years with friends, many of them dissident Jews. Albert Fried—my loving mentor and most careful reader—has shaped my thinking on these matters more than anyone, and has showered me with kindnesses too numerous to mention. In the course of editing this book I have often traded ideas with Leonard Benardo and Eyal Press, two of the sharpest minds and warmest souls I have encountered. I have also drawn upon the generous contributions of Sasha Abramsky, Ammiel Alcalay, Sinan Antoon, David Epstein, Edith Fried, Michelle Garcia, Amira Hass, Riva Hocherman, Baruch Kimmerling, Leela Jacinto, Daniel Lazare, Scott Malcomson, Arno Mayer, Thom Powers, Sol Resnik, Bruce Robbins, Marc Ribot, Joe Sacco, Elliott Sharp, Mustapha Tlili, Jennifer Washburn, Jennifer Weiss, and Michael Wrezin.

Finally, I wish to thank three remarkable people: my sister, Sarah Shatz, who has taught me more than she knows; my mother, Leslie Shatz, whose rebel heart is a constant inspiration; and my father, Stephen Shatz, to whom I owe my passion for ideas, and my love of justice.

PERMISSIONS